T0202912

Lecture Notes in Computer Science 14711

Founding Editors

Gerhard Goos
Juris Hartmanis

The series Lecture Notes in Computer Science (LNCS), including its subseries Lecture Notes in Artificial Intelligence (LNAI) and Lecture Notes in Bioinformatics (LNBI), has established itself as a medium for the publication of new developments in computer science and information technology research, teaching, and education.

LNCS enjoys close cooperation with the computer science R & D community, the series counts many renowned academics among its volume editors and paper authors, and collaborates with prestigious societies. Its mission is to serve this international community by providing an invaluable service, mainly focused on the publication of conference and workshop proceedings and postproceedings. LNCS commenced publication in 1973.

Vincent G. Duffy
Editor

Digital Human Modeling and Applications in Health, Safety, Ergonomics and Risk Management

15th International Conference, DHM 2024
Held as Part of the 26th HCI International Conference, HCII 2024
Washington, DC, USA, June 29 – July 4, 2024
Proceedings, Part III

 Springer

Editor
Vincent G. Duffy
Purdue University
West Lafayette, IN, USA

ISSN 0302-9743   ISSN 1611-3349 (electronic)
Lecture Notes in Computer Science
ISBN 978-3-031-61065-3   ISBN 978-3-031-61066-0 (eBook)
https://doi.org/10.1007/978-3-031-61066-0

This Springer imprint is published by the registered company Springer Nature Switzerland AG
The registered company address is: Gewerbestrasse 11, 6330 Cham, Switzerland

If disposing of this product, please recycle the paper.

Foreword

This year we celebrate 40 years since the establishment of the HCI International (HCII) Conference, which has been a hub for presenting groundbreaking research and novel ideas and collaboration for people from all over the world.

The HCII conference was founded in 1984 by Prof. Gavriel Salvendy (Purdue University, USA, Tsinghua University, P.R. China, and University of Central Florida, USA) and the first event of the series, "1st USA-Japan Conference on Human-Computer Interaction", was held in Honolulu, Hawaii, USA, 18–20 August. Since then, HCI International is held jointly with several Thematic Areas and Affiliated Conferences, with each one under the auspices of a distinguished international Program Board and under one management and one registration. Twenty-six HCI International Conferences have been organized so far (every two years until 2013, and annually thereafter).

Over the years, this conference has served as a platform for scholars, researchers, industry experts and students to exchange ideas, connect, and address challenges in the ever-evolving HCI field. Throughout these 40 years, the conference has evolved itself, adapting to new technologies and emerging trends, while staying committed to its core mission of advancing knowledge and driving change.

As we celebrate this milestone anniversary, we reflect on the contributions of its founding members and appreciate the commitment of its current and past Affiliated Conference Program Board Chairs and members. We are also thankful to all past conference attendees who have shaped this community into what it is today.

The 26th International Conference on Human-Computer Interaction, HCI International 2024 (HCII 2024), was held as a 'hybrid' event at the Washington Hilton Hotel, Washington, DC, USA, during 29 June – 4 July 2024. It incorporated the 21 thematic areas and affiliated conferences listed below.

A total of 5108 individuals from academia, research institutes, industry, and government agencies from 85 countries submitted contributions, and 1271 papers and 309 posters were included in the volumes of the proceedings that were published just before the start of the conference, these are listed below. The contributions thoroughly cover the entire field of human-computer interaction, addressing major advances in knowledge and effective use of computers in a variety of application areas. These papers provide academics, researchers, engineers, scientists, practitioners and students with state-of-the-art information on the most recent advances in HCI.

The HCI International (HCII) conference also offers the option of presenting 'Late Breaking Work', and this applies both for papers and posters, with corresponding volumes of proceedings that will be published after the conference. Full papers will be included in the 'HCII 2024 - Late Breaking Papers' volumes of the proceedings to be published in the Springer LNCS series, while 'Poster Extended Abstracts' will be included as short research papers in the 'HCII 2024 - Late Breaking Posters' volumes to be published in the Springer CCIS series.

I would like to thank the Program Board Chairs and the members of the Program Boards of all thematic areas and affiliated conferences for their contribution towards the high scientific quality and overall success of the HCI International 2024 conference. Their manifold support in terms of paper reviewing (single-blind review process, with a minimum of two reviews per submission), session organization and their willingness to act as goodwill ambassadors for the conference is most highly appreciated.

This conference would not have been possible without the continuous and unwavering support and advice of Gavriel Salvendy, founder, General Chair Emeritus, and Scientific Advisor. For his outstanding efforts, I would like to express my sincere appreciation to Abbas Moallem, Communications Chair and Editor of HCI International News.

July 2024   Constantine Stephanidis

HCI International 2024 Thematic Areas and Affiliated Conferences

- HCI: Human-Computer Interaction Thematic Area
- HIMI: Human Interface and the Management of Information Thematic Area
- EPCE: 21st International Conference on Engineering Psychology and Cognitive Ergonomics
- AC: 18th International Conference on Augmented Cognition
- UAHCI: 18th International Conference on Universal Access in Human-Computer Interaction
- CCD: 16th International Conference on Cross-Cultural Design
- SCSM: 16th International Conference on Social Computing and Social Media
- VAMR: 16th International Conference on Virtual, Augmented and Mixed Reality
- DHM: 15th International Conference on Digital Human Modeling & Applications in Health, Safety, Ergonomics & Risk Management
- DUXU: 13th International Conference on Design, User Experience and Usability
- C&C: 12th International Conference on Culture and Computing
- DAPI: 12th International Conference on Distributed, Ambient and Pervasive Interactions
- HCIBGO: 11th International Conference on HCI in Business, Government and Organizations
- LCT: 11th International Conference on Learning and Collaboration Technologies
- ITAP: 10th International Conference on Human Aspects of IT for the Aged Population
- AIS: 6th International Conference on Adaptive Instructional Systems
- HCI-CPT: 6th International Conference on HCI for Cybersecurity, Privacy and Trust
- HCI-Games: 6th International Conference on HCI in Games
- MobiTAS: 6th International Conference on HCI in Mobility, Transport and Automotive Systems
- AI-HCI: 5th International Conference on Artificial Intelligence in HCI
- MOBILE: 5th International Conference on Human-Centered Design, Operation and Evaluation of Mobile Communications

List of Conference Proceedings Volumes Appearing Before the Conference

1. LNCS 14684, Human-Computer Interaction: Part I, edited by Masaaki Kurosu and Ayako Hashizume
2. LNCS 14685, Human-Computer Interaction: Part II, edited by Masaaki Kurosu and Ayako Hashizume
3. LNCS 14686, Human-Computer Interaction: Part III, edited by Masaaki Kurosu and Ayako Hashizume
4. LNCS 14687, Human-Computer Interaction: Part IV, edited by Masaaki Kurosu and Ayako Hashizume
5. LNCS 14688, Human-Computer Interaction: Part V, edited by Masaaki Kurosu and Ayako Hashizume
6. LNCS 14689, Human Interface and the Management of Information: Part I, edited by Hirohiko Mori and Yumi Asahi
7. LNCS 14690, Human Interface and the Management of Information: Part II, edited by Hirohiko Mori and Yumi Asahi
8. LNCS 14691, Human Interface and the Management of Information: Part III, edited by Hirohiko Mori and Yumi Asahi
9. LNAI 14692, Engineering Psychology and Cognitive Ergonomics: Part I, edited by Don Harris and Wen-Chin Li
10. LNAI 14693, Engineering Psychology and Cognitive Ergonomics: Part II, edited by Don Harris and Wen-Chin Li
11. LNAI 14694, Augmented Cognition, Part I, edited by Dylan D. Schmorrow and Cali M. Fidopiastis
12. LNAI 14695, Augmented Cognition, Part II, edited by Dylan D. Schmorrow and Cali M. Fidopiastis
13. LNCS 14696, Universal Access in Human-Computer Interaction: Part I, edited by Margherita Antona and Constantine Stephanidis
14. LNCS 14697, Universal Access in Human-Computer Interaction: Part II, edited by Margherita Antona and Constantine Stephanidis
15. LNCS 14698, Universal Access in Human-Computer Interaction: Part III, edited by Margherita Antona and Constantine Stephanidis
16. LNCS 14699, Cross-Cultural Design: Part I, edited by Pei-Luen Patrick Rau
17. LNCS 14700, Cross-Cultural Design: Part II, edited by Pei-Luen Patrick Rau
18. LNCS 14701, Cross-Cultural Design: Part III, edited by Pei-Luen Patrick Rau
19. LNCS 14702, Cross-Cultural Design: Part IV, edited by Pei-Luen Patrick Rau
20. LNCS 14703, Social Computing and Social Media: Part I, edited by Adela Coman and Simona Vasilache
21. LNCS 14704, Social Computing and Social Media: Part II, edited by Adela Coman and Simona Vasilache
22. LNCS 14705, Social Computing and Social Media: Part III, edited by Adela Coman and Simona Vasilache

47. LNCS 14730, HCI in Games: Part I, edited by Xiaowen Fang
48. LNCS 14731, HCI in Games: Part II, edited by Xiaowen Fang
49. LNCS 14732, HCI in Mobility, Transport and Automotive Systems: Part I, edited by Heidi Krömker
50. LNCS 14733, HCI in Mobility, Transport and Automotive Systems: Part II, edited by Heidi Krömker
51. LNAI 14734, Artificial Intelligence in HCI: Part I, edited by Helmut Degen and Stavroula Ntoa
52. LNAI 14735, Artificial Intelligence in HCI: Part II, edited by Helmut Degen and Stavroula Ntoa
53. LNAI 14736, Artificial Intelligence in HCI: Part III, edited by Helmut Degen and Stavroula Ntoa
54. LNCS 14737, Design, Operation and Evaluation of Mobile Communications: Part I, edited by June Wei and George Margetis
55. LNCS 14738, Design, Operation and Evaluation of Mobile Communications: Part II, edited by June Wei and George Margetis
56. CCIS 2114, HCI International 2024 Posters - Part I, edited by Constantine Stephanidis, Margherita Antona, Stavroula Ntoa and Gavriel Salvendy
57. CCIS 2115, HCI International 2024 Posters - Part II, edited by Constantine Stephanidis, Margherita Antona, Stavroula Ntoa and Gavriel Salvendy
58. CCIS 2116, HCI International 2024 Posters - Part III, edited by Constantine Stephanidis, Margherita Antona, Stavroula Ntoa and Gavriel Salvendy
59. CCIS 2117, HCI International 2024 Posters - Part IV, edited by Constantine Stephanidis, Margherita Antona, Stavroula Ntoa and Gavriel Salvendy
60. CCIS 2118, HCI International 2024 Posters - Part V, edited by Constantine Stephanidis, Margherita Antona, Stavroula Ntoa and Gavriel Salvendy
61. CCIS 2119, HCI International 2024 Posters - Part VI, edited by Constantine Stephanidis, Margherita Antona, Stavroula Ntoa and Gavriel Salvendy
62. CCIS 2120, HCI International 2024 Posters - Part VII, edited by Constantine Stephanidis, Margherita Antona, Stavroula Ntoa and Gavriel Salvendy

https://2024.hci.international/proceedings

Preface

Software representations of humans, including aspects of anthropometry, biometrics, motion capture and prediction, as well as cognition modeling, are known as Digital Human Models (DHM), and are widely used in a variety of complex application domains where it is important to foresee and simulate human behavior, performance, safety, health and comfort. Automation depicting human emotion, social interaction and functional capabilities can also be modeled to support and assist in predicting human response in real-world settings. Such domains include medical and nursing applications, work, education and learning, ergonomics and design, as well as safety and risk management.

The 16th Digital Human Modeling and Applications in Health, Safety, Ergonomics and Risk Management (DHM) Conference, an affiliated conference of the HCI International Conference 2024, encouraged papers from academics, researchers, industry and professionals, on a broad range of theoretical and applied issues related to Digital Human Modeling and its applications.

The research papers contributed to this year's volumes span across different fields that fall within the scope of the DHM Conference. The role of DHM in the design and evaluation of various technologies has been explored, emphasizing the importance of the field for personalized and useful systems and applications, that advance user experience and foster communication, collaboration and learning. A significant number of submissions addressed DHM in assistive technologies for older adults, individuals with impairments and persons suffering from injuries. Furthermore, contributions have brought to the foreground the significance of DHM in healthcare interventions, and in technologies to support mental health and well-being, bridging the gap between human physiology and technological innovation. Finally, ergonomics constituted a topic that received focus this year, elaborating on the impact of DHM on ergonomic solutions for safety in work environments and the design of smart technologies.

Three volumes of the HCII 2024 proceedings are dedicated to this year's edition of the DHM conference. The first focuses on topics related to Digital Human Modeling for Design and Evaluation; User Experience and Assistive Technologies; and User Experience, Communication, and Collaboration. The second focuses on topics related to Healthcare Design and Support; Technology in Mental Health and Wellbeing; and Artificial Intelligence and Health Applications. The third focuses on topics related to Work, Safety, and Ergonomics; Ergonomics, Artificial Intelligence and Smart Technologies; and Advanced Technologies for Training and Learning.

The papers of these volumes were accepted for publication after a minimum of two single-blind reviews from the members of the DHM Program Board or, in some cases, from members of the Program Boards of other affiliated conferences. I would like to thank all of them for their invaluable contribution, support and efforts.

July 2024   Vincent G. Duffy

15th International Conference on Digital Human Modeling and Applications in Health, Safety, Ergonomics and Risk Management (DHM 2024)

Program Board Chair: **Vincent G. Duffy**, *Purdue University, USA*

- Karthik Adapa, *UNC Chapel Hill, USA*
- Giuseppe Andreoni, *Politecnico di Milano, Italy*
- Pedro Arezes, *University of Minho, Portugal*
- Hasan Ayaz, *Drexel University, USA*
- Aydin Azizi, *Oxford Brookes University, UK*
- Angelos Barmpoutis, *University of Florida, USA*
- Simone Borsci, *University of Twente, Netherlands*
- Andre Calero Valdez, *University of Lübeck, Germany*
- Yaqin Cao, *Anhui Polytechnic University, P.R. China*
- Ignacio Castellucci, *Universidad de Valparaíso, Chile*
- Damien Chablat, *CNRS/LS2N, France*
- Karen Chen, *North Carolina State University, USA*
- Bong Jun Choi, *Soongsil University, Korea*
- Denis Coelho, *Jönköping University, Sweden*
- Clive D'Souza, *University of Pittsburgh, USA*
- H. Onan Demirel, *Oregon State University, USA*
- Yi Ding, *Anhui Polytechnic University, P.R. China*
- Manish Kumar Dixit, *Texas A&M University, USA*
- Ehsan Esfahani, *University at Buffalo, USA*
- Martin Fleischer, *Technical University of Munich, Germany*
- Martin Fränzle, *Oldenburg University, Germany*
- Afzal Godil, *National Institute of Standards and Technology, USA*
- Wenbin Guo, *University of Florida, USA*
- Sogand Hasanzadeh, *Purdue University, USA*
- Bochen Jia, *University of Michigan, USA*
- Genett Isabel Jimenez Delgado, *Institucion Universitaria de Barranquilla IUB, Colombia*
- Jari Kaivo-oja, *Turku School of Economics, University of Turku, Finland*
- Taina Kalliokoski, *University of Helsinki, Finland*
- Jeong Ho Kim, *Oregon State University, USA*
- Woojoo Kim, *Kangwon National University, Korea*
- Steffi Kohl, *Zuyd University of Applied Sciences, Netherlands*
- Richard Lamb, *East Carolina University, USA*
- Nicola Francesco Lopomo, *Università degli Studi di Brescia, Italy*
- Siu Shing Man, *South China University of Technology, P.R. China*
- Alexander Mehler, *Goethe University Frankfurt, Germany*

- Jörg Miehling, *Friedrich-Alexander-Universität Erlangen-Nürnberg (FAU), Germany*
- Salman Nazir, *University of Southeastern Norway, Norway*
- Peter Nickel, *Institute for Occupational Safety and Health of the German Social Accident Insurance (IFA), Germany*
- Ashish Nimbarte, *West Virginia University, USA*
- Joseph Nuamah, *Oklahoma State University, USA*
- Miguel Ortiz-Barrios, *Universitat Politecnica de Valencia, Spain and Universidad de la Costa (CUC), Colombia*
- Nicola Paltrinieri, *NTNU, Norway*
- Thaneswer Patel, *North Eastern Regional Institute of Science and Technology, India*
- Xingda Qu, *Shenzhen University, P.R. China*
- Qing-Xing Qu, *Northeastern University, P.R. China*
- Erwin Rauch, *Free University of Bolzano, Spain*
- Arto Reiman, *University of Oulu, Finland*
- Deep Seth, *Mahindra University, India*
- Fabio Sgarbossa, *NTNU, Norway*
- Jieun Shin, *University of Florida, USA*
- Thitirat Siriborvornratanakul, *National Institute of Development Administration, Thailand*
- Beatriz Sousa Santos, *University of Aveiro, Portugal*
- Hendrik Stern, *Universität Bremen, Germany*
- Lesley Strawderman, *Mississippi State University, USA*
- Youchao Sun, *Nanjing University of Aeronautics and Astronautics, P.R. China*
- Zhengtang Tan, *Hunan Normal University, P.R. China*
- Leonor Teixeira, *University of Aveiro, Portugal*
- Renran Tian, *IUPUI, USA*
- Joseph Timoney, *Maynooth University, Ireland*
- Vinay V. Panicker, *National Institute of Technology Calicut, India*
- Dustin Van der Haar, *University of Johannesburg, South Africa*
- Kuan Yew Wong, *Universiti Teknologi Malaysia (UTM), Malaysia*
- Shuping Xiong, *Korea Advanced Institute of Science and Technology, Korea*
- James Yang, *Texas Tech University, USA*

The full list with the Program Board Chairs and the members of the Program Boards of all thematic areas and affiliated conferences of HCII 2024 is available online at:

http://www.hci.international/board-members-2024.php

HCI International 2025 Conference

The 27th International Conference on Human-Computer Interaction, HCI International 2025, will be held jointly with the affiliated conferences at the Swedish Exhibition & Congress Centre and Gothia Towers Hotel, Gothenburg, Sweden, June 22–27, 2025. It will cover a broad spectrum of themes related to Human-Computer Interaction, including theoretical issues, methods, tools, processes, and case studies in HCI design, as well as novel interaction techniques, interfaces, and applications. The proceedings will be published by Springer. More information will become available on the conference website: https://2025.hci.international/.

General Chair
Prof. Constantine Stephanidis
University of Crete and ICS-FORTH
Heraklion, Crete, Greece
Email: general_chair@2025.hci.international

https://2025.hci.international/

Contents – Part III

Ergonomics, Artificial Intelligence and Smart Technologies

Advanced Technologies for Training and Learning

Work, Safety, and Ergonomics

Ergonomic Improvement and Simulation Analysis of Armrests for Uncomfortable Working Environments

Weichao Lin⬚, Siu Shing Man, Kang Ran, Meng Zhang, Guolue Xu, and Liang Chen$^{(\boxtimes)}$⬚

School of Design, South China University of Technology, Guangzhou, China
{ssman6,earchen}@scut.edu.cn

Abstract. With the prevalence of portable laptops, the limitations of computer workstations are gradually diminishing, and any location furnished with a desk and chair can now function as a workspace. However, it must be acknowledged that frequently having the arm in an uncomfortable working position while operating the mouse is not uncommon. This phenomenon can be attributed to desk and chair design, individual height differences, and workplace requirements. Prolonged use of a computer in incorrect postures may lead to health issues, such as carpal tunnel syndrome, which can harm the wrists and joints and result in persistent pain. Therefore, various armrest products have emerged in the market to assist workers in adjusting their working postures and reducing the occurrence of health problems, such as carpal tunnel syndrome. However, not all arm support products effectively assist users in achieving ergonomic positioning, especially in unfriendly work environments. This research aims to enhance the existing structure of armrests to tackle this problem. 12 male and female subjects representing the 5th, 50th, and 95th percentiles of standard height were selected. These subjects were then asked to engage in computer-related activities using a computer and a mouse. Subsequently, the Rapid Upper Limb Assessment method and SAMMIE software were employed for posture analysis. This study utilized Autodesk Fusion 360 software to redesign the armrest and conducted simulation experiments to perform a comprehensive comparative analysis before and after the improvement.

Keywords: Ergonomics · Armrest · Structural improvement · Rapid Upper Limb Assessment · Simulation · Carpal tunnel syndrome

1 Introduction and Background

In modern society, computers have become indispensable for learning and work. Sitting in front of the computer with a mouse in hand has become the norm for students and office workers. However, if the desk height, chair height, and desk-chair distance are not appropriate, it can result in the worker's right arm

V. G. Duffy (Ed.): HCII 2024, LNCS 14711, pp. 3–14, 2024.
https://doi.org/10.1007/978-3-031-61066-0_1

being suspended in mid-air and the wrist being bent. Maintaining improper work postures for a prolonged period can injure the muscles and joints of the wrist, elbow, and arm, increasing the risk of developing carpal tunnel syndrome. Symptoms of carpal tunnel syndrome include numbness, pain, and weakness in the lateral three fingers of the hand, with the middle finger being the most significantly affected. In addition, the numbness and pain worsen when flexing the elbow, raising the forearm, or flexing the wrist. Patients may also exhibit a positive Tinel's sign over the carpal tunnel and swelling and tenderness in the wrist. For patients who have suffered from the condition for a long time, the nerve damage can be severe, potentially leading to atrophy of the thenar muscles and loss of thumb function.

Ergonomic mouse designs can guide users into more natural wrist postures [2]. By comparing regular mice and ergonomic mice in experiments, it was found that workers using ergonomic mice experienced less wrist pressure, thus reducing the risk of carpal tunnel syndrome [4]. However, some experiments have also found that workers using regular horizontal mice had advantages in work efficiency and effectiveness [5]. Therefore, when selecting mouse designs, it is necessary to consider the trade-off between work efficiency and work posture. In addition to improving mouse design, studies have found that gel mouse pads can reduce ulnar deviation, and palm rests can reduce wrist extension, even when using regular horizontal mice [6]. Table 1 shows the dimensions of desks and chairs in the dormitory of the South China University of Technology (SCUT) International Campus. The SCUT is a prestigious academic institution in mainland China, known for its outstanding achievements in science and engineering. However, students have received widespread complaints regarding the desks and chairs in the newly constructed international campus dormitories. Investigations reveal that most students find the desk height and chair design in the dormitories impractical, with a significant disparity in height causing discomfort during study or work. Prolonged work periods contribute to arm and wrist strain, resulting in fatigue and discomfort. Many students have attempted to address this issue by purchasing armrests; however, the currently available products fail to meet their needs. We believe that addressing this problem is of significant practical importance.

According to the principles documented in Chinese ergonomic textbooks [1], the recommended height difference between the working desk and chair should be between 27.0–30.0 cm. Specifically, for males, the recommended range is 28.0–30.0 cm, while for females, it is 27.0–29.0 cm. However, the height difference between the desks and chairs at the International Campus of SCUT reaches 39.0 cm, which significantly exceeds the recommended range. This makes it an unsuitable working environment from an ergonomic perspective. Given practical constraints that prohibit the modification or redesign of the existing desks and chairs on a large scale, our proposed solution focuses on improving the design of the current mouse armrest to alleviate improper postures.

Table 1. Dimensions of desks and chairs in the dormitory.

Desk		Chair	
Horizontal length	90.00 cm	Seat width	47.50 cm
Depth	53.00 cm	Depth	50.50 cm
Thickness	2.30 cm	Seat height	37.00 cm
Height	76.00 cm		

2 Product Analysis

2.1 Market Analysistitle

We conducted market research on a specific e-commerce platform in China and found that armrest products can generally be categorized into two groups. The first category consists of single-board armrests that clamp onto the desktop. These armrests are secured to the desktop using bolts, which extend the product's planar structure to the edge of the desk. However, the ability to adjust the height may vary among products in this category. The second category consists of multi-adjustable armrests that resemble multi-joint mechanical arms. These armrests have rotational degrees of freedom, which enable users to adjust the angle. Since single-board armrests clamped to the desktop clearly cannot meet the requirements of the specific working environment discussed in this paper, we will only discuss multi-adjustable armrest products.

Certain models offer both height-adjustable and non-height-adjustable variants within multi-section adjustable armrest products, as outlined in Table 2.

Table 2. Two types of multi-section adjustable armrest products.

	Product image	Structure	Adjustable range
Height-adjustable			Section1: Rotate around y-axis; Section2: Rotate around y-axis, lift up around x-axis; Section3: Rotate around y-axis;
Non-height-adjustable			Section1: Rotate around y-axis; Section2: Rotate around y-axis; Section3: Rotate around y-axis;

2.2 Structural Analysis

To determine the direction for improvement, we utilized reverse engineering to reconstruct the structure of the product, followed by a structural analysis. Simulation results for joint movement indicate that the range of motion for each hinge is approximately 105°. Adjusting the rotational angle of the joints enables different flexion and extension states, as illustrated in Fig. 1.

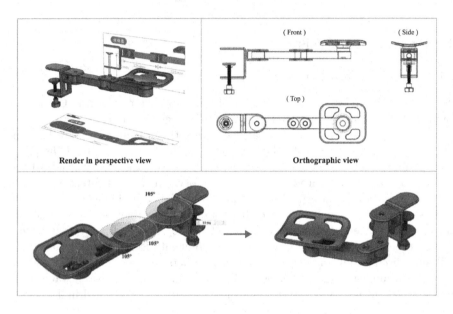

Fig. 1. Reverse modeling and structural analysis of non-height-adjustable armrest.

2.3 Improvement

The main goal of the enhancement is to add a new feature to the armrest, allowing its supporting surface to lower below the level of the desktop. This innovation aims to provide users with increased adjustability to accommodate diverse working environments. To achieve the added height adjustability, each joint incorporates two degrees of freedom, allowing rotation around the Y-axis and the X-axis. To achieve this, we consider implementing a structure similar to a spherical joint, as depicted in Fig. 2. Furthermore, to accommodate variations in the working postures of different users' elbows and arms, we have integrated a spherical joint and a 360-degree rotation mechanism into the end-supporting surface, as shown in Fig. 3. The final product enhancement design is depicted in Fig. 4.

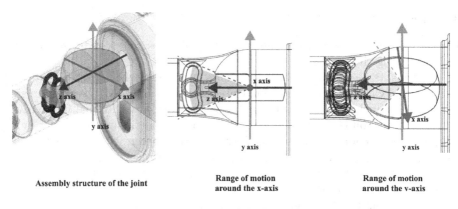

Assembly structure of the joint   Range of motion around the x-axis   Range of motion around the v-axis

Fig. 2. Assembly structure and range of motion of ball joints.

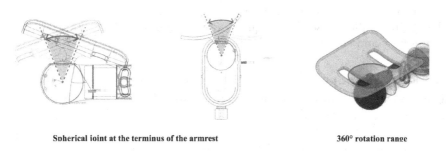

Spherical joint at the terminus of the armrest   360° rotation range

Fig. 3. The improved armrest has a support surface with a spherical joint.

Fig. 4. Different views of the enhanced armrest.

3   Experiment Research

3.1   Subject

We recruited 12 students from the International Campus of the SCUT as participants. Specifically, we selected six males and six females who represented the 5th, 50th, and 95th percentiles of standard height for both genders. These participants were chosen from diverse academic disciplines and colleges to ensure the wide-ranging applicability of the study results.

3.2   Process

For each participant, the following experimental steps were conducted before and after using the armrest:

Participants used student desks and chairs provided by the dormitories at the International Campus of South China University of Technology. The experimental workspace included a computer and a mouse, with no additional interfering devices or items on the work surface. In this environment, participants sat in a self-perceived comfortable posture in front of the computer, with their left hand naturally placed and their right forearm resting on the desktop. If assessing the posture of the armrest, participants were required to adjust it to an appropriate angle, allowing the right forearm to rest naturally on the armrest. The right hand naturally grasped the mouse. Participants sequentially completed two tasks while researchers assessed their working posture.

The two tasks employed refer to the experimental design used in previous related studies [3]. These tasks require extensive mouse movements to evaluate the usability and effectiveness of armrests.

Task 1 - Data Re-Entry (20 min). Participants were assigned to enter four-digit numbers into two worksheets within the same Excel file. Initially, random four-digit numbers were placed in random rows on the first worksheet, with a minimum of 20 empty rows between each number. Participants had to memorize these numbers and their respective rows and columns on the first worksheet. Subsequently, they re-entered them into the corresponding rows and columns on the target worksheet (Sheet 30 in the same Excel file).

Task 2 - Balloon Shooting (5 min). In this task, participants aimed to shoot as many balloons as possible. The balloons started at zero diameter and gradually expanded to their maximum diameter, bursting and disappearing. The balloons would appear within a window measuring 18 cm in width and 12 cm in height. Participants were instructed to shoot as many balloons as possible within the given time frame.

The researchers documented the participants' postures both before and after using the armrest. Posture recording involved using smartphones for photography and direct observation. The smartphone was positioned 80 cm away from the participant, capturing side, top, and rear views. The observation focused on working postures, exertion loads, and muscle usage of the right hand, neck, torso, and feet.

For posture assessment, the Rapid Upper Limb Assessment (RULA) method was employed. This method categorized the elements of human movement into two major groups: the wrist and arm, and the neck, torso, and legs. RULA scores were assigned based on the recorded results, enabling the determination of the participants' ergonomic performance levels. This method was utilized to assess the postures of participants before and after using the armrest, providing an evaluation of the effectiveness and usability of the armrest. The assessment steps are outlined in Table 3.

Table 3. Specific steps for applying the RULA assessment.

Step	Content
1	Assessment of the Upper Arm
2	Assessment of the Lower Arm
3	Wrist Assessment
4	Wrist Rotation Assessment
5	Wrist and Arm Posture Score
6	Wrist and Arm Posture Combined with Muscle Effort Assessment
7	Wrist and Arm Posture Combined with Load Level Assessment
8	Wrist and Arm Total Score
9	Neck Assessment
10	Trunk Assessment
11	Leg Assessment
12	Neck, Trunk, and Leg Posture Score
13	Neck, Trunk, and Leg Posture Combined with Muscle Effort Assessment
14	Neck, Trunk, and Leg Posture Combined with Load Level Assessment
15	Neck, Trunk, and Leg Total Score
16	Final Score

4   Results and Discussion

4.1   RULA Analysis

Without Armrest. Analysis results, as shown in Table 4, revealed that among the 12 participants, 11 exhibited a risk level of 2, with only one participant (No. 8) reaching a risk level of 3. Further investigation revealed that Participant 8 had a spinal curvature issue, which led to an elevated trunk score in the RULA assessment and consequently resulted in a higher risk level. This result indicates that users with poor posture face an increased risk.

The risk level of 2 for the remaining 11 participants indicates the presence of ergonomic risks that require further improvement in the working environment. This result also implies that prolonged work in this environment does not meet ergonomic requirements, potentially leading to fatigue or discomfort in the upper limbs. This result emphasizes the need for environmental enhancements.

Table 4. RULA analysis results of working postures without armrest support.

No.	Height	Gender	Score	Risk	Response
1	158	Female	4	2	Further investigation and necessary improvement
2	158	Female	4	2	Further investigation and necessary improvement
3	161	Female	4	2	Further investigation and necessary improvement
4	161	Female	3	2	Further investigation and necessary improvement
5	175	Female	3	2	Further investigation and necessary improvement
6	175	Female	4	2	Further investigation and necessary improvement
7	162	Male	4	2	Further investigation and necessary improvement
8	162	Male	5	3	Immediate investigation and improvement required
9	172	Male	3	2	Further investigation and necessary improvement
10	174	Male	3	2	Further investigation and necessary improvement
11	181	Male	3	2	Further investigation and necessary improvement
12	181	Male	3	2	Further investigation and necessary improvement

Combining observational methods with RULA analysis, we observed that participants had higher scores and significant variations in the right upper limb, right lower limb, right wrist, and right wrist twist. In contrast, the scores for the neck, torso, and legs were relatively low and stable. This suggests that in this working environment, issues related to fatigue and discomfort are more pronounced in the right upper limb.

With Improved Armrest. Following the utilization of the armrest, we selected female participants whose heights corresponded to the 5th, 50th, and 95th percentiles for a subsequent round of RULA analysis. The results, as shown in Table 5, indicated that all participants maintained a risk level of 2. Although the risk level after using the armrest remained unchanged compared to the baseline without the armrest, we speculate that the difference in height between the chair and table, combined with the inability to adjust them, resulted in the right upper limb being significantly further away from the center. Consequently, the addition of the armrest did not result in a significant improvement.

Table 5. RULA analysis results of working postures with armrest support.

No.	Height	Gender	Score	Risk	Response
1	158	Female	3	2	Further investigation and necessary improvement
2	158	Female	3	2	Further investigation and necessary improvement
3	161	Female	3	2	Further investigation and necessary improvement
4	161	Female	3	2	Further investigation and necessary improvement
5	175	Female	3	2	Further investigation and necessary improvement
6	175	Female	3	2	Further investigation and necessary improvement

Despite the consistent level of risk, there was a change in the total assessment score. The four risk levels in RULA analysis are categorized based on the total assessment score, where a higher score indicates an increased work-related risk. Therefore, examining changes in the total assessment score allows us to evaluate the effectiveness of the armrest in adjusting working posture. We used a paired-sample t-test to analyze the differences in the total score of the assessment.

The results of the paired-sample t-test, as shown in Table 6, revealed a significant p-value of 0.025**. This result suggests a significant difference between the total assessment scores without the armrest (mean = 3.67) and with the armrest (mean = 3). The significant decrease in the total assessment score after adding the armrest indicates a lower ergonomic risk level. This result suggests that the armrest we designed enhances the comfort of the right upper limb during prolonged mouse usage in a dormitory setting. Further observations revealed improvements in the condition of the right lower limb, right wrist, and right wrist twist after using our designed armrest. To validate this hypothesis further, we conducted simulations in SAMMIE.

Table 6. Paired samples T-test on the total scores of the two RULA assessments.

		Mean	N	SD.	SE. Mean	t	Sig (2-tailed)
Pair	Without Armrest	3.67	6	0.516	20.211	1.362	0.025
	With Armrest	3.00	6	0.000	0.000		

4.2 Simulation Analysis

Without Armrest. In this section, the SAMMIE human factors analysis software was utilized to analyze the posture of participants with different body types while using the mouse without the armrest, as shown in Fig. 5 and Fig. 6. For the 5th percentile male, all assessed metrics were within a reasonable range. However, for the 50th percentile male, the "Twist" metric for the forearm was abnormal, indicating a need for forearm and palm rotation towards the body. Similarly, the male at the 95th percentile exhibited abnormal "Twist" metrics, which necessitated a rotation of the forearm and palm towards the body.

As for the 5th percentile female, all metrics were within acceptable limits. In the case of the 50th percentile female, all metrics were generally acceptable. However, the "Twist" metric for the forearm was at the upper limit of the reasonable range, indicating potential issues. Similarly, the female at the 95th percentile displayed abnormal "Twist" metrics, requiring a rotation of the forearm and palm towards the body.

In summary, the common issue identified among participants was related to forearm posture. Specifically, the upper arm failed to extend to the required angle, resulting in inadequate axial rotation of the forearm during posture adjustment. Additionally, it was observed that the forearm and palm joints, which serve as support structures, were resting on the edge of the desk. This positioning has the potential to cause joint discomfort when used for extended periods of time.

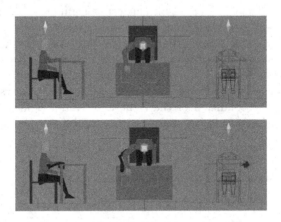

Fig. 5. Simulation analysis has been conducted on two situations: with armrest and without armrest in SAMMIE software.

With Improved Armrest. To validate the effectiveness of the improved armrest design in addressing the previously mentioned posture issues, we conducted a posture analysis using models that represent the 5th, 50th, and 95th percentiles of female body types. This analysis was performed after incorporating the improved armrest. Simulation results indicate a reduction in the "Twist" metric for the forearm, bringing it within a reasonable range for all participants. This result suggests that our armrest design can alleviate discomfort during prolonged mouse usage in a dormitory setting, particularly for female users. This improvement is likely applicable to male participants as well, as it caters to users at both the 5th and 95th percentiles. This result demonstrates the design's suitability for individuals with heights ranging from the 5th to the 95th percentiles. In conclusion, the redesigned armrest is effective, versatile, and reliable in addressing ergonomic issues related to the arm and wrist during mouse usage.

Without armrest :

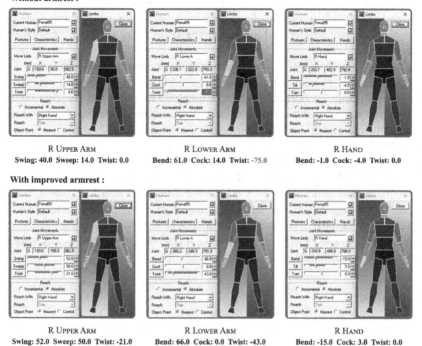

R UPPER ARM
Swing: 40.0 Sweep: 14.0 Twist: 0.0

R LOWER ARM
Bend: 61.0 Cock: 14.0 Twist: -75.0

R HAND
Bend: -1.0 Cock: -4.0 Twist: 0.0

With improved armrest :

R UPPER ARM
Swing: 52.0 Sweep: 50.0 Twist: -21.0

R LOWER ARM
Bend: 66.0 Cock: 0.0 Twist: -43.0

R HAND
Bend: -15.0 Cock: 3.0 Twist: 0.0

Fig. 6. Numerical representation of changes in the comfort of arm segments with arm-rest support in SAMMIE software (illustrated with a 95th percentile Chinese female).

4.3 Conclusion

This study conducted RULA assessments and SAMMIE analyses on the working postures of students at the International Campus of SCUT while using a mouse in dormitory settings. Identified ergonomic risks in this working environment guided the design of an armrest to improve users' working postures. The effectiveness of the improved armrest design was verified through simulation experiments.

Results from RULA assessments and SAMMIE analyses highlighted discomfort during mouse usage in dormitories, primarily related to the posture of the right hand. Specific ergonomic risks include excessive axial twist of the forearm, significant pressure on the palm joint and wrist from the desk edge, and a substantial difference in seat height, leading to unnatural forearm placement.

To address these ergonomic issues, an existing multi-adjustable armrest available in the market was modified to improve the twisting conditions of the right forearm, wrist, and hand. The main improvement to the armrest was the addition of a feature that allows the supporting surface to be lowered below the desktop. This improvement was achieved by incorporating a spherical joint, which enhances adjustability. Simulations in SAMMIE with armrest and human models showed that posture metrics for participants of varying heights and genders were within normal ranges. Additionally, the total score in RULA assessments significantly decreased.

This study demonstrated the effectiveness, versatility, and reliability of the redesigned armrest in addressing ergonomic issues related to arm and wrist strain during mouse usage in dormitory environments. The proposed solution offers a practical approach to enhancing working postures in particular work environments, reducing the discomfort caused by prolonged mouse use. Furthermore, this methodology can serve as a valuable reference and guide for addressing similar ergonomic issues in different contexts. Future research may extend to long-term application studies in real working environments, gathering extensive user feedback and conducting testing. Continuous optimization, based on user opinions and suggestions, can further enhance the ergonomic performance of the product. Evaluating the long-term effects of armrests in reducing discomfort and improving work efficiency provides a reference for scientifically rational improvements to armrests and similar assistive products.

References

1. Ding, Y.: Ren Ji Gong Cheng Xue, 3rd edn. Beijing Institute of Technology Press (2005)
2. Gaudez, C., Cail, F.: What's the best computer mouse? A comparative study of wrist angles and carp extensor activity when using three mice. Comput. Methods Biomech. Biomed. Eng. **20**(sup1), 89–90 (2017)
3. Jovanović, S., Šimunič, B.: Effect of ergonomic armrest® forearm support on wrist posture related to carpal tunnel pressure during computer mouse work. Int. J. Ind. Ergon. **86**, 103220 (2021)
4. Keir, P.J., Bach, J.M., Rempel, D.: Effects of computer mouse design and task on carpal tunnel pressure. Ergonomics **42**(10), 1350–1360 (1999)
5. Lourenço, M.L., Pitarma, R.A., Coelho, D.A.: Horizontal and vertical handheld pointing devices comparison for increasing human systems integration at the design stage. In: Nunes, I. (eds.) Advances in Human Factors and System Interactions, vol. 497, pp. 15–24. Springer, Cham (2017). https://doi.org/10.1007/978-3-319-41956-5_2
6. Schmid, A.B., Kubler, P.A., Johnston, V., Coppieters, M.W.: A vertical mouse and ergonomic mouse pads alter wrist position but do not reduce carpal tunnel pressure in patients with carpal tunnel syndrome. Appl. Ergon. **47**, 151–156 (2015)

Ergonomics for Work-Life Balance: A Systematic Review

Abhijeet Ambesange, Akhila Chandrasekaran[(✉)], and Vincent G. Duffy

Purdue University, West Lafayette, IN 47906, USA
{aambesan,chand199,duffy}@purdue.edu

Abstract. In modern times, work has started bleeding outside of corporate offices. The notion of a routine nine-to-five at a designated desk or workstation has become limited with the advent of non-traditional work cultures and environments. Computers and cloud storage facilities have introduced several 24x7 operations. Organizations offer various levels of flexibility with respect to workload and work timings. COVID-19 moved a lot of jobs into peoples' homes– jobs that were considered impossible to perform from a remote location. In the face of all this, the working population continues to steadily grow older. This study aims to analyze the effects of traditional and non-traditional employment conditions on the present-day working population and Work-Life Balance (WLB). Also surveyed are some studies that offer solutions to common workplace ergonomic hazards, physiological as well as psychological. Content Analysis tools like maxQDA, VOS Viewer, CiteSpace and Google Ngram Viewer were used for this purpose.

Keywords: workplace · ergonomics · working population

1 Introduction and Background

The impact of ergonomics on WLB is a multifaceted area that encompasses various aspects of workplace design, human factors, and employee well-being. Research has indicated that the application of ergonomics can significantly influence the quality of work life, reduce musculoskeletal disorders, and enhance productivity. Furthermore, ergonomic conditions have been found to be effective in promoting employee happiness, satisfaction, and self-esteem in the workplace. The goal of ergonomics is to create safe, comfortable, and productive workplaces that take into account individuals' abilities and limitations, thereby contributing to a positive WLB.

Ergonomics plays a crucial role in mitigating age-related injuries and addressing obstacles faced by older workers in the workplace, thereby contributing to a more inclusive and supportive work environment. Additionally, ergonomic-driven workplace design and modifications have been highlighted as highly effective in determining appropriate work conditions, preventing workers' exposure to ergonomic risks, and accommodating medical restrictions, ultimately contributing to improved WLB.

Moreover, the incorporation of ergonomics training into office workplaces has been shown to enhance the effective use of work environments and knowledge workers'

V. G. Duffy (Ed.): HCII 2024, LNCS 14711, pp. 15–29, 2024.
https://doi.org/10.1007/978-3-031-61066-0_2

sense of control and environmental satisfaction, thereby positively impacting WLB. Understanding the technical aspects of ergonomic applications can lead to changes in the office environment that favorably affect management's bottom line while reducing health hazards for employees, thus contributing to a healthier WLB.

Overall, the integration of ergonomics into workplace design and practices has the potential to significantly impact WLB by promoting physical well-being, job satisfaction, and a supportive work environment for employees across various industries and demographics.

2 Purpose of Study

The aim of this study is to understand the challenges faced by the employees of this day and age with regard to various parameters like the industry, age, the pandemic, etc. and explore lower management level solutions to bureaucratic measures. Job satisfaction has come to be analogous to WLB, and it has been known to improve productivity, hence, it is a lucrative area of study.

3 Data Collection

3.1 Textbook References

In the course IE 578 Applied Ergonomics, the text "Handbook of Human Factors and Ergonomics" (fourth and fifth editions) edited by Gavriel Salvendy and Waldemar Karwowski was used as the reference. This study has referred to the chapters 9: Emotional Design and 14: Workplace Design.

The chapter "Emotional Design" by Zhou, Ji, and Jiao (2021) discusses the significance of emotional design in web interfaces. It emphasizes the importance of creating designs that evoke positive emotions in users, leading to a more engaging and satisfying user experience. The chapter delves into the theoretical foundations of emotional design, such as the influential model proposed by Norman, and provides practical guidance on incorporating emotional elements into web design. Additionally, it explores the impact of emotional design on user behavior and decision-making, highlighting its relevance in creating successful and user-centric web interfaces.

On the other hand, the chapter "Workplace Design" by Smith and Johnson (2020) focuses on the ergonomic and human factors considerations in designing work environments. It covers various aspects of workplace design, including spatial layout, furniture, lighting, and environmental factors, with the aim of enhancing employee well-being, productivity, and satisfaction. The chapter emphasizes the importance of considering human factors in workplace design, such as anthropometry and user-centered design principles, to create work environments that promote health, safety, and efficiency (Marmaras & Nathanael, 2012).

In summary, the chapter on emotional design provides insights into creating emotionally engaging web interfaces, while the chapter on workplace design offers comprehensive guidance on designing ergonomic and user-centered work environments.

3.2 Methodology

Keywords and Search Strategy. Phrases like "ergonomics for work-life balance", "effects of ergonomics on work-life balance", and "ergonomics and work-life balance" were used to generate search results on platforms like Scopus, scite.ai, Google Scholar, Research Gate, Web of Science and Purdue Libraries. The obtained results were filtered to obtain recent articles in journals and publications relating to Ergonomics and Industrial Engineering. After going through the abstracts of the results in the first couple of pages, a new search phrase was used since results are generally arranged in decreasing order of relevance (Figs. 1, 2 and 3).

The search results obtained are tabulated below (Table 1):

Table 1. Total number of articles generated in each source

Source	Number of Articles
Scopus	68
Scite.ai	268,761
Google Scholar	136,000
Research Gate	100
Web of Science	101
Purdue Libraries	5780

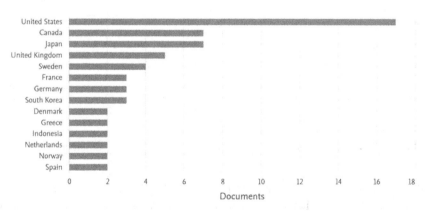

Documents by country or territory
Compare the document counts for up to 15 countries/territories.

Fig. 1. Country wise number of publications

Concept Mapping. In order to create an organized visualization of ideas, VOS viewer and CiteSpace were used. A text file was imported into the VOS Viewer software from

Documents by subject area

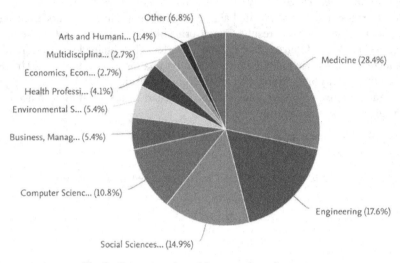

Fig. 2. Documents by subject area from Scopus

Documents per year by source

Compare the document counts for up to 10 sources.   Compare sources and view CiteScore, SJR, and SNIP data

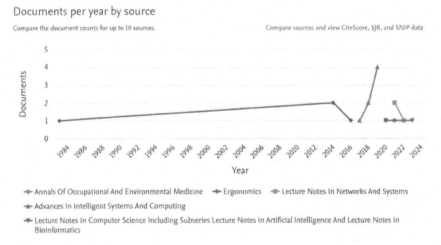

Fig. 3. Trend showing number of documents published per year by different sources

the Web of Science website, containing the titles of all the search results, citations, and authors. The below figure helps understand what keywords appear in the titles and how they relate to each other, thereby giving an idea of what all the publications indicate (Fig. 4).

Another tool used for this purpose is CiteSpace and is also undertaken by importing the text file into the software. The result is basically a grouping of articles based on

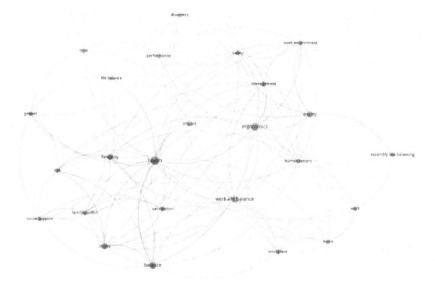

Fig. 4. Co-Occurrence Analysis using VOS Viewer

certain keywords. This, again, helps visualize the main patterns in scientific literature in this particular area (Fig. 5).

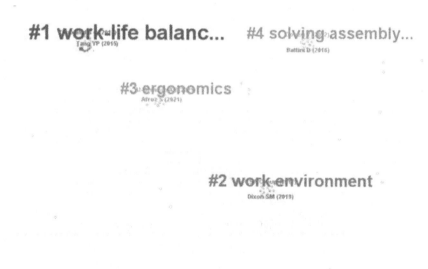

Fig. 5. Clusters Analysis of citations using CiteSpace

Trend Analysis. Two main tools were used to examine the trends within the topic: ergonomics and WLB, namely Google Ngram and Scopus. As the heading suggests, it is used to identify patterns and emerging subject areas (Fig. 6).

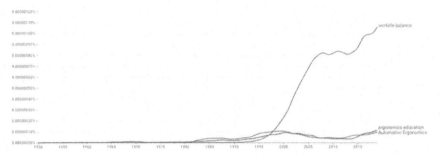

Fig. 6. Trend of WLB in comparison to ergonomics education and automotive er gon. It clearly shows the emergent and rising popularity of WLB.

The below trend diagram shows the trend in terms of number of publications with respect to the year of publication. This also demonstrates WLB as a emergent topic with rising popularity and publication (Fig. 7).

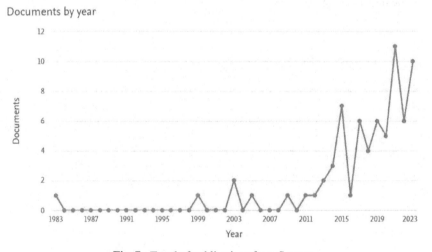

Fig. 7. Trend of publications from Scopus

4   Discussion and Conclusions

4.1   Content Analysis

Out of the 23 articles chosen, the following represents the number of studies that examined each location (Fig. 8).

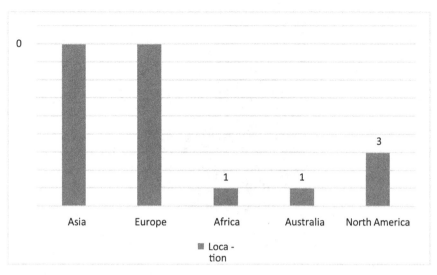

Fig. 8. Articles chosen by location

Six of the chosen studies alluded to remote work and the perceived effects of it are shown in the below chart (Fig. 9).

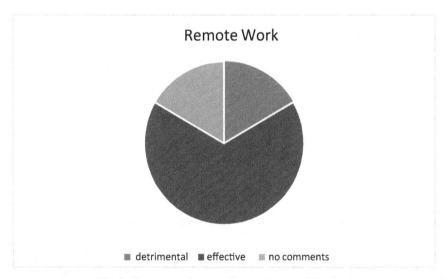

Fig. 9. Remote work according to chosen publications

Four articles inspect the effects of COVID-19 on the WLB of remote working employees.

Figures 10 and 11 show the number of studies based on their types.

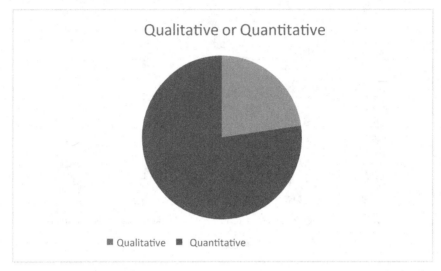

Fig. 10. Number of Qualitative versus Quantitative studies based on their results

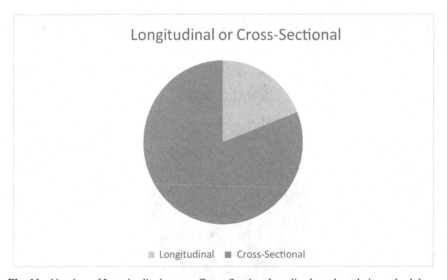

Fig. 11. Number of Longitudinal versus Cross-Sectional studies based on their methodology

The wordcloud below generated using maxQDA analyzes the content of the chosen publications and points out the commonly occurring terms. This helps understand the most pertinent ideas of the literature synthesized (Fig. 12 and Table 2).

4.2 Insights

The advent of remote working has brought significant changes to the landscape of work life, which has led organizations and individuals to re-evaluate traditional work-related

Fig. 12. Wordcloud of the chosen research papers

norms and their effects on personal life. This article examines the impact of telecommuting on work-life balance and provides an overview of four different perspectives presented in Articles 1, 9, 16 and 23.

Implementation of operational information systems and reliance on cloud resources, as emphasized in Article 1, contribute to the smooth operation of remote work environments. However, the constant availability and expectations of 24x7 operations can blur the lines between work and personal life, which can lead to increased stress. Emphasis is placed on the joint assessment of transport and the social family, which highlights the need for strategies that respond to the challenges of telecommuting without jeopardizing work-life balance.

Article 9 emphasizes the importance of maintaining a balance between the main job and the work environment. Although ergonomic changes can improve efficiency, it is important to avoid possible negative effects on workers and their welfare The static positions and repetitive movements associated with remote work can lead to physical discomfort and health problems, highlighting the need for organizations to implement ergonomic principles in remote workspaces to ensure a healthy work-life balance.

Article 16 sheds light on employee telecommuting preferences. The vast majority want to continue working remotely, which means a change in attitude towards flexible working arrangements. Although this preference can promote a better work-life balance by allowing employees to adjust their work schedules, it also emphasizes the need for organizations to adapt practices to support remote work and address the challenges associated with it.

The psychological and social effects of telecommuting presented in Article 23 draw attention to the potential challenges telecommuters face. Social isolation, lack of teamwork and concerns about workplace safety affect the complex interaction between work and personal life. Employers are advised to consider the psychological well-being of employees and ensure that remote work does not create a feeling of isolation or insecurity.

To sum up, it can be stated that remote work offers both opportunities and challenges in balancing work and family life. The introduction of functional information systems

Table 2. Lexical term analysis conducted using maxQDA. This provides a foundation for easing the literature survey task.

Word	Word length	Freque... ▼	%	Rank
✦ work	4	2307	2.94	1
✦ health	6	711	0.91	2
✦ study	5	702	0.90	3
✦ al	2	630	0.80	4
✦ et	2	628	0.80	5
✦ worker	6	473	0.60	6
✦ high	4	471	0.60	7
✦ use	3	408	0.52	8
✦ age	3	406	0.52	9
✦ employee	8	396	0.51	10
✦ hour	4	387	0.49	11
✦ risk	4	373	0.48	12
✦ factor	6	366	0.47	13
✦ time	4	366	0.47	13
✦ job	3	364	0.46	15
✦ burnout	7	333	0.43	16
✦ shift	5	323	0.41	17
✦ life	4	314	0.40	18
✦ model	5	312	0.40	19

and ergonomic principles can increase efficiency, but it is important to be oriented in the psychological and social aspects of remote work. Finding a balance between functional demands, individual preferences and well-being is critical for organizations striving to create a sustainable and supportive telecommuting environment.

Article 3 discusses the complex dynamics of different work schedules through latent class analysis and highlights important implications for work-life balance. The identification of six different types of work schedules shows that flexibility combined with regular working hours significantly contributes to both subjective health and work-life balance. This finding suggests that organizations that promote flexible schedules within a standardized framework can create an environment that promotes employee well-being. On the other hand, the analysis shows the adverse effects of extended working hours, even when accompanied by flexibility. Rigid schedules that offer less control are considered acceptable as long as they avoid extended working hours. The overall message is clear: a balanced approach combining flexibility with reasonable working hours is essential to optimize employee health and work-life balance.

Article 14 shifts the focus to the specific context of hospital nurses, providing insight into the impact of changing schedules on different aspects of their lives. The study shows a significant difference between clockwise (CW) and counterclockwise (CCW) rotation schedules. Nurses on CW rounds reported sleeping more hours during their shift and feeling more rested at the start of their shift than their CCW counterparts. Importantly, CCW rotation nurses expressed the perception that work has a greater impact on their private lives, interfering with family and social relationships. This highlights the complex interplay between rotation orientation and the general well-being of nurses and highlights the need for healthcare organizations to consider the nuances of shift scheduling to mitigate potential negative effects and promote a healthier work-life balance for nursing staff.

Article 19 provides valuable insights into the impact of different work shifts on work-life balance, highlighting the links between evening, Saturday and Sunday work and different aspects of well-being. The results show that evening work is associated with a significantly increased risk of poor work-life balance, highlighting the potential challenges individuals face when their work extends into the evening hours. In addition, the study identifies a link between Saturday work and poor work-life balance and accidents at work, suggesting a possible strain in personal and professional life during weekends. Similarly, Sunday work is associated with poor work-life balance and work-related health problems, indicating that working on a traditional day off can upset people and their ability to maintain a healthy balance between work and personal life.

These findings have significant implications for organizations and decision makers seeking to improve work-life balance. Employers may need to review evening, Saturday and Sunday working hours as they are aware of the potential negative impact on employees and their general well-being. Preventive measures, such as providing alternatives or accommodation for those working less frequent days, can help create a more supportive work environment. In addition, the study emphasizes the importance of awareness of the potential health effects of non-traditional working hours and emphasizes the need for a comprehensive workplace policy that prioritizes employee well-being and work-life balance, even across sectors. Which require longer or unusual working hours.

Musculoskeletal disorders (MSDs) present a major challenge to work-life balance, as evidenced by the reviews in Articles 4 and 13. Article 4 highlights the prevalence of SLEs in the upper body, particularly in the neck, shoulders, and hands, indicating the physical burden that work-related stressors can place on workers. The mention of intervention training to reduce stress suggests a proactive approach to mitigate the impact of these disorders on employees. By addressing the root causes of TULE and providing targeted training, organizations may be able to improve the well-being of their work-force and thereby promote a healthier work-life balance. In addition, the emphasis on reducing absenteeism highlights the possibility of mitigating the negative effects of STDs not only on individuals and their physical health, but also general work ability and productivity.

Article 13 expands the debate by linking poor work-life balance to increased work-related injuries and musculoskeletal pain. The study highlights a broader perspective, noting that research on work-life balance is still limited in some regions, such as Korea, compared to Europe and the United States. The association between longer working hours and an increased risk of occupational accidents emphasizes the importance of scheduling working hours to maintain a healthy work-life balance. In addition, the recognition that employees who are dissatisfied with their lives have a higher risk of accidents at work highlights the link between mental well-being and physical health. This shows that considering work-life balance is crucial not only to prevent MSDs, but also to reduce the risk of occupational accidents, highlighting the need for comprehensive wellness programs.

Counterintuitive to logical belief, Article 24 has uncovered that the work-from-home culture is not as attractive as it is advertised to be. It tends to lock people in their houses, dealing with family while also juggling work which actually heightens stress.

In short, it can be stated that the impact of musculoskeletal diseases on work-life balance is profound and affects not only physical health, but also general job satisfaction and job security. Addressing these issues requires a holistic approach that includes targeted interventions, ergonomic improvements, and a focus on employees' psychological well-being. Organizations that prioritize the prevention of sexually transmitted diseases and the promotion of a healthy work-life balance are likely to create a more sustainable and supportive work environment for their employees.

4.3 Summary

To summarize, it can be stated that the research project on the topic "Ergonomics for the balance of work and family life" learns about the multifaceted impact of ergonomic aspects in the evolving landscape of modern working life. Examining the dynamics of telecommuting in Articles 1, 9, 16, and 23 highlights the transformative potential of telecommuting as operational information systems and cloud resources increase efficiency. However, constant connectivity and 24x7 operations emphasize the delicate balance needed to prevent potential tensions from intruding into personal life. Article 3 supports this narrative by underscoring the importance of flexible schedules with reasonable working hours to optimize both subjective health and work-life balance.

The complex relationship between shift work and work-life balance illuminated by Articles 14 and 19 adds to the precision of our understanding. The particular challenges faced by healthcare workers, especially nurses, in managing shift schedules and the potential stress caused by evening, Saturday and Sunday wrk highlight the need for tailored measures. This knowledge is invaluable to organizations looking to create supportive practices that meet the diverse needs of their workforce, especially in industries that require non-traditional work hours.

The research project also looks at physical well-being through the lens of musculoskeletal disorders according to Sects. 4 and 13. The prevalence of upper body TUL conditions such as neck, shoulder and forearm discomfort highlights the need for targeted interventions. Intervention training to reduce stress and the link between poor work-life balance and increased work-related accidents underscore the importance of comprehensive wellness programs. These programs, as proposed in Article 13, must consider the broader context of employee satisfaction, and recognize the complex relationship between mental well-being and physical health.

In the current environment where remote work has become more common, ergonomic policy appears as a key factor in shaping the future of work. In the light of this research project, organizations and decision-makers have the opportunity to proactively plan work environments that contribute to the overall well-being of employees. By implementing ergonomic principles, promoting flexible schedules, and considering the diverse needs of the workforce, organizations can foster a stimulating work culture that increases job satisfaction, reduces absenteeism, and ultimately promotes a harmonious work-life balance. As the world continues to evolve, the importance of ergonomics in navigating the complexities of modern work cannot be overstated, making it a critical aspect for the work of the future.

5   Strengths and Limitations

The main strength of this project is that it has a very good mix of literature from all over the world. Also, there are a good number of longitudinal studies that monitor the effects of the solutions they suggest on their subjects' WLB. In addition to this, 20 of the 25 references were published in the last five years, making this study very up to date.

The limitations of this study have to be that most of the reference articles related mainly to desk jobs and not physical labor; and even the ones that did had a very low sample size. Also, only four of the studies provide qualitative data. While the bulk of quantitative data does help test and confirm something, qualitative data is what helps learn and understand the results thus obtained.

6   Future Work

The literature devoted to ergonomics for WLB is quite few and far between. As Jiang & Duffy (2021) suggests, the results can be applied in other fields as well, namely education and automation. COVID-19 caused educational institutions to resort to remote instruction and this caused lowered levels of motivation among students. Controllers who oversee automations tend to get fatigued and miss malfunctions during human monitoring. It is a lucrative avenue to explore – ergonomic changes to improve the delivery of online instruction and effectiveness of human monitoring of automation.

References

Gopinathan, S., Raman, M.: Ergonomic quality, playing a role in ensuring work life balance among Malaysian ICT workers. Procedia Soc. Behav. Sci.a Soc. Behav. Sci. **211**, 1210–1215 (2015). https://doi.org/10.1016/j.sbspro.2015.11.161

Marhaendra, T.: The ergonomic holistic management strategy against the covid-19 pandemic. Int. J. Curr. Sci. Res. Rev. **04**(11) (2021). https://doi.org/10.47191/ijcsrr/v4-i11-11

Brauner, C., Wöhrmann, A., Frank, K., Michel, A.: Health and work-life balance across types of work schedules: a latent class analysis. Appl. Ergon.on. **81**, 102906 (2019). https://doi.org/10.1016/j.apergo.2019.102906

Heidarimoghadam, R., Mohammadfam, I., Babamiri, M., Soltanian, A., Khotanlou, H., Sohrabi, M.: Study protocol and baseline results for a quasi-randomized control trial: an investigation on the effects of ergonomic interventions on work-related musculoskeletal disorders, quality of work-life and productivity in knowledge-based companies. Int. J. Ind. Ergon. **80**, 103030 (2020). https://doi.org/10.1016/j.ergon.2020.103030

Coleman, D., et al.: SS02. vascular surgeon burnout – a report from the society for vascular surgery wellness task force. J. Vasc. Surg. **69**(6), e97 (2019). https://doi.org/10.1016/j.jvs.2019.04.103

Mikellidou, C., Boustras, G., Nicolaidou, O., Dimopoulos, C., Anyfantis, I., Messios, P.: Work-related factors and individual characteristics affecting work ability of different age groups. Saf. Sci. **128**, 104755 (2020). https://doi.org/10.1016/j.ssci.2020.104755

Weale, V., Wells, Y., Oakman, J.: The work-life interface: a critical factor between work stressors and job satisfaction. Pers. Rev. **48**(4), 880–897 (2019). https://doi.org/10.1108/pr-09-2016-0226

Aziz, R., Munap, R., Nor, S., Zakir, N., Jufri, N., Kadir, M.: A case study of a service organisation in Malaysia: employees' work-life balance, work commitment & leadership style on job satisfaction during remote working. Adv. Int. J. Bus. Entrep. SMEs **5**(15), 31–40 (2023). https://doi.org/10.35631/aijbes.515004

Finna, H., Forgacs, T.: enhancement of human performance with developing ergonomic workplace environment and providing work-life balance. Perspect. Innov. Econ. Bus. 59–61 (2010). https://doi.org/10.15208/pieb.2010.50

Sutarto, A., Nubli, A.: Multimodal stress-management intervention improves physiological, psychological, and productivity of assembly-line workers. Ind. Eng. Manag. Syst. **19**(4), 812–824 (2020). https://doi.org/10.7232/iems.2020.19.4.812

Andersen, L., Pedersen, J., Thorsen, S., Rugulies, R.: High physical work demands have worse consequences for older workers: prospective study of long-term sickness absence among 69 117 employees. Occup. Environ. Med. **78**(11), 829–834 (2021). https://doi.org/10.1136/oemed-2020-107281

Giakoumis, D., Votis, K., Altsitsiadis, E., Segkouli, S., Paliokas, I., Tzovaras, D.: Smart, personalized and adaptive ICT solutions for active, healthy and productive ageing with enhanced workability (2019). https://doi.org/10.1145/3316782.3322767

An, J., et al.: Association of work–life balance with occupational injury and work-related musculoskeletal pain among Korean workers. Ann. Occup. Environ. Med. **32**(1) (2020). https://doi.org/10.35371/aoem.2020.32.e20

Shiffer, D., et al.: Effects of clockwise and counterclockwise job shift work rotation on sleep and work-life balance on hospital nurses. Int. J. Environ. Res. Public Health **15**(9), 2038 (2018). https://doi.org/10.3390/ijerph15092038

Chim, J., Chen, T.: Prediction of work from home and musculoskeletal discomfort: an investigation of ergonomic factors in work arrangements and home workstation setups using the covid-19 experience. Int. J. Environ. Res. Public Health **20**(4), 3050 (2023). https://doi.org/10.3390/ijerph20043050

Jones, A., Fan, J., Thomas-Olson, L., Zhang, W., McLeod, C.: Continuation of telework in the post-pandemic era: healthcare employees' preference and determinants. Healthc. Manag. Forum **36**(4), 256–262 (2023). https://doi.org/10.1177/08404704231170733

Labriola, M., Lund, T., Burr, H.: Prospective study of physical and psychosocial risk factors for sickness absence. Occup. Med. **56**(7), 469–474 (2006). https://doi.org/10.1093/occmed/kql058

Abarqhouei, N., Nasab, H.: Total ergonomics and its impact in musculoskeletal disorders and quality of work life and productivity. Open J. Saf. Sci. Technol. **01**(03), 79–88 (2011). https://doi.org/10.4236/ojsst.2011.13008

Greubel, J., Arlinghaus, A., Nachreiner, F., Lombardi, D.: Higher risks when working unusual times? A cross-validation of the effects on safety, health, and work–life balance. Int. Arch. Occup. Environ. Health **89**(8), 1205–1214 (2016). https://doi.org/10.1007/s00420-016-1157-z

Cetrano, G., et al.: How are compassion fatigue, burnout, and compassion satisfaction affected by quality of working life? Findings from a survey of mental health staff in Italy. BMC Health Serv. Res. **17**(1) (2017). https://doi.org/10.1186/s12913-017-2726-x

Golisch, K., Sanders, J., Rzhetsky, A., Tatebe, L.: Addressing surgeon burnout through a multi-level approach: a national call to action. Curr. Trauma Rep. **9**(2), 28–39 (2023). https://doi.org/10.1007/s40719-022-00249-x

Zhou, F., Ji, Y., Jiao, R.J.: Emotional design. In: Salvendy, G., Karwowski, W. (eds.) Handbook of Human Factors and Ergonomics (2021). https://doi.org/10.1002/9781119636113.ch9

Marmaras, N., Nathanael, D.: Workplace design. In: Salvendy, G. (ed.) Handbook of Human Factors and Ergonomics (2012). https://doi.org/10.1002/9781118131350.ch21

Palumbo, R.: Let me go to the office! an investigation into the side effects of working from home on work-life balance. Int. J. Public Sect. Manag.ct. Manag. **33**(6/7), 771–790 (2020). https://doi.org/10.1108/ijpsm-06-2020-0150

Mostafa, B.: The effect of remote working on employee's wellbeing and work-life integration during pandemic in Egypt. Int. Bus. Res. **14**(3), 41 (2021). https://doi.org/10.5539/ibr.v14n3p41

Jiang, J., Duffy, V.G.: Modern workplace ergonomics and productivity – a systematic literature review. In: Stephanidis, C., Duffy, V.G., Krömker, H., Fui-Hoon Nah, F., Siau, K., Salvendy, G., Wei, J. (eds.) HCII 2021. LNCS, vol. 13097, pp. 509–524. Springer, Cham (2021). https://doi.org/10.1007/978-3-030-90966-6_35

Ergonomic Evaluation of a VTOL Aircraft Using RAMSIS

Vani Chawla[✉], Rashmila Mahajan, Vincent G. Duffy[✉], and Martin Pohlmann

Purdue University, West Lafayette 47906, USA
{chawla42,mahaja44,duffy}@purdue.edu,
mpohlmann@human-solutions.com

Abstract. In this lab report, we have conducted an ergonomic evaluation for pilots in vertical take-off and landing for an aircraft using RAMSIS as a part of our course (IE 578: Applied Ergonomics) requirement at Purdue University. The report covers a holistic evaluation of various factors like reachability, outside visibility, comfort level, obstructions, acuity, and reflection for different anthropometries. The recommendations suggested in the class lab sessions and literary sources, as cited in the report, have been used for improvising the ergonomic design. Further, the changes in the above parameters, as demonstrated in the report, are devised to suit the range of the defined samples. The analysis provided insights into the importance of the mentioned factors and areas for improvement to create an ergonomic design.

Keywords: Ergonomic · Anthropometry · Aircraft

1 Introduction and Background

Efficiency and safety are critical in the aviation industry. As the central nervous system of any airplane, the cockpit is essential to maintaining both of these vital components. In order for pilots to operate an aircraft comfortably and successfully—especially on lengthy flights or important missions—the cockpit's layout and design must take their demands into consideration. One of the topics studied during the research for this report highlights the importance of eye level and visual angle as areas of improvement that can lead to enhanced cockpit ergonomics. For effective resolution of these problems, the study also suggests modifying seating adjustment restrictions with respect to height [1].

The simulation results in RAMSIS are dependent on the different anthropometries, e.g., as mentioned in one of the articles studied by the authors. In the article from scite.ai, the data points of the Korean male helicopter pilots show higher homogeneity than US pilots. Figure 1 shows the differences in the mean of various parameters like body weight, head, trunk, etc. for the Korean and US pilots. As a result, the ergonomic analysis and, thus, the aircraft design will differ for Korean and US pilots [2, 3].

© The Author(s), under exclusive license to Springer Nature Switzerland AG 2024
V. G. Duffy (Ed.): HCII 2024, LNCS 14711, pp. 30–48, 2024.
https://doi.org/10.1007/978-3-031-61066-0_3

Table 3. Comparison of Korean male helicopter pilots, Korean male civilians and US Army male personnel.

Body part	Code	ADs	Korean helicopter pilots (n = 94)		Korean civilians (n = 1800)		KP versus KC			US Army (n = 1774)		KP versus UA		
			M_{KP}	SD_{KP}	M_{KC}	SD_{KC}	M_{KP-KC}	M_{KP}/M_{KC}	SD_{KP}/SD_{KC}	M_{UA}	SD_{UA}	M_{KP-UA}	M_{KP}/M_{UA}	SD_{KP}/SD_{UA}
Whole body	AD1	Stature	173.0	5.2	170.0	7.0	3.0**	1.02	0.74**	175.6	6.7	−2.6**	0.99	0.77**
	AD2	Weight	73.3	8.6	69.3	10.5	4.0**	1.06	0.81*	78.5	11.1	−5.1**	0.93	0.77**
Head and trunk	AD3	Sitting height	93.1	2.9	91.9	3.6	1.2**	1.01	0.80*	91.4	3.6	1.7**	1.02	0.81**
	AD4	Sitting eye height	81.3	3.0	80.4	3.5	0.9**	1.01	0.87	79.2	3.4	2.1**	1.03	0.88
	AD5	Sitting acromial height	60.9	2.7	59.4	2.9	1.4**	1.02	0.93	59.8	3.0	1.1**	1.02	0.90
	AD6	Biacromial breadth	40.1	1.7	39.5	2.4	0.6**	1.02	0.72**	39.7	1.8	0.4*	1.01	0.97
	AD7	Chest circumference	100.1	5.0	95.6	6.9	4.5**	1.05	0.72**	102.3	6.5	−2.2**	0.98	0.76**
	AD8	Chest depth	19.3	1.6	20.9	2.0	N/C	N/C	N/C	24.3	2.1	N/C	N/C	N/C
	AD9	Hip breadth	37.6	1.8	34.9	2.1	2.7**	1.08	0.89	36.7	2.5	1.0**	1.03	0.73**
	AD10	Waist circumference	84.2	6.6	81.2	8.5	3.0**	1.04	0.78**	86.2	8.6	−2.1**	0.98	0.76**
Upper limbs	AD11	Elbow-to-fingertip length	46.1	1.7	44.6	2.3	1.5**	1.03	0.75**	48.4	2.3	−2.3**	0.95	0.73**
	AD12	Forearm-to-forearm breadth	48.9	3.9	47.3	4.8	1.6**	1.03	0.82*	54.6	4.4	−5.7**	0.89	0.90
	AD13	Shoulder-to-elbow length	34.9	1.4	33.5	1.8	1.4**	1.04	0.81*	36.9	1.8	−2.0**	0.94	0.80**
	AD14	Thumb-tip reach	76.6	3.0	N/A	N/A	N/A	N/A	N/A	80.1	3.9	−3.5**	0.96	0.76**
Lower limbs	AD15	Buttock-to-knee length	57.6	2.4	56.8	2.7	0.8**	1.01	0.86	61.6	3.0	−4.0**	0.93	0.79**
	AD16	Buttock-to-popliteal length	47.6	2.1	46.5	2.7	1.0**	1.02	0.77**	50.0	2.7	−2.5**	0.95	0.79**
	AD17	Foot length	25.2	1.0	24.9	1.3	0.3**	1.01	0.74**	27.0	1.3	−1.8**	0.93	0.73**
	AD18	Knee height	51.9	2.2	50.7	2.6	1.1**	1.02	0.84*	55.9	2.8	−4.0**	0.93	0.78**
	AD19	Popliteal height	41.4	1.7	39.7	2.3	1.7**	1.04	0.73**	43.4	2.5	−2.0**	0.95	0.68**
	AD20	Thigh circumference	57.2	3.6	55.9	4.5	1.3**	1.02	0.80**	59.7	4.9	−2.4**	0.96	0.72**
	AD21	Thigh clearance	16.3	1.2	15.2	1.6	1.1**	1.07	0.71	16.8	1.3	−0.5**	0.97	0.92

Notes: KP, Korean helicopter pilots; KC, Korean civilians; UA, US Army. *P < .05; **P < .01; N/C: not comparable due to use of different landmarks; N/A: not available.

Fig. 1. Differences in the parameters for Korean and US Pilots

Further, several other ergonomic design elements are studied by the authors, including industry standards and airplane cockpits of the new generation, to better understand the importance of ergonomic design and pay closer attention to the different functionalities Articles from several literary resources, including Purdue Library, have been used in this report to better understand ergonomic design and simplify the process [4].

2 Hypothesis

This report explores the question of "What are the important factors for an ergonomic design?". The author answers this question by applying the different functionalities in RAMSIS that are related to Ergonomic design. Trade-offs are analyzed, and the importance of ergonomic considerations gets highlighted as various tasks are performed. The authors also use Google NGram to study the trends for the phrases "ergonomics, anthropometry, and cockpit". The results are shown in the graph below. It can be inferred that the term "ergonomics" gained popularity in the year 2000 and then, after a dip in 2010, has been used at a stable rate. Further, "anthropometry" has been used at a constant rate throughout the years [5] (Fig. 2).

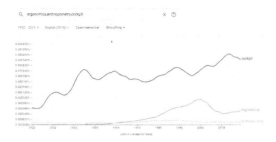

Fig. 2. Shows the Google NGram view for the phrases (cockpit, ergonomics, anthropometry)

3   Procedure

Below are the steps followed for Task 1 to Task 6 as per the 'RAMSIS_lab2_IE 578_Purdue 9-14 updated 10-4' (Tables 1, 2, 3, 4, 5 and 6).

3.1   Task 1 – Creating Body Measurements

Table 1. (a). This table represents the steps for Task 1.

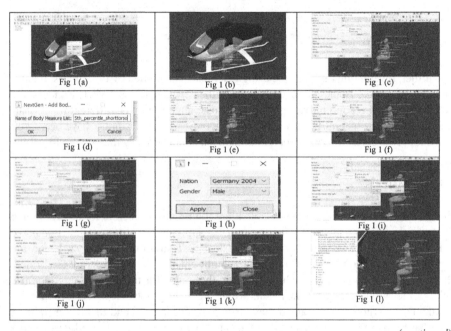

(continued)

Table 1. (*continued*)

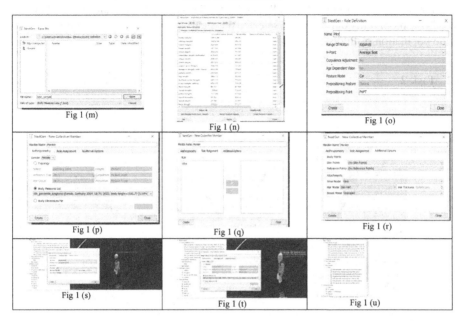

Table 1. (b). This table describes the steps for Task 1.

Step 1	Fig 1 (a) and Fig 1 (b) shows the initiation of Body Builder Plugin and the creation of female manikin with Germany 2004 as nation
Step 2	Fig 1 (c) shows the creation of anthropometric database of Female.
Step 3	Fig 1 (c) shows the change in control measurements to reference year 2023, 5th percentile body height, medium waist and short torso.
Step 4	Fig 1 (d) showcases the naming of the body measurement list to '5th_percentile_shorttorso'
Step 5	Fig 1 (e) to Fig 1 (k) depict the creation of manikins of all the variants like female medium torso 5th percentile, female long torso 5th percentile, male short, medium and long torso 95th percentile. Also, a male of medium torso 50th percentile is created. Fig (l) shows all the created manikins under the Body Measure Lists
Step 6	Fig 1 (m) and Fig 1 (n) shows the steps to save the file and view individual measurements of created manikins. After this the Project Manager Plug in is initiated
Step 7	The role of 'Pilot' is created as shown in Fig 1 (o), Range of motion, H-point, posture model and prepositioning point are also defined.
Step 8	A female manikin with long torso 5th percentile is selected instead of selecting from the available database as shown in Fig (p). The Body measurement list that was created earlier is used to assign the Pilot, as shown Fig 1 (q). Lastly The Gino shoes are put as shown in Fig 1 (r)
Step 9	Similarly, the other 6 manikins are created using a Body Measurement List as seen in Fig 1 (s) to Fig (u)

This task is the beginning of ergonomic analysis for Pilots with various anthropometries, ranging from short female to tall female and short male to tall male. The percentile depicts the probability of Pilots with selected physical characteristics among the majority of the population of Pilots.

3.2 Task 2

Table 2. **(a).** This table represents steps for Task 2.

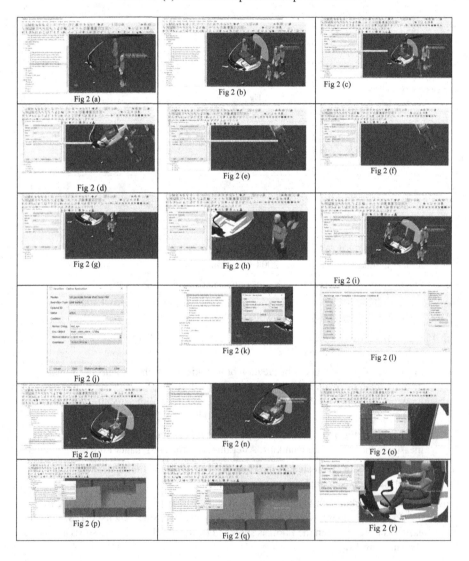

Table 2. (b). This table describes the steps for Task 2.

Step 1	As seen in Fig 2 (r) and Fig 2 (a), the Ergonomic Plug in was reactivated
Step 2	Fig 2 (r) shows activation of additional skin points like HAR_3_10 ('Right_Graspingpoint) for 5th percentile male manikin with medium torso.
Step 3	All these skin points are copied and pasted to other female manikins as seen in Fig (a) and Fig 2 (b)
Step 4	All the skin points were also copied to the Male manikins as seen in the Fig (b)
Step 5	From Fig 2 (c) to Fig 2 (j) the constraints are defined for H point, Left heel, Right heel, Right Pedal, Left Pedal. Fig 2 (j) shows the vision limited to lower_vision_plane_-17 deg. Fig 2 (h) shows the torso angle to be 20 deg.
Step 6	As seen in Fig 2 (k) using the special copy and paste options all the constraints are copied for other manikins as well.
Step 7	As seen in Fig 2 (l) the posture calculation is started. Fig 2 (m) shows the manikin sitting in the Pilots position after running the Posture calculation. Fig (n) shows all the manikins in sitting position once the Posture calculation is executed for all the manikins.
Step 8	As shown in Fig (o) the H-points are copied for all the manikins. Fig 2 (p) and Fig 2 (q) show the horizontal distance calculated between the 2 H-points (the foremost and the rearmost) to be 154mm.

3.3 Task 3

Table 3. **(a).** This table represents the steps for Task 3.

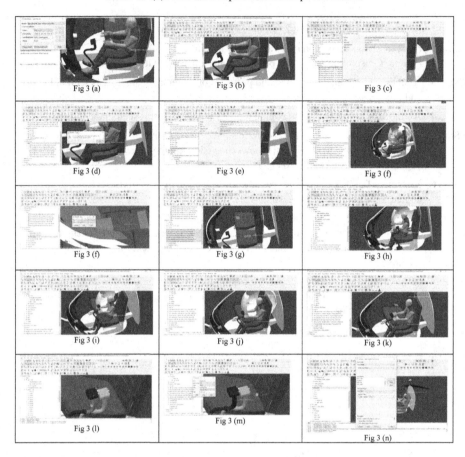

Table 3. **(b).** This table describes the steps for Task 3.

Step 1	In Fig 3 (a) and Fig 3 (b) the grasping points which were created in task 2 are identified. Fig 3 (c) shows the creation of a reachability envelope for the 50th percentile male with medium torso. This can be done by going to the Analysis option on the taskbar and selection in the function Define Reach.
Step 2	In Fig 3 (d), Fig 3 (e) and Fig 3 (f) the user can see the reachability spheres that are created for all the manikins using the Define Reach option
Step 3	With the help from 'Geometry' option on the taskbar, an intersection between the SRP_Y-plane and the foremost sphere, rearmost sphere is created as seen in Fig 3 (f) and Fig 3 (g)
Step 4	Fig 3 (g) and Fig 3 (h) show the difference between the position of the control lever. As shown in fig (h) the control lever is translated to be inside the rearmost reach envelope.

(continued)

Table 3. (*continued*)

Step 5	Then a visual check was conducted and the control lever was observed to be too close to the foremost manikin. In Fig 3 (i) the control lever is re-adjusted to fit between the legs of all the manikins.
Step 6	A duplicate control lever is created as suggested in the lab 2 procedure by copying the item and pasting it to the interior Geometry of the aircraft as seen in Fig 3 (j). It was observed, that the taller manikins need the control lever to be even farther away due to their long hands. Hence, the position of duplicate control lever was adjusted accordingly in the Fig 3 (k).
Step 7	A common grasping point is made on both the control levers to enable distance calculation. Distance between the rearmost and the frontmost control lever was measured to be 106mm as seen in the Fig 3 (m) and Fig 3 (n)

3.4 Task 4

Table 4. (**a**). This table represents the steps for Task 4.

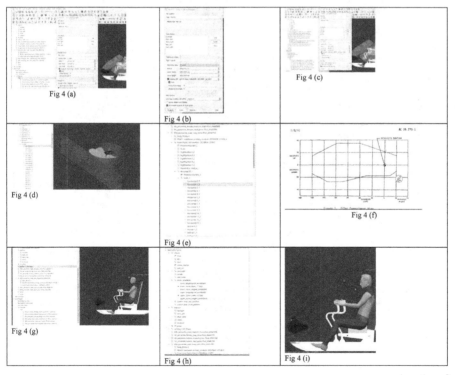

(*continued*)

Table 4. (*continued*)

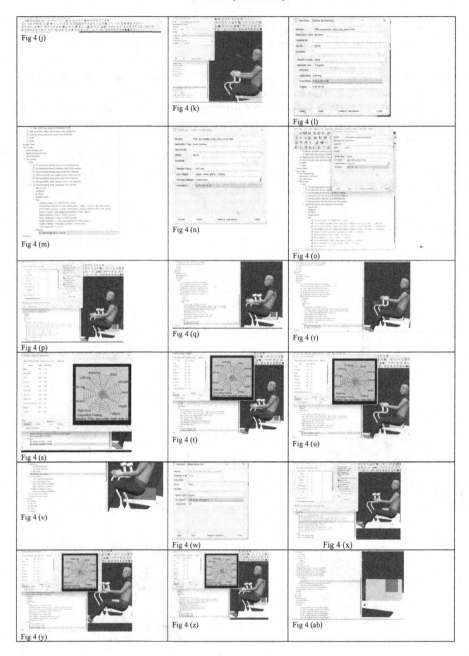

Table 4. (b). This table describes the steps for Task 4.

Step 1	As seen in Fig 4 (a), the manikin with the highest eye-point location (95th percentile male with long torso) is activated
Step 2	As seen in Fig 4 (a) and Fig 4(b) the Outer Field Sight Analysis is being run. It can be found in the Cognitive Plug-in option on the taskbar. The user selects the (active) Manikin and then add the objects.
Step 3	Fig 4 (b) and Fig 4(c) shows the objects such as the vehicle exterior (fuselage and doors) being added. The type is selected as Cylinder in the XY-Plane with 5000mm radius with the wind off the cylinder in the front (180°). The scale is selected to be in 5°-increments.
Step 4	Fig (d) shows a cylinder with 5000mm radius. The cylinder is winded up in the front (180°).
Step 5	To run comparisons, we hide the projections from the window in Fig 4 (e)
Step 6	Fig 4(f) and Fig (g) shows the DOT's recommendations from Pilot Compartment View Design Considerations (especially 0° vertical line). Our result shows that the current upward limit for the Manikin is ~ 7° upwards from the Manikin's eye position, which will cause a problem in terms of visibility outside of the aircraft of the Manikin. This is which is way too less as compared to our recommendation value of at least 22°.
Step 7	Fig 4 (h) shows the Vision Geometry. The lower boundary is 17° and upper boundary is 22°. The Manikin needs to be above the lower boundary and below the upper boundary. Fig 4 (i) shows the need for posture calculation as the current Manikin's eye point is outside of the ideal boundaries.
Step 8	Fig 4 (j) shows how to add a new limit surface constraint by clicking on Define Restriction on the taskbar.
Step 9	The Restriction Type is selected as Limit Surface for the active Manikin and for orientation we make sure that the z value is negative to ensure mid-eye is below that surface as shown in Fig 4 (k)
Step 10	To ensure head remains upright, we define another constraint – Direction as shown in Fig 4 (l)
Step 11	Before clicking on posture calculation, we save original posture, in order to do comparison. To do so, go to Operations>Add posture as structure tree. It will appear as shown in Fig 4 (m)
Step 12	Now we run Posture Calculation with the 2 new tasks – Defining a new constraint to put the Manikin's eye below the tangent to ensure Manikin can see forward and upward by 22°. The second constraint is the Limit Surface to ensure mid-eye is not restricted by VTOL surface as shown in Fig 4 (n) and Fig 4 (o)
Step 13	The Posture Calculation is run as shown in Fig 4 (p)

(*continued*)

Table 4. (*continued*)

Step 14	Fig 4 (q) shows the second posture being saved after posture calculation with the 2 new tasks. Fig 4 (r) shows the first posture. The author shows both the images to showcase difference in postures and evaluate tradeoffs in terms of visibility and comfort for the Manikin. The manikin with the 2nd posture has visibility but no comfort.
Step 15	Fig 4 (s) shows the discomfort analysis that is done for the Manikin with the 2nd posture. We can clearly see that there is a feeling of discomfort, even though the Manikin has great visibility
Step 16	Fig 4 (t) emphasizes that the Manikin with the 2nd posture has good visibility but discomfort, especially for legs and neck
Step 17	The same analysis is done for the 1st posture of the Manikin. In Fig 4 (u) it is seen that there is comfort for the Manikin, but no visibility (as originally analyzed)
Step 18	We now look at a resolution to have minimum trade off by focusing on Height and length adjustment. The extended travel surface is selected, this increases the H-point position on the complete surface as shown in Fig 4 (v)
Step 19	We change the task for the H-point that was previously defined as shown in Fig 4 (w) and run the Posture calculation as in Fig 4 (x)
Step 20	Fig 4 (y) shows the manikin after running this calculation. It can be seen that the comfort is improved, while there is still outside visibility for the Manikin in this position. This posture is saved
Step 21	Fig 4 (z) shows the previous posture, and we can observe that the Manikin underwent a vertical travel on the seat
Step 22	Fig 4 (ab) shows the two H Points for the Manikin and the vertical seat adjustment that we performed in order to minimize trade-offs in terms of comfort and outside visibility

3.5 Task 5

Table 5. **(a).** This table represents the steps for Task 5.

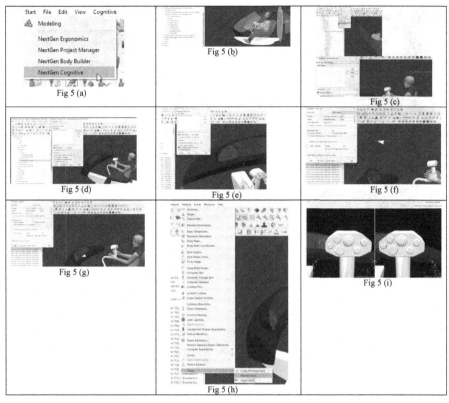

(*continued*)

Table 5. (*continued*)

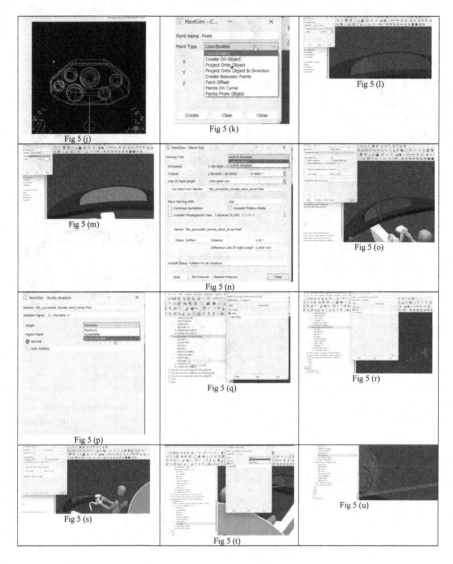

Table 5. (b). This table describes the steps for Task 5.

Step 1	To begin the obstruction analysis, NextGen Cognitive function is enables as shown in the Fig 5 (a).
Step 2	Fig 5 (b) shows the activation of one of the manikins (95th percentile male with long torso)
Step 3	In order to analyze the view from manikin's position, 'Direct Vision' function from the Analysis option is selected as shown in the Fig 5 (c).
Step 4	Into the 'Direct Vision' tab, manikin's mid eye position is selected. To study the obstruction created by an object in the path of screen view. The object here is control lever and hence view object is selected as *control_lever_front_position* inside the dialogue box as shown in Fig 5 (d). The geometry object to be viewed is selected as *control_display* and the simulation is computed as seen in Fig 5 (e).
Step 5	Inside the aircraft, a Pilot will adjust its vision angle to look in the direction of screen. Hence, the vision angle of manikin is changed from the default upright position to -25 deg, for the manikin to view the screen as seen in Fig 5 (f) and Fig 5 (g). Now, to analyze the view from the interior of aircraft, 'Interior View' option is selected as in Fig 5 (h). The pink dotted lines on display and control lever in Fig 5 (i) and Fig (j) shows the region of overlap for the manikin's view. To summarize, some view of the left screen or right screen is blocked by control lever. The recommendations are either changing the position of the screen at center or to be higher than the lever or increasing the height of the manikin's seat. Fig 5 (j) shows the wire diagram for the objects.
Step 6	As shown in Fig 5 (k) and Fig 5 (l), using the NextGen – Create Geometry tab, an object is created at the center of the display. Fig 5 (m) shows the exact location of the created object on the center_display. Fig 5 (n) and Fig 5 (o) shows the manikin looking directly at the object. Now we conduct the Acuity Analysis that is 'deciding the most suitable size of readable letter/number on the screen' as shown in Fig 5 (p). Fig 5 (q) and Fig 5 (r) shows the minimum value of letter to be 4mm and recommended value to be 7.12mm for a manikin with 5th percentile short torso female.
Step 7	Now, the manikin with longest legs that is the one with shortest torso (95th percentile male short torso) is selected. Since the manikin is farthest from the screen in compared to other manikins due to long legs, the recommended value of letter height will change for readability.
Step 8	Fig 5 (s) shows the manikin looking at the object previously created.
Step 9	Fig 5 (t) and Fig 5 (u) provide the result of acuity analysis for farthest manikin that is the minimum height of object is 5mm and recommended is 8mm.

3.6 Task 6

Table 6. (a). This table represents the steps for Task 6.

Fig 6 (a)	Fig 6 (b)	Fig 6 (c)
Fig 6 (d)	Fig 6 (e)	Fig 6 (f)
Fig 6 (g)	Fig 6 (h)	Fig 6 (i)
Fig 6 (j)	Fig 6 (k)	Fig 6 (l)
Fig 6 (m)	Fig 6 (n)	Fig 6 (o)
Fig 4 (p)	Fig 4 (q)	Fig 4 (r)

Table 6. (b). This table describes the steps for Task 6.

Step 1	As seen in Fig 6 (a), the 5th percentile female manikin is activated. We also activate the center display and the window surface.
Step 2	As seen in Fig 6 (b) we choose the Reflection Analysis function in the Cognitive Plug-in. For night-time reflection the reflection geometry is the windshield and view object are center display. We also put reflection cone in the no-show zone. F
Step 3	Fig 6 (c) shows the area where the display gets reflected in the windshield. Intensity is not given; it is more geometry based.
Step 4	Fig (d) and Fig (e) show the reflection analysis for left_sidewindow and right_sidewindow. Both of them have an empty folder under the Reflection Analysis, hence the display window does not have any reflections on either window.
Step 5	Fig 4 (f) shows the day-time reflections for the display. The reflection cone represents the direction from which sun light must come to be reflected in the display for a specific eye-location. We ensure that the cone is not going through any window surface as shown in Fig 6 (g).
Step 6	Fig 6 (h) shows the creation of a duplicate center_display which can be used to optimize reflections.
Step 7	Fig 6 (i) shows the Translate function being applied to the copied display surface so that the reflection cone does not aim at any window surface and day-time reflections are thus eliminated.
Step 8	Fig 6 (j) shows the rotation of the copied display panel around 5mm on y-axis. We also rotate along the z-axis as shown in and get the optimized result as in Fig 6 (k).
Step 9	Fig 6 (l) and Fig 6 (m) show the calculation for night-time reflections with optimized display location. We were able to reduce the area of reflection and also change its location.
Step 10	Fig 6 (n) shows the creation of boundary spline of the display surface.
Step 11	Fig 6 (o) and Fig (p) shows the copy of the upper part of the boundary (spline) and its translation in +x and +z direction by 50mm.
Step 12	Fig 6 (q) shows the creation of a surface between original spline and translated spline to partially block reflection cone.
Step 13	Fig 6 (r) shows the final reflection analysis including the created hood surface and the display surfaces.

4   Conclusion

As intended in the introduction, we have studied the key factors involved in an ergonomic VTOL design using RAMSIS. Below are some observations from this analysis:

4.1   Observations

1. We were able to delve deeper into RAMSIS's features in Lab 2, which also underlined how crucial ergonomic design is to both the geometry of automobiles and aircraft. We

were able to comprehend a variety of cockpit design elements, including reachability, comfort, and outside visibility. RAMSIS was an excellent tool all around.

2. Importance of Trade-Offs – After performing the activity, we were able to comprehend how trade-offs play a crucial part in ergonomic design. One of the tasks allowed us to change postures for Manikins on the basis of their visibility outside the aircraft and the comfort level that they are provided while operating the vehicle.

4.2 Parameter Specific Discussion

Parameter	Changes made in RAMSIS for improving the ergonomic functionality
Reachability	In order to make the control lever assessable for short as well as tall manikins, the range is defined for its flexible design and operation. The intersection between the reach envelopes and the SRP_Y plane was also computed for a comfortable seating arrangement for all the test manikins. Further, the article referenced has been very helpful in understanding this aspect with respect to various anthropometries. The article uses data points (body measurement points) for 90th percentiles of the pilot population which is in parallel to the 95th percentiles for the male population [1]
Outside Visibility	The graph in Fig. 4 (f) shows the ideal range of upper- and lower-angle views when a pilot is sitting in an upright position with zero eye-level inclination. As per our observation, the original position of the manikin was not meeting the view requirements, and hence changes for the mid-eye angle with the upper vision plane were made to achieve the intended result. However, after assessing the comfort level of the manikin with the adjusted posture, the head of the manikin was colliding with the aircraft geometry thereby putting strain on the left and right leg. This could result in discomfort and long-term health risks for the pilot
Comfort	In order to mitigate the discomfort and health risks for a pilot manikin, the H-point was readjusted towards the back of the seat. As shown in Fig. 4 (y), in discomfort analysis, the comfort level of the manikin is improved with devised changes
Obstructions	Similarly, there were observations made for assessing the visibility of the screen (the part that is in the interior of the aircraft geometry). The control lever was blocking the complete view of the screen, either through left-eye, right-eye, or mid-eye positions for the manikin. The lab demo recommended the angular adjustments for all three eye inclinations. However, viewing the entire screen simultaneously was not possible. Finally, the recommendations to adjust the seat height or display position were given in order to meet the requirements. But as per the instructor, the aircraft's upper frame and manikin's head might again collide, and the designer will enter the loop for managing deliverables. To resolve this issue, trade-offs or prioritization between certain requirements came into play for an ergonomic design. If the pilot is going to view the instructions less often from the obstructed screen area, we can keep the option for the pilot to readjust himself or herself on their own

(continued)

(*continued*)

Acuity	Here, we defined the size of the letters or numbers to ensure readability for the pilot on the screen, irrespective of different anthropometries. In RAMSIS, depending on whether the test sample is short or long, the tool provides the recommended height of the letter for clear readability for the manikin. Accordingly, the height of letters was noted for the manikin with shorter and longer torsos and size criteria was finalized
Reflections	Translation and Rotation of display allowed us to re-direct the reflection into a completely new direction, ensuring it is not going through the window surfaces. For day-time reflection, the orientation of the display played a crucial part. For night-time reflection, we were able to reduce the actual area on which the reflection is seen and move the reflections to a higher area in the display. Additionally, Day time reflections include reflecting geometries in the car and Night time reflections having internal light sources and reflection being created on window surfaces

5 Limitations

Below are some limitations that we observed during the analysis of ergonomic design:

1. RAMSIS does not take into account human error while performing an analysis. The simulation results, if built on the basis of one error and referenced multiple times, could result in the domino effect of human error.
2. Outside weather conditions are not always considered in RAMSIS. This makes maintaining an ergonomic design difficult for the user.
3. RAMSIS simulation results are dependent on the pre-defined body measurements. Non-ideal human postures are not considered during analysis.
4. Industry Standards: Depending on the airline and country of manufacture, the ideal ergonomic values may differ, making it challenging to have a single ideal value for reference.
5. Integration challenges with some operating systems, such as Mac OS, are faced while installing RAMSIS.
6. For reflection calculation, RAMSIS focuses more on the geometry aspect and gives the user an understanding of where the reflection falls. It does not give information on the intensity of the reflection, which might be useful for improving design.
7. The manikin configured in RAMSIS also has built-in limitations as to how it can move and be positioned. For example, when reaching far, a human tends to move his arm forward and even twist his back to reach further. However, as per our experience and as cited in the report, manikins do not mimic this human behavior [6].
8. RAMSIS, by default, only offers one sitting technique, known as Neutral Posture inside a Posture Model. Inexperienced users may struggle to get accurate results when evaluating drivers with different body proportions using defined Posture calculation feature. In that case, the users need to define the specific skin points and map them to the geometry as done in this lab 2 exercise [7].

6   Literature Review

The authors use multiple literature resources, such as Scite.ai, Google Ngram, and Purdue Library, in this report. Each resource provides the authors with different functionalities, ensuring that information is accessible and the report sufficiently covers the topic at hand. These resources provide insights into the topics of RAMSIS, VTOL, ERGONOMIC DESIGN, and LIMITATIONS and allow the reader to critically think and discern relevant facts, ultimately leading to knowledge gain and an enhancement to the credibility of their own work.

References

1. PurdueLibrary.   chrome-extension://efaidnbmnnnibpcajpcglclefindmkaj/https://www-tandfo nline-com.ezproxy.lib.purdue.edu/doi/pdf/10.1080/10803548.2015.1126456?needAccess=tru e. Accessed 18 Oct 2023
2. Scite.ai.   https://scite.ai/search?q=Anthropometric%20evaluation%20of%20cockpit%20d esigns. Accessed 18 Oct 2023
3. Lee, W., et al.: An anthropometric analysis of Korean male helicopter pilots for helicopter cockpit design. Ergonomics 5(56), 879–887 (2013). https://doi.org/10.1080/00140139.2013. 776703
4. Zhang, Y., Sun, Y., Chen, Y.-C.: A framework for ergonomics design of transport category airplane cockpit. Procedia Eng. 80, 573–580 (2014). https://doi.org/10.1016/j.proeng.2014. 09.113
5. GoogleNGram.   https://books.google.com/ngrams/graph?content=ergonomics%2Canthrop ometry%2Ccockpit&year_start=1920&year_end=2019&corpus=en-2019&smoothing=3. Accessed 18 Oct 2023
6. Johansson, I., Larsson, M.: Master's Thesis 2007:122 CIV Evaluation of the Manikin Building Function in EM-RAMSIS When Using Motion Capture (n.d.). Accessed 1 Nov 2023
7. Gao, Y., Kaiser, R., Wagner, P.-O., Abendroth, B., Paternoster, S.: Driving posture assessment: a new approach. In: Black, N.L., Neumann, W.P., Noy, I. (eds.) IEA 2021. LNNS, vol. 221, pp. 639–646. Springer, Cham (2021). https://doi.org/10.1007/978-3-030-74608-7_78

A Systematic Literature Review of Ergonomics in Transportation Focused on Driver Fatigue and Safety

Skyler Doss(✉), Siddharth Lavu, and Vincent G. Duffy

Purdue University, West Lafayette, IN 47907, USA
{dosss,lavu,duffy}@purdue.edu

Abstract. Within the field of ergonomics, there has always been some focus on challenges related to transportation. Transportation as a focus is unique, as the environment is extremely dynamic, driving performance can be affected by a wide variety of variables, there are many emerging vehicle technologies, and it involves an inherently dangerous activity being performed by humans who are prone to error. To delve further into both the persistent and emerging topics of interest related to ergonomics in transportation, bibliometric analysis was performed and analyzed, with a focus on safety, more specifically driver fatigue. This study involved a systematic literature review using tools such as Scopus, VOSViewer, MaxQDA, CiteSpace, Web of Science, and Google Scholar. The procedures for conducting analysis with each tool will be described, and the leading authors, journals, and areas of further research are identified. The findings of this study suggest that ergonomics within transportation, specifically ergonomic considerations related to driver fatigue and safety, is an area within ergonomics and human factors engineering that has had persistent challenges along with many emerging areas but also needs further research to expand on the academic knowledge available surrounding this topic.

Keywords: Ergonomics in Transportation · Transportation Safety · Driver Fatigue · Literature Review · Bibliometric Analysis

1 Introduction and Background

While the topic of transportation is extremely broad and interacts with many different areas of society, human factors engineers and ergonomists play a vital role in addressing the many challenges that arise. Importantly, many safety advancements such as intelligent cruise control technology have influenced the many protective systems which are employed around the world and are defending the public against injuries and death [1].

Because of the wide range of challenging areas related to ergonomics in transportation, there are many different topics that could be of focus. Chapter 58: Human Factors and Ergonomics in Motor Vehicle Transportation from the 4th edition of the Handbook of Human Factors and Ergonomics [2] served as a basis for different topics that could be researched in this literature review. Generally, the material covered includes information

© The Author(s), under exclusive license to Springer Nature Switzerland AG 2024
V. G. Duffy (Ed.): HCII 2024, LNCS 14711, pp. 49–64, 2024.
https://doi.org/10.1007/978-3-031-61066-0_4

for human factor engineers and ergonomists to design and evaluate vehicles to improve the safety, performance, and usability of vehicles. This includes background material and design guidelines for vehicular safety systems, ride quality, driver performance, controls and displays, distraction and workload assessments, review of roadway systems, and analysis of crash databases and statistics [3].

Because transportation and safety have been topics of focus for the entire history of ergonomics, there has been some professional focus to address these issues. There are many groups with an interest in transportation and safety related ergonomic issues, such as a technical committee within the International Ergonomics Association named Transport Ergonomics and Human Factors (TEHF) that has attempted to address some challenges in this area, but because many groups are studying at local levels, inconsistencies in standards and outcomes are an existing challenge.

2 Purpose of Study

In the most recently published version at the time of this writing, the 5th edition of the Handbook of Human Factors and Ergonomics, there was no chapter highlighting ergonomics in transportation. However, there is mention of driving in Chapter 7 on Mental Workload, which was related to task performance in driving studies [4]. An article published in 2011 in the 43rd volume of *Accident Analysis and Prevention* demonstrated clear evidence linking sleep with impaired driving performance and roadway accidents [5].

This study looks to further expand on these topics of ergonomics in transportation by seeking to summarize the current efforts being made with research in the area of transportation safety focused on driver fatigue and performance, and to analyze metadata to better understand trends and the future direction of research in this area.

3 Procedure

3.1 Identification of Topic and Key Words

To identify key terms to use in the systematic literature review for the topic of ergonomics in transportation, a word cloud was first created. Figure 1 represents a word cloud generated from the most frequently used words of the Handbook of Human Factors 4th edition textbook chapter on transportation [2], excluding common prepositions and other frequent words which conveyed no information and were removed, to better visualize word usage of the chapter to form a basic understanding of transportation in ergonomics.

From Fig. 1, there were a few words that stood out and formed the basis for the keywords that were later used in the research procedure that follows. Of the most frequently used words that are found in the largest font of the word cloud, the words "driving", "driver", "systems", "safety", and "performance".

This word cloud analysis led to the narrowing of choice of topic for this study to Ergonomics in Transportation focused on Driver Fatigue and Safety, as this topic directly relates to all the above frequently occurring words and therefore represents a current focus on the field of ergonomics within transportation. This further lead to the

Fig. 1. A word cloud generated using MaxQDA software to represent the most frequently occurring words from Chapter 58: Human Factors and Ergonomics in Motor Vehicle Transportation from the 4th edition of the Handbook of Human Factors and Ergonomics.

terms of "driver fatigue" and "safety" being chosen as the items to be searched in the different selected databases.

Fatigue can take a variety of different forms when applied to transportation and specifically for drivers, and some such fatigue related events identified by Arnold et al. include falling asleep while driving, crashing, and near misses [6]. Fatigue was chosen over other terms such as sleepiness, as this was found to be less frequently used in academic literature and more difficult to measure. However, some studies did try to assign a measure to sleepiness, such as by relating it to factors such as the time of day, the time since awakening and the duration of prior sleep [7]. The other search term used, "safety", is broad and can be hard to measure in scientific studies. However, there are approaches that can be taken to measure safety in terms of an operationally measurable variable, such as in Mollicone et al. where safety in relation to transportation was directly related to hard-braking events as they are easily observed and correlated to collisions and near-crashes [8].

3.2   Data Collection

Data collection for the systematic review process was performed by using the previously chosen search terms with various databases to gather metadata that can then be analyzed. This process and methodology were modeled after similar procedures seen in Kanade [9] as well as in Duffy [10]. For the data collection in this analysis, a keyword search for both "Driver Fatigue" and "Safety" was done for three different databases, Scopus [11], Web of Science [12], and Google Scholar [13]. The search done on Google Scholar contained a much higher volume of results as compared to the other databases, so a second search on Google Scholar was done, limited to results since 2019 (Table 1).

Table 1. Keyword Search Result Counts per Database.

Database	Keywords Used	Number of Results
Scopus	"Driver Fatigue" and "Safety"	637
Web of Science	"Driver Fatigue" and "Safety"	1,246
Google Scholar (Articles since 2019)	"Driver Fatigue" and "Safety"	8,270
Google Scholar (All time)	"Driver Fatigue" and "Safety"	20,800

3.3 Trend Analysis

The trend analysis is based off the results found from searches on both Scopus and Web of Science. Both of these databases offered tools from their website to analyze search results from the keyword search done previously. The search was performed with terms "Driver Fatigue" and "Safety" without any other filters applied to results. Figure 2, showing results only from Web of Science, clearly represents an upward trend of articles published per year for these terms in the last 20 years, with an increase or same number of publications each year. 2022 showed the most publications of 137.

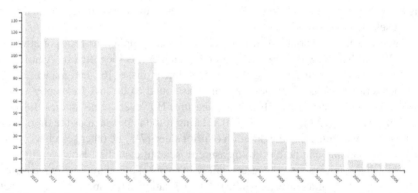

Fig. 2. A graph showing the Number of Publications per Year on Web of Science for search terms "Driver Fatigue" and "Safety".

Analysis of the results from the Scopus search, found in Fig. 3, show a similarly upward trend of articles published per year. There were some year-to-year declines in results, but 2008 to 2010 is the only period that showed declines lasting more than one year. However, both database search results show a greater increase in results per year than previously found in the data, showing that this topic should continue to experience growth in research and publications per year. Therefore, it is clear from both results from Scopus and Web of Science that the areas of Driver Fatigue and Safety are a growing topic of research and an emerging area needing further study.

A search utilizing Google Ngram, a tool that illustrates and compares trends in usage of specified terms in books for a defined time period [14], was performed with terms related to Ergonomics in Transportation that were also found from review of

Documents by year

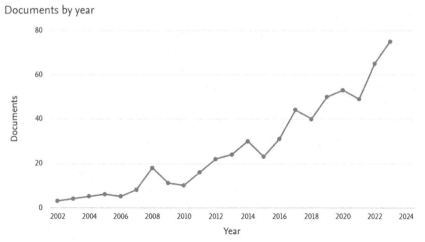

Fig. 3. A graph showing the Number of Publications per Year on Scopus for search terms "Driver Fatigue" and "Safety".

the Handbook of Human Factor's chapter of Transportation [2]. This included terms such as "older drivers", "job scheduling", "collision avoidance", and "driver fatigue". While nearly all of these terms showed an upward trend of usage in the past five years, "driver fatigue" showed as the least used of these terms in the search, which showed that compared to other areas of ergonomics in transportation, more research and publication on driver fatigue can be done (Fig. 4).

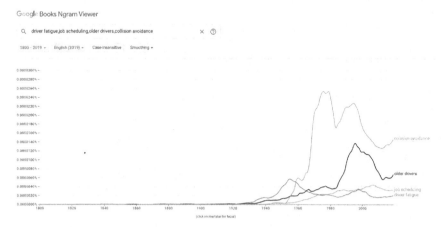

Fig. 4. A Google NGram search of various terms related to Ergonomics in Transportation.

3.4 Content Analysis

To begin content analysis, another leading table was created of the articles from the Web of Science search with the highest citations, as this list represents the most referenced articles that have formed the basis of research within the field. A list of these articles, along with the number of citations for each article over each of the past three years along with total number of citations is shown in Table 2.

Table 2. Leading Articles by Citation Count for Web of Science Keyword Search.

Article	2021 Citations	2022 Citations	2023 Citations	Average per Year	Total Citations
A critical review of the psychophysiology of driver fatigue Feb 2001 I Lal, SKL and Craig, A	67	59	39	31.09	715
Real-time nonintrusive monitoring and prediction of driver fatigue Jul 2004 I Ji, Q; Zhu, ZW and Lan, PL	24	20	9	24.35	487
Detecting Driver Drowsiness Based on Sensors: A Review Dec 2012 I Sahayadhas, A; Sundaraj, K and Murugappan, M	57	43	30	34.83	418
Driver fatigue: Electroencephalography and psychological assessment May 2002 I Lal, SKL and Craig, A	37	30	14	17.5	385
DRIVER FATIGUE Jun 1994 I BROWN, ID	18	10	8	11.37	341
Driver fatigue: The importance of identifying causal factors of fatigue when considering detection and countermeasure technologies May 2009 I May, JF and Baldwin, CL	43	22	24	18.27	274

(*continued*)

Table 2. (*continued*)

Article	2021 Citations	2022 Citations	2023 Citations	Average per Year	Total Citations
Development of an algorithm for an EEG-based driver fatigue countermeasure 2003 | Lal, SKL; Craig, A; (…); Nguyen, H	19	13	9	12.38	260
Can SVM be used for automatic EEG detection of drowsiness during car driving? Jan 2009 | Yeo, MVM; Li, XP; (…); Wilder-Smith, EPV	30	22	12	17.13	257
EEG-Based Spatio-Temporal Convolutional Neural Network for Driver Fatigue Evaluation Sep 2019 | Gao, ZK; Wang, XM; (…); Zuo, SY	65	57	60	47.6	238
Driver Behavior Analysis for Safe Driving: A Survey Dec 2015 | Kaplan, S; Guvensan, MA; (…); Karalurt, Y	49	39	18	26	234

The table showcases leading articles on driver fatigue, highlighting their citation counts over three years. Lal and Craig's critical review on psychophysiology leads with consistent citations since 2001, maintaining a high average of 31.09 per year. Similarly, Sahayadhas et al.'s sensor-based drowsiness detection review sustains a notable average of 34.83. Gao et al.'s 2019 study gains traction, steadily accumulating citations with a high average of 47.6. Interestingly, older works, like Brown's 1994 article, sustain relevance with consistent albeit lower citation counts. The trends suggest sustained interest in established research while newer technological approaches, like EEG-based neural networks, gain increasing attention, reflecting the evolution of fatigue detection methodologies in driver safety research.

Figure 5, a network visualization generated via VOSViewer using Scopus keyword search data, illustrates prevalent terms and their co-occurrences. Dominant words include "driver fatigue" and "fatigue," indicating their significant usage. Additionally, terms such as "fatigue detection," "humans," "motor transportation," "accidents," and "accident prevention" appear prominently within the network. This visualization highlights the interconnectedness and frequency of these specific terms, emphasizing their close association within the context of the research data, likely indicating their vital roles in discussions surrounding driver fatigue and safety within the realm of transportation studies.

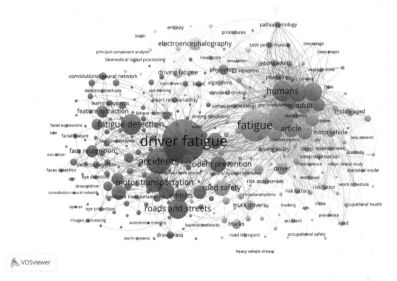

Fig. 5. Network Visualization from VOSViewer of co-occurrences from the Scopus keyword search results data.

Figure 6 lists keywords related to driving and safety, their occurrences, and total link strength. "Fatigue" and "driver fatigue" are prominent keywords, indicating a significant focus on the impact of tiredness on driving. The table quantifies the frequency and connectivity of these terms in literature, offering insights into prevalent research themes and potential areas for further exploration.

In summary, the figure provides a visual representation of the most common keywords related to driving safety and fatigue, and their frequency and connectivity in literature. It can be used to identify research trends and areas worthy of more research.

3.5 Co-citation Analysis

The bar graph in Fig. 7 examining document counts across various countries or territories within the context of driver safety and fatigue reveals interesting insights. China emerges as the leader, boasting a substantial number of documents exceeding 200, indicating a significant focus or perhaps a prevalent issue in this area within the country. The United States and India closely follow, suggesting a comparable level of attention or research in these regions concerning driver safety and fatigue-related topics.

Interestingly, Australia, Canada, and the United Kingdom show similar document counts, signifying a moderate but relatively lower emphasis on this subject compared to the leading nations. Taiwan, South Korea, Malaysia, and Germany exhibit even fewer

Keyword	Occurrences	Total link strength
fatigue	139	1893
driver fatigue	214	1892
human	105	1804
humans	79	1425
automobile driving	68	1208
car driving	67	1196
adult	55	1113
article	60	1065
male	50	1004
traffic accident	54	937
female	44	912
accidents, traffic	44	808
accidents	101	782
automobile drivers	84	773
roads and streets	76	704
motor transportation	71	677
fatigue detection	79	621
safety	49	617
road safety	56	602

Fig. 6. Keywords with number of Occurrences from VOSViewer content analysis of Scopus keyword search.

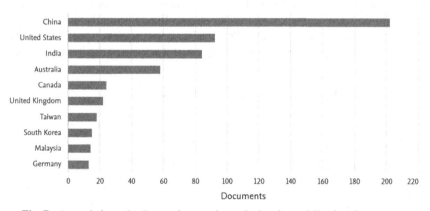

Documents by country or territory

Compare the document counts for up to 15 countries/territories.

Fig. 7. A graph from the Scopus keyword search showing publications by country.

document counts, suggesting a comparatively lesser emphasis or possibly a different focus in their research on driver safety and fatigue. This distribution of document counts indicates varying degrees of attention and research emphasis across different countries, shedding light on potential disparities in concerns, priorities, or approaches to addressing driver safety and fatigue-related issues globally (Table 3).

Table 3. Web of Science Record Count by Country for Keyword Search.

Countries/Regions	Record Count	% of Total Records in Search
CHINA	407	32.717
USA	120	9.646
AUSTRALIA	74	5.949
ENGLAND	55	4.421
INDIA	45	3.617
CANADA	30	2.412
TAIWAN	23	1.849
GERMANY	22	1.768
SOUTH KOREA	20	1.608
SPAIN	17	1.367

The Scopus Top Sources for the keyword search showcase diverse publications. "Lecture Notes in Electrical Engineering" leads with 16 records, potentially exploring technology applications. "Transportation Research Part F Traffic Psychology and Behaviour" follows, emphasizing behavioral aspects with 15 records. "Accident Analysis and Prevention" and "SAE Technical Papers" contribute 14 and 12 records, respectively, focusing on safety and technical details. Journals like "Journal of Safety Research," "Safety Science," and "Traffic Injury Prevention" collectively offer insights into safety practices. Additionally, conferences or compilations like "Lecture Notes in Computer Science" and "Transportation Research Procedia" provide varied perspectives, spanning technology, psychology, safety, and interdisciplinary studies in transportation (Table 4).

Table 4. Scopus Top Sources for Keyword Search.

Source Title	Records from Source
Lecture Notes In Electrical Engineering	16
Transportation Research Part F Traffic Psychology And Behaviour	15
Accident Analysis And Prevention	14
SAE Technical Papers	12
Lecture Notes In Computer Science Including Subseries Lecture Notes In Artificial Intelligence And Lecture Notes In Bioinformatics	11
Journal Of Safety Research	10
Transportation Research Record	10
Safety Science	7
Traffic Injury Prevention	7
Transportation Research Procedia	7

The data from the Web of Science highlights significant sources in transportation safety and analysis. "Accident Analysis and Prevention" and its variant are prominent, representing about 3.62% of total records, indicating a focus on accident studies. IEEE journals like "IEEE Access" and "IEEE Transactions on Intelligent Transportation Systems" contribute about 2.5% collectively, showcasing technological aspects. Journals like "Sensors" and "Sensors Basel Switzerland" account for 2.26%, implying a sensor-centric approach. Safety-focused journals like "Journal of Safety Research" and "Safety Science" collectively constitute 1.77%. The emphasis spans accident prevention, intelligent transportation systems, sensor technologies, and behavioral psychology in traffic safety research, portraying a multidisciplinary approach in the field (Table 5).

Table 5. Web of Science Top Sources Keyword Search.

Publication/Source Titles	Record Count	% of Total Records in Publication
ACCIDENT ANALYSIS AND PREVENTION	23	1.85%
ACCIDENT ANALYSIS PREVENTION	22	1.77%
IEEE ACCESS	17	1.37%
IEEE TRANSACTIONS ON INTELLIGENT TRANSPORTATION SYSTEMS	14	1.13%
SENSORS	14	1.13%
SENSORS BASEL SWITZERLAND	14	1.13%
JOURNAL OF SAFETY RESEARCH	13	1.05%
TRANSPORTATION RESEARCH PART F TRAFFIC PSYCHOLOGY AND BEHAVIOUR	13	1.05%
TRANSPORTATION RESEARCH RECORD	10	0.80%
SAFETY SCIENCE	9	0.72%

In the Scopus leading authors table for keyword searches, several researchers stand out. Matthews, G., Neubauer, C., Wang, F., and Williamson, A. demonstrate prolific output with 7–8 documents each. Craig, A., Di Stasi, L.L., and Zhang, H. follow closely with 5–6 documents. Their collective contributions indicate diverse expertise across transportation safety, psychology, and technology, offering robust insights in the field (Table 6).

To further explore and analyze the leading authors of articles, the data from the Scopus keyword search was exported as a .RIS file type and imported into the VOSViewer software, similar to what was done earlier with the keyword analysis map [15]. VOSViewer was then utilized to analyze the connections between some of the leading authors from the keyword search and map these relationships into a network

Table 6. Scopus leading authors table for keyword searches.

Author	Documents
Matthews, G	8
Neubauer, C	7
Wang, F	7
Williamson, A	7
Craig, A	6
Di Stasi, L.L	6
Zhang, H	5
Catena, A	4
Dawson, D	4
Filtness, A.J	4

visualization. The minimum number of documents for an author to be considered for this analysis was set to five, which narrowed the initial field of 1788 authors down to 30 with over five documents included in the search, as this would represent the leading authors in the field of driver fatigue and safety.

From the analysis, there is an obvious cluster of 24 of the 30 authors with more than five documents included in the search. From further analysis of some of these connected authors, most are from universities in China, with some being located geographically close to each other. Such an example is Wang, H., found in the purple dot near the center of the cluster, who is from the School of Mechanical Engineering and Automation in Northeastern University, in Shenyang, China, and his connection to Wang, L., found in green near the top of the cluster, who is also from Shenyang, China, but he is from Shenyang Institute of Engineering (Fig. 8).

4 Discussion

Driver fatigue is a significant concern in transportation safety, as it can impair a driver's ability to make decisions, slow down reaction time, decrease attention, and contribute to an increase in the number of accidents [16]. With more than 9.5 million Americans working overnight or rotating shifts and one-third of United States commutes exceeding 30 min, the implications for traffic and occupational safety are significant [17]. Driver fatigue is a major problem in safety-critical work situations as well as in public traffic [18]. It is well understood that driver fatigue is a contributing factor in up to 20% of collisions in the UK, which are 50% more likely to result in a fatality or serious injury [19]. The impact of operator fatigue on safety performance is a major issue in the railroad industry [20].

Fig. 8. Network visualization of different authors from VOSViewer using data from the Scopus keyword search.

To address driver fatigue, various detection methods have been proposed to assist drivers in driving safely and improve traffic safety. These methods include detecting yawning based on subtle facial action recognition [21], a fatigue driving detection algorithm based on facial multi-feature fusion [22], and a fatigue detection system for high-speed trains based on driver vigilance using a wireless wearable EEG. Furthermore, studies have shown that critical incidents are more likely to occur at certain times of the day and at certain periods within a duty, emphasizing the need for effective fatigue detection and management systems [23]. Some commercial approaches to driver fatigue in the trucking industry include detection systems to analyze the state of the driver to help reduce incidents related to impairment [24].

In addition to driver fatigue, the ergonomic design of transportation systems and workstations plays a crucial role in ensuring the safety and well-being of transport workers. Problems in transport workers are closely related to ergonomic issues [25]. The ergonomics design of transport category airplane cockpits is of great importance to the efficiency of flight crew operation and has a major impact on flight safety [23]. Furthermore, the use of ergonomic measures related to musculoskeletal complaints among construction workers has been found to be essential for ensuring the safety and health of workers [26].

In conclusion, driver fatigue is a significant concern in transportation safety, with implications for both occupational and public traffic safety. Effective fatigue detection methods and ergonomic design of transportation systems and workstations are crucial for mitigating the risks associated with driver fatigue and ensuring the safety and well-being of transport workers.

5 Conclusion and Future Work

5.1 Conclusion

Ergonomics within the realm of transportation, particularly concerning the crucial aspect of mitigating driver fatigue and ensuring safety, remains an imperative field demanding persistent focus and sustained efforts. Despite notable strides in technology and the evolution of safety measures, the enduring challenges associated with driver fatigue emphasize the ongoing necessity for comprehensive research and proactive interventions. This review underscores the dynamic and evolving nature of this domain, emphasizing the indispensable requirement for interdisciplinary approaches that address the multifaceted dimensions of transportation safety.

Moreover, the burgeoning corpus of literature signifies an increasing acknowledgment of the intricate and pivotal role played by human factors in establishing and maintaining safe and efficient transportation systems. As such, continued dedication to both research and practical implementation is crucial, not only for a nuanced understanding of driver fatigue and safety concerns but also for the effective deployment of strategies aimed at safeguarding individuals on the road while optimizing transportation efficiency.

5.2 Potential Directions for Further Research

1. Behavioral Studies: A deeper exploration of the behavioral components influencing driver fatigue and safety stands as a pivotal avenue for future research. This involves delving into the psychological and cognitive aspects of drivers, understanding their decision-making processes, stressors, and attentional patterns. Moreover, developing tailored interventions and comprehensive training programs could significantly mitigate driver fatigue issues, enhancing overall safety on the roads.
2. Technological Innovations: Continuous exploration and development of emerging technologies offer promising avenues for combatting driver fatigue. Advanced systems like AI-driven fatigue detection mechanisms or adaptive vehicle designs that actively minimize risks associated with fatigue-related impairments present critical areas for further exploration. Integrating these technologies seamlessly into transportation systems could offer preventive measures against potential accidents caused by driver fatigue.
3. Global Collaboration: Encouraging and fostering collaborations among researchers and institutions across nations is paramount. This collaborative approach facilitates the exchange of diverse perspectives, methodologies, and regional insights, leading to a comprehensive understanding of transportation safety concerns. By addressing regional disparities and pooling expertise, a collective effort can be made towards establishing universal safety standards and best practices.

4. Longitudinal Studies: Initiating and conducting longitudinal studies can offer substantial insights into the long-term efficacy and sustainability of implemented safety measures and technological interventions. Tracking the impact of these interventions over extended periods not only validates their effectiveness but also informs policymakers and stakeholders about their continuous relevance and potential areas for improvement.

In essence, the multifaceted nature of ergonomics in transportation, particularly concerning driver fatigue and safety, necessitates a holistic approach encompassing behavioral, technological, collaborative, and longitudinal research endeavors. This comprehensive strategy is essential not only for addressing immediate challenges but also for establishing a robust foundation for the continual enhancement of transportation safety and efficiency globally.

References

1. Hancock, P.A.: How human factors and ergonomics save lives. Appl. Ergon. **98**, 103585 (2022). https://doi.org/10.1016/J.APERGO.2021.103585
2. Green, P.A.: Human factors and ergonomics in motor vehicle transportation. In: Handbook of Human Factors and Ergonomics, pp. 1596–1614 (2012). https://doi.org/10.1002/9781118131350.ch58
3. Eby, D.: Human Factors and Ergonomics in Motor Vehicle Transportation, pp. 1538–1569 (2006). https://doi.org/10.1002/0470048204.ch59
4. Hancock, G.M., Longo, L., Young, M.S., Hancock, P.A.: Mental workload. In: Handbook of Human Factors and Ergonomics, pp. 203–226 (2021). https://doi.org/10.1002/9781119636113.ch7
5. Williamson, A., Lombardi, D.A., Folkard, S., Stutts, J., Courtney, T.K., Connor, J.L.: The link between fatigue and safety. Accid. Anal. Prev. **43**(2), 498–515 (2011). https://doi.org/10.1016/j.aap.2009.11.011
6. Arnold, P.K., Hartley, L.R., Corry, A., Hochstadt, D., Penna, F., Feyer, A.M.: Hours of work, and perceptions of fatigue among truck drivers. Accid. Anal. Prev. **29**(4), 471–477 (1997). https://doi.org/10.1016/S0001-4575(97)00026-2
7. Åkerstedt, T., Connor, J., Gray, A., Kecklund, G.: Predicting road crashes from a mathematical model of alertness regulation -: the sleep/wake predictor. Accid. Anal. Prev. **40**(4), 1480–1485 (2008). https://doi.org/10.1016/j.aap.2008.03.016
8. Mollicone, D., et al.: Predicting performance and safety based on driver fatigue. Accid. Anal. Prev. **126**, 142–145 (2019). https://doi.org/10.1016/j.aap.2018.03.004
9. Kanade, S.G., Duffy, V.G.: Use of virtual reality for safety training: a systematic review. In: Duffy, V.G. (ed.) Digital Human Modeling and Applications in Health, Safety, Ergonomics and Risk Management. Health, Operations Management, and Design, pp. 364–375. Springer, Cham (2022). https://doi.org/10.1007/978-3-031-06018-2_25
10. Duffy, T., Duffy, V.G.: Moderating stress in task design and motivation: a systematic review. In: V.G., Ziefle, M., Rau, P.-L.P., Tseng, M.M. (eds.) Human-Automation Interaction: Mobile Computing Duffy, pp. 415–430. Springer, Cham (2023). https://doi.org/10.1007/978-3-031-10788-7_25
11. Scopus. https://www.scopus.com/. Accessed 15 Dec 2023
12. Web of Science. https://www.webofscience.com/wos/woscc/basic-search. Accessed 15 Dec 2023

13. Google Scholar. https://scholar.google.com/. Accessed 15 Dec 2023
14. Michel, J.-B., et al.: Quantitative analysis of culture using millions of digitized books. Science **331**, 176–182 (2011). https://doi.org/10.1126/science.1199644
15. van Eck, N.J., Waltman, L.: VOS Viewer: Visualizing Scientific Landscapes [Software] (2010). https://www.vosviewer.com
16. Yin, J., Hu, J., Mu, Z.: Developing and evaluating a mobile driver fatigue detection network based on electroencephalograph signals. Healthc. Technol. Lett. **4**(1), 34–38 (2017). https://doi.org/10.1049/htl.2016.0053
17. Lee, M.L., et al.: High risk of near-crash driving events following night-shift work. Proc. Natl. Acad. Sci. **113**(1), 176–181 (2016). https://doi.org/10.1073/pnas.1510383112
18. Wang, F., Wang, H.: Study of driving fatigue alleviation by transcutaneous acupoints electrical stimulations. Sci. World J. **2014**, 450249 (2014). https://doi.org/10.1155/2014/450249
19. Guest, A.J., et al.: Attenuated cardiovascular reactivity to acute psychological stress predicts future fatigue symptoms in truck drivers. J. Occup. Environ. Med. **65**(3) (2023). https://journals.lww.com/joem/fulltext/2023/03000/attenuated_cardiovascular_reactivity_to_acute.6.aspx
20. Yan, R., Wu, C., Wang, Y.: A preliminary study for exploring high-speed train driver fatigue using eye-gaze cue. In: Proceedings of the 2016 2nd International Conference on Artificial Intelligence and Industrial Engineering (AIIE 2016), pp. 187–190, Atlantis Press (2016). https://doi.org/10.2991/aiie-16.2016.43
21. Yang, H., Liu, L., Min, W., Yang, X., Xiong, X.: Driver yawning detection based on subtle facial action recognition. IEEE Trans. Multimedia **23**, 572–583 (2021). https://doi.org/10.1109/TMM.2020.2985536
22. Li, K., Gong, Y., Ren, Z.: A fatigue driving detection algorithm based on facial multi-feature fusion. IEEE Access **8**, 101244–101259 (2020). https://doi.org/10.1109/ACCESS.2020.2998363
23. Zhang, Y., Sun, Y., Chen, Y.: A framework for ergonomics design of transport category airplane cockpit. Procedia Eng. **80**, 573–580 (2014). https://doi.org/10.1016/j.proeng.2014.09.113
24. Horberry, T., et al.: Human-centered design for an in-vehicle truck driver fatigue and distraction warning system. IEEE Trans. Intell. Transp. Syst. **23**(6), 5350–5359 (2022). https://doi.org/10.1109/TITS.2021.3053096
25. Kurniawan, B., Rahfiludin, Z., Setyaningsih, Y., Nurjazuli, N.: Ergonomic risk, muscle tension, lactic acid, and work performance on transport workers at fish auction. Media Kesehatan Masyarakat Indonesia **18**(2), 50–56 (2022). https://doi.org/10.30597/mkmi.v18i2.19739
26. Boschman, J.S., Frings-Dresen, M.H.W., van der Molen, H.F.: Use of ergonomic measures related to musculoskeletal complaints among construction workers: a 2-year follow-up study. Saf. Health Work **6**(2), 90–96 (2015). https://doi.org/10.1016/j.shaw.2014.12.003

A Literature Review of Trends in Personal Protective Equipment

Alexandra Favazza, Andrew Frosti, and Vincent G. Duffy[(✉)]

Purdue University, 610 Purdue Mall, West Lafayette, IN 47907, USA
{afavazza,afrosti,duffy}@purdue.edu

Abstract. Personal Protective Equipment (PPE) is used in varying degrees across any industry where the work poses a threat to human safety. It ranges from protective glasses worn by a machinist to full-on hazmat suits used to work in areas with high radiation and everywhere in between. The impact of PPE is undeniable as it allows industrial entities to protect their workers from serious harm as well as shielding them from liability. By adequately using the appropriate and properly fitted PPE for any given task the risk of injury can be drastically reduced. This can clearly be illustrated by the U.S. Bureau of Labor Statistics which found that the rate of non-fatal workplace injuries or illness decreased by 70% from 1972 to 2018 [1]. The increased attention to PPE has paid dividends in worker safety since its popularization in the 1970s, and even today industry leaders in professional safety groups are hard at work to develop PPE that is safer and more accessible than ever before.

Keywords: Personal Protective Equipment (PPE) · Industry Safety · Workplace Accident · Safety Ergonomics · Anthropometry

1 Introduction and Background

The topic of personal protection equipment (PPE) is vital to many industries for the basic protection of their workers. From the U.S Department of Labor-Occupational Safety and Health Association (OSHA) PPE is equipment worn to minimize exposure to hazards that cause serious workplace injuries and illness. For companies to maintain their workforce, they must protect their employees by following industry standards for basic safety protocols [2]. PPE can range from eye and ear protection to gowns and full suits depending on the hazards the job may present.

The focus of PPE first showed importance in the 1920s, then became a serious topic of interest in the 1970s. There have always been hazardous jobs in the workforce, but engineers have access to more capabilities than ever to create the best gear and equipment for workplace environment safety.

Furthermore, Personal Protective Equipment is a crucial part of industrial engineering because it allows human workers to safely work in industrial settings without significant risk of injury. Proper PPE improves efficiency, keeps workers safe, limits

© The Author(s), under exclusive license to Springer Nature Switzerland AG 2024
V. G. Duffy (Ed.): HCII 2024, LNCS 14711, pp. 65–82, 2024.
https://doi.org/10.1007/978-3-031-61066-0_5

company liability, and allows workers to use industrial machinery they wouldn't be able to otherwise.

Beyond industrial engineering, a focus on PPE is valuable in any setting where human injury is at risk. This includes factory workers, inspectors, medical professionals, and much more. A recent example is the focus placed on PPE to combat Covid-19. National broadcasts went out throughout 2020 to educate the population on the proper use of PPE to protect themselves, and the Human Factors and Ergonomics Society even had a hand in developing safe practices for the use and reuse of COVID-19 PPE. Industries everywhere are working to optimize their use of PPE to mitigate human liability.

Although we have made great strides in worker safety and PPE over the past 50 years, we still have a long way to go on making PPE accessible and tailored to an increasingly diverse workforce. For example, women are far more likely to be put at risk than their male counterparts due to ill-fitting safety gear. A survey conducted by the Center for Construction Research and Training asked 174 female workers about their experience with PPE, and found that 77% of them had been put at risk due to ill-fitting safety gear. This goes to show that a traditionally male-dominated trade, like construction, is not adapting fast enough to a changing workforce to adequately protect employees.

Finally, human factors and ergonomics are closely tied to personal protective equipment since PPE directly interfaces with human workers. As such it is imperative that designers of PPE have a good understanding of human factors and anthropometry. The Human Factors and Ergonomics Society works to develop anthropometric standards that are used to evaluate the fit of industry protective equipment, per "ISO 15537:2004 Principles for selecting and using test persons for testing anthropometric aspects of industrial products and designs." [5]. This helps ensure that a wide variety of people with different body types can effectively and safely use well-fitted PPE.

This systematic literature review aims to explore the history and applications of PPE, from the past to future developments [26, 27]. PPE is a generalized term that is used across multiple industries, ranging from automotive, medical, aviation, and civil engineering work. PPE is a vital piece of equipment for the safety of persons in various environments. Historically it ranges from basic protection gear such as ear muffs or safety eyeglasses to guards on automated arms on assembly lines. The constriction of these materials is not quite as simple. Safety testing is conducted for any piece of equipment or clothing considered PPE to ensure it holds up to its standards, which are set by material properties and also by OSHA. Thanks to rapidly developing technologies across a myriad of industries, PPE has become more important than ever and will need to remain an evolving field of study and relevance.

1.1 Definitions

Personal Protective Equipment: Personal protective equipment, commonly referred to as "PPE", is equipment worn to minimize exposure to hazards that cause serious workplace injuries and illnesses. These injuries and illnesses may result from contact with chemical, radiological, physical, electrical, mechanical, or other workplace hazards. Personal protective equipment may include items such as gloves, safety glasses and shoes, earplugs or muffs, hard hats, respirators, coveralls, vests, and full-body suits.

Workplace Accident: According to OSHA a workplace accident is an unplanned event that results in personal injury or property damage during or arising out of work performed in the course and the scope of employment [3].

Anthropometry: Anthropometry is the science that defines physical measures of a person's size, form, and functional capacities. Applied to occupational injury prevention, anthropometric measurements are used to study the interaction of workers with tasks, tools, machines, vehicles, and personal protective equipment—especially to determine the degree of protection against dangerous exposures, whether chronic or acute [4].

2 Purpose of Study

While research into PPE was first popularized in the early 1970s with the founding of OSHA and the rise of labor and workplace safety regulations, the last five years have seen a surge in research spearheaded by the response to COVID-19, but still readily apparent in other industries. This study will seek to understand what is driving PPE as an emerging topic as well as a mainstay of scientific research. Bibliometric analysis will allow us to understand what topics of PPE are driving most modern research as well as where that research is taking place. Data was collected using a wide variety of databases including Scopus and Google Scholar, and then visualized using metadata tools like Citespace, Scopus, google Ngram, and Nvivo.

3 Procedure

To analyze relevant findings related to PPE along with its use within multiple industries and future work for innovation, a bibliometric analysis was conducted along with data searching tools. This analysis measures the engagement of researchers and the relevance of PPE related to ergonomics in society. A trend analysis, keyword search analysis, identification of emergence, and general data collection will be discussed all concerning PPE.

The sources referenced in this literature review are intended to assist in the bibliometric analysis of the topic of PPE in ergonomics and to relate current and previous research conducted to the relevance of the topic of PPE in society. Scopus, CiteSpace, Google nGram, and VOSviewer are examples of analysis tools that aid in understanding the prevalence of PPE. Research articles from various sites such as Scopus, Google Scholar, and PubMed are referenced to expand on the importance of PPE and how it is currently and previously understood, researched, and applied in various applications and work settings.

3.1 Identifying Driving Factors of PPE Research

See Table 1.

Table 1. A tabulation of the documents found using Scopus to search for PPE and Workplace Accidents using various filters.

Search Terms	Database	Search Parameters	Number of Articles
Personal Protective Equipment	Scopus	No Restrictions	17,776
	Scopus	1972–2023	17,749
	Scopus	Engineering Documents	2.577
Workplace Accident	Scopus	No Restrictions	9,472
	Scopus	1972–2023	9,469
	Scopus	Engineering Documents	2.915
Anthropometry	Scopus	No Restrictions	94,932
	Scopus	1972–2023	92,424
	Scopus	Engineering Documents	5,547

3.2 Data Visualization Methods

The citation methods used for this systematic literature review were inspired by: "Methodology for Systematic Literature Review Applied to… - IEEE Xplore." IEEE Conference Publication. Accessed November 27, 2023. https://ieeexplore.ieee.org/abstract/document/8363388.

The following methods were used to find trends, relationships, and current research being conducted for PPE in multiple applications (medical, industrial, automotive, etc.)

1. CiteSpace analysis research articles for trends in the representation of a topic and linkages between authors.
2. VOSViewer is used to construct a bibliometric network of relations between authors and publications.
3. Google nGram displays a string of frequencies of searched topics compared to their relevance factor in time.

4 Results and Discussion

4.1 Trends in PPE Research

The focus of PPE first showed importance in the 1920s, then became a serious topic of interest in the 1970s. There have always been hazardous jobs in the workforce, but engineers have access to more capabilities than ever to create the best gear and equipment for workplace environment safety [5].

The key search terms used were "personal protection equipment". It can be inferred from the data displayed in Fig. 1 that the COVID-19 pandemic was a large cause of the spike seen in 2020 for articles published related to personal protection equipment (Fig. 2).

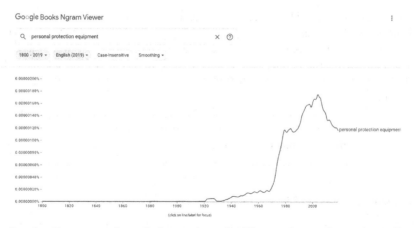

Fig. 1. Google nGram comparison of a keyword search of "personal protection equipment" and displaying its relevance between the years of 1800 to 2019.

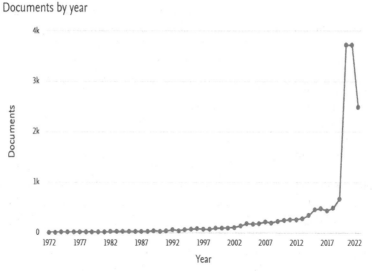

Fig. 2. Number of documents about personal protective equipment published in Scopus from 1972 to 2022.

According to Scopus, in 2017 432 documents related to PPE were released compared to 3,718 documents released in 2021. I would attribute this to the global focus on PPE regarding coronavirus that has been ongoing since 2020. This accounts for the surge in over 8 times as many documents released compared to just 4 years prior. An astonishing 43.4% of Scopus PPE documents are related to the medical field, while the next largest field was engineering with only 9.3%. This of course begs the question of does this trend extends to other industries across this same five-year period, or is it isolated to medical PPE?

When examining solely engineering-related documents we found that 98 PPE documents were released in Scopus in 2017, and 314 were released in 2021, which is over 3 times as many. This means that although the trend did not exist to the same extent it did in the medical field, the global focus on PPE in recent years is not solely based on COVID-19, which solidifies PPE as both a stable of ergonomics and an emerging technology.

It is difficult to tell in the figure above but Scopus articles first started being submitted around 1972 and saw a steady increase until 2020 when a massive influx of submissions coincided with the beginning of the Covid-19 pandemic. In 2022 this number started to decline as the Covid was better understood and less widespread.

4.2 Leading Sources of PPE Research

Through our research, we have identified several leading articles related to PPE and ergonomics summarized in Table 2 below. Of the five top articles four of them are about medical PPE, one of which is specifically about Covid-19, and the fifth is about PPE for construction workers. This reflects the recent national focus on medical PPE to combat a global pandemic. Specifically, the leading PPE article discusses how medical PPE, which is often cumbersome, impacts the ability of medical professionals to do their jobs. Reduced visibility, reduced dexterity, and overheating are just some of the factors that could result in mistakes being made [23]. This is particularly interesting because the most cited article has nothing to do with improving the effectiveness of PPE, but rather to prevent it from getting in the way.

The second leading article surveyed construction workers to identify the physical pain they experience during their jobs. This data will be used to develop new PPE specifically targeted to reduce these aches and pains [24]. Finally, the third leading article is about minimizing the risk of contagion during an endoscopic procedure. The article also discusses the importance of considering additional factors when selecting PPE, such as patient allergies to some synthetic materials and the ability of surgeons to do their job despite PPE being in the way [25]. These articles give us a better idea of not only what the leading topics in today's research are, but ideas as to where they will go in the future.

The main topic of PPE demonstrated in many of these articles that related to COVID-19 was equipment that can be made to fit-for-all or fit for a general population was highlighted throughout many articles. The benefit of a universal fit is fast production times, simple manufacturing equipment (non-variable), and overall low cost to produce, which then means the product can be more affordable to purchase. The other caveat to COVID-19 was the governmental requirements for certain PPE and disinfecting procedures in public spaces. This nuance caused a massive bottleneck in the manufacturing industry by a large request for production of the PPE, shortage of materials, low staffing, and high demand.

These research articles referenced in this systematic review have been identified as overlapping [6, 15], as they are both about personal protection equipment during the COVID-19 pandemic. These articles were cross-checked by comparing the Scopus information about the index keyword used.

Table 2. Identified 5 top leading articles about PPE and ergonomics were cited the most, using Scopus as an identification source. 85 articles were identified as related to PPE in ergonomics using the general keyword search tool in Scopus from 2010 to 2022.

Author	Article Title	Leading Keywords	# of Citations
Martina Loibner	Scopus - Document details - Limiting factors for wearing personal protective equipment (PPE) in a health care environment evaluated in a randomised study	Adult; Body Temperature; Ergonomics	93
S. Eaves	Scopus - Document details - Building healthy construction workers: Their views on health, wellbeing and better workplace design	Ageing; Construction ergonomics; Health and wellbeing; Participatory ergonomics	91
Marcos C. Pedrosa	Scopus - Document details - Minimizing occupational hazards in endoscopy: Personal protective equipment, radiation safety, and ergonomics	clinical study; data base; ergonomics	76
Massimiliano Sorbello	Scopus - Document details - Aerosol boxes and barrier enclosures for airway management in COVID-19 patients: a scoping review and narrative synthesis	aerosol box; aerosol-generating procedures; COVID-19; droplets; intubation box; tracheal intubation	75
Lorna K.P. Suen	Scopus - Document details - Self-contamination during doffing of personal protective equipment by healthcare workers to prevent Ebola transmission	Adult; Aerosols; Environmental Exposure; Female	75

Additionally, we have identified the top 5 research institutions for PPE development which are summarized in Table 3 below. Unsurprisingly they are all either medical research institutions or larger research institutions that have a strong presence in the medical field. What is more surprising is just how much more research was conducted at the top institution, The National University of Singapore. The National University of Singapore has nearly twice as many research documents as the next four highest institutions combined.

This is likely partially because the University of Singapore is being evaluated as a single entity whereas other institutions like Harvard Medical School have its research counted separately from the main Harvard University's total. Regardless, this doesn't adequately explain this discrepancy. Therefore, we are forced to conclude that medical PPE and likely other forms of PPE are prioritized highly at the National University of Singapore, as that priority is reflected in the sheer volume of their research.

Table 3. The Top 5 leading institutions in the research of personal protection equipment from topic search in Scopus. Researchers were identified by referencing the key search words "Ergonomics" and "PPE". The results were then filtered by the highest number of citations with the keywords used to search. This data is based on results matching documents since 2019.

Institution	Country	# of Documents
National University of Singapore	Singapore	1984
University Hospital Bern,	Switzerland	316
Medizinische Universität Graz	Austria	308
Università degli Studi di Firenze,	Italy	202
Harvard Medical School,	United States	197

An additional analysis was conducted using VOSViewer and CiteSpace for a co-author analysis that represents relations in the field of ergonomics, specifically related to personal protection equipment, and can be seen in Figs. 3 and 4 below. The VOSViewer analysis displays an intricate web of relations between authors in Fig. 3. In Fig. 4, it can be inferred that many articles are cross-referenced by each other, which is represented by the smaller clusters encircled by a larger cluster.

4.3   PPE in Various Industrial Applications

Given the dominance of the medical field in PPE research and the enormous spike in research published at the start of the Covid-19 pandemic, we thought it would be more diverse and interesting to examine keywords used only in engineering articles about PPE as shown in the word cloud above. In this word cloud, we see the biggest words are personal, protective, equipment, safety, arc, and flash, The first four words are fairly self-explanatory, but arc and flash show that a significant amount of research is focusing on PPE to protect workers from electrical arcing and bright flashes that could damage retinas.

If we look around these core words (see Fig. 5) we can see keywords that give us clues about what types of PPE is being discussed most and what sorts of hazards they are intended to guard against. For example, clothing is a large word, which would lead us to believe that there is a large focus on PPE clothing rather than accessories like glasses or a harness. Potential risk words include fire, electrical, and pesticide which show there is a wide variety of dangers PPE needs to guard against.

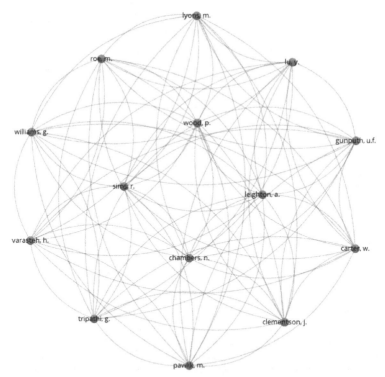

Fig. 3. Analysis conducted in VOSviewer. This co-analysis of author relations represents the authors and their relations to others in the field of ergonomics. The authors referenced in this article [5] are all co-authors from a research study of one-size-fits face shields for users during the 2020 COVID-19 pandemic to decrease the variability and cost, but allow face shields to be most accessible to users.

Personal Protective Equipment is a crucial part of industrial engineering because it allows human workers to safely work in industrial settings without significant risk of injury. Proper PPE improves efficiency, keeps workers safe, limits company liability, and allows workers to use industrial machinery they wouldn't be able to otherwise.

While PPE is an integral part of industrial engineering it also exists in any setting where human injury is at risk. This includes factory workers, inspectors, medical professionals, and much more. A recent example is the focus placed on PPE to combat Covid-19. National broadcasts went out throughout 2020 to educate the population on the proper use of PPE to protect themselves, and the Human Factors and Ergonomics Society even had a hand in developing safe practices for the use and reuse of COVID-19 PPE [20]. Industries everywhere are working to optimize their use of PPE to mitigate human liability (Fig. 6).

We were surprised to see arc and flash and some of the biggest keywords in our word cloud generated by nVivo, which prompted us to search through Scopus to see how many articles were published relating to arc personal protective equipment. In total there are 214 articles, whose distribution can be seen in the figure above. It looks like

Fig. 4. Analysis conducted in CiteSpace. This co-citation analysis pairs articles that have been cited together within multiple other articles. Ninety-one (91) records were discovered in Web of Science based on the key search terms "ergonomics" and "PPE". These 91 articles were then analyzed by citation occurrence. It should be noted that there were no citation bursts discovered within these 91 reference articles.

PPE to protect people from electrical arcs was not researched thoroughly until 1996 and became more popular around 2004. This is interesting because electrical arcing has been a danger to people since the widespread implementation of electrical power, and arc welding was developed as far back as the late 19th century. There was likely some technological innovation that increased the rate of human exposure to electrical arcs around 2004, which contributed to further research into arc PPE.

4.4 Relevance to Human Factors and Ergonomics

Trends in PPE are related to several chapters in the 5th edition of the Handbook of Human Factors and Ergonomics, but two of them are of particular interest. First, the entire 25th chapter titled Use of Personal Protective Equipment is highly relevant to our literature review of trends in PPE as it details the applications for several PPE devices including respirators, helmets, and much more. Section 2 of Chapter 25, Selection of Respiratory Protective Devices for Different Types of Workplaces [17], starting on page 669 is especially relevant for recent research in PPE as it has been focused on developing better masks to guard against viral infection. The chapter is largely about the use of industrial respirators that filter out gasses and particles either through the use of a filter

Fig. 5. Word cloud generated by nVivo using keywords from engineering documents about PPE on Scopus.

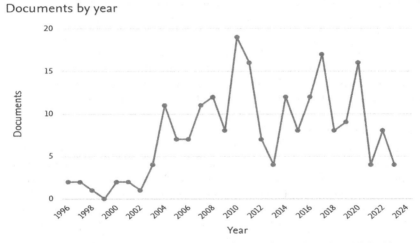

Fig. 6. The number of documents about arc personal protective equipment published in Scopus from 1996 to 2023.

or an external oxygen tank. These devices may not be directly related to the medical-grade masks discussed in the future work section, but the principles of selecting the proper breathing device for a given situation can still be applied.

The second related chapter is Chapter 11: 3D Anthropometry and its Applications in Product Design [18]. As discussed earlier, since PPE is equipment that is worn by and interfaces directly with humans it is important that PPE can fit different body types.

Anthropometry can be used to simulate human proportions and aid in the rapid design and prototyping of PPE. Section 5 of this chapter titled, Application in Product Design, discusses how this data can be used to aid design processes for both static and dynamic applications, which PPE is often subject to both. Their discussion of adapting to different body dimensions and height and weight percentiles is also particularly relevant.

PPE challenges are also relevant to our work in vehicle interiors that was performed in RAMSIS for Lab 2. In that lab, students were asked to position cockpit controls in such a manner that they were comfortable for pilots ranging from a 5th percentile female to a 95th percentile male representing a wide range of body types and pilot sizes. These same lessons can be applied to the development of PPE. Protective gear is only effective if it adequately fits the wearer. If it is too loose or too tight, not only will it distract workers from their jobs, but could cause them to take it off while performing dangerous work if it is too uncomfortable. Finally, PPE is directly related to multiple chapters we discussed in the 5th edition Handbook of Human Factors and Ergonomics, as discussed in the preceding paragraphs.

5 Conclusions and Future Work

5.1 Importance of PPE Research

PPE research is often limited in scope to a particular industry. After all, there are significant differences in the PPE needs among different industries. Medical professionals don't need the same protective gear factory workers do and vice versa. This literature review seeks to better understand commonalities and differences in the challenges faced by different industries in developing and employing PPE. For example, protective eyewear sizes do not vary that much between individuals with different body types in the same way more full-body gear would. Therefore, protective eyewear companies don't need to worry as much about developing different products that fit various sizes of workers.

PPE developers also need to be aware of more recent changes to their customer demographics. Certain fields like construction have been male-dominated for decades and are now seeing more and more women step into those roles. Women need different-sized hard hats and safety vests, but these aren't particularly difficult engineering problems to solve. PPE companies can easily resize existing products to fit the new workforce, but the greater issue is in the distribution and implementation of appropriately sized PPE and the impact that has on construction companies. Some companies could be reluctant to purchase new safety equipment for women, which could lead to either women wearing poorly fitted men's safety equipment or the company refusing to hire women at all.

There were various articles found that pertained to the development and future of PPE, especially after the events of the COVID-19 pandemic. Table 4 outlines the articles that were identified for future work on an analysis for PPE. These articles will be used to expand on the impact PPE had during the pandemic and the outcomes of further improvements for PPE during critical times.

5.2 Societal Influences

Society needs to put a greater emphasis on making PPE accessible and tailored to an increasingly diverse workforce. For example, women are far more likely to be put at

Table 4. A brief list of key articles, found from a co-citation analysis will be used for a more depth of analysis regarding the topic of PPE. This analysis will aid in the understanding of the new methodology that is being used to ensure the safety and protection of persons.

Article Title	Citation	Intentions for Review
Human factors issues of working in personal protective equipment during the COVID-19 pandemic [7]	Hignett, S., Welsh, R., Banerjee, J Human factors issues of working in personal protective equipment during the COVID-19 pandemic (2021) Anaesthesia, 76 (1), pp. 134–135 http://onlinelibrary.wiley.com/journal/10.1111/(ISSN)1365-2044 doi: https://doi.org/10.1111/anae.15198	This article will aid as a general overview of PPE concerns due to the COVID-19 pandemic
Headaches due to external compression [8]	Krymchantowski, A.V Headaches due to external compression (2010) Current Pain and Headache Reports, 14 (4), pp. 321–324. Cited 52 times doi: https://doi.org/10.1007/s11916-010-0122-x	Face masks and shields were common PPE tools that were required in many working settings during the COVID-19 pandemic. This article will aid in understanding the effects face masks had and the ergonomic impact it had on a person's head
Unmasking the myths surrounding use of barrier face coverings during the COVID-19 pandemic [9]	Liew, C.H., Flaherty, G.T Unmasking the myths surrounding use of barrier face coverings during the COVID-19 pandemic (2020) Int. J. Travel Med. Global Health, 8 (4), pp. 134–136	This article will serve as an opposing view to the use of face masks and other PPE during the pandemic
The Supply of Personal Protective Equipment (PPE) during the COVID-19 Pandemic. [10]	Davies, G (2020) The Supply of Personal Protective Equipment (PPE) during the COVID-19 Pandemic D.o.H.a.S. Care National Audit Office: https://www.nao.org.uk/wp-content/uploads/2020/11/The-supply-of-personal-protective-equipment-PPE-during-the-COVID-19-pandemic.pdf	This research will explore the limitations of PPE
Facial anthropometric differences among gender, ethnicity, and age groups [11]	Zhuang, Z., Landsittel, D., Benson, S., Roberge, R., Shaffer, R Facial anthropometric differences among gender, ethnicity, and age groups (2010) Annals of Occupational Hygiene, 54 (4), pp. 391–402 doi: https://doi.org/10.1093/annhyg/meq007	This research supports the use of face masks by gaining insights to the design of facemasks by understanding the anthropometrics for general populations

(continued)

Table 4. (*continued*)

Article Title	Citation	Intentions for Review
Comfort evaluation of hearing protection [12]	Hsu, Y.-L., Huang, C.-C., Yo, C.-Y., Chen, C.-J., Lien, C.-M Comfort evaluation of hearing protection (2004) International Journal of Industrial Ergonomics, 33 (6), pp. 543–551 www.elsevier.com/locate/ergon doi: https://doi.org/10.1016/j.ergon.2004.01.001	This analysis will support the use of ear protection and how to make it more ergonomically comfortable for the user
Hearing protectors: Noise attenuation and comfort [13]	Gerges, S.N.Y Hearing protectors: Noise attenuation and comfort (2010) 39th International Congress on Noise Control Engineering 2010, INTER-NOISE 2010, 1, pp. 34–52 ISBN: 978-161782396-1	Along with anthropometric research, this article will give perspective to another type of personal protective equipment for the ears
Factors contributing to discomfort or dissatisfaction as a result of wearing personal protective equipment. [14]	Akbar-Khanzadeh, F Factors contributing to discomfort or dissatisfaction as a result of wearing personal protective equipment (1998) Journal of human ergology, 27 (1–2), pp. 70–75	Research conducted will analyze PPE as a general topic and dissatisfaction by the users

risk than their male counterparts due to ill-fitting safety gear. A survey conducted by the Center for Construction Research and Training asked 174 female workers about their experience with PPE, and found that 77% of them had been put at risk due to ill-fitting safety gear [14]. This goes to show that a traditionally male-dominated trade, like construction, is not adapting fast enough to a changing workforce to adequately protect employees.

Human factors and ergonomics are closely tied to personal protective equipment since PPE directly interfaces with human workers. As such it is imperative that designers of PPE have a good understanding of human factors and anthropometry. The Human Factors and Ergonomics Society works to develop anthropometric standards that are used to evaluate the fit of industry protective equipment, per "ISO 15537:2004 Principles forselecting and using test persons for testing anthropometric aspects of industrial products and designs." [20]. This helps ensure that a wide variety of people with different body types can effectively and safely use well-fitted PPE.

One of the listed ten ways to analyze new and existing research is to carefully consider your background information. This helps to interpret trends that we are seeing in the metadata we have gathered. For example, our research shows that there was a sharp increase in PPE-related research documents in 1972 and again in 2020. To understand these trends, we need to remember the major events of those eras that would have a profound influence on the development and research of PPE. For example, the coronavirus pandemic began in 2020 which sparked national debate on effective PPE measures. Naturally, this led to a large increase in PPE documents submitted to scientific databases.

In 1971, the Occupational Health and Safety Administration or (OSHA) was founded which sought to standardize workplace safety practices across the nation. OSHA's influence mandated programs like inspections, mandatory workplace accident reporting, and a plethora of other safety improvements that extend to PPE [21]. By examining metadata trends, we don't currently understand it is best to dig into the historical context and background information available to get a better understanding of the full picture. After all, metadata can tell us what kinds of trends occurred in a topic, but not why they occurred, which is why background information creates new ways to gain insight into the metadata,

5.3 Covid-19 PPE

In our literature review of PPE the most popular field was the medical field and the most popular sub-topic was Covid-19-related PPE. Of those articles, a consistent focus was on developing products that can adapt to and fit a diverse population. The benefits of developing a one-size-fits-all product include cheaper manufacturing costs, easier distribution, and in turn a more affordable product for the general public. There are certainly cases when a more tailored approach is required for individuals like health care workers with high rates of exposure, but for the general public, the benefits of a one-size-fits-all approach far outweigh the negatives.

Other articles discussed how government and company policies on PPE and disinfecting created a significant manufacturing challenge for the industry. People were required to wear masks and gloves and disinfect surfaces which created a massive demand for these sanitation and PPE products that the current supply chain was not prepared for. This is why a lot of more recent research has been conducted on the manufacturing and distribution of these products as opposed to new product development.

5.4 Industrial PPE

Since the medical industry makes up over 40% of all PPE research in popular databases, more so in recent years. We wanted to shift our perspective to investigate engineering-related PPE research and see what topics were prevalent. Our analysis showed that some of the most popular research topics for this field were PPE to protect people from electrical arcs and bright flashes that could damage retinas. I suspect that this is due to an increase in electrical work done in the last few decades. As more and more technology become electronic, the risk of electrocution and the need for electrical PPE has subsequently increased. I expect this trend to continue over the next ten years as companies leverage renewable energy sources to develop more electric cars, appliances, and devices.

5.5 Future Work

Unsurprisingly, much of the future work related to PPE research is centered around the medical field and Coronavirus as seen by the various references and cited articles in this co-author analysis. The medical field has historically dominated the bulk of PPE research and that trend has only become more pronounced since 2020. One area of particular interest is in developing better masks to protect people from viral infections. Nowadays, it is pretty common for people to own cloth masks to cover their faces to prevent them from inhaling airborne diseases, but cloth masks can only do so much. That is why new research is underway to develop smarter, cheaper, and more effective masks.

The National Science Foundation (NSF) is funding Northwestern University to create smart masks that use batteryless electronic sensors to send data to the mask's wearer without the need for maintenance or recharging. This would remove the burden of maintaining further equipment placed on the mask wearer and would allow them to gain actual data on whether or not they have been exposed to harmful pathogens [22]. This will allow hospitals to receive real-time data from PPE to better track the rate of infection and maintain a healthy workforce.

Another project funded by the NSF is being conducted by the University of Central Florida to develop antiviral nanofilms that can actively fight and kill germs rather than just prevent them from entering the human body. The project aims to use bio-compatible particles embedded with ultraviolet light to create new antiviral coatings (https://www.nsf.gov/awardsearch/shoAward?AWD_ID=2027489&HistoricalAwards=false. [15]). A development like this could yield significant results in reducing the amount of pathogens that healthcare workers are exposed to at work. The last 3 years have impressed scientists with the need for smarter and more effective masks, and with research like this, I expect to see big developments in the next few years.

References

1. Improving the National Statistics. U.S. Bureau of Labor Statistics. https://www.bls.gov/opub/btn/volume-9/nearly-50-years-of-occupational-safety-and-health-data.htm. Accessed 27 Nov 2023
2. Personal Protective Equipment - Overview. Occupational Safety and Health Administration. https://www.osha.gov/personal-protective-equipment. Accessed 27 Nov 2023
3. Fleiss, A.: How Does Osha Define an Accident? Rebellion Research, 15 May 2023. https://www.rebellionresearch.com/how-does-osha-define-an-accident-workplace-accident
4. Anthropometry. Centers for Disease Control and Prevention, 30 August 2022. https://www.cdc.gov/niosh/topics/anthropometry/default.html
5. Kozłowski, E., Młyński, R.: Selection of earmuffs and other personal protective equipment used in combination. Int. J. Environ. Res. Public Health **16**(9), 1477 (2019). https://doi.org/10.3390/ijerph16091477
6. Gunputh, U.F., et al.: Design and Manufacture of One-Size-Fits-All Healthcare Face Shields for the NHS during the COVID-19 Pandemic. SSRN, 26 October 2022. https://papers.ssrn.com/sol3/papers.cfm?abstract_id=4258668

7. Hignett, S., Welsh, R., Banerjee, J.: Human factors issues of working in personal protective equipment during the COVID-19 pandemic. Anaesthesia **76**(1), 134–135 (2021). http://onlinelibrary.wiley.com/journal/https://doi.org/10.1111/(ISSN)1365-2044. https://doi.org/10.1111/anae.15198

8. Krymchantowski, A.V.: Headaches due to external compression. Curr. Pain Headache Rep. **14**(4), 321–324 (2010). https://doi.org/10.1007/s11916-010-0122-x

9. Liew, C.H., Flaherty, G.T.: Unmasking the myths surrounding use of barrier face coverings during the COVID-19 pandemic. Int. J. Travel Med. Global Health **8**(4), 134–136 (2020)

10. Davies, G.: The Supply of Personal Protective Equipment (PPE) during the COVID-19 Pandemic D.o.H.a.S. Care National Audit Office (2020). https://www.nao.org.uk/wp-content/uploads/2020/11/The-supply-of-personal-protective-equipment-PPE-during-the-COVID-19-pandemic.pdf

11. Zhuang, Z., Landsittel, D., Benson, S., Roberge, R., Shaffer, R.: Facial anthropometric differences among gender, ethnicity, and age groups. Ann. Occup. Hyg. **54**(4), 391–402 (2010). https://doi.org/10.1093/annhyg/meq007

12. Hsu, Y.-L., Huang, C.-C., Yo, C.-Y., Chen, C.-J., Lien, C.-M.: Comfort evaluation of hearing protection. Int. J. Ind. Ergon. **33**(6), 543–551 (2004). www.elsevier.com/locate/ergon. https://doi.org/10.1016/j.ergon.2004.01.001

13. Gerges, S.N.Y.: Hearing protectors: Noise attenuation and comfort. In: 39th International Congress on Noise Control Engineering 2010, INTER-NOISE 2010, 1, pp. 34–52 (2010). ISBN 978-161782396-1

14. Akbar-Khanzadeh, F.: Factors contributing to discomfort or dissatisfaction as a result of wearing personal protective equipment. J. Hum. Ergol. **27**(1–2), 70–75 (1998)

15. NSF AWARD SEARCH: Award # 2027489 - rapid: Conformal, anti-viral nanofilms on personal protective equipment materials to combat coronavirus transmission/sequestration (capture). https://www.nsf.gov/awardsearch/showAward?AWD_ID=2027489&HistoricalAwards=false. Accessed 27 Nov 2023

16. Guidance Documents. Centers for Disease Control and Prevention. https://www.cdc.gov/coronavirus/2019-ncov/communication/guidance-list.html. Accessed 27 Nov 2023

17. Bartkowiak, G., et al.: Use of personal protective equipment. In: Salvendy, G., Karwowski, W. (eds.) Handbook of Human Factors and Ergonomics. Wiley, Hoboken (2021)

18. Ma, L., Niu, J.: Three-dimensional (3D) anthropometry and its applications. Essay. In: Salvendy, G., Karwowski, W. (eds.) Handbook of Human Factors and Ergonomics. Wiley, Hoboken (2021)

19. The Front Line: News from the field (2023) in ISE Magazine, pp. 12–13, June 2023

20. Published*standards*from*ISO*technical*Committee159*(ergonomics ... - HFES. https://www.hfes.org/portals/0/documents/Published-Standards-ISO-TC159-SC3.pdf. Accessed 27 Nov 2023

21. Salvendy, G., Karwowski, W.: Handbook of Human Factors and Ergonomics. Wiley, Hoboken (2021)

22. NSF AWARD SEARCH: Award # 2032408 - rapid: Low-cost, batteryless Smart Personal Protective Equipment (PPE) tackling the COVID-19 pandemic. https://www.nsf.gov/awardsearch/showAward?AWD_ID=2032408. Accessed 27 Nov 2023

23. Loibner, M., Hagauer, S., Schwantzer, G., Berghold, A., Zatloukal, K.: Limiting factors for wearing personal protective equipment (PPE) in a health care environment evaluated in a randomised study. PLoS ONE **14**(1), e0210775 (2019). https://doi.org/10.1371/journal.pone.0210775

24. Eaves, S., Gyi, D.E., Gibb, A.G.F.: Building healthy construction workers: their views on health, wellbeing and better workplace design. Appl. Ergon. **54**(May), 10–18 (2016). https://doi.org/10.1016/j.apergo.2015.11.004

25. Varadarajulu, S., Wong Kee Song, L.-M., Tierney, W.: Minimizing occupational hazards in endoscopy: personal protective equipment, radiation safety, and ergonomics. GIE J. (2010). https://www.giejournal.org/article/S0016-5107(10)00144-6/fulltext

26. Torres, G.M.S., Backstrom, J., Duffy, V.G.: A systematic review of workplace stress and its impact on mental health and safety. In: Gao, Q., Zhou, J., Duffy, V.G., Antona, M., Stephanidis, C. (eds.) Human-Computer Interaction, HCII 2023. LNCS, vol. 14055, pp. 610–627. Springer, Cham (2023). https://doi.org/10.1007/978-3-031-48041-6_41

27. Kuratomi, D., Shin, C., Duffy, V.G.: Systematic literature review on the advances of wearable technologies. In: Duffy, V.G., Krömker, H., A. Streitz, N., Konomi, S. (eds.) Human-Computer Interaction, HCII 2023. LNCS, vol. 14057, pp. 78–95. Springer, Cham (2023). https://doi.org/10.1007/978-3-031-48047-8_5

Improving Construction Safety: The Role of Workplace Stressors and Personality Traits on Near-Miss Recognition of Workers'

Shashank Muley$^{(\boxtimes)}$ and Chao Wang

Bert S. Turner Department of Construction Management, Louisiana State University, Baton Rouge, LA 70803, USA
smuley1@lsu.edu

Abstract. The construction industry, despite safety enhancements, remains hazardous. Hazard identification and near-miss reporting are pivotal in preventing accidents. However, the dynamic nature of construction work and workplace stress can impede safety recognition ability. Despite previous studies employing stress loading to assess workers' safety behavior and its influence on hazard recognition among construction workers, there has been no empirical investigation into the direct impact of mental and auditory stressors on workers' psychophysiological indicators during near-miss recognition activities. This study investigates the impact of personality traits and stress on construction workers' cognitive abilities during near-miss recognition tasks. Thirty-five participants underwent an eye-tracking experiment with mental and auditory stressors. Personality traits were assessed through self-reported questionnaires, while physiological data were collected using wearable devices. Results revealed increased stress levels during stressor trials, significantly affecting cognitive load and visual attention. Workers with low conscientiousness and openness/intellect exhibited heightened attention to "fatal four" near-miss opportunities. The findings emphasize the influence of workplace stressors on construction workers' cognitive abilities during near-miss recognition and establish a significant relationship between personality traits and performance in recognizing near-miss incidents. This study provides evidence supporting the development of personalized training programs tailored to at-risk individuals. By addressing specific personality traits associated with lower near-miss identification abilities, these tailored programs aim to enhance workers' recognition skills. Therefore, the contribution from this study would work towards fostering a robust safety culture within the construction sector, aligning to achieve zero incidents and promote overall workplace safety.

Keywords: Visual Sensing · Big 5 · Occupational Stress

1 Introduction

Despite continuous efforts to enhance construction safety, the construction industry remains one of the most dangerous and stressful sectors for the workforce. In recent years, stakeholders in the construction industry have implemented various measures to

V. G. Duffy (Ed.): HCII 2024, LNCS 14711, pp. 83–95, 2024.
https://doi.org/10.1007/978-3-031-61066-0_6

decrease accidents and minimize fatal injuries. Previous studies estimated that construction accidents incurred a yearly cost surpassing $11 billion in 2002, amounting to 15% for private construction sectors [1]. Fatal and non-fatal accidents in the construction sector majorly occurred in areas such as falls, caught-in/between incidents, struck-by accidents, and electrocutions. A study conducted by The Center for Construction Research and Training (CPWR) reported 6,694 fatalities due to falls, 3,326 fatalities due to struck-by incidents, 1,166 fatalities due to caught-in-between incidents, and 1,474 fatalities due to electrocutions between 2011 and 2020 [2]. To reduce accidents in construction hazard identification stands out as a crucial preventive measure with significant potential to reduce injury rates. Moreover, enhancing construction safety statistics is attainable through the efficient identification and reporting of near-miss incidents, which can play a pivotal role in eliminating accidents. To cut down on safety accidents it is vital to understand and address the importance of near-miss reporting by promoting safety behavior. Any individual who promotes health and safety in the workplace is considered to showcase safety behavior [3]. The dynamic nature of the construction workplace introduces numerous factors that can alter the safety behavior of workers and impair their ability to identify and address hazards. Additionally, workplace stressors can induce occupational stress in workers, affecting their performance in recognizing hazards. Hazard recognition is considered a crucial preventive measure in ensuring workplace safety and reducing injury rates. Recent efforts have been made to identify, analyze, and implement strategies aimed at evaluating the hazard recognition skills of construction workers under stress through physiological and psychological indicators. A study conducted to explore the impact of workers' personalities on their hazard recognition ability showcased that individuals with extrovert and conscientious personalities have a significant relationship with their recognition performance [4]. Whereas, a different study explored the impact of task stressors on workers' cognitive processing and attention allocation during electrical activity [5].

Despite previous studies employing stress loading to assess workers' safety behavior and its influence on hazard recognition among construction workers, there has been no empirical investigation into the direct impact of mental and auditory stressors on workers' personality parameters and physiological indicators during near-miss recognition activities. Hence, this study investigates the impact of mental and auditory stressors on cognitive load and their relationship with personality traits during near-miss recognition activity.

2   Related Work

2.1   Impact of Workplace Stress on Worker Safety Behavior in Construction Industry

Construction workplace personnel are exposed to active and passive factors that can compromise an individual's productivity and safety at large. An integral part of the Construction safety climate is hazard mitigation which is dependent on active hazard recognition and the decision-making process conducted by each person on the construction site. Each individual on-site consumes a huge amount of internal cognitive resources to handle and evaluate external information [6].

A large amount of cognitive load can be manifested in multiple dimensions in terms of mental load, mental effort, workplace stress, and work performance as described in a general model manifested in a study [7]. The integral aspect of work-related stress also known as mental stress is mental fatigue, increased stress can induce mental fatigue that could occur when individuals' cognitive abilities are overloaded leading to a lowered performance in safety hazard detection [8]. Previous literature indicated that workers under stressful conditions tend to become hypervigilant while searching for potential safety information in the workplace environment leading to unsafe acts caused by human error [9]. Accordingly, increased human errors lead to individuals' unsafe behavior and curtail safety performance. Some studies suggest that stress imposed by workplace stressors hinders cognitive processes such as hazard recognition performance and risk perception, leading to flawed judgment and unpredictable decision-making [10]. Therefore, exposure to mental stressors on the worksite can overwhelm the limited capacity of cognitive resources at the disposal causing a reduction in attention [11]. Further, increased levels of mental stress can disrupt workers' ability to focus in hazardous situations on the job site making them inefficient in identifying, intervening, and reporting near-misses.

Similarly, the effect of auditory stress and the safety risks manufactured due to noise exposure cannot be underestimated, essentially for workers' safety behavior that demands high cognitive ability to limit incidents [12]. The cognitive performance of construction workers is affected by noise emissions significantly when they are exposed to high-frequency noise for a longer duration [13]. Therefore, workers' ability to identify, evaluate, and mitigate unsafe incidents depends on their safety behavior which can be affected by high cognitive loading due to the presence of workplace stressors.

2.2 Use of Physiological Parameters and Eye Tracking in Safety Assessment and Cognitive Load

The human body reacts to any changes in physical, mental, and environmental that can trigger stress observed by variations in the physiological parameters of an individual. Stress manifests a biological reaction that triggers the human body to release hormones that activate a fight-or-flight response because of which the sympathetic nervous system (SNS) is activated [14]. There are several methods available to measure stress, but the most common one uses subjective assessment which would not be suitable for the complex and dynamic nature of the construction industry. In recent years, use of real-time monitoring of physiological parameters has been utilized to evaluate human physiology and behavior variation and their correlation to accidents. Heart rate, skin temperature, heart rate variability, and electrodermal activity as some of the indicators that can measure changes in human physiology because of variations in external stimuli. Among these, heart rate (HR) which is the number of times the heart contracts/beats per minute (bpm), and electrodermal activity (EDA) is fluctuation in electrical signals due to changes in skin moisture level measured in microsiemens (μS) are the most commonly utilized parameters to assess body response to changes in stress levels [15, 16].

Similarly, eye-tracking technology has proven to be an efficient tool to evaluate workers' ability to identify and assess safety on the job site. Saccade and fixations have been identified as vital eye movement in safety studies where saccade matrices such as saccade amplitude and direction track cognitive activity that influences each oculomotor selection [17], and fixation-derived matrices such as fixation duration and fixation count can characterize individuals' attentional variations during visual sensing [18]. Some studies have explored the correlation between visual information processing through eye-tracking and social gazing behavior [19, 20]. The results from these studies suggest a strong relationship between gazing behavior and the personality of an individual. Including fixation-derived matrices pupil diameter can provide vital information regarding individuals' cognitive load in visual sensing studies. Previous research shows that cognitive load can be measured using subjective and physiological measurements. Among them, pupil response that falls under the umbrella of physiological parameters is an effective way to measure cognitive load. A study conducted to evaluate the relationship between pupil size and mental activity for problem-solving reported that pupil diameter increases as cognitive load increases [21]. Additionally, further study conducted demonstrated that pupil dilatation is related to interest, emotionality, and mental activity [22].

3   Material and Methods

3.1   Participants

A total of 44 participants were invited to be recruited for this study out of which 9 participants were excluded from the study due to exclusion criteria or incomplete fixation data. The remaining 35 participants (30 males, 5 females) with an age range of 18 to 50 years and construction industry experience ranging from <1 to 12 years were selected for this study. All participants had normal or correlated-to-normal vision and were healthy to participate in the study. Before starting the experiment, participants were required to fill out a questionnaire regarding their demographic, construction experience, and medical history (for example, eye problems). If the participants had any medical history, they were requested to opt out of this study. Non-Clinicals experiments on visual attention and eye movement usually require a smaller sample size than traditional survey-style studies, as the eye tracking matrix captures dozens of eye matrices and fixation across multiple trials. Based on G*Power analysis and within the subject's experimental design, 30 participants were enough to satisfy participants per variable. We collected 5 additional participants to increase the power.

3.2   Stimuli Images and Area of Interest (AOIs)

The near-miss event is categorized as an incident that may or may not lead to an accident or loss of property. Images from the construction site and web-scrapping were collected to generate a pool of images for the final section of stimuli images. Special care is taken into consideration to collect images that show potential fatal four hazards within the vicinity of construction workers that can be categorized as near-miss. The area of interest (AOI) on each image was manually marked and verified by safety experts for validation. The final image data set used for this study included 54 images, with 42 images containing 48 well-balanced fatal four near-miss AOIs and twelve images were false positive with no near-miss. AOIs for this research were categorized into one of the following fatal four areas Slip, Trip & Fall (On the same level, from an elevated level), Struck-By (Falling object, machinery, PPE violation, standing under the suspended object, etc.), Caught-in-Between (Between two moving objects, one stationary and one moving object, trench/excavation collapse, pinch point), Electrocution (Contact with live circuits without PPE, contact with energized source, improper use of tools or cords, etc.).

3.3 Research Instruments

Experimental data collection involved the use of two validated wearable devices and a state-of-the-art visual sensing device. Participants EDA activity as physiological data were gathered using the E4 Empathic Wristwatch, manufactured by Empatica Inc., Cambridge, MA, US. The E4 wristband is equipped with Photoplethysmography (PPG), Electrodermal activity (EDA), a 3-axis accelerometer, and Optical thermometer sensors. This wearable sensor records EDA data at a sampling rate of 4 Hz. To collect heart rate data of participants the polar H10 heart rate sensor manufactured by Polar Electro, Inc., Finland with a data collecting frequency of 1 Hz was utilized. The polar H10 heart rate sensor has been considered a gold standard of high precision and accuracy for heart rate monitoring. Both wearable sensors were collected to 2 different iOS devices that collected and uploaded data in real-time to the collection server. To assess visual sensing and collect eye-tracking data during the near-miss recognition experiment, Tobii Glasses 2 was used. This instrument has been used in the past for studies conducted in construction safety research. Tobii Pro Glasses 2 (manufactured by Tobii AB Company, Danderyd Municipality, Sweden), will be used in this study to capture the visual behavior of participants (Fig. 1c). The device has a gaze sampling frequency of 100 Hz, and camera angle ranges of 82° (horizontal) and 52° (vertical). Before the actual data collection for the experiment, a pilot study was conducted to assess the feasibility and reliability of using the devices.

3.4 Experimental Methodology

A controlled eye-tracking experiment with repeated measure design was conducted to assess how workplace stressors (mental and auditory) influence workers' cognitive loading during near-miss recognition. Participants were asked to identify near-miss scenarios using images taken from real construction sites under three different conditions on two separate days to facilitate the removal of carryover effects. Each participant completed the baseline condition followed by two stressor conditions in randomized order. All the experimental procedures were approved by the Institutional Review Board (IRB) at the university level.

In this study experimental procedure included five steps that are illustrated below:

- **Step 1**: Before the experiment trial all participants were requested to complete a pre-experiment task that included the completion of a demographic questionnaire, mini-marker personality survey, and near-miss and construction fatal-four AV training.
- **Step 2**: Upon arrival for the first visit, participants were briefed about the entire experiment. Post-briefing, participants were requested to sign a consent form and confirm the completion of the pre-experiment task. They were then asked to complete a training evaluation quiz, testing their knowledge regarding the 'fatal-four near-misses.' The desired passing rate was set at 70%. Once the desired rate was achieved they were equipped with wearable sensors and a visual sensing eye-tracker while being seated in a position. After sensor calibration was performed data collection devices were checked for consistency to initiate the experimental trial.
- **Step 3**: Each participant began the experiment with a baseline non-stressor trail, which included non-stress resting activity followed by a fatal-four near-miss recognition eye-tracking activity. The directions provided to participants in the eye-tracking experiment were to identify fatal four near misses. Each image stimulus appeared on the screen for exactly 15 s then the screen went blank for the non-specified period. During this period participants were asked to answer questions related to near-miss they observed on screen. This information was used to confirm observers' awareness of identifying near-misses to validate eye-tracking data.
- **Step 4**: After completing the baseline non-stressor trial, participants were given a 5-min rest period to reduce experiment-related fatigue. They then completed either a mental stressor trial or the auditory stressor trial. In the mental stressor trial participants were asked to transform a four-digit number while sitting at a self-selected pace for 10 min, this method of artificially inducing stress has been used in previous studies [23]. After completing mental stressor activity participants complete eye-tracking experiments with different sets of images. Whereas, in auditory stress trial participants were exposed to high-level (>85 dBA) construction noise of range between 90–100 dBA projected towards participants from two speakers placed 70 cm diagonal on either side of the monitor followed by the near-miss recognition task. The order of these stressor trials was counterbalanced for all participants to avoid any order effects.
- **Step 5**: During the second visit, participants were equipped with sensors and an eye-tracking device. Calibration was performed, and the participant completed either the mental stressor trial or auditory stressor trial based on the pre-defined experimental series. After completion, the sensors were removed, and participants were free to leave. Figure 1 demonstrates sensor placement and Fig. 2 the experiment setup.

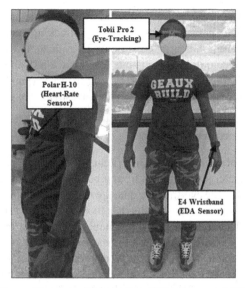

Fig. 1. Sensor Placement (Eye-tracker, EDA sensor, and HR Sensor)

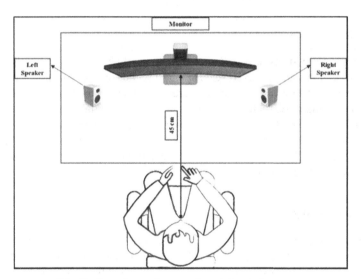

Fig. 2. Experiment Setup and participant placement

4   Data Analysis

4.1   Eye-Tracking Data Processing

Eye-tracking matrices were extracted for each participant by mapping the eye-tracking raw data on areas of interest related to near-miss opportunities. Tobii Pro Lab version 1.142.1 was used for data processing, this program provides a comprehensive platform to analyze eye gaze data from raw video collected with a combination of visual and analytical tools for sensing assessment. Extraction of eye-tracking matrices was conducted for all participants under all three trial conditions. To evaluate the impact of workplace stressors on near-miss recognition, participants' cognitive load using pupil diameter was selected for analysis. The selection of eye-tracking matrices (pupil diameter) depends on the identification process and cognitive demand investigated in previous studies [24].

4.2 Pupil Diameter Extraction

To evaluate the impact of cognitive load on participants during the near-miss recognition experiment, pupil diameter was extracted from processed eye-tracking data for all three experimental conditions. The eye-tracking data file was exported for each participant and was filtered for eye movement type classified as fixation. Left and right pupil diameters (millimeters) were collected for each AOI hit on mapped images. In normal conditions, there is a limited statistical difference between the left and right pupil diameters corresponding to the same person. We used the pupil diameter of the left eye and removed the missing data generated in the experiment, as the previous study proposed [25]. The pupil diameter for each participant (35) corresponding to AOI (16) for all (3) experimental trials were exported to be analyzed in SPSS.

4.3 Personality Assessment

The Big 5 personality traits were validated through a reliability assessment. Personality traits data collection uses the Likert scale to measure the subjective evaluation of participants' personality factors. Although there are several acceptable methods to analyze a questionnaire's reliability, such as split half and inter-rater reliability, Cronbach's alpha is considered the most reliable one. Based on reliability assessment Cronbach's alpha coefficients for all personality factors ($\alpha > 0.70$) were greater than the widely suggested acceptable value (i.e., coefficient equal to or greater than 0.70), although some studies suggest the proper threshold to be 0.60 [26].

4.4 Statistical Analysis

Once all data collection for all participants was completed for 3 stressor conditions, a normality test was conducted on pupil diameter using the Shapiro-Wilk test. Based on the results of the normality test pupil diameter violated the assumptions of normality $p < 0.05$. Therefore, a non-parametric statistical test was conducted. As the same participant was exposed to three conditions (1 non-stress and 2 stress conditions), the Friedman one-way repeated measure analysis of variance by rank was used to evaluate the impact of workplace stressor conditions on workers' cognitive loading through near-miss recognition. Additionally, in case of significant difference, pairwise comparison using the Wilcoxon Signed Ranks test was conducted with a significance of $p < 0.05$. Correlation between personality traits and pupil diameter for near-miss recognition was conducted using Kendall's tau (non-parametric) method.

5 Results

The statistical analysis and descriptive results are presented based on impact and correlation analysis. The scores of each participant for personality traits were validated with a reliability assessment. Additionally, a descriptive mean plot for personality traits for 35 participants showcases well well-balanced personality profile. Personality traits of extraversion, agreeableness, conscientiousness, and openness/intellect provide a mean score of above average with the exception of neuroticism as shown in Fig. 3.

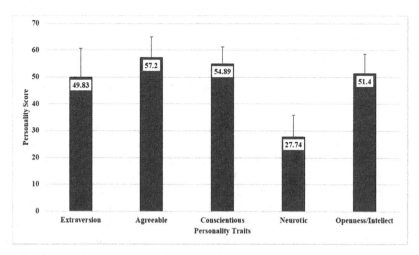

Fig. 3. Descriptive plot of personality traits vs average personality score (n = 35)

The physiological parameters were collected to observe the induction of workplace stressors. Wilcoxon single rank test was conducted to observe significant variation in physiological parameters (EDA) during all three stressor conditions. The finding provides statistical significance between EDA for baseline and mental stressor trials with significant increases in participants' stress levels during mental stressor activity ($F = -3.767$, $p < 0.05$), and a similar trend is observed in auditory ($F = -3.464$, $p < 0.05$) stressors trial compared to the baseline trial. In Fig. 4 it can be observed that standardized EDA values increase from baseline to mental stressors and from baseline to auditory stressor trial providing evidence of induced stress in participants. Whereas HR standardized value reduces from mental to auditory but increases from baseline to mental stressor trial.

5.1 Effect of Workplace Stressors on Cognitive Load During Near-Miss Recognition

The Friedman test showed that the construction workers' pupil diameter during the near-miss recognition task was statistically significant impacted by workplace stressors (non-stress, mental, and auditory) conditions, ($\chi^2 (2) = 19.252, p = <0.001$). The result provides evidence that the presence of workplace stressors has a significant impact on

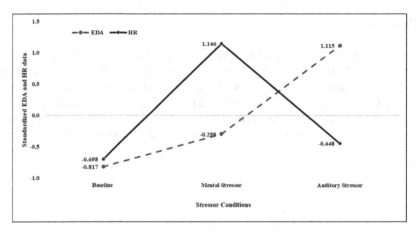

Fig. 4. Stressor condition vs standardized EDA and HR data

workers' cognitive load during near-miss recognition activity. To identify specific stressor differences, post hoc using the Wilcoxon single rank test was conducted (Table 1). Pairwise comparison showcased statistical significance between baseline and auditory stressor trials ($z = -5.469$, $p < 0.001$). However, there was no significant difference observed between the baseline and mental stressor trail. Although there was no significant difference observed during the induction of mental stressor trial, the pupil diameter increased from 2.454 to 2.635 which is an indication of increased cognitive loading under stress. Whereas, in the case of auditory stressors, pupil diameter increased from 2.454 to 2.977 which corresponds to elevated cognitive load.

Table 1. Variation in participants. Pupil diameter across different stressor conditions during eye-tracking activity.

Parameter	Experimental Trial	Mean	Std	Z-Value	Sig. (2-tailed)
Pupil Diameter	Baseline	2.454	1.400		
	Vs Mental Stressor	2.635	1.240	−1.438	0.15
	Vs Auditory Stressor	2.977	0.874	−5.469	**< 0.001***

Note: Z-Test statistics from Wilcoxon Signed Ranks Test, *p-value < 0.05

5.2   Association Between Personality Traits and Pupil Diameter

To evaluate the association between personality traits and pupil diameter during a near-miss recognition experiment Kendall tau correlation analysis was conducted with personality traits as independent variable and pupil diameter as response variable. Based on the results, a positive association with statistical significance is observed between extraversion and pupil diameter during non-stress ($r = 0.085$, $p = 0.004 < 0.01$) and auditory stressor trail (r = 0.090, p = 0.002 < 0.01). However, conscientiousness (r = 0.108, p = 0.001 < 0.01) showcases a positive association with statistical significance with pupil diameter for the baseline trial. In addition to extraversion and conscientiousness, a positive correlation with statistical significance is observed between openness/intellect (r = 0.060, p = 0.041 < 0.05) and pupil diameter for the auditory stressor trial. Due to the positive correlation between extraversion, conscientiousness, and openness/intellect with pupil diameter during baseline and auditory stressors, it can be observed that individuals with high personality scores showed increased pupil diameter which is an indication of increased cognitive load. However, between baseline and auditory trials for extraversion personality traits increased cognitive load with association was observed as shown in Table 2.

Table 2. Correlation Analysis (Personality Traits vs Pupil Diameter) for different experimental conditions.

Personality traits	Statistics	BT_Pupil Dia	MT_Pupil Dia	AT_Pupil Dia
Extraversion	Correlation Coefficient	.085**	0.03	.090**
	Sig. (2-tailed)	**0.004**	0.304	**0.002**
	N	560	560	560
Agreeable	Correlation Coefficient	0.038	0.01	−0.014
	Sig. (2-tailed)	0.201	0.725	0.635
	N	560	560	560
Conscientious	Correlation Coefficient	.108**	−0.001	0.048
	Sig. (2-tailed)	**<.001**	0.98	0.101
	N	560	560	560
Neurotic	Correlation Coefficient	−0.049	−0.038	0.014
	Sig. (2-tailed)	0.097	0.193	0.639
	N	560	560	560
Openness/Intellect	Correlation Coefficient	−0.008	0.028	.060*
	Sig. (2-tailed)	0.78	0.343	**0.041**
	N	560	560	560

**. Correlation is significant at the 0.01 level (2-tailed)
*. Correlation is significant at the 0.05 level (2-tailed)
BT-Baseline Trial, MT-Mental Stressor Trail, AT-Auditory Stressor Trial

6 Conclusion

This study investigated the impact of workplace stressors, such as mental and auditory stressors, on cognitive load and their relationship with personality traits during near-miss recognition activities. The results indicate that inducing mental stress and auditory stress through stressor activities and high-frequency noise, respectively, affected participants' pupil diameter during recognition tasks, influencing their cognitive load towards near-miss identification. In comparison to mental stressors, auditory stressors had a more profound impact on participants, suggesting that workers become more aware of situations on the site when exposed to noisy environments. Furthermore, the influence analysis revealed that workers with high extraversion, conscientiousness, and openness/intellect exhibited a higher increased pupil diameter, indicative of cognitive loading during "fatal four" near-miss opportunities. Therefore, workers who are highly extroverted, pragmatic, and curious demonstrated increased awareness through cognitive load when encountering near-miss scenarios.

The findings of this study provide empirical evidence regarding the influence of workplace stressors on construction workers' pupil diameter during near-miss recognition tasks. Additionally, it establishes a connection between workers' personality traits and cognitive load during near-miss recognition. These findings offer valuable insights into how workplace stress induced by mental and auditory stressors can impair workers' cognitive abilities to accurately identify near-miss incidents. Moreover, this study paves the way for the development of human behavior safety intervention programs and stress management strategies tailored to individuals with increased cognitive load, resulting in reduced identification abilities. These tailored programs have the potential to contribute to fostering a robust safety culture within the construction sector, ultimately facilitating a decrease in incidents towards achieving net zero occurrences.

Disclosure of Interests. The authors have no competing interests to declare that are relevant to the content of this article.

References

1. Waehrer, G.M., et al.: Costs of occupational injuries in construction in the United States. Accid. Anal. Prev. **39**(6), 1258–1266 (2007). https://doi.org/10.1016/j.aap.2007.03.012
2. CPWR. Construction Focus Four (2022). https://www.cpwr.com/research/data-center/data-dashboards/construction-focus-four-dashboard/
3. Burke, M.J., et al.: General safety performance: a test of a grounded theoretical model. Pers. Psychol. **55**(2), 429–457 (2002). https://doi.org/10.1111/j.1744-6570.2002.tb00116.x
4. Hasanzadeh, S., et al.: Role of personality in construction safety: investigating the relationships between personality, attentional failure, and hazard identification under fall-hazard conditions. J. Constr. Eng. Manag. **145**(9) (2019). https://doi.org/10.1061/(ASCE)CO.1943-7862.0001673
5. Pooladvand, S., Hasanzadeh, S.: Impacts of stress on workers' risk-taking behaviors: cognitive tunneling and impaired selective attention. J. Constr. Eng. Manag. **149**(8), 04023060 (2023). https://doi.org/10.1061/Jcemd4.Coeng-13339
6. Shaw, M.L., Shaw, P.: Optimal allocation of cognitive resources to spatial locations. J. Exp. Psychol. Hum. Percept. Perform. **3**(2), 201–211 (1977). https://doi.org/10.1037//0096-1523.3.2.201
7. Paas, F.G.W.C., Vanmerrienboer, J.J.G.: Variability of worked examples and transfer of geometrical problem-solving skills - a cognitive-load approach. J. Educ. Psychol. **86**(1), 122–133 (1994). https://doi.org/10.1037/0022-0663.86.1.122
8. Li, J., et al.: Evaluating the impact of mental fatigue on construction equipment operators' ability to detect hazards using wearable eye-tracking technology. Autom. Constr. **105** (2019). https://doi.org/10.1016/j.autcon.2019.102835

9. Kaber, D., et al.: The effect of driver cognitive abilities and distractions on situation awareness and performance under hazard conditions. Transp. Res. Part F-Traffic Psychol. Behav. **42**, 177–194 (2016). https://doi.org/10.1016/j.trf.2016.07.014

10. Liang, Q., et al.: Unveiling the mechanism of construction workers' unsafe behaviors from an occupational stress perspective: a qualitative and quantitative examination of a stress–cognition–safety model. Saf. Sci. **145**, 105486 (2022). https://doi.org/10.1016/j.ssci.2021.105486

11. Hockey, G.R.: Compensatory control in the regulation of human performance under stress and high workload; a cognitive-energetical framework. Biol. Psychol. **45**(1–3), 73–93 (1997). https://doi.org/10.1016/S0301-0511(96)05223-4

12. Arezes, P.M., Miguel, A.S.: Risk perception and safety behaviour: a study in an occupational environment. Saf. Sci. **46**(6), 900–907 (2008). https://doi.org/10.1016/j.ssci.2007.11.008

13. Smith, A., Wellens, B.: Noise and occupational health and safety. In: First European Forum on Efficient Solutions for Managing Occupational Noise Risks, Noise at work (2007)

14. Leung, M.-Y., Chan, I.Y.S., Yu, J.: Preventing construction worker injury incidents through the management of personal stress and organizational stressors. Accid. Anal. Prev. **48**, 156–166 (2012). https://doi.org/10.1016/j.aap.2011.03.017

15. Jebelli, H., Choi, B., Lee, S.: Application of wearable biosensors to construction sites. II: assessing workers' physical demand. J. Constr. Eng. Manag. **145**(12), 04019080 (2019). https://doi.org/10.1061/(Asce)Co.1943-7862.0001710

16. Habibnezhad, M., et al.: Comparison of ironworker's fall risk assessment systems using an immersive biofeedback simulator. Autom. Constr. **122**, 103471 (2021). https://doi.org/10.1016/j.autcon.2020.103471

17. Zhang, Q., et al.: Visual attention and cognitive process in construction hazard recognition: study of fixation-related potential. Autom. Constr. **148**, 104756 (2023)

18. Xu, Y., et al.: Robust segmentation and localization of structural planes from photogrammetric point clouds in construction sites. Autom. Constr. **117**, 103206 (2020). https://doi.org/10.1016/j.autcon.2020.103206

19. Perlman, A., Sacks, R., Barak, R.: Hazard recognition and risk perception in construction. Saf. Sci. **64**, 22–31 (2014). https://doi.org/10.1016/j.ssci.2013.11.019

20. Rauthmann, J.F., et al.: Eyes as windows to the soul: gazing behavior is related to personality. J. Res. Pers. **46**(2), 147–156 (2012). https://doi.org/10.1016/j.jrp.2011.12.010

21. Hess, E.H., Polt, J.M.: Pupil size in relation to mental activity during simple problem-solving. Science **143**(3611), 1190–1192 (1964). https://doi.org/10.1126/science.143.3611.1190

22. Hess, E.H., Polt, J.M.: Pupil size as related to interest value of visual stimuli. Science **132**(3423), 349–350 (1960). https://doi.org/10.1126/science.132.3423.349

23. Kahneman, D.: Attention and effort, vol. 1063. Citeseer (1973)

24. Fu, H., et al.: Influence of cues on the safety hazard recognition of construction workers during safety training: evidence from an eye-tracking experiment. J. Civil Eng. Educ. **150**(1), 04023009 (2024). https://doi.org/10.1061/JCEECD.EIENG-1882

25. Wu, X., Xue, C., Zhou, F.: An experimental study on visual search factors of information features in a task monitoring interface. In: Kurosu, M. (ed.) HCI 2015. LNCS, vol. 9171, pp. 525–536. Springer, Cham (2015). https://doi.org/10.1007/978-3-319-21006-3_50

26. Van Griethuijsen, R.A., et al.: Global patterns in students' views of science and interest in science. Res. Sci. Educ. **45**, 581–603 (2015)

Navigating the Ergonomic Challenges of Remote Work: A Closer Look at Neck and Lower Back Pain

Chung Tia[✉] and Vincent G. Duffy

Purdue University, West Lafayette, IN 47907, USA
{ctia,duffy}@purdue.edu

Abstract. Exploring the Importance of Home Office Equipment in an Evolving Remote Work Landscape. This study investigates how home office equipment influences the comfort and productivity of telecommuters, with a particular focus on the evolving remote work landscape accelerated by the COVID-19 pandemic. Recognizing the heightened importance of home office ergonomics, the research explores the impact of ergonomic features on user well-being and work performance in telecommuting scenarios. Utilizing a comprehensive methodology that encompasses ergonomic assessments, user surveys, and potential real-world observations, the study delves into the nuanced relationship between home office equipment design and telecommuting outcomes. Preliminary findings underscore the pivotal role of ergonomic elements, such as adjustability and user-friendly interfaces, in shaping positive user experiences. The paper also addresses the sudden surge in remote work prompted by COVID-19, emphasizing the critical need for tailored ergonomic solutions in home work environments to optimize the remote work experience amidst the challenges posed by the global health crisis.

Keywords: Remote work · Ergonomics · Telecommuting · Productivity · Stress

1 Introduction and Background

1.1 Introduction

The global shift toward remote work, escalated by the widespread adoption forced by the COVID-19 pandemic, has revolutionized traditional work dynamics. With this transformative change comes the inevitable need to examine the impact of home office equipment on the comfort and productivity of telecommuters (Hedge et al. 2006). This study aims to delve into the nuances of home office ergonomics, exploring how the design and features of workspaces within domestic environments influence the well-being and performance of individuals adapting to this evolving remote work landscape. The COVID-19 pandemic has not only accelerated this transition but also underscored the importance of understanding how ergonomic considerations can shape the success of telecommuting experiences. By investigating the intricate relationship between home office equipment design and telecommuting results, this research is looking to offer valuable insights, contributing to the ongoing dialogue on optimizing the remote work experience.

V. G. Duffy (Ed.): HCII 2024, LNCS 14711, pp. 96–109, 2024.
https://doi.org/10.1007/978-3-031-61066-0_7

Ergonomic challenges of remote work is important to both individuals and society because as companies have started to adopt to work from home environments, it is important to understand the ergonomic implications that come along with it. Employees need to work in an ergonomically healthy environment in order to produce at their highest level.

1.2 Background

The transition to remote work has introduced a number of ergonomic challenges reshaping the traditional work environment. Employees are now tasked with creating workspaces in home settings, often lacking proper ergonomic setups, leading to concerns about maintaining healthy work postures while working on laptops or makeshift workstations (Hedge, Ray, & Shor et al. 2006). This shift poses a heightened risk of musculoskeletal issues due to prolonged periods of sedentary work without proper ergonomic support (Straker et al. 2020). The absence of ergonomic office furniture like adjustable chairs and desks further compounds these challenges, impacting employee health and well-being (Robertson et al. 2010). Moreover, limited space, technological constraints, and distractions in home environments contribute to eye strain, fatigue, and decreased job satisfaction among remote workers (Berg-Beckhoff, Nielsen, & Ladekjær Larsen et al. 2020). As remote work continues to evolve, addressing these ergonomic challenges becomes paramount to fostering a healthy and productive workforce in this dynamic work landscape.

Google nGram Viewer was used as a bibliographic analysis tool in this research to better understand the trends of the following keywords: Ergonomics, neck pain, and remote work. From Fig. 1 below, it can be observed that remote work has not been as prevalent compared to ergonomics or neck pain. In addition to Google nGram, software such as VOSViewer and Citespace were also utilized for content analysis (Liu, Li et al. 2022). The purpose of these software is to help guide the research process in understanding the prevalence of the research topic within other research articles (Cho, Min Ho et al. 2023).

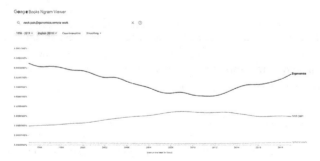

Fig. 1. Google nGram analysis of keywords: Ergonomics, neck pain, and remote work ("Google Ngram," n.d.)

2 Purpose

The purpose of this study is to comprehensively assess and analyze the ergonomic challenges faced by remote employees in home office environments. By investigating the impact of ergonomic factors on the comfort, health, and productivity of telecommuters, this research aims to identify the key elements influencing remote work experiences (Jones & Smith et al. 2019). Additionally, this study seeks to explore potential solutions and recommendations to mitigate ergonomic challenges, providing valuable insights for optimizing work from home environments and enhancing the overall well-being and performance of individuals engaged in remote work. This research aims to consolidate progress made in this field and assess their effectiveness. It explores whether these endeavors have yielded positive outcomes by utilizing diverse tools capable of analyzing metadata, such as VOSviewer, CiteSpace, NVivo, and Scopus.

3 Procedures

3.1 Data Collection

The literature review for this research was performed by extracting metadata from various databases such as SpringerLink and Scopus to analyze.

Table 1. Keyword search within different databases and their respective results

Database	Search keywords	Search settings	Number of articles
SpringerLink	"Telecommuting"	None	3,559
SpringerLink	"Work from home"	Year > 2022	205,051
SpringerLink	"Covid related ergonomics"	None	3,759
Scopus	"home ergonomics"	None	1,312
Scopus	"Telecommuting"	Year > 2020	1,577

Table 1. Above shows the different database utilized to search for keywords and their corresponding results. From these results we can observe that the keywords "Work from home" searched in the SpringerLink databases yielded the most results. This can be related to the broadness of these terms.

3.2 Trend Analysis

Trend analysis was performed by utilizing the metadata gathered from databases like Web of Science and Scopus. Databases like Web of Science and Scopus contain built in analysis tools to assist researchers in understanding the results of their searches. The following figures are examples of trend analysis graphs generated by the databases' features.

The utilization of Web of Science as a comprehensive database plays an important role in facilitating robust research opportunities for researchers across various disciplines. The platform offers multifaceted tools and features that enhance the efficiency of literature exploration, citation tracking, and scholarly impact assessment.

Accessing Web of Science allows researchers to delve into an extensive repository of academic articles, enabling them to initiate their inquiry by utilizing search functionalities. This includes the use of keywords and filters to narrow down search results based on publication date, document type, author, and other relevant criteria. The comprehensive search results provide researchers with a broad spectrum of publications including titles, authors, abstracts, and publication details, facilitating a preliminary overview of available literature.

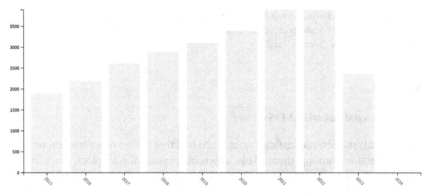

Fig. 2. Trend diagram for the number of article found on Web of Science database using the search terms "Homework design" ("Web of Science," n.d)

Shown in the figure above is a graphical depiction of the number of articles related to the keywords "Homework design" from 2015 to 2024 found in the Web of Science database. From the bar graph we can observe that the trend for this search has been increasing in a steady pace since the year 2015 with its peak occurring in the years 2021 & 2022. The results of those years generated over 3500 articles. The topic of "Homework design" has become more and more relevant as of late. Figure 3 below shows similar results utilizing the Scopus database.

In Fig. 3 above, a trend analysis was performed using the Scopus database from results yielded from the search for "Ergonomics and telecommuting". Similar to Fig. 2, we notice that there is a sharp increase between 2019 and 2022 in our results with the peak happening around 2022. The utilization of Scopus analysis tool features will be discussed later on.

The observations from both trend analyses can be due to the Covid-19 pandemic directly effecting work place environments for the majority of society during this global shutdown for the better part of two years.

Documents by year

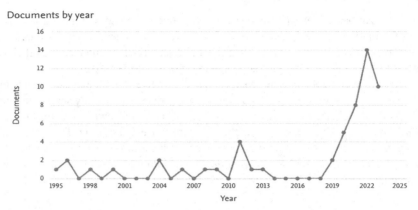

Fig. 3. Trend by year generated from Scopus for articles found in topic search "Ergonomics and telecommuting". There is a sharp increase in this trend from 2019 to 2022 which coincides with the Covid-19 pandemic ("Scopus," n.d.)

4   Results

4.1   Content Analysis with VOSviewer

Co-citation analysis identifies articles referenced together within other articles, revealing the interconnections among them. This approach reveals the level of association or connectivity between scholarly works. VOSviewer was the software utilized to facilitate the co-citation analysis process, refining metadata obtained from the Scopus database.

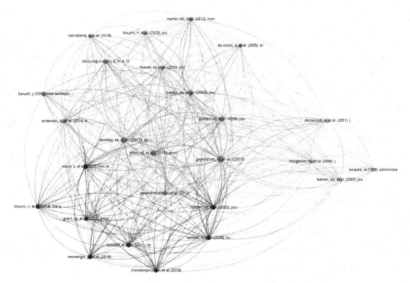

Fig. 4. Co-citation analysis performs using VOSviewer software with data collected from Scopus database ("VOSviewer," n.d.)

Figure 4 above was generated by VOSviewer depicting the interconnectivity of all the articles. This analysis contained 30,449 articles, however for the article to be considered in the analysis, it had to be cited at least 20 times. This criterion was satisfied by only 26 articles. The figure below, Fig. 5, represents the metadata collected by VOSviewer and shows the number of citations each article contains. The "Total link strength" correlates to the size of the data point in Fig. 4. The higher the link strength, the larger the representation.

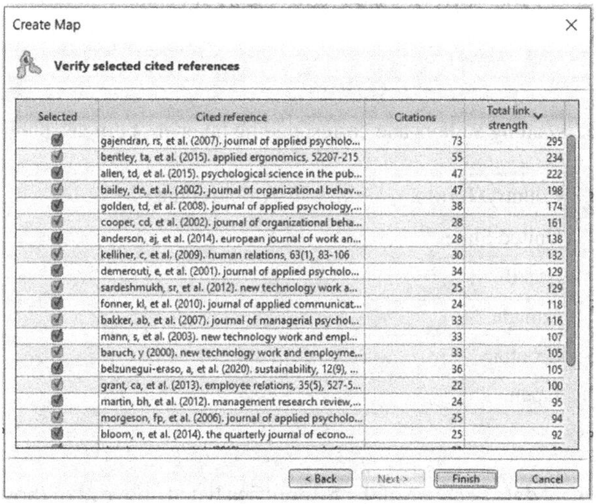

Selected	Cited reference	Citations	Total link strength
☑	gajendran, rs, et al. (2007). journal of applied psycholo...	73	295
☑	bentley, ta, et al. (2015). applied ergonomics, 52207-215	55	234
☑	allen, td, et al. (2015). psychological science in the pub...	47	222
☑	bailey, de, et al. (2002). journal of organizational behav...	47	198
☑	golden, td, et al. (2008). journal of applied psychology,...	38	174
☑	cooper, cd, et al. (2002). journal of organizational beha...	28	161
☑	anderson, aj, et al. (2014). european journal of work an...	28	138
☑	kelliher, c, et al. (2009). human relations, 63(1), 83-106	30	132
☑	demerouti, e, et al. (2001). journal of applied psycholo...	34	129
☑	sardeshmukh, sr, et al. (2012). new technology work a...	25	129
☑	fonner, kl, et al. (2010). journal of applied communicat...	24	118
☑	bakker, ab, et al. (2007). journal of managerial psychol...	33	116
☑	mann, s, et al. (2003). new technology work and empl...	33	107
☑	baruch, y (2000). new technology work and employme...	33	105
☑	belzunegui-eraso, a, et al. (2020). sustainability, 12(9), ...	36	105
☑	grant, ca, et al. (2013). employee relations, 35(5), 527-5...	22	100
☑	martin, bh, et al. (2012). management research review,...	24	95
☑	morgeson, fp, et al. (2006). journal of applied psycholo...	25	94
☑	bloom, n, et al. (2014). the quarterly journal of econo...	25	92

Fig. 5. Co-citation analysis cited references from VOSviewer ("VOSviewer," n.d)

4.2 Leading Tables from Scopus Analysis

Scopus identifies leading authors in a keyword search by analyzing citation data and the frequency of publication associated with the searched keywords. Through citation analysis, it recognizes authors with substantial impact and influence in a specific field. Author profiles in Scopus exhibit publication history, citation metrics, collaborations, and affiliations, offering a comprehensive overview of an author's contributions and standing in the research community. This combination of citation data and collaborative networks enables Scopus to highlight prominent authors within a given research domain.

Table 2 below represents the leading authors when researching respective leading keywords utilizing Scopus database. The number of articles the author wrote related to the leading keywords are also included in the table. From 1995–2023 Atul H. Goel has published 23 articles related to the keywords "Human, Computer, & Neck Pain".

Utilizing a similar methodology, Scopus is capable of identifying the leading countries in various research fields, providing valuable insights into global research contributions and impact. The following table, Table 3, lists the leading countries with written articles related to the keywords "ergonomics" and "telecommuting" utilizing the Scopus database.

Table 2. Leading authors and corresponding number of articles published

Author	Years active	Leading keywords	Article count
El Kadri Filho, Fauzi	2022–2023	Ergonomics, Telecommuting	3
Coombes, Brooke K	2009–2023	Neck pain, Remote work	2
Holden, Richard J	2005–2022	Work from home, ergonomics	12
Goel, Atul H	1995–2023	Human, Computer, Neck pain	22
Dai, Fei	2007–2023	Musculoskeletal, Ergonomics, Remote work	2

Table 3. Leading authors and corresponding number of articles published

Country/Territory	Article count
United States	16
Brazil	8
Canada	7
Croatia	3
Japan	3

Table 3 is relevant data because of the 5 countries listed above, 2 of those countries are on the list of countries most severally affected by the Covid-19 pandemic. According to the research article, "COVID-19 in the Age of Artificial Intelligence: A Comprehensive Review" the United States of America, and Brazil are 2 of the most affected countries by Covid-19 (Jamil et al. 2021). This correlates to Table 3 because the most affected countries are publishing articles related to ergonomic challenges with remote work hence concluding that the Covid-19 pandemic is a direct impact to the surge in the telework directive. Figure 6 below is a graph from "COVID-19 in the Age of Artificial Intelligence: A Comprehensive Review" displaying the number of Covid-19 cases in each country.

4.3   Content Analysis with NVIVO

When all articles intended to be analyzed were collected, we were able to perform content analysis and generate a wordcloud utilizing the NVIVO software. All articles were uploaded to the NVIVO software in.txt documents to create the wordcloud. The wordcloud is created by extracting the most frequently used words and compiling them to form a shape. Word clouds are widely used for quick insights into the key themes or most frequently mentioned terms within a body of text. They're often employed in data visualization to summarize text-based information, making it easy to identify prevalent topics or patterns within a dataset. Figure 7 below is the result of the generated wordcloud on the content analysis tool.

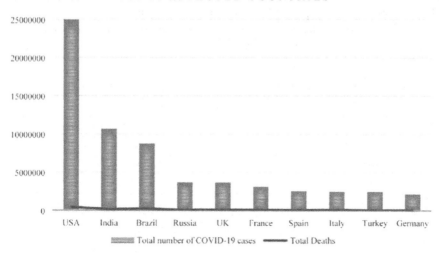

Fig. 6. A graph from "COVID-19 in the Age of Artificial Intelligence: A Comprehensive Review" displaying the number of Covid-19 cases in each country (Jamil et al. 2021).

Fig. 7. Wordcloud generated by utilizing the NVivo tool ("NVivo," n.d.)

In the wordcloud figure above, the words in the center of the wordcloud in the orange represent the most pertinent words mentioned in the articles used to create this figure. Words like "office", "discomfort", and "internet" are all important terminology for this research study.

Often irrelevant filler words appear to be the most prevalent words that appear within an article thus effecting the results of the wordcloud content analysis. A method to reduce those words is to introduce a filter to exclude words less than 5 letters in each word. This significantly reduces the number of filler words like "a", "the", "it", etc. which do not show any significance to the content of the articles. After performing the initial filtration of the list of words, we then proceeded to manually remove any irrelevant terms from the remainder of the list. The figure below is a portion of the word list utilized to generate the NVivo word cloud (Fig. 8).

Word	Length	Count	Weighted Percentage (%)
office	5	109	0.56
study	5	107	0.55
chair	5	105	0.54
saddle	6	101	0.52
standard	8	91	0.46
discomfort	10	80	0.41
internet	8	80	0.41
trial	5	80	0.41
spinal	6	78	0.40
research	8	74	0.38
subjects	8	73	0.37
block	5	69	0.35

Fig. 8. Word list extracted by the NVivo tool to generate the wordcloud ("NVivo," n.d.)

4.4 CiteSpace Citation Analysis

In the CiteSpace software, there is a citation burst feature that is designed to identify sudden spikes or increases in the frequency of citations attributed to a particular research topic within a specific timeframe. This function operates by analyzing citation data over time, aiming to recognize instances where there is a significant surge in citations beyond the expected or typical frequency. It calculates the strength of these bursts by comparing observed citation counts during specified time periods to anticipated counts based on historical citation patterns. These bursts are then visually depicted in timelines, presenting spikes that signify notable periods of increased attention or interest in a specific scholarly article. Researchers use this tool to identify pivotal moments or influential publications within a field, helping to understand the progression of academic interest and the impact of research contributions over time. Figure 9 below is the citation burst analysis performed using the Citespace software.

The figure above depicts the top 7 articles with the strongest "Citation Bursts" among 198 qualified records as process by the CiteSpace software. The application filters the articles which are cited the most often and indicates the years in which they are cited. Of those 7 articles, 2 of them are relevant to "homework design".

Top 7 References with the Strongest Citation Bursts

References	Year	Strength	Begin	End	2015 - 2023
Felstead A, 2017, NEW TECH WORK EMPLOY, V32, P195, DOI 10.1111/ntwe.12097, DOI	2017	3.52	2020	2023	
Dingel JI, 2020, J PUBLIC ECON, V189, P0, DOI 10.1016/j.jpubeco.2020.104235, DOI	2020	4.29	2021	2023	
Kniffin KM, 2021, AM PSYCHOL, V76, P63, DOI 10.1037/amp0000716, DOI	2021	3.66	2022	2023	
Gerding T, 2021, WORK, V68, P981, DOI 10.3233/WOR-205294, DOI	2021	2.82	2022	2023	
Barrero JM, 2021, 28731 NAT BUR EC RES, V0, P0	2021	2.82	2022	2023	
Tavares AI, 2017, INT J HEALTHCARE, V3, P30, DOI 10.5430/ijh.v3n2p30, DOI	2017	2.34	2022	2023	
Delanoeije J, 2019, HUM RELAT, V72, P1843, DOI 10.1177/0018726718823071, DOI	2019	2.34	2022	2023	

Fig. 9. Citation burst analysis performed on Citespace software ("Citespace," n.d.)

5   Discussion

5.1   Emergence of Remote Work

Globally, the contextual implications of teleworking have garnered considerable attention from researchers, as shown evidently in comprehensive reports discussing its multifaceted advantages and limitations. Paramount among these considerations are the critical focuses of cultivating an optimal ergonomic situation, establishing relationships between employees and management, fostering a culture of work autonomy, and strategically managing workloads – all of which play vital roles in mitigating potential detriments associated with telework, extending beyond the realm of musculoskeletal disorders (MSD). The literature reviewed accentuates the prevalence of suboptimal ergonomic conditions precipitated by the sudden and widespread implementation of lockdowns (Fadel et al. 2023). Notably, individuals with a history of lower back pain (LBP) experienced amplified discomfort during teleworking amid lockdown measures, albeit notably mitigated among those with dedicated, well-organized home office spaces (Bodin et al. 2023). Despite the scarcity of comprehensive evidence, a discernible trend suggests that strategic ergonomic interventions hold promise in curbing the incidence of MSD. Consequently, imperative future research endeavors should delve into comprehensive ergonomic interventions, encompassing educational initiatives, training modules, and tailored equipment provisions to address the nuanced needs of remote workers (Fadel et al. 2023).

Ergonomic challenges within remote work is certainly an emerging area within the realm of applied ergonomics. As telework becomes an increasingly popular method of work, employees are attached to their work computers for longer periods of time. During the research process for this research paper, an analysis was performed on the metadata collected from the Scopus database showing the number of articles related to the topic's keywords throughout the years. In the Fig. 3, we can clearly observe that there has been a sharp increase in the number of articles related to the keywords "ergonomics" and "telecommuting" in the last few years, especially starting in 2019. This is directly correlated to the Covid-19 pandemic.

Despite the challenges of the Covid-19 pandemic, there have been many actions taken to address the issue. Companies have started health and wellness programs, flexible work policies, and specialized furniture and equipment cater to remote work setups. These corporate wellness programs extend support to remote employees, emphasizing a multidisciplinary approach to creating a holistic and health-conscious work environment beyond traditional office settings.

5.2 Neck Pain from Telework

Using most mobile device tasks that require users to look downwards or to hold their arms out in front of them to read the screen can lead to fatigue and pain in the neck and shoulders (Fares et al., 2017). Although the quoted statement refers to the usage of mobile devices, the posture for the use of work computers are similar, neck in a downward position, arms and shoulders extended in front of the person. Improper ergonomics over elongated periods of time leads to eventual neck, shoulder, and lower back pain.

5.3 Benefits of Telework

I have found that a majority of employees prefer telework environments. Over half of all respondents reported that they would like to telework post-pandemic all the time (Jones et al. 2023). The National Science Foundations studies show that telework is a win-win-win for managers, employees and the environment. The study reveals that the majority of agency employees telework, and that 87 percent hold a positive view of telework in the federal government. The majority of managers who directly supervise teleworkers find those employees' productivity increases or remains the same while teleworking. Additionally, there are a multitude of benefits to telecommuting (Simeli et al. 2023). Teleworking can help achieve sustainable development goals (SDG) set by the United Nations (Tsekouropoulos et al. 2023).

Over the last decade, height-adjustable workstations are being introduced in office spaces that allow workers to alternate between sitting and standing posture, by raising and lowering the work surface accordingly. Typically, most industry solutions are electrically driven for easy and fast adjustment. A large number of recent studies have shown the benefits of such a solution for reducing back-pain (Agarwal, Steinmaus, & Harris-Adamson, 2018) and alleviating worker discomfort with no negative effects on productivity (Karakolis & Callaghan, 2014). This is especially important for work from home settings as employee apartments could potentially not have the required space to have a proper work space set-up. The use of a standing desk could help lower the potential for back-pain due to extended time spent in the sitting down position.

As telework continues to be an increasingly popular form of employment, an area of improvement that can help prevent musculoskeletal diseases is by creating new office equipment that allows for employees to prevent these ergonomic challenges. From the article, "Telework" Benefits Employers, Employees, and the Environment", it says that employees show an increased productivity when working from home. The environment also benefits from this as telecommute requires less traffic. Remote work comes with both benefits and cautions. Currently, most homeworkers are found to be in less-than-ideal environments (Chim et al. 2023). Showing that there is still a plethora of areas in which organizations need to improve upon.

6 Future Work

The proliferation of remote work has significantly altered the setting of modern employment by offering flexibility and convenience but also presenting its own set of ergonomic challenges. These issues often lead to various health problems, including neck pain (Hedge, 2016). Ergonomics is the study of designing equipment and devices that fit the human body and its movements. In the context of telework, ergonomic issues arise due to inadequate home office setups, prolonged sitting, and repetitive movements (Amick et al. 2003).

Poor workstation ergonomics contribute significantly to neck pain among those who work from a remote setting. Many individuals lack proper office equipment, resulting in having to use kitchen tables or sofas as makeshift workstations. These setups rarely offer proper support for maintaining a neutral spine and head position. This leads to individuals eventually adopting incorrect postures, like craning their necks forward or slouching (Sharan et al., 2014). Prolonged sitting in telework, exacerbates neck pain by causing muscle stiffness and reduced blood circulation, further aggravating musculoskeletal issues (Hedge, 2016).

Repetitive movements when using devices like laptops or mobile devices without ergonomic accessories, can strain the neck muscles due to awkward postures. Continuous use of these devices without proper support leads to tension in the shoulders and neck, contributing to discomfort and pain (Sharan et al., 2014).

Addressing these ergonomic challenges requires a multilayered approach. Educating remote workers about proper ergonomics and providing guidelines for setting up an ergonomic home office is crucial (Amick et al. 2003). Employers also play a pivotal role by offering resources or allowances to provide employees with proper office furniture and equipment. By incorporating simple adjustments like using a supportive chair or integrating regular breaks to stretch, individuals can significantly alleviate neck pain associated with remote work (Hedge 2016).

Technological advancements offer potential solutions to improve ergonomics in remote work. Wearable devices or applications that remind individuals to take breaks, adjust their posture, or perform stretching exercises can mitigate the negative effects of prolonged sitting and repetitive movements (Amick et al., 2003). Dynamic workstations, such as standing desks or adjustable workstations, also promote movement and variation in posture, reducing strain on the neck and other body parts (Sharan et al. 2014).

In conclusion, the ergonomic challenges posed by remote work significantly contribute to neck pain among individuals. Addressing these challenges necessitates a concerted effort from both employees and employers to implement proper ergonomic practices and leverage technological advancements to create healthier work environments (Hedge 2016).

References

Amick, B.C., Robertson, M.M., Moore, A.: Workplace-based return-to-work interventions: a systematic review of the quantitative literature. J. Occup. Rehabil. **13**(4), 277–291 (2003)

Berg-Beckhoff, G., Nielsen, G., Ladekjær Larsen, E.: Systematic review: work environment and ergonomic aspects of home offices. Work 65(2), 377–393 (2020)

Chim, J.M.Y., Chen, T.L.: Prediction of Work from Home and Musculoskeletal Discomfort: An Investigation of Ergonomic Factors in Work Arrangements and Home Workstation Setups Using the COVID-19 Experience. MDPI. (Accessed 21 November 2023)

Cho, M.H., Kamalraj, A.R., Duffy, V.G.: Literature review on human-automation interaction: relation between work from home and virtual environments. In: International Conference on Human-Computer Interaction, pp. 16–36. Springer Nature Switzerland, Cham (2023)

CiteSpace. http://cluster.cis.drexel.edu/~cchen/citespace/

Fadel, M., Bodin, J., Cros, F., Descatha, A., Roquelaure, Y.: Teleworking and Musculoskeletal Disorders: A Systematic Review. MDPI (2023)

Gadge, K., Innes, E.: An Investigation into the Immediate Effects on Comfort, Productivity and Posture of the Bambach Saddle Seat and a Standard Office Chair. (Accessed 26 November 2023)

Google Ngram. https://books.google.com/ngrams

Hedge, A., Dorsey, J.: The effects of office chairs on comfort and productivity during telecommuting. In: Human Factors and Ergonomics Society Annual Meeting Proceedings (2006)

Hedge, A., Ray, E., Shor, R.: Remote office ergonomic self-evaluation. Hum. Fact. Ergon. Soc. Annual Meeting Proc. **50**(19), 2028–2032 (2006)

Jones, A.M., Fan, J., Thomas-Olson, L., Zhang, W., McLeod, C.B.: Continuation of Telework in the Post-Pandemic Era: Healthcare Employees' Preference and Determinants. Healthcare Manag. Forum (2023)

Jones, A., Smith, B.: Remote Work and Ergonomic. J. Remote Work **8**(3), 112–125 (2019). https://joaournals.sagepub.com/doi/epdf/, https://doi.org/10.1177/084047042311 70733?src=getftr.Challenges

Liu, L., Guo, F., Zou, Z., Duffy., V.G.: Application, development and future opportunities of collaborative robots (cobots) in manufacturing: a literature review. Inter. J. Human–Comput. Interact. 1–18 (2022)

Marmaras, N., Nathanael, D.: Workplace Design. In: Salvendy G. (ed.) Handbook of Human Factors and Ergonomics, 5th ed., pp. 379–370. Wiley & Sons, Incorporated (2021)

Marras, W.S., Karwowski, W.: Basic Biomechanics and Workplace Design. In: Salvendy G. (ed.) Handbook of Human Factors and Ergonomics, 5th ed., pp. 343–345. Wiley & Sons, Incorporated (2021)

Mendeley. https://www.mendeley.com/

National Science Foundation. (Accessed 21 November 2023). https://www.nsf.gov/news/news_s umm.jsp?cntn_id=111252

NVivo. https://help-nv.qsrinternational.com/20/win/Content/about-nvivo/about-nvivo.htm

Rasheed, J., Jamil, A., Ali, H.A., Al-Turjman,R.A.:. COVID-19 in the Age of Artificial Intelligence: A Comprehensive Review (2021)

ResearchGate. https://www.researchgate.net

Robertson, M.: Ergonomics in the home office. Proc. Human Fact. Ergon. Soc. Annual Meeting **54**(15), 1218–1222 (2010)

Saes-Silva, E., et al.: Remote Work and Back Pain during the COVID-19 Pandemic in Adults and Older Population in South Brazil. Ciência & Saúde Coletiva (2022)

Simeli, I., et al.: Benefits and Challenges of Teleworking for a Sustainable Future: Knowledge Gained through Experience in the Era of COVID-19. Sustainability (Switzerland) **15** (2023). https://www-scopus-com.ezproxy.lib.pur due.edu/record/display.uri?eid=2-s2.0   85167874988&origin=resultslist&sort=plf-f&src=s&sid=8d001713e4dcc0970d9dc4e85be05921&sot=b&sdt=b&s=TITLE-ABS-KEY%28benefits+of+telework%29&sl=35&sessionSearchId=8d001713e4dcc0970d9dc4e85be0592

Scopus. https://www.scopus.com/search/form.uri?display=basic&zone=header&origin=#basic

SpringerLink. https://link.springer.com

Straker, L., Coenen, P., Dunstan, D., Gilson, N., Healy, G: .Sedentary Work - Evidence on an Emergent Work Health and Safety Issue - Final Report. Safe Work Australia (2020)

de Macedoa, T.A.M., et al.: Ergonomics and Telework: A Systematic Review (2020). Accessed at https://content.iospress.com/download/work/wor203224?id=work%2Fwor203224

VOSviewer. https://www.vosviewer.com/

Weston, E.B., Hassett, A.L., Khan, S.N., Weaver, T.E., Marras, W.S.: Cognitive Dissonance Increases Spine Loading in the Neck and Low Back (2023)

Integrating Extended Reality (XR) in a Smart Factory Environment: Systematic Review

Nachiket Vatkar[1,2(✉)], Chanho Shin[1,2], and Vincent G. Duffy[1]

[1] Purdue University School of Industrial Engineering, West Lafayette, IN 47907, USA
{nvatkar,shin243,duffy}@purdue.edu
[2] Flex Laboratories, West Lafayette, IN 47906, USA

Abstract. The main goal of this work is to study the integration of extended reality in the setting of Smart Factories. In order to investigate this topic a systematic review is conducted by performing bibliometric analysis followed by a cluster analysis. Bibliometric metadata as well as performance metrics for key search terms were collected with the use of Scopus and Web of Science databases. Then network analysis was conducted using VOSviewer and Citespace of the collected metadata. From the cluster analysis key works were identified and NVivo was used to perform a lexical analysis in order to perform a reappraisal and review of the topic at hand. Finally Zotero was used to create a bibliography. Through this work it was shown that Extended Reality and Smart factories have great academic interest independently, however the integration of extended reality within a smart factory environment is a relatively new and emerging topic with a great scope for new research. This partly due to the limited adoption of Smart Factories in the manufacturing industry globally as this industry is still transitioning into Industry 4.0. Following the discussion of analysis results future work derived from relevant NSF awarded grants has also been discussed.

Keywords: Extended Reality(XR) · Smart Factory · VOSviewer · nVivo · Citespace · Zotero · Web of Science · Scopus

1 Introduction and Background

The extended Reality Environments are really helpful to establish simulation for the manufacturing process of smart factories. It will help humans to find defects before they build the actual facility, so it will decrease the waste of time and money significantly. Advanced technologies such as robots, XR(extended reality), and other assistive devices to build complete smart factories which could operate with limited human interaction, i.e. working towards higher levels of automation.

Manufacturing, specifically advanced manufacturing, is a core concept within the field of industrial engineering. A smart factory is a new-age approach that could facilitate and enhance advanced manufacturing in various industries, ranging from automotive to electronics. In addition, extended reality systems that could be integrated into such smart factories could further enhance the automation and output during production. This combined effort of extended reality integrated in smart factories can also contribute to the

V. G. Duffy (Ed.): HCII 2024, LNCS 14711, pp. 110–128, 2024.
https://doi.org/10.1007/978-3-031-61066-0_8

study of operations research and optimization, which are other core concepts within the field of industrial engineering. The basic building blocks for the development of smart factories, with integrated XR technology can be traced back to work done in various fields. Mechanical and mechatronics engineering has contributed to the development of relevant hardware such as assembly line robots and subtractive/additive manufacturing machines. Such hardware developments are complemented by relevant software contributions made by computer scientists and engineers. Such a multidisciplinary approach has enabled industrial engineers to integrate all these technologies together to create smart factories of the future.

Currently, the key limitation lies in the funding and adaptability of 'smart factories' in commercial settings. Commercial manufacturing is still slow to adapt to the rapid technological advancements driven by industry 4.0. Commercial adoption of smart factories will allow the manufacturing industry to establish industry 4.0 as the new standard.

In our report, the chosen topic draws from two crucial chapters within the 5th edition of the Handbook of Human Factors and Ergonomics: Chapter 30, titled "Extended Reality (XR) Environments" by Kay M. Stanney, Hannah Nye, Sam Haddad, Kelly S. Hale, Christina K. Padron, and Joseph V. Cohn, and Chapter 44, "Human–Robot Interaction" by Jessie Y.C. Chen and Michael J. Barnes. Chapter 30 delves into the foundation of the selected subject, elaborating on Extended Reality (XR) and the ergonomic implications in constructing such systems. The chapter explicates, "Virtual Reality technology involves simulating an entire virtual world, including assets and the world itself, and presenting that in an HWD such that the users' view and perception of the real world is obstructed" (Cipresso et al. 2018) (Stanney et al. 2021). Conversely, Chapter 44 explores the potential synergy between Extended Reality and Smart Factories. It illuminates the possibility of leveraging ergonomics in human-robot interactions within smart factories, contemplating the prospect of employing extended reality systems to potentially enhance safety and various parameters for factory workers. Chen and Barnes (2021) articulate, "As robots evolve from tools to human teammates, the dynamics of their interactions also change dramatically. The type of human-robot communications can take many different forms, from traditional human-computer interaction to language-based and multimodal interaction."

1.1 Relevant Definitions

Extended Reality
Extended Reality (XR) is an umbrella term encompassing Virtual Reality (VR), Augmented Reality (AR), and Mixed Reality (MR) (Park & Kim, 2022). XR technologies create computer-mediated indirect experiences, allowing users to develop high-quality skills in realistic and immersive environments (Otero-Varela et al., 2023). Moreover, XR simulators utilizing VR, AR, and MR technologies offer advantages over physical simulators, as they can be used by multiple users and provide real-time instruction and feedback (Yoo et al., 2022). Furthermore, the integration of XR technologies, such as AR, VR, and MR, with simulation in Quality 4.0 (quality management within industry 4.0), offers numerous advantages (Ahmed et al., 2022). Overall, XR encompasses a wide range of technologies that extend reality and offer diverse applications in different domains.

Smart Factory

Smart Factory refers to a modern manufacturing facility that integrates advanced technologies, such as cyber-physical (XR) systems, the Internet of Things (IoT), artificial intelligence, and data analytics, to optimize the manufacturing process, improve efficiency, and enable flexibility in production. The concept of smart manufacturing has gained momentum in both industry and academia, driven by the need to adapt to highly competitive market demands, customize production, and move towards digitalization (Mittal et al. (2016) Ding et al. 2019; Calì, 2021). Smart factories are at the core of the modern production and manufacturing industry, playing a pivotal role in realizing the principles of Industry 4.0, which emphasizes the digital transformation of manufacturing processes and the integration of smart technologies across the entire supply chain (Ding et al. 2019; Calì, 2021). The vision of smart manufacturing involves leveraging digital technologies to increase the interconnection and cooperation of resources within plants and along the supply chain, leading to enhanced competitiveness and efficiency (Calì 2021). Automation is a key aspect of smart factories, with the complete automation of work processes, including the use of robots, intelligent manufacturing cells, and computer control mechanisms, to produce products without human supervision and intervention (Kosem et al. 2021). Additionally, the integration of smart sensors and advanced control systems in smart factories enables improved monitoring, control, and optimization of the manufacturing processes (Vadde et al., n.d.).Overall, smart factories represent a paradigm shift in manufacturing, leveraging cutting-edge technologies to create agile, efficient, and interconnected production environments.

2 Methodology

The basis of the methodology used for this work is derived from three papers. The first is titled "Green Supply Chain Management: A Review and Bibliometric Analysis.", which was published in the international journal of production economics. (Fahimnia, Sarkis, and Davarzani 2015). The second is titled "Application, Development and Future Opportunities of Collaborative Robots (Cobots) in Manufacturing: A Literature Review", which was published in International Journal of Human–Computer Interaction (Liu et al. 2024). The third is titled "Literature Review on Human-Automation Interaction: Relation Between Work from Home and Virtual Environments", which was published in the HCI International 2023 – Late Breaking Papers (Cho, Ravi Kamalraj, and Duffy 2023). The review process consisted of two main analysis approaches, the first is through bibliometric analysis and the second is through network analysis. Bibliometric analysis was first conducted using key databases such as Web of Science and Scopus to identify relevant literature pertaining to the topics of extended reality and smart factory. Through these databases key leading tables and trend metrics were derived. From the leading tables for each of the key word searches, prominent authors and leading affiliations were determined. Following this key trend, the number of papers published per year was also obtained to help speak to the relevance of the areas of extended reality and smart factories in academia. Following the basic bibliometric, metadata of complete records were compiled and used as input for network analysis, with the help of the VOS viewer and citespace softwares. Using this VOS viewer, co-occurrence, co-authorship and co-citation analysis was conducted as well as a citation burst was generated using citespace. The key findings from co-citation analysis and citation burst were then used to further narrow down the list of key literature to 8 papers for the areas of extended reality and smart factory each, i.e. 16 critical pieces of literature identified. Following this process, we used the NVivo software to perform further lexical analysis on the shortlisted literature, resulting in the formation of two critical word clouds that will help guide the reappraisal and review process that will be discussed in future sections. The tools used are introduced in the following sub sections.

2.1 Analysis Tools

2.1.1 Bibliometric Analysis Tools (Database)

Web of Science
Web of Science is a paid-access platform that provides citations, references, and other academic resources. It also has some features to analyze the data such as the number of articles per year or the number of papers of each author. Through Academic institution accounts, students can have free access, so they see vast amounts of resources for their research.

Scopus
Scopus is a database of peer-reviewed literature and web sources for tracking, visualizing and analyzing research. Similar to Web of Science, it helps a lot to find the resource and analyze the data such as number of articles and tendency of each keyword. Through the academic institution account, students can find papers for free.

2.1.2 Cluster/Network Analysis Tools

VOS viewer
Vosviewer is a software tool to visualize and construct bibliometric data. Once the user puts a text file of citations or other information, the tool analyzes interactions between authors or most used words in articles. It has many features for data visualization based on co-citation, co-authorship, and others.

Cite Space
Citespace is a tool that visualizes data in text similar to VOSViewer. It analyzes the written information and shows visualized data with connections of each other, so the user can easily see clusters, authors, and words that are mostly used or connected. It is a free tool for everyone and the program is written in Java. In the context of this work, Cite space was primarily used to create citation bursts, which allow for a time based on relevant historical articles found through a co-citation analysis.

2.1.3 Lexical Analysis and AI Tools

Nvivo
nVivo is the premier software to analyze and visualize qualitative data. The data can be from surveys, interviews, field notes, and others. In this project, nVivo is used to generate

word clouds and lexical analysis of given papers from Web of Science and Scopus. It is a very good tool to find patterns of data that the user puts in.

Scite.ai

Scite.ai is Artificial Intelligence powered platform for research to analyze and provide context of citation of scientific papers. It uses deep learning algorithms and natural language processing techniques, so it can generate paragraphs based on actual scientific data. Since what it generates is based on certified papers, users can trust its work.

3 Results

In this research, Scopus and Web of Science became the main database to analyze the Extended Reality and Smart Factory in terms of current situation and tendency of its direction. Thanks to the amazing development of Virtual Reality technology, it was found that the interest in the topic has arisen rapidly in the last 10 years. As Pivot Table and VOS viewer shows, the rank for authors with most citations and the clusters for co-citation were visualized. Citespace delved into time-based citation bursts, highlighting influential papers, while co-authorship analysis brought the result of clustered author relationships and global collaborations. Through utilizing another software nVivo, word cloud is generated based on co-citation analysis and 16 chosen articles related to Smart Manufacturing and Extended Reality, most used terms were selected and arranged in a shape. This multifaceted approach has given a comprehensive understanding of how Smart Factory and Extended Reality research are evolving.

3.1 Search Results

Two databases were used to search for the topic of Extended Reality and Smart Factory which are Web of Science and Scopus. To get high quality data from both databases, various keywords were used for searching; with use of different search words, it was found that small variation caused the large difference in number of articles. To extract the data, Harzing's Publish or Perish software was chosen and the result of the number of papers are shown in the table below.

Table 1. Search terms and all databases used

Database	Key Word Used	Number of Results
Web Of Science	"human robot" interaction"	23834
Scopus	"human AND robot AND interaction"	39098
Web Of Science	"Extended Reality"	10402
Scopus	"extended AND reality"	1448
Web Of Science	"Smart Factory"	3994
Scopus	"Smart Factory"	6669
Web Of Science	"Extended Reality AND Smart Factory"	15
Scopus	"Extended Reality AND Smart Factory"	22

3.2 Trends

3.2.1 Emergence Metric

Using the keywords "Smart Factory", "Extended Reality", and "Smart Factory and Extended Reality", The team conducted searching in Scopus for articles and conference papers. The result has shown a trendline that draws the growth of the topic over the last couple of decades. For the Smart Factory, the number has increased dramatically since 2015 and it reached over 500 papers during late 2010's and early 2020's. The topic became popular in the mid 2010's, and it is expected to be more in future. A similar situation happened to Extended Reality. It has gradually increased from a couple decades ago thanks to the interests in VR technology. The possible reason could be the invention of the VR headset, and it boosted up the research. However, the number of articles for both Smart Factory and Extended Reality has shown very low numbers since the area is a unique topic. With current technologies, it is hard to conduct research, but it is expected to be increase in future with advanced equipment.

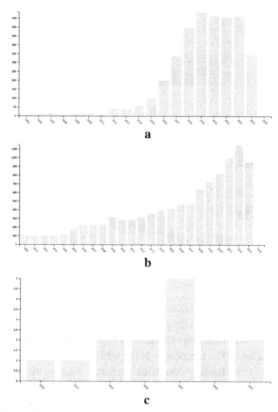

Fig. 1. a) The number of documents related to Smart Factory by year, b) The number of documents related to Extended Reality by year, c) The number of documents related to both Extended Reality and Smart Factory by year

3.2.2   Authors and Affiliations

Using Web of Science, the Tables 2a and 2b for leading affiliations for both Smart Factory and Extended reality, respectively, were generated. For Smart Factory, Sungkyunkwan University is leading in the topic showing competitive numbers with the second highest leading affiliations. For Extended Reality, the University of California system is shown as the leading affiliation, but it is not showing a huge difference compared to the second highest (Table 1).

Table 2. a) WOS leading affiliations for smart factory, b) WOS leading affiliations for extended reality.

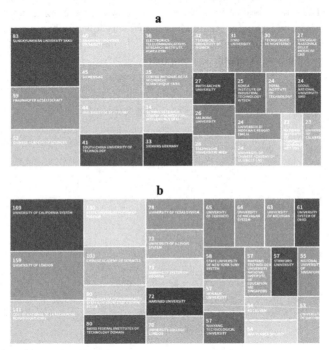

Similarly, another analysis was done through the Web of Science, but it is based on the leading authors instead of the leading affiliations. As shown in Table 3a, Jeong J is the leading author with 46, and Lee J has the second highest number of 36. The interesting thing is that there are a lot of Korean people at the table, it is because in previous analysis, South Korea was one of the leading countries for Smart Factory research. The Table 3b also shows the leading authors for the Extended Reality topic as well.

Based on the raw metadata collected as shown in Tables 3 and 4, two Pivot tables were made for each keyword, Smart Factory and Extended Reality and shown in Fig__ below. The chart shows rankings of authors with numbers of articles they published. The data is drawn from Web of Science and the team used Bibexcel to organize it based on the number of articles of each author. Then using the excel software two pivot tables are

Table 3. a) WOS leading authors for smart factory, b) WOS leading authors for extended reality.

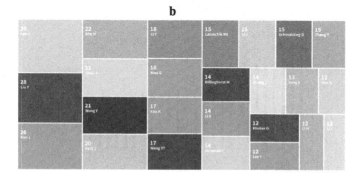

created. Figure 2a shows that there is one author with the highest number of publications that makes a noticeable difference from the one with second highest articles. In Fig. 2b, Top three authors for Extended Reality topics show good performance compared to the rest of them. This table can be meaningful in that it shows who is leading the field.

3.3   Cluster Analysis

Plain text files were extracted from the Web of Science database that contained metadata for search results of relevant papers related to our key search terms. This data included paper title, authors, full record of references, etc. This data was put in the VOS Viewer to conduct network analysis. Data was visualized as clusters based on various factors (Fig. 3).

3.3.1   VOS Viewer Analysis

Through the VOS Viewer software Co-occurrence analysis was conducted for Smart Factory with the 15 threshold value and the result is shown in Fig. 5. Total of 1000 words were chosen with 47 clusters, and the word that has the most number is smart factory which is at the center, and other words with big numbers are centered at each cluster. For the co-occurrence analysis related to Extended Reality, the cluster formation

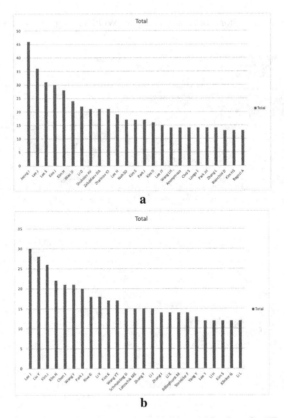

Fig. 2. a) Pivot table chart for "Smart Factory", b) Pivot table chart for "Extended Reality"

followed a very similar pattern to that of the analysis for Smart Factory. The 1000 keywords were chosen based on 1 minimum threshold and it formed 46 clusters (Fig. 4).

The next analysis is for co-citation, and it shows the relationships between authors based on citations. The co-citation analysis for Smart Factory with 10 minimum thresholds indicates 91 authors with 5 clusters. As shown in Fig. 7, there are some authors with a big size of nodes in each cluster, which means that they have a higher number of co-citation numbers. For the co-citation analysis for Extended Reality, the result shows 83 authors and 7 big clusters with 10 minimum threshold, but unlike Smart Factory, there is one big node at the center for the Milgram, P, who has the highest number of co-citation.

Using the co-citation analysis through VOS viewer, top 10 articles were chosen for both Smart Factory and Extended Reality. The software chooses those articles not based on the raw number of citations, but based on the link number, so it selects only the articles with high quality. Some references are in chicago formats below (Fig. 5).

CiteSpace is used to conduct a time based analysis of the metadata retrieved from Web of Science for the key terms searched. The citation burst is shown in Figs. 13 and 14 for the search terms of "Extended Reality" and "Smart Factory" respectively. Through these citation bursts it can be seen that through a co-citation analysis, which papers

a

b

Fig. 3. a) VOS Viewer using Web Of Science, Co-occurrence for "Smart Factories", 15 minimum thresholds. 1000 keywords, 47 clusters, b) VOS Viewer using Web Of Science, Co-occurrencefor "Extended Reality", 1 minimum thresholds. 1000 keywords, 46 clusters

were highly co-cited and the time period of relevance of these papers from a co-citation perspective. Hence some of these papers can selected for more in depth analysis to gain more relevant insights into the topic at hand (Fig. 6).

Co-authorship analysis for the Smart Factory has shown 4 clusters with 46 authors based on 1 threshold. There is one author on the left side who is well connected with all the clusters and there are others who are in the middle of the clusters. Analysis for Extended Reality shows interesting visualization that it has only 2 clusters with 26 authors. There is one author in the middle of 2 clusters and the one on the left is well connected with each other.

The last analysis is co-authorship analysis but country based; 50 countries are forming 12 clusters. For the Smart Factory, South Korea is the leading country for this topic and next one is People's China. There are 3 big countries leading the smart factories. However, in the analysis for Extended Reality, There are 13 clusters with 57 countries, but each country is well connected to each other compared to Smart Factory.

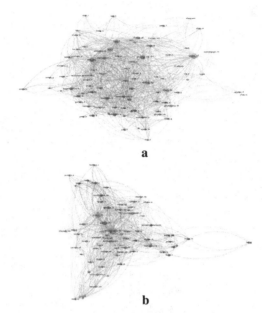

a

b

Fig. 4. a) VOS Viewer using Web Of Science for co-citation analysis of "Smart Factories", 10 minimum threshold, 91 items, 5 clusters, b) VOS Viewer using Web of Science for co-citation analysis of "Extended Reality", 10 minimum threshold, 83 items, 7 clusters

3.3.2 Lexical Analysis

Total of 16 articles from multiple databases were chosen based on the results of the co-citation analysis to generate word clouds for both Smart Manufacturing and Extended Reality through nVivo software. The articles were ingested into the program and it formed the word clouds based on most common terms. In Fig. 8a, the most used words for Extended Reality are shown at the center with bigger size compared to other words such as metaverse and virtual. In Fig. 8b, manufacturing, smart, automation are selected as most used words for chosen articles. This type of analysis is useful for future research in that it shows the trend based on terms, so people can expect what is being popular in academia.

Similarly, Lexical search was conducted through the nVivo with the articles chosen for both Smart Factory and Extended Reality. This has the same purpose as generating word clouds, however, it shows the actual number of words used in the article. This is better version of visualizing in a shape in that it gives number not the size (Fig. 9).

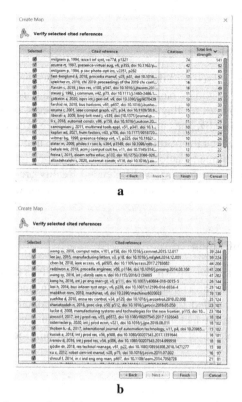

Fig. 5. a) Top 10 articles as reviewed for Extended Reality in VOS Viewer co-citation analysis, b) Top 10 articles as reviewed for Smart Factory in VOS Viewer co-citation analysis.

Top 1 References with the Strongest Citation Bursts

References	Year	Strength	Begin	End	2016 - 2020
Weichert F, 2013, SENSORS-BASEL, V13, P6380, DOI 10.3390/s130506380, DOI	2013	1.86	2016	2017	

a

Top 13 References with the Strongest Citation Bursts

References	Year	Strength	Begin	End	2018 - 2023
Lee Jay, 2015, MANUFACTURING LETTERS, V3, P18, DOI 10.1016/j.mfglet.2014.12.001, DOI	2015	5.97	2018	2019	
Radziwon A, 2014, PROCEDIA ENGINEER, V69, P1184, DOI 10.1016/j.proeng.2014.03.108, DOI	2014	4.80	2018	2019	
Lasi H, 2014, BUS INFORM SYST ENG+, V6, P239, DOI 10.1007/s12599-014-0334-4, DOI	2014	3.03	2018	2019	
Wang SY, 2016, COMPUT NETW, V101, P158, DOI 10.1016/j.comnet.2015.12.017, DOI	2016	2.91	2018	2020	
Zhong RY, 2017, ENGINEERING-PRC, V3, P616, DOI 10.1016/J.ENG.2017.05.015, DOI	2017	2.11	2018	2019	
Hofmann E, 2017, COMPUT IND, V89, P23, DOI 10.1016/j.compind.2017.04.002, DOI	2017	2.31	2019	2020	
Theben K D, 2017, INTERNATIONAL JOURNAL OF AUTOMATION TECHNOLOGY, V11, P4, DOI 10.20965/IJAT.2017.P0004, DOI	2017	4.06	2020	2021	
Osterrieder P, 2020, INT J PROD ECON, V221, P0, DOI 10.1016/j.ijpe.2019.08.011, DOI	2020	4.35	2021	2023	
Buchi G, 2020, TECHNOL FORECAST SOC, V150, P0, DOI 10.1016/j.techfore.2019.119790, DOI	2020	3.30	2021	2023	
Strozzi F, 2017, INT J PROD RES, V55, P6572, DOI 10.1080/00207543.2017.1326643, DOI	2017	2.68	2021	2023	
Alcácer V, 2019, ENG SCI TECHNOL, V22, P899, DOI 10.1016/j.jestch.2019.01.006, DOI	2019	2.27	2021	2023	
Sjödin DR, 2018, RES TECHNOL MANAGE, V61, P22, DOI 10.1080/08956308.2018.1471277, DOI	2018	2.16	2021	2023	
Soimu S, 2018, IEEE T IND INFORM, V14, P4724, DOI 10.1109/TII.2018.2852491, DOI	2018	2.03	2021	2023	

b

Fig. 6. a) Citation burst from CiteSpace for Extended Reality, b) Citation burst from CiteSpace for Smart Factory

4 Discussion

4.1 Topic Relevance

Google Ngram is a web-based tool that analyzes and shows the words frequency and phrases in the database of google based on the keywords that user puts. It is based on the huge amount of resources for linguistic and cultural aspects, so it is possible for the tool to enable users to visualize the change of language usage over time for comparison. The Google Ngram has given the result that compared to the numbers for Smart Factory and Extended Reality, Human Factors and Ergonomics have much higher numbers. The reason is because Smart Factory and Extended Reality are relatively new topics compared to Human Factors and Ergonomics, so the accumulated data has a significant gap (Fig. 10).

4.2 Application Justification

The manufacturing industry has grown significantly, especially in the 20th century during the industrial revolution. In the 21st century, the manufacturing industry is going through another such revolution, called Industry 4.0, with the introduction of automation and robotics. The goal of smart factories is to reach a certain level of autonomy while maintaining a sustainable level of human-robot interaction. Tools such as Extended

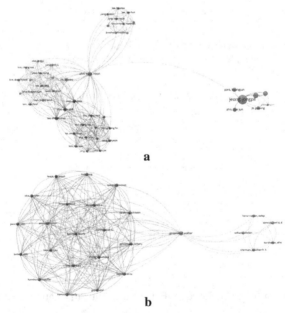

Fig. 7. a) VOS Viewer using Web Of Science, co-authorship for "Smart Factories". 46 authors, 4 clusters, b) VOS Viewer using Web Of Science, co-authorship for "Extended Reality". 26 authors, 2 clusters, c) Countries based Co-authorship for "Smart Factories", 50 items, 12 clusters, d) Countries based Co-authorship for "Extended Reality", 57 items, 13 clusters

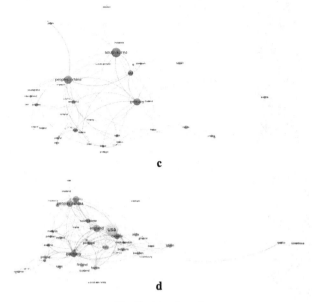

Fig. 7. (*continued*)

Fig. 8. a) Word cloud generated by nVivo for Extended Reality, b) Word cloud generated by nVivo for Smart Factory

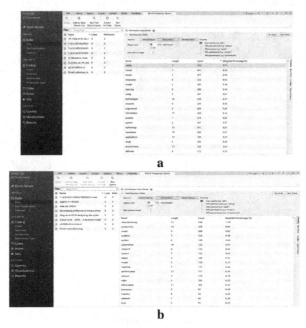

Fig. 9. a) Lexical search in nVivo for Extended Reality, b) Lexical search in nVivo for Smart Factory

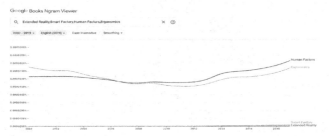

Fig. 10. Google nGram graph showing interest trends for the key words: "Smart Factory", "Extended Reality", "Human Factors", and "Ergonomics."

Reality can be used to optimize the layout, planning, and output of these Factories. The synthesis of Extended reality within a Smart Factory is an emerging area of research. Not only are each of the individual topics novel and of particular interest for many researchers, but the combination of these topics in the context of research related to Industry 4.0 further adds to the importance and novelty of this topic.

4.3 Academic Justification

Figures 1a-1c below show the trend of publications by year for the topics of "Smart Factory", "Extended Reality" and extended reality AND smart factory respectively. From these diagrams both the topics of "Smart Factory" and "Extended Reality" have an increasing number of publications each year, showing their emergence and growth in academia. However, Fig. 1c shows very limited literature with searching for the combined key word extended reality AND smart factory. Hence showing that despite the prominence of the individual areas of study there is limited current work related to the integration of extended reality systems within smart factories. Hence this topic is unique as it can help bridge the gap between and help to explain the application of XR within the context of a smart factory.

Table 2 highlights key academic justification behind the investigation of the topic at hand. Comparing the number of publications in 2016 vs the number of publications in 2022, there is a clear increase in the number of publications. For the search term Smart Factory there is an increase from 166 publications from 2016 to 563 publications in 2022, which is an increase of 64.7%. On the other hand, for the Search term of Extended Reality there is an increase from 466 publications in 2016 to 1146 publications in 2022, which is an increase of 59.3%.

Table 4. Table of # of publications in 2016 vs 2022 based on Web of Science search for the relevant topics.

Search Term	# of publications 2016	# of publications 2022
Smart Factory	199	563
Extended Reality	466	1146

4.4 Topic Reprisal

The landscape of technology in skill acquisition transformed significantly, particularly with the emergence of Head-Mounted Displays (HMDs). HMDs revolutionized skill development across cognitive, psychomotor, and affective domains [Cipresso et al. 2018]. The pivotal shift occurred in 2013 when Oculus Rift's initial developer versions introduced a new era of consumer-priced Virtual Reality (VR) technology, democratizing access to this innovation [Jensen and Konradsen 2018]. Subsequently, an influx of competitors flooded the market, expanding the reach of HMDs for research, education, and public use. Industries swiftly harnessed Augmented Reality (AR) for remote guidance and intricate tasks like maintenance, while VR found prevalence in layout planning and virtual training applications [Jensen and Konradsen 2018]. To fortify organizational capabilities in navigating these technological advancements, the integration of practical experiences and knowledge through learning factories becomes imperative [Fast-Berglund, Gong, and Li 2018].

The evolution towards Smart Factories and Industry 4.0 epitomizes collaborative cyber-physical systems, promising a transformative industrial future [Ivanov et al. 2016]. Automation within production isn't merely about replacing human labor; it should converge with organizational success and sustainable societal and environmental development [Kosem, Markič, and Gorenc Zoran 2021]. Smart manufacturing amalgamates present and future manufacturing assets with cutting-edge technologies like cyber-physical systems such as extended reality systems, the Internet of Things (IoT), cloud computing, artificial intelligence, and data science [Kusiak 2018]. This paradigm shift underpins the forthcoming industrial revolution, redefining manufacturing landscapes and processes. Cyber-physical (XR) systems blur the boundaries between physical and digital realms, notably in preventive maintenance scenarios where real-time digital parameters mirror the physical wear and tear of machinery [Lasi et al. 2014]. Industry 4.0's focus on smart manufacturing encompasses the entire production ecosystem, orchestrating intelligent, autonomous manufacturing resources at shop floors and factories, streamlining the supply chain [Ding et al. 2020]. This transformative approach conceptualizes cyber-physical systems as the backbone of smart shop floors, orchestrating intelligent manufacturing resources.

The convergence of these technological realms not only reshapes industrial landscapes but also transcends into the larger fabric of societal progress, emphasizing sustainable development and redefining the conventional paradigms of production, efficiency, and interconnectedness within the manufacturing sphere.

5 Conclusion

Extended Reality is growing rapidly nowadays due to its unlimited possibility of application. It was not feasible until 2010's, but thanks to the development of technology, it became more realistic than ever. Many companies, such as Meta are working on their project to bring VR technology to the real world, and it will be applied to our daily life soon. Smart Factory is another topic which is rising in both academic and industry. A lot of leading manufacturers are already utilizing Smart Manufacturing for the next generation to increase productivity and efficiency. The XR technology can be used to boost the production system by helping and supporting the work force for simulating and analyzing various situations in the field.

Through running multiple analyses with different software. Both of them are actively researched separately, however, the combination of them are in the early stages. Looking at the bright side, the combination of both topics has huge potential that can lead humanity to a more developed manufacturing system. Further development for each of them is still required since both of them are not perfect in that the technology cannot support combining them, but when it is done, applying the XR technology to Smart Manufacturing will be the next hot topic.

6 Future Work

Based on the current bibliometric analysis and keywords used in this work on the nsf.gov database, some potential awarded grants were identified. These works could form a potential basis for future works related to our selected topic. A grant related to the area of extended reality titled: "Collaborative Research: An Extended Reality Factory Innovation for Adaptive Problem-solving and Personalized Learning in Manufacturing Engineering" that was awarded on August 1, 2023. The principal investigators for this work are Dr. Faisal Aqlan, Dr. Jason Saleem and Dr. Marci DeCaro from the University of Louisville. Finally, related to the topic of human-robot interaction in a Smart Factory is a grant titled: "NRI: INT: COLLAB: Manufacturing USA: Intelligent Human-Robot Collaboration for Smart Factory" awarded in 2019 to THE RESEARCH FOUNDATION FOR THE STATE UNIVERSITY OF NEW YORK. The principal investigator for this work is Dr. Zhaozheng Yin. These works provide a very comprehensive basis for potential future work to allow for an organic continuation of this work.

References

Ahmed, A., Olsen, J., Page, J.: Integration of six sigma and simulations in real production factory to improve performance – a case study analysis. Inter. J. Lean Six Sigma **14**(2), 451–482 (2023). https://doi.org/10.1108/IJLSS-06-2021-0104

Alizadehsalehi, S., Hadavi, A., Huang, J.C.: From BIM to extended reality in aEC industry. Autom. Constr. **116**, 103254 (2020). https://doi.org/10.1016/j.autcon.2020.103254

Azuma, R., Baillot, Y., Behringer, R., Feiner, S., Julier, S., MacIntyre, B.: Recent advances in augmented reality. IEEE Comput. Graphics Appl. **21**(6), 34–47 (2001). https://doi.org/10.1109/38.963459

Calì, M.: Smart Manufacturing technology. Appl. Sci. **11**(17), 8202 (2021). https://doi.org/10.3390/app11178202

Chen, J.Y.C., Barnes, M.J.: Human–robot interaction. In: Salvendy, G., Karwowski, W. (eds.) Handbook of human factors and ergonomics, 1st ed., 1121–42. Wiley (2021). https://doi.org/10.1002/9781119636113.ch44

Cho, M.H., Kamalraj, A.R., Duffy, V.G.: Literature review on human-automation interaction: relation between work from home and virtual environments. In: Kurosu, M., et al. (eds.) HCI International 2023 – Late Breaking Papers, A14054:16–36. LNCS. Springer Nature Switzerland, Cham (2023). https://doi.org/10.1007/978-3-031-48038-6_2

Cipresso, P., Giglioli, I.A.C., Raya, M.A., Riva, G.: The past, present, and future of virtual and augmented reality research: a network and cluster analysis of the literature. Front. Psychol. **9**, 2086 (2018). https://doi.org/10.3389/fpsyg.2018.02086

Ding, K., Lei, J., Zhang, F., Wang, Y., Wang, C.: Analyzing the cyber-physical system-based autonomous collaborations among smart manufacturing resources in a smart shop floor. Proc. Instit. Mech. Eng. Part B: J. Eng. Manufact. **234**(3), 489–500 (2020). https://doi.org/10.1177/0954405419875340

Extended Reality Affiliations Leading Table. https://www.webofscience.com/wos/woscc/analyze-results/84a9d977-f932-4e3f-9504-c2f1ffb4b8ff-b9de4bf9 (Accessed 7 December 2023)

Extended Reality Author Leading Table. https://www.webofscience.com/wos/woscc/analyze-results/84a9d977-f932-4e3f-9504-c2f1ffb4b8ff-b9de4bf9 (Accessed 7 December,2023)

Extended Reality Publications by Year. https://www.webofscience.com/wos/woscc/analyze-results/84a9d977-f932-4e3f-9504-c2f1ffb4b8ff-b9de4bf9 (Accessed 7 December 2023)

Fahimnia, B., Sarkis, J., Davarzani, H.: Green supply chain management: a review and bibliometric analysis. Int. J. Prod. Econ. **162**, 101–114 (2015). https://doi.org/10.1016/j.ijpe.2015.01.003

Fast-Berglund, Å., Gong, L., Li, D.: Testing and validating extended reality (xr) technologies in manufacturing. Proc. Manufact. **25**, 31–38 (2018). https://doi.org/10.1016/j.promfg.2018.06.054

Flavián, C., Ibáñez-Sánchez, S., Orús, C.: The impact of virtual, augmented and mixed reality technologies on the customer experience. J. Bus. Res. **100**, 547–560 (2019). https://doi.org/10.1016/j.jbusres.2018.10.050

Hwang, G., Lee, J., Park, J., Chang, T.-W.: Developing performance measurement system for internet of things and smart factory environment. Int. J. Prod. Res. **55**(9), 2590–2602 (2017). https://doi.org/10.1080/00207543.2016.1245883

Ivanov, D., Dolgui, A., Sokolov, B., Werner, F., Ivanova, M.: A dynamic model and an algorithm for short-term supply chain scheduling in the smart factory industry 4.0. Int. J. Prod. Res. **54**(2), 386–402 (2016). https://doi.org/10.1080/00207543.2014.999958

Jensen, L., Konradsen, F.: A review of the use of virtual reality head-mounted displays in education and training. Educ. Inf. Technol. **23**(4), 1515–1529 (2018). https://doi.org/10.1007/s10639-017-9676-0

Kosem, U., Markič, M., Zoran, A.G.: Automation of work processes and night work. Data **6**(6), 56 (2021). https://doi.org/10.3390/data6060056

Kusiak, A.: Smart manufacturing. Int. J. Prod. Res. **56**(1–2), 508–517 (2018). https://doi.org/10.1080/00207543.2017.1351644

Lasi, H., Fettke, P., Kemper, H.-G., Feld, T., Hoffmann, M.: Industry 4.0. Bus. Inf. Syst. Eng. **6**(4), 239–242 (2014). https://doi.org/10.1007/s12599-014-0334-4

Lee, J., Bagheri, B., Kao, H.-A.: A Cyber-physical systems architecture for industry 4.0-based manufacturing systems. Manufact. Lett. **3**(January), 18–23 (2015). https://doi.org/10.1016/j.mfglet.2014.12.001

Liu, L., Guo, F., Zou, Z., Duffy, V.G.: Application, development and future opportunities of collaborative robots (cobots) in manufacturing: a literature review. Inter. J. Hum. Comput. Interact. **40**(4), 915–932 (2024). https://doi.org/10.1080/10447318.2022.2041907

Mittal, S., Khan, M.A., Wuest, T.: Smart manufacturing: characteristics and technologies. in: product lifecycle management for digital transformation of industries. In: Harik, R., Rivest, L., Bernard, A., Eynard, B., Bouras, A. (eds.), vol. 492, pp. 539–548. Springer International Publishing, Cham (2016). https://doi.org/10.1007/978-3-319-54660-5_48

NSF Award Search: Award # 1954548 - NRI: INT: COLLAB: Manufacturing USA: Intelligent Human-Robot Collaboration for Smart Factory. https://www.nsf.gov/awardsearch/showAward?AWD_ID=1954548 (Accessed 6 December 2023)

NSF Award Search: Award # 2302833 - Collaborative Research: An Extended Reality Factory Innovation for Adaptive Problem-Solving and Personalized Learning in Manufacturing Engineering. https://www.nsf.gov/awardsearch/showAward?AWD_ID=2302833&HistoricalAwards=false (Accessed 6 December 2023)

Otero-Varela, L., et al.: Extended reality as a training method for medical first responders in mass casualty incidents: a protocol for a systematic review. Muhammad Shahzad Aslam. PLOS ONE **18**(3), e0282698 (2023). https://doi.org/10.1371/journal.pone.0282698

Park, S.-M., Kim, Y.-G.: A Metaverse: taxonomy, components, applications, and open challenges. IEEE Access **10**, 4209–4251 (2022). https://doi.org/10.1109/ACCESS.2021.3140175

Smart Factorty Publications by Year. https://www.webofscience.com/wos/woscc/analyze-results/f40e6cf5-824c-4f7e-bed1-f75b93b5abbb-b9de75c9 (Accessed 7 December 2023)

Smart Factory Affiliations Leading Table. https://www.webofscience.com/wos/woscc/analyze-results/f40e6cf5-824c-4f7e-bed1-f75b93b5abbb-b9de75c9 (Accessed 7 December 2023)

Smart Factory Author Leading Table. https://www.webofscience.com/wos/woscc/analyze-results/f40e6cf5-824c-4f7e-bed1-f75b93b5abbb-b9de75c9 (Accessed 7 December 2023)

Stanney, K.M., Nye, H., Haddad, S., Hale, K.S., Padron, C.K., Cohn, J.V.:. "Extended reality (xr) environments. In: Salvendy, G., Karwowski, W. (eds.) Handbook of Human Factors and Ergonomics, 5th ed., pp. 782–815. Wiley (2021). https://doi.org/10.1002/9781119636113.ch30

Vadd, S., Kamarthi, S.V., Berry, N.M.: Smart sensors in a flow-line manufacturing system: an agent-based simulation. In: International Conference on Integration of Knowledge Intensive Multi-Agent Systems, Westin Hotel, Waltham, MA, USA, pp. 635–40. IEEE (2005).. https://doi.org/10.1109/KIMAS.2005.1427158

Yoon, H.: Opportunities and challenges of smartglass-assisted interactive telementoring. Appli. Syst. Innovat. **4**(3), 56 (2021). https://doi.org/10.3390/asi4030056

Research on the Risk of Radar Antenna Array Maintenance Operations in Real Working Conditions Based on Intelligent Evaluation Tools

Jingluan Wang[1](✉), Huizhong Zhang[1], Zhongjian Han[2], Yu Fan[2], and Dengkai Chen[1]

[1] Key Laboratory of Industrial Design and Ergonomics, Ministry of Industry and Information Technology, Northwestern Polytechnical University, Xi'an 710072, China
wangjingluan1@163.com
[2] The 20th Research Institute of China Electronics Technology Group Corporation, Xi'an 710072, China

Abstract. The assessment of worker posture load risk, as they interact with their work environment, is pivotal in evaluating biomechanical overload and preventing work-related musculoskeletal disorders (WMSDs). This paper investigates the application of artificial intelligence (AI) algorithms for posture risk assessment in authentic work settings. Workers' actions were recorded using smartphones, and key posture frames were extracted through pose recognition algorithms from these video samples. The key frames were digitally skeletalized, and their pose load was assessed using the Rapid Upper Limb Assessment (RULA) method. A total of 9431 key frames were extracted from a 32-min video of a single worker performing a task, after conducting two repetitive experiments. The findings demonstrate the efficacy of the method in recognizing key postures within actual work scenarios. Achieving a joint recognition accuracy of 84.6%. Moreover, 89.1% of the assessed tasks in radar antenna array maintenance resulted in upper arm scores exceeding 3 points, indicating a significant risk. This research lays a robust foundation for establishing a human-centric Industry 5.0 system, facilitating the online, real-time assessment of human posture risks.

Keywords: intelligence · risk assessment of work posture · RULA · radar antenna array · human-centric

1 Introduction

Work-related musculoskeletal disorders (WMSDs) are defined as injuries or diseases of muscles, nerves, tendons, joints, cartilage, etc. that are associated with workplace exposure to risk factors. WMSD is the second most common work-related issue globally and a hot research topic. Previous studies have shown that the incidence of diseases related to WMSD is higher in the large-scale equipment manufacturing industry, with maintenance workers being the most significant.

The radar antenna array is an important component to ensure that the radar system achieves functions such as search, tracking, and weapon guidance. It consists of thousands of components and is extremely susceptible to damage during use. Therefore, the

radar antenna array faces very frequent maintenance tasks such as component disassembly and assembly, and a single maintenance operation takes a long time (about half
an hour). Maintenance personnel need to perform frequent high-load upper limb operations, which poses a great threat to their physical health. Although industrial automation
has been widely used in production and manufacturing, it has not yet been popularized in large-scale equipment maintenance operations [3, 4]. When carrying out these
maintenance tasks, the main reliance is on the manual operation of the upper limbs
of the operators, and the manual operation process often maintains a bad posture with
high repeatability of actions and high external loads. Poor maintenance posture can lead
to muscle bone compression, insufficient blood supply, and subsequently cause muscle
soreness and injury. Long term maintenance tasks can also lead to stiffness and weakness
in the wrists and hands of maintenance personnel, reducing work efficiency, increasing
the potential risks of WMSDs, and even causing safety accidents [5].

WMSDs are not only a personal health issue, but also pose a threat to the country's economy. This not only hinders sustainable economic growth, but also incurs high
healthcare costs. Therefore, studying the dangerous postures of maintenance workers
during the work process is crucial for improving the ergonomic level of the existing
working environment and reducing the incidence of WMSDs. Ergonomic researchers
need to propose sustainable solutions to improve workers' WMSDs, maintain full work
cycle efficiency, and help workers create a safe, comfortable, and healthy working environment. This also responds to the call of Industry 5.0- "putting people at the center
and improving human well-being" [7]. Therefore, this study focuses on the core of the
workplace - "people". Studying the task risks of workers during the homework process
from the perspective of homework posture is a real scenario job risk assessment.

The traditional methods of homework risk assessment are mainly divided into three
categories: subjective reporting, physiological indicator measurement, and observation
evaluation [8]. The evaluation method based on subjective reports guides workers to
express their musculoskeletal symptoms or fatigue during the homework process through
interviews, questionnaires, and other means. Furthermore, utilizing relevant knowledge
such as statistics to analyze the musculoskeletal disorders and work risks of workers.
NMQ, DMQ, NASA-TLX, Borg, and other questionnaires or scales are the most common
subjective report based evaluation methods [9]. Frasie [10] used Borg CR10 to evaluate
shoulder fatigue during handling tasks, demonstrating that the Borg scale is an effective
tool for detecting shoulder risk in workers. The subjective report based evaluation method
has a lower cost and has been proven to be an effective method for job risk assessment
in different fields and personnel such as factories, schools, hospitals, etc. However, such
a method still requires extremely professional knowledge accumulation to accurately
discover the features hidden in the questionnaire data.

The evaluation method based on physiological indicator measurement relies on sensors directly connected to workers to monitor human physiological indicators related
to work. Physiological indicators usually include heart rate, electroencephalography,
electrodermal stimulation, respiratory rate, body temperature, and so on [11, 12]. The
decrease in frequency domain data of electromyography indicates fatigue in the human
body. This measurement method can obtain very accurate human related parameters and
has great advantages in pathological mechanisms and laboratory research, but it is not

suitable for industrial site evaluation [13]. Because directly fixing the sensor to the subject may cause discomfort, especially with wired sensors, which can also limit worker behavior.

The observation based evaluation method involves expert evaluators observing the work process and workplace environment of workers at industrial sites, and recording the risky factors in the work. Then input it into evaluation rules such as OWAS, REBA, RULA, NIOSH, QEC, etc. to determine the level of job risk [14, 15]. The observation and evaluation method is widely applicable and commonly used for industrial site evaluation, as direct observation of workers does not affect their normal work [16].

The maintenance of radar antenna arrays often takes about half an hour. Subjective reports are difficult to achieve real-time evaluation, and measurements based on physiological indicators are not suitable for industrial site evaluation. Manual observation and evaluation methods are time-consuming and labor-intensive in processing massive data. Therefore, this study is based on the intelligent algorithm proposed in previous laboratory research [17]. Apply intelligent evaluation tools to practical cases. Targeting the maintenance task of radar antenna arrays, non-intrusive video recording is used to obtain the posture data of maintenance personnel, analyze the angle and status of maintenance posture. Using RULA evaluation method to conduct risk assessment of work posture, and finally providing optimization guidance for high-risk work posture, aiming to improve the work efficiency and comfort of radar antenna array maintenance personnel.

2   Materials and Methods

2.1   Experimental Scenarios and Maintenance Tasks

This study was approved by the 20th Research Institute of China Electronics Technology Corporation. A study was conducted on the maintenance task of a certain type of vehicle mounted radar antenna array, as shown in Fig. 1. Front size: wide × high × Thickness = 2600 mm × 2550 mm × 500 mm. The TR component in the upper left corner of the radar antenna array is one of the components that is prone to failure, so the maintenance process here has been selected as the research task point. When a malfunction occurs, the maintenance worker needs to use an electric screwdriver to unscrew the screws on the cover plate of the faulty area, open it, and repair the faulty component. After the repair is completed, the cover plate needs to be reinstalled. A single repair takes a long time, during which frequent upper limb operations may occur, which can easily cause upper limb fatigue and pose certain risks.

The TR component module is located in the main frame under the cover plate at position 2 in the upper left corner of the array. The maintenance work is divided into two processes: disassembly and installation. The specific process is as follows: ① Remove the cover plate ② TR component cable ③ Remove the TR component screw ④ Replace the TR component ⑤ Install the component screw ⑥ Connect the component cable ⑦ Install the cover plate 2, as shown in Fig. 2.

Fig. 1. Real maintenance scenario of a certain type of vehicle mounted radar antenna array.

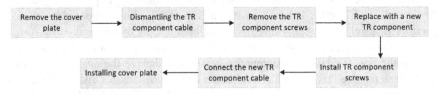

Fig. 2. TR component module maintenance task process.

2.2 Experimental Data Collection

In order to reduce costs and improve the usability of ergonomic evaluation. This study used smartphones to capture videos of maintenance personnel performing tasks throughout the entire process. In order to obtain the flexion and extension angles of the upper limbs of maintenance personnel in the sagittal plane, the posture information collection equipment for this experiment was arranged in the direction of two o'clock on the right side of the subjects, as shown in Fig. 3. Before the experiment, adjust the angle and position of the device to ensure that the viewfinder of each acquisition device can capture all the limbs of the subject. At the same time, adjust the deployment posture (pitch) angle of the radar vehicle array to ensure that the test personnel can vertically remove the top screw of the array cover plate with tools in hand. By recording the key working postures and videos of maintenance personnel on the side. A total of 32 min of maintenance operation videos were obtained, and after unfolding by frame, 9431 key operation posture images were selected.

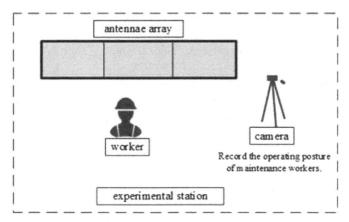

Fig. 3. Experimental environment settings.

2.3 Data Analysis Methods

The analysis of maintenance task video data is based on attitude recognition algorithms. A large number of laboratory studies have been conducted in previous studies [8, 17] to determine the accuracy of attitude recognition algorithms. This study is conducted in real work scenarios to further explore the engineering application value of the proposed method. Because a single maintenance task often takes about half an hour, the generated basic data samples are too large, the algorithm operation pressure is high, and the effective recognition rate is low. Therefore, for the continuous recognition of long-term homework posture, the posture recognition algorithm is improved by optimizing the frame by frame unfolding part of the video code, improving the clarity of the image after frame by frame unfolding, and reducing the impact of image ghosting [15].

Evaluate the recognized human task posture data using the RULA evaluation method. The RULA method divides the body into two groups, A and B, for evaluation and scoring. Group A includes both arms, forearms, and wrists. Group B includes the neck, torso, and feet. According to the angle of each body part corresponding to each static posture, check the comparison table to obtain the score of the corresponding part. Then evaluate the total score based on the scores of Group A and Group B. Different scores indicate different levels of posture load. The higher the score, the higher the posture load level. This study focuses on hand manipulation tasks, therefore paying more attention to the posture load of the upper limbs. Use the RULA evaluation method to score the upper limbs of radar antenna array maintenance workers. The scoring rules are shown in Table1.

Table 1. Table captions should be placed above the tables.

Upper arm posture	score	Additional score	Lower arm posture	score	Additional score
0° –20° or 0° –20°	1	+1 Arm extension +1 Shoulder lift −1 Support arm weight	60°–100	1	+ 1 Lower arm external expansion
20° –45 or >20°	2				
45° –90° or >20°	3		0°–60° or >25 100	2	
> 90°	4				

3   Evaluation Results

This section will use intelligent evaluation tools, including attitude recognition algorithms and RULA evaluation, to identify and assess the working posture of radar antenna array maintenance personnel. The maintenance task videos collected on site are input into the intelligent evaluation tool for human joint point recognition, and the human operation posture skeleton is reconstructed from the original image. Figure 4 shows the recognition results of key operational poses on the radar antenna array. Due to the large amount of data, 150 recognition result images were randomly selected for display. From the Fig. 4, it can be seen that when workers work continuously, the recognition of human joint points is relatively accurate, and the recognition of the skeleton of the upper limb work posture is still relatively complete, which can effectively track the changes in the worker's work posture. When there is severe occlusion on the left side, there is also a situation where the joint points are not recognized.

Fig. 4. Key working posture skeleton recognition effect.

This study further extracted recognition accuracy scores for the three joint points of the right shoulder, right elbow, and right wrist, as shown in Fig. 5. The accuracy score for right shoulder joint recognition is 0.808 (0.037), the accuracy score for right elbow joint recognition is 0.851 (0.046), and the accuracy score for right wrist joint recognition is 0.878 (0.052). In addition, we also counted the proportion of unrecognized joints, with 2.3% of work posture images not recognizing the right shoulder joint, 3.4% of work posture images not recognizing the right elbow joint, and 5.5% of work posture images not recognizing the right wrist joint. Although the recognition accuracy of intelligent evaluation tools in real industrial maintenance environments is slightly lower compared to laboratory results, the overall recognition accuracy of joint points has also reached over 80%, and the loss rate is also less than 6%. This is still a good result in the risk assessment of work posture in the on-site environment.

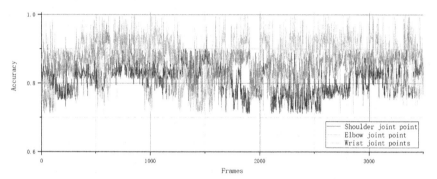

Fig. 5. Accuracy score for identifying joint points.

Using the coordinate data of the joint points, the angles of the upper and lower arms of the radar maintenance personnel were calculated. Figure 6 shows the process of the changes in the angles of the upper and lower arms of the maintenance personnel throughout the entire operation process. During the entire 32-min homework process, the average upper arm angle reached 90.51° (± 40.25°). The proportion of work postures with upper arm angles greater than 90° reached 45.3%, work postures with angles between 90° and 45° accounted for 44.2%, and work postures with angles less than 45° accounted for 10.5%. The average lower arm angle of radar maintenance personnel is 59.14° (± 38.22°), with 15.7% working positions having a forearm bending angle greater than 100°, 35.8% working positions having a normal angle between 60° and 100°, and 48.5% working positions having a lower angle than 60°.

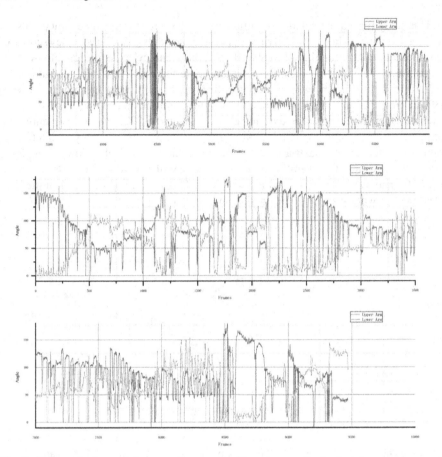

Fig. 6. Changes in the angle between the upper and lower arms of radar maintenance personnel.

Based on intelligent evaluation and recognition, the RULA evaluation method was used to further assess the risk of upper and lower arm angles in radar maintenance operations, as shown in Fig. 7. In the radar maintenance task, the average upper arm score reached 3.29 ($\pm$ 0.77), and 89.1% of the work positions scored higher than 3 (with the highest upper arm risk score of 4). The average lower arm score reached 1.63 ($\pm$ 0.48), and 63.5% of the homework positions scored 2.

In order to improve the operational efficiency and comfort of radar antenna array maintenance personnel, this study analyzed the highest risk sub task of dismantling the top screws of the cover plate 2 (Subtask A) and the lowest risk sub task of dismantling the bottom screws of the cover plate 2 (Subtask B) from the maintenance operation video. In these two sub tasks, the comparison of the angles of the maintenance personnel's upper and lower arms is shown in Fig. 8, and the comparison of the risk assessment scores of the upper and lower arms is shown in Fig. 9.

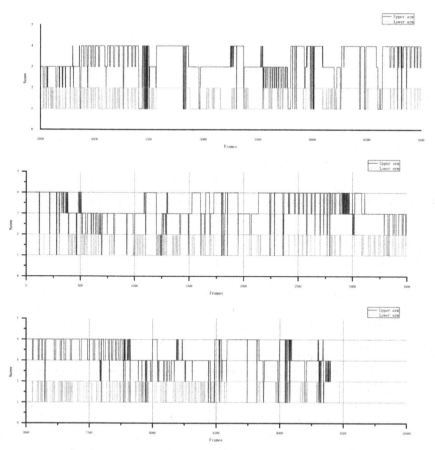

Fig. 7. Changes in risk assessment scores for upper and lower arms of radar maintenance personnel.

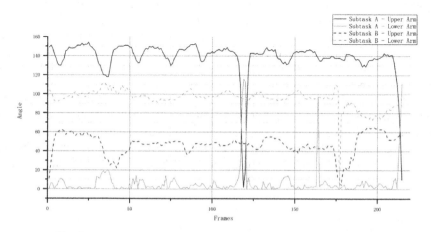

Fig. 8. Comparison of upper and lower arm angles for two subtasks.

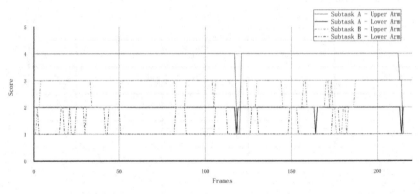

Fig. 9. Comparison of Risk Assessment Scores for Upper and Lower Arms in Two Subtasks.

4 Discussion

This study adopted an intelligent maintenance posture recognition and risk assessment method, and conducted a comprehensive evaluation of radar antenna array maintenance operations under the condition that the actual working environment does not interfere with the normal work of maintenance personnel, exploring the adverse posture of radar antenna array maintenance operations. This study applies the intelligent evaluation tools proposed in previous studies to actual case assessments, which will provide a more convenient and realistic tool for risk assessment in the field of ergonomics in the future.

In terms of joint recognition accuracy, the actual joint recognition accuracy in the environment is 0.846, which is slightly worse than the results of previous laboratory studies [8], but slightly better than the results of Chen et al. [18] (0.712). The complexity of the background environment makes the recognition process more difficult to determine. In addition, we also found an interesting point that the accuracy of shoulder joint recognition is lower than that of wrist joint recognition, but the loss rate is much lower. We understand that it is because workers wear heavier workwear, which obstructs the recognition of shoulder joints and exposes the wrist more. However, due to the greater mobility of the wrist, it is also easy for the wrist joints to be lost in recognition.

During the entire radar maintenance task, the average upper arm angle of the maintenance personnel's work posture reached 90° and remained at a relatively large angle, posing a high risk to the workers' upper arms. The angle of the lower arm of the maintenance personnel's work posture is relatively small, which is related to the fact that the work posture is usually a straight arm operation. The RULA evaluation method was used to assess the risk level of key work postures for maintenance personnel, and the results further proved the high risk of radar maintenance tasks. Finally, by comparing the perspectives and risk assessment scores of the two sub tasks, it was found that the height of the work surface is the main factor contributing to the high risk of radar maintenance operations.

5   Conclusions

Maintenance workers often need to interact with various mechanical equipment and handheld tools. Frequent upper limb operations bring them many potential risks. This study uses intelligent evaluation tools to evaluate the upper limb operations of radar antenna array maintenance workers. Compared with the current research that mainly focuses on laboratory simulation tasks, this study applies pose recognition algorithms and intelligent evaluation tools to real work scenarios, improving the application value of artificial intelligence algorithms. Lowered the threshold for the use of ergonomic evaluation methods. The research results show that high load postures account for a higher proportion in maintenance tasks. In subsequent research, it is necessary to analyze the high load posture during the maintenance process and find ways to solve the high load risk posture. Efforts should be made to improve the ergonomic level of maintenance operations through multi-channel optimization.

Acknowledgments. This work was supported by the "Basic Strengthening Plan Foundation of China" [grant number: 2021-JCJQ-JJ-1018], the "Innovation Foundation for Doctor Dissertation of Northwestern Polytechnical University" [grant number: CX2023049] and the "National Key R&D Program of China" [grant number: 2021YFC2800600].

Disclosure of Interests. The authors have no competing interests to declare that are relevant to the content of this article.

References

1. Liang, J., Jia, N., Zhang, F., et al.: Shoulder work-related musculoskeletal disorders and related factors of workers in 15 industries of China: a cross-sectional study. BMC Musculoskelet. Disord. **23**(1), 952 (2022)
2. Yang, Y., Lyu, L., Han, Z., et al.: Ergonomics assessment of the overhead maintenance of vehicle-mounted radar antenna using digital human modelling. Adv. Design Res. **1**(2), 63–70 (2023)
3. Ozdemir, R., Sarigol, I., AlMutairi, S., et al.: Fuzzy multi-objective model for assembly line balancing with ergonomic risks consideration. Int. J. Prod. Econ. **239**, 108188 (2021)
4. Battini, D., Berti, N., Finco, S., et al.: WEM-Platform: A real-time platform for full-body ergonomic assessment and feedback in manufacturing and logistics systems. Comput. Indust. Eng. **164**, 107881 (2022)
5. Clément, J., Raison, M., Rouleau, D.: Reproducibility analysis of upper limbs reachable workspace, and effects of acquisition protocol, sex and hand dominancy. J. Biomech. **68**, 58–64 (2018)
6. Buchbinder, R., Hartvigsen, J., Maher, C.: The lancet series call to action to reduce low value care for low back pain: an update. Pain **161**(Supplement 1), 57–64 (2020)
7. Wang, L.: A futuristic perspective on human-centric assembly. J. Manuf. Syst. **62**, 199–201 (2022)
8. Wang, J., Chen, D., Zhu, M., et al.: Risk assessment for musculoskeletal disorders based on the characteristics of work posture. Autom. Constr. **131**, 103921 (2021)
9. Aziz, A., Karuppiah, K., Suhaimi, N., et al.: Footrest intervention: association between prolonged standing and perceived exertion in the body parts among industrial workers using Borg's scale questionnaire. Int. J. Ind. Ergon. **76**, 102898 (2020)

10. Frasie, A., Bertrand-Charette, M., Compagnat, M., et al.: Validation of the Borg CR10 Scale for the evaluation of shoulder perceived fatigue during work-related tasks. Appl. Ergon. **116**, 104200 (2024)

11. Venugopal, G., Navaneethakrishna, M., Ramakrishnan, S.: Extraction and analysis of multiple time window features associated with muscle fatigue conditions using sEMG signals. **41**(6), 2652–2659 (2014)

12. Strimpakos, N., Georgios, G., Eleni, K., et al.: Issues in relation to the repeatability of and correlation between EMG and Borg scale assessments of neck muscle fatigue. J. Electromyogr. Kinesiol. **15**(5), 452–465 (2005)

13. Peternel, L., Fang, C., Tsagarakis, N., et al.: A selective muscle fatigue management approach to ergonomic human-robot co-manipulation. Robot. Comput.-Integrated Manufact. **58**, 69–79 (2019)

14. Su, J., Chang, J., Indrayani, N., et al.: Machine learning approach to determine the decision rules in ergonomic assessment of working posture in sewing machine operators. J. Safety Res. **87**, 15–26 (2023)

15. Huang, K., Jia, G., Wang, Q., et al.: Spatial relationship-aware rapid entire body fuzzy assessment method for prevention of work-related musculoskeletal disorders. Appl. Ergon. **115**, 104176 (2024)

16. Micheletti, C., Giustetto, A., Caffaro, F., et al.: Risk assessment for musculoskeletal disorders in forestry: a comparison between rula and reba in the manual feeding of a wood-chipper. Int. J. Environ. Res. Public Health **16**(5), 793 (2019)

17. Wang, J., Chen, D., Zhang, X., et al.: Real-time anthropometric data-driven evaluation method for complex console layout design. Comput. Ind. Eng. **183**, 109463 (2023)

18. Su, K., Yu, D., Xu, Z., et al.: Multi-person pose estimation with enhanced channel-wise and spatial information. In: 2019 IEEE/CVF Conference on Computer Vision and Pattern Recognition (CVPR), Long Beach, CA, USA, pp. 5674–5682 (2019)

Trend Analysis of AR-Assisted Assembly Visualization Design Based on Bibliometrics

Lei Wu, Yufan Lin, and Junfeng Wang[✉]

School of Mechanical Science and Engineering, Huazhong University of Science and
Technology, Wuhan 430074, People's Republic of China
wangjf@hust.edu.cn

Abstract. Based on the bibliometric method, this study systematically comprehended the global characteristics of the research on visualization design for AR-assisted assembly, investigated the current research hotspots and theoretical foundations of visualization design for AR-assisted assembly, and explored the new trends of future development. Taking the relevant literature collected by Web of Science as the data source, the VOSviewer scientific bibliometric method was comprehensively used to sort out and visualize the research lineage in terms of publication trends, high-frequency keywords, high-frequency areas, organizations, main publications, and highly cited papers. The conclusion of the study shows that in the research field of visualization design for AR-assisted assembly, China and the United States are tied for the first place in terms of the number of publications, Germany ranks second and Italy ranks third. The top three important research institutions are Northwestern Polytechnic University, National University of Singapore and University of Patras. The main research hotspots are augmented reality, design, system, assembly, visualization, maintenance, industry 4.0. In this paper, the research status, development trend, and research hotspots in the research field of visualization design for AR-assisted assembly are visualized and analyzed, which is of corresponding guiding significance to the related researchers.

Keyword: AR-assisted assembly · Visualization design · Bibliometrics · VOSviewer

1 Introduction

Assembly refers to the assembly of several components following the established installation sequence and accuracy requirements, under the specifications, reasonable process flow, and then after appropriate debugging to meet the inspection specifications, and finally become a finished product. In product manufacturing, assembly is the last process of the production process, but also a critical step. Assembly is an important stage in the product development process, the assembly workload accounts for 20% to 70% of the entire product development workload, an average of 45%, and the assembly time accounts for 40% to 60% of the entire manufacturing time [1], the assembly in the overall production costs accounted for 30% to 50% or more. Therefore, the improvement of product assembly process planning is the key to improve the manufacturing process chain.

V. G. Duffy (Ed.): HCII 2024, LNCS 14711, pp. 141–152, 2024.
https://doi.org/10.1007/978-3-031-61066-0_10

Currently, many high-end complex products (such as automobiles, engines, aerospace equipment, etc.) assembly process is difficult to automate, still rely on manual operation, especially for highly customized or highly complex products. For example, in automobile manufacturing, the assembly of the body and chassis is usually automated, while the final assembly of the interior and electrical equipment is usually manual. The assembly process faces problems such as the large number of assembly steps, the need for empirical skill in the assembly process, and the high degree of similarity of the assembled parts, which places extreme demands on the operators. As programs become more flexible and reconfigurable, interfaces that support manual assembly become increasingly necessary.

Augmented reality is a technology that superimposes computer-generated virtual information on a real environment and finally displays it through a display device. The most important feature of augmented reality lies in the real-time fusion of virtual reality, by mixing and blending the reality with the superimposed annotations and information, a clearer view can be created [2], so augmented reality has a significant advantage in conveying technical information in the industrial field [3]. Augmented assembly refers to the use of augmented reality technology to assist the assembly process, through the superimposition of appropriate virtual information in the real assembly environment, such as three-dimensional models, text, animation, to provide instruction information for the operator in the assembly process, aiming to enhance the assembly efficiency, improve the quality of the assembly, and reduce the cost of assembly training. The AR-assisted assembly system can provide workers with a virtual and real complementary assembly environment, so that the workers can obtain the information needed during the assembly operation promptly, such as the current operation steps, the parts to be assembled, the assembly skills and precautions, and whether or not the assembly is correct. Compared with the traditional assembly instruction manuals, the assisted assembly system can alleviate the cognitive and memorization burden of the operators, thus significantly improving assembly efficiency and reducing assembly error.

Complex product assembly instruction information has many contents (e.g., operation sequence, tool use, quality requirements, auxiliary material selection, safety warning, etc.), and the traditional paper assembly instruction document mainly expresses the information in the form of text and static pictures. Under the augmented reality environment, the expression of assembly instruction information has increased the number of 3d models, 3d animations, and other forms of visualization (e.g., video, dynamic labeling, etc.) [4]. Inappropriate use of assembly guidance information can easily lead to assembly errors, and it has been pointed out that 60% of assembly errors are caused by misinterpretation of the information [5], and the expression of assembly guidance information has a significant role in augmented visualization assembly guidance aimed at assisting the operator [6].

2   Methods

2.1   Experiment Methodology

The bibliometric method is one of the mainstream methods of literature research, VOSviewer software utilizes the means of visualization of the scientific knowledge map, both visualizes knowledge graphics, but also serializes knowledge genealogy can intuitively and accurately show the evolution of a discipline or knowledge field in a certain period and trend trends in the development of the evolution of the course of movement, has become an important tool that has been widely used in the study of bibliometrics.

In this paper, VOSviewer is adopted as the research tool platform, and the research literature on visualization design of AR-assisted assembly published in the Web of Science database during 1999–2023 is downloaded and exported from the Web of Science database in txt format, and then imported into VOS viewer software in accordance with the needs of the research content, and then analyze the data.

2.2   Experiment Data Source

To ensure the quality and academic value of the research, the core data collection of the Web of Science database is selected as the literature data source of this paper. In the process of literature data collection, the core data collection of the Web of Science database is selected as the literature source, and the search condition is "subject: (assembly) AND subject: (AR OR Augmented Reality) AND subject: (interface design OR user interface OR visualization OR visual design OR graphic design OR graphic)", and after a rigorous process, we select the core data collection of Web of Science database as the literature source. After strict screening and elimination of the literature that did not meet the theme of AR-assisted assembly, a total of 319 articles were selected as research samples.

3   Experiment Results

3.1   Publication Trends

A total of 355 documents were retrieved from 1999–2023, and a total of 36 documents were excluded according to the exclusion criteria, resulting in the inclusion of 319 research documents. As shown in Fig. 1, from the number of studies, the number of publications on AR-assisted assembly visualization design in WOS from 1999 to 2023 shows a rapid growth trend over time: 2 publications in 2004, 25 publications in 2016, 44 publications in 2022, and 21 publications in 2023. This indicates that the overall academic interest in visualization design research for AR-assisted assembly is increasing and it has become a research hotspot.

3.2   High-Frequency Keywords

Based on the data acquisition method in the previous section, the keywords frequency of the research literature on visualization and design for AR-assisted assembly in WOS

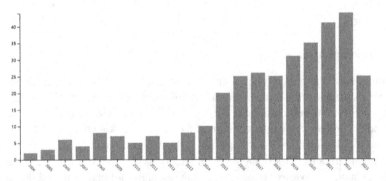

Fig. 1. Publication trends of AR-assisted assembly visualization design

from 1999 to 2023 were sorted, as shown in Table 1 and Fig. 2. The keywords frequency from high to low are augmented reality, design, system, assembly, visualization, maintenance, and industry 4.0. Among them, maintenance, industry 4.0, manufacturing, remote collaboration, and human-robot collaboration appeared 24, 23, 11, 9, and 6 times, respectively, indicating that these are popular application areas of AR-assisted assembly. Augmented reality, virtual reality, mixed reality, simulation, tracking, framework, and human-centered computing appear 177, 23, 20, 12, 7, and 6 times respectively, indicating that these are the hot technologies related to AR-assisted assembly. Direction. As shown in Fig. 2, different colors represent different clusters, and the color, size, and clustering results of the nodes are used to interpret the strength of different clusters and their interaction relationships.

Table 1. High-frequency co-occurrences keywords

No	Keyword	Freq	No	Keyword	Freq
1	augmented reality	177	11	manufacturing	11
2	design	47	12	technology	10
3	system	30	13	performance	9
4	assembly	27	14	remote collaboration	9
5	visualization	27	15	tracking	8
6	maintenance	24	16	augmented reality applications	7
7	industry 4.0	23	17	framework	7
8	virtual reality	23	18	human-centered computing	7
9	mixed reality	20	19	interface	7
10	simulation	12	20	human-robot collaboration	6

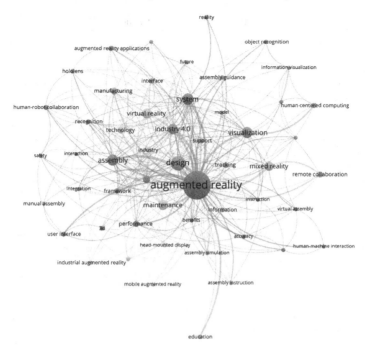

Fig. 2. Time visualization of high-frequency co-occurrence keywords

3.3 High-Frequency Areas

The number of papers indexed by SCI and the citation frequency reflect the overall scientific research strength and influence of a country/region. A total of 44 countries/regions, including China, USA, Germany, Italy, Singapore, etc., have published research papers on visualization design for AR-assisted assembly, which were retrieved from the Web of Science core collection database. Sorting the countries/regions of AR-assisted assembly visualization design research in Web of Science from 1999–2023, the countries/regions with top 10 publications are shown in Table 2.

Using VOSviewer software to make a cooperation relationship graph between countries in the world of AR-assisted assembly visualization design research, the size of the circle in the graph indicates the degree of activity and the number of articles published in a certain country/region, and the distance of the connecting line between the countries/regions indicates the degree of cooperation between the countries/regions, and the smaller the distance is, the closer the cooperation is between the countries/regions. The smaller the distance, the closer the cooperation between countries/regions. From Fig. 3, it can be seen that China and the USA are the most active countries with 53 articles published, followed by Germany with 44 articles published, but China's research started later, and Singapore and Finland started relatively earlier.

Table 2. The top 10 most high-frequency areas

No	Country / Region	Amount
1	China	53
2	USA	53
3	Germany	44
4	Italy	17
5	Singapore	13
6	Australia	10
7	Greece	10
8	Japan	9
9	France	8
10	Portugal	8

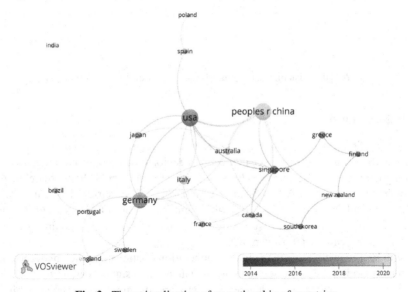

Fig. 3. Time visualization of co-authorship of countries

3.4 Organizations

Through the analysis, the research papers in this field involve 298 research institutions, and the top 10 research institutions are shown in Table 3. Northwestern Polytechnic University has 22 publications in the research field of visualization and design for AR-assisted assembly from 1999–2023, which is higher than that of the second-ranked institutions such as National University of Singapore (9 articles) and University of Patras (9 articles). Figure 4 represents a diagram of the cooperation between important research institutions in this field, from which it can be seen that the cooperation between each research institution, in which the cooperation between each research institution is weak and needs to be strengthened.

Table 3. The top 10 most productive organizations

No	Organization	Amount
1	Northwestern Polytechnic University	22
2	National University of Singapore	9
3	University of Patras	9
4	Iowa State University	7
5	University of South Australia	6
6	Politecnico di Bari	5
7	Virginia Polytechnic Institute and State University	5
8	Columbia University	4
9	Huazhong University of Science and Technology	4
10	National Tsing Hua University	4

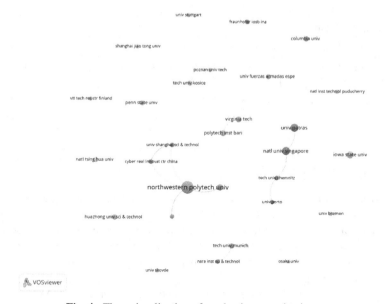

Fig. 4. Time visualization of productive organizations

3.5 Main Publications

An analysis of journals in a particular field of study identifies the core journals that are SCI sources in that field. The impact factor is a method of calculating the influence of a journal, i.e., the total number of citations of papers published by a journal in the previous two years in the year of counting divided by the total number of papers published by the journal within the previous two years. A total of 262 journals in this field participated, and the top 10 journals in terms of the number of publications are shown in Table 4. International journal of advanced manufacturing technology, the first journal in terms of the number of publications, has an impact factor of 3.4. The second and the third publications with the highest number of published papers were conference paper publications. Computers in industry, the fourth journal with the highest number of publications, has an impact factor of 10.

Table 4. The top 10 most productive publications

No	Main publications	Amount
1	International Journal of Advanced Manufacturing Technology	20
2	Lecture Notes in Artificial Intelligence	17
3	Procedia CIRP	10
4	Computers in Industry	7
5	Robotics and Computer-integrated Manufacturing	6
6	Applied Sciences-Basel	5
7	Journal of Manufacturing Systems	5
8	CIRP Annals-manufacturing Technology	4
9	2022 IEEE Conference on Virtual Reality and 3D User Interfaces Abstracts and Workshops (VRW 2022)	4
10	International Symposium on Mixed and Augmented Reality	4

3.6 Highly Cited Papers

The citation frequency of an article reflects, to a certain extent, the degree of attention paid to a certain research work, and can show the extent to which scientific papers are used and valued in the research process, as well as their role and status in academic communication. In the current research evaluation, the citation frequency is increasingly used as an indicator of the importance of a paper. The top 10 cited frequency papers in this field are shown in Table 5.

"Augmented reality applications in design and manufacturing" by AYC Nee et al. from the department of mechanical engineering, National University of Singapore, published in 2012, reviews the research and development of augmented reality applications in design and manufacturing applications research and development, as well as its technical challenges and industrial applications, and explores human factors and interactions in AR systems and future trends and developments.

"A comprehensive survey of augmented reality assembly research" by Wang, Xiaogang et al. from the National University of Singapore, provides a brief overview of the technical features, characteristics, and wide range of applications of AR-based assembly systems published between 1990 and 2015, and discusses current constraints and future trends.

Table 5. The top 10 highly cited papers

No	Highly cited papers	Citations
1	Augmented reality applications in design and manufacturing	409
2	A comprehensive survey of augmented reality assembly research	266
3	Augmented reality on large screen for interactive maintenance instructions	124
4	CAD model based virtual assembly simulation, planning and training	105
5	Augmented Reality-Based Manual Assembly Support with Visual Features for Different Degrees of Difficulty	104
6	Augmented reality application to support remote maintenance as a service in the Robotics industry	103
7	Augmented reality (AR) applications for supporting human-robot interactive cooperation	97
8	AR-based interaction for human-robot collaborative manufacturing	94
9	Using Augmented Reality to Facilitate Piping Assembly: An Experiment-Based Evaluation	93
10	Evaluating the Microsoft HoloLens through an augmented reality assembly application	88

4 Discussion

4.1 AR-Assisted Assembly Visualization in Comparison to Traditional Assembly

Most studies have shown that AR-assisted assembly information visualization is significantly improved compared to traditional paper-based manual, particularly in terms of improving assembly performance (reduction in assembly time and reduction in assembly errors). Fiorentino (2014) presented an empirical study evaluating the effectiveness of interactive augmented reality instruction-assisted maintenance, where 14 participants performed four maintenance tasks in a complete four maintenance tasks on a motorcycle engine using both paper manuals and AR-enhanced instructions, and statistical analysis proved that the augmented instructions significantly reduced the overall execution time and error rate of the participants [7]. Moghaddam (2021) used an electromechanical component of an engine to instruct the assembly process in both a paper manual and a helmeted AR approach, and the findings, on the other hand, showed that both approaches had almost the same load levels in six aspects of TLX, but the helmet AR approach had a significant advantage in reducing assembly errors [8]. Qin (2023) proposed an electroencephalogram (EEG)-based assessment of the workload of assembling a timber frame for construction, along with a task performance analysis of completion rate and accuracy. The use of an AR head-mounted display improved assembly efficiency and significantly increased completion rates compared to paper displays. The AR display group maintained a lower cognitive load and less fluctuation (standard deviation) throughout the assembly process [9].

However, some studies also showed that the overall cognitive load of AR-assisted assembly increased instead compared to the traditional mode, which may be related to the individual operator, the assembly object and complexity, the weight of the AR hardware, the field of view angle, etc. Deshpande (2018) designed the assembly of multilayered office furniture by applying the quantitative metrics of the number of parts, symmetry, and the use of screws for both simple and complex two types of assembly tasks, and the post-test TLX analysis showed that the helmet AR approach slightly increased the overall workload over the paper manual approach to assisted assembly, which correlated with the weight and field of view angle of the AR helmet. The data also showed that the AR approach can significantly reduce the completion time of complex assembly tasks and the number of assembly errors [10]. Chu (2020) used the arch assembly of Chinese architectural structures as an example, and the TLX scores of paper manuals, 3D virtual animation browsing, and hand-held AR obtained through the experiments showed that the hand-held mobile AR approach had the highest overall workload and the second highest cerebral load, which may be attributed to the following reasons caused by the operator's unfamiliarity and discomfort with the interaction method of AR-assisted assembly [11].

4.2 AR-Assisted Assembly Visualization Between Different Carriers

There are various ways of presenting AR, such as screen-based AR, handheld AR, and helmet-based AR, and these different vehicles can also significantly affect the practical use of AR-assisted assembly visualization. In most studies, screen-based AR brings minimal mental load to workers, while hand-held and helmet-mounted AR performs poorly due to the heavy hand or head burden. Alves (2022) evaluated three different AR-based methods, which set up an assembly task with 18 blocks to build three different assemblies, and the TLX data showed that screen-fixed AR has the least mental load, hand-held AR and helmet-mounted AR have the least mental load, and hand-held AR and helmet-mounted AR have the least mental load. Helmet-mounted ARs performed poorly due to the high hand or head occupancy burden [12].

4.3 AR-Assisted Assembly Visualization in Visual Design

In the AR environment, there are a wider variety of visualization options. Research has shown that dynamic information is more efficient and less cognitively taxing than static information, and that text attributes have a great impact on assembly efficiency and quality (blue text on a white background with outlines is more readable). Pictures reduce the assembly time and cognitive load of the assembler compared to text and numbers. Different auxiliary information shows different effects in tasks of different complexity (showing hand movements reduces harder assembly times).

Hou L (2013) conducted LEGO model assembly experiments using AR, and the animated AR system showed shorter task completion times, fewer assembly errors, and a lower total task load. Experimental results also showed a shorter learning curve and improved task performance related to working memory for novice assemblers when using AR training [13]. Hou L (2013) found that AR training helped both male and female beginner assemblers learn the assembly process more quickly and that 3D manual-based training was more effective for male beginner assemblers [14]. Hou L (2015) evaluated the performance of a prototype scenario through collaborative development and obtained that AR-assisted assembly improves accuracy and reduces errors, with animated forms of AR performing better than static AR [15]. Gattullo M (2015) conducted experiments to investigate the effect of attributes such as font type, size, color, and texture of the assembly text message on assembly time and errors, showing that textual attributes have a large impact on both assembly efficiency and quality [16]. Wang, X (2016) study focused on validating the effectiveness of different auxiliary information in AR, including the assembly interface, operator hand movements, and handheld components. Whether each type of information was effective in providing guidance was obtained by measuring performance (assembly time, errors in the process) by filling out the NASA-TLX questionnaire as well as by interviews: showing operator hand motion reduced harder assembly times, and hand modeling gave the operator a visual cue to quickly and roughly locate the assembly interface in large unseen areas, and then to pinpoint the location in smaller areas through haptic perception. However, the effectiveness of information containing handheld components is not obvious, as positional deviations between actual and virtual objects may reduce human hand-eye coordination [17]. Brolin, Anna Z (2016) showed in an experimental study of pedal bike assembly in a mixed-flow model that the use of a combination of textual and digitally-expressed guidance information for the assembly operation would increase the cognitive load, whereas guidance information in the form of pictures was able to reduce the product assembly time and the cognitive load of assemblers [18].

5 Conclusion

In this paper, based on the bibliometric data in the AR-assisted assembly visualization design, we analyze the relevant literature included in the WOS database from 1999 to 2023. The conclusion of the study shows that China and the United States are the activist countries in the research field of AR-assisted assembly visualization design, followed by Germany, and Italy is ranked third. The main research hotspots are augmented reality, design, system, assembly, visualization, maintenance, industry 4.0.

Strengths and limitations of this study: the data analysis of this study objectively and clearly demonstrates the general trend of global research on visualization design for AR-assisted assembly as well as the boundaries of the research, which can be used as a reference for researchers who are interested in carrying out more in-depth studies in this field. However, there are some limitations, this study only collected articles from the Web of Science database, so it may have missed other relevant articles in the literature. In addition, since this study only included publications published in the Web of Science core collection, publications in other databases that were not examined may have hidden some ideas in this research area.

Acknowledgments. The authors acknowledge the support from the National Natural Science Foundation of China (72271100).

References

1. Liu, J., et al.: The State-of-the-art, connotation and developing trends of the products assembly technology. J. Mech. Eng. **54**(11), 2–28 (2018)
2. Keil J., Schmitt F., Engelke T., et al.: Augmented Reality Views: Discussing the Utility of Visual Elements by Mediation Means in Industrial AR from a Design Perspective. In: Chen, Je.Y. C., Fragomeni, G. (eds.) Virtual, Augmented and Mixed Reality: Applications in Health, Cultural Heritage, and Industry, pp. 298–312. Springer International Publishing (2018). https://doi.org/10.1007/978-3-319-91584-5_24
3. Gattullo, M., et al.: What, how, and why are visual assets used in industrial augmented reality? a systematic review and classification in maintenance, assembly, and training (from 1997 to 2019). IEEE Trans. Visual Comput. Graphics **28**(2), 1443–1456 (2022)
4. Li, W., Wang, J., Jiao, S., et al.: Research on the visual elements of augmented reality assembly process. Virt. Real. Intell. Hardware. **1**(6), 622–634 (2019)
5. Johansson P., Malmsköld L., Fast-Berglunå., et al.: Challenges of handling assembly information in global manufacturing companies. J. Manufact. Technol. Manag. **31**(5), 955–976 (2020)
6. Wang, J., Li, W., Fu, Y., Wu, L.: Research progress on human factor adaptability in augmented reality assisted assembly. J. Mech. Eng. **58**(18), 16–30 (2022)
7. Fiorentino, M., et al.: Augmented reality on large screen for interactive maintenance instructions. Comput. Industry. **65**(2), 270–278 (2014)
8. Moghaddam, M., Wilson, N.C., Modestino, A., et al.: Exploring augmented reality for worker assistance versus training. Adv. Eng. Inform. **50**(4), 101410 (2021)
9. Qin, Y., Bulbul, T.: An EEG-Based mental workload evaluation for AR head-mounted display use in construction assembly task. J. Constr. Eng. Manag. **149**(9), 04023088 (2023)
10. Deshpande, A., Kim, I.: The effects of augmented reality on improving spatial problem solving for object assembly. Adv. Eng. Inform. **38**, 760–775 (2018)
11. Chu, C.H., Liao, C.J., Lin, S.C.: Comparing augmented reality-assisted assembly functions-a case study on dougong structure. Appl. Sci. **10**(10), 3383 (2020)
12. Alves, J.B., Marques, B., Ferreira, C., et al.: Comparing augmented reality visualization methods for assembly procedure. Virt. Reality **26**(1), 235–248 (2022)
13. Hou, L., Wang, X.Y., Bernold, L., et al.: Using animated augmented reality to cognitively guide assembly. J. Comput. Civ. Eng. **27**(5), 439–451 (2013)
14. Hou, L., Wang, X.Y.: A study on the benefits of augmented reality in retaining working memory in assembly tasks: a focus on differences in gender. Autom. Constr. **32**, 38–45 (2013)
15. Hou, L., Wang, X.Y., Truijens, M.: Using Augmented reality to facilitate piping assembly: an experiment-based evaluation. J. Comput. Civ. Eng. **29**(1), 05014007 (2015)
16. Gattullo, M., Uva, A.E., Fiorentino, M., et al.: Legibility in Industrial AR: text Style, Color Coding, and Illuminance. IEEE Comput. Graphics Appl. **35**(2), 52–61 (2015)
17. Wang, X., Ong, S.K., NEE, A.Y.C.: Multi-modal augmented-reality assembly guidance based on bare-hand interface. Adv. Eng. Inform. **30**(3), 406–421 (2016)
18. Brolin, A,Z.: An Investigation of Cognitive Aspects Affecting Human Performance in Manual Assembly. Doctoral dissertation, Loughborough University (2016)

Research on the Process Efficiency of Metro Security CheckSystem Under the Perspective of Spatial Guidance

Yihong Yuan, Haoze Zhang[✉], Ruolei OuYang, Jinbang Tan, and Yaodong Shen

South China University of Technology, Guangzhou, China
975882285@qq.com

Abstract. Metro is one of the most important forms of public transportation in Chinese cities. With the continuous expansion and development of metro networks in China's major cities, ensuring the safety of passengers has become a key part of metro operation and management. However, there are some efficiency and human factors engineering deficiencies in the current metro security system. Some researchers have studied the efficiency of subway security systems and their influencing factors in subway or railroad stations. However, in actual subway stations, the spatial guidance in front of and behind the screening area is also one of the causes of congestion in the screening area. This study focuses on the deficiencies of spatial guidance in the subway, and the resulting congestion in the subway station, which leads to a reduction in the efficiency of the screening system. The implementation plan of this study is to explore the spatial guidance system of Guangzhou Metro, summarize the influencing factors of congestion, quantify and extract data for the influencing factors, and establish a model and data analysis. The interview method was used to invite volunteers to participate, and the information from the interviews was used for data statistics to quantify the influencing factors caused by the spatial guidance system, to establish an appropriate model for the influencing factors, and to determine the significant influencing factors of the spatial guidance on the congestion of people with respect to the data fed back from the model. The collected data and information are coded using the rooted theory research method, analyzed with the help of auxiliary software, and finally, three categories of first-level core influence factors of site layout design, guide signs, and human factors and corresponding second- and third-level subcategories are refined, and a system of influence factors on the efficiency of the process of the security system under the perspective of spatial guidance is constructed.

Keywords: Subway security screening · Spatial guidance · Human factors engineering · Rootedness theory

1 Introduction

Metro is one of the most important forms of public transportation in Chinese cities, and it is the preferred choice for citizens to travel in a fast and convenient way. With the continuous expansion and development of metro networks in China's major cities, ensuring

V. G. Duffy (Ed.): HCII 2024, LNCS 14711, pp. 153–161, 2024.
https://doi.org/10.1007/978-3-031-61066-0_11

passenger safety has become a key aspect of metro operation and management. Therefore, China's subways have adopted strict security measures, including the screening of passengers' luggage and passengers themselves. However, there are some efficiency and human factors engineering deficiencies in the current metro security system. Several researchers have studied the efficiency of metro security systems and their influencing factors in subway or railroad stations, and previous work has focused on analyzing the factors of security equipment, staff, security processes, and passengers themselves in the security screening area. However, in actual subway station scenarios, the spatial guidance before and after the screening area is also one of the reasons for the phenomenon of congestion in the screening area. Without good spatial guidance, the flow of people entering and leaving the security check area will further increase the congestion and confusion in the security check area. This study focuses on the inadequacy of spatial guidance in the subway, and the resulting congestion in the subway station, which in turn leads to a reduction in the efficiency of the security system. Information was collected through field research using user interviews, and the results were quantitatively evaluated to determine the main factors contributing to congestion. It is hoped that a set of guidelines can be provided for the management and planning of urban subway stations.

1.1 Methods

In order to better discover the deficiencies of spatial guidance in the subway, we conducted an in-depth study on the security service time and its influencing factors before and after passengers pass through the security machine during the peak period. The main research methods are as follows:

1.2 Pre-experimental Planning

1. Field collection of videos of the security check process in subway stations within Guangzhou City was used to comprehensively examine objective elements such as spatial layout, guidance system and manual evacuation in subway stations;
2. Use interviews to collect user experience data and quantify and analyze the results using the method of programmed rooting theory;
3. Combined with the final quantitative data, establish a set of universally adaptable model of the factors influencing the process efficiency of the security check system under the perspective of spatial guidance, analyze the influencing factors and validate the model, and finally give suggestions to improve the efficiency of the security check.

1.3 Location Selection and Research

The field research location was selected Zhujiang New City subway station, the reason is that the subway station is a metro station in the center of Guangzhou City with a large flow of passengers, its internal passages are more and more complex structure, there are more security checkpoints, so it is representative, but also more likely to reveal the actual problem. We choose Friday night at 8:00 p.m. to collect materials at the intersection of the eight passages in Zhujiang New City, and record the situation of each entrance and exit through video, photographs, notes, etc., which mainly include security check gates, object security check machines, entry and exit swipe gates, and diversion fences.

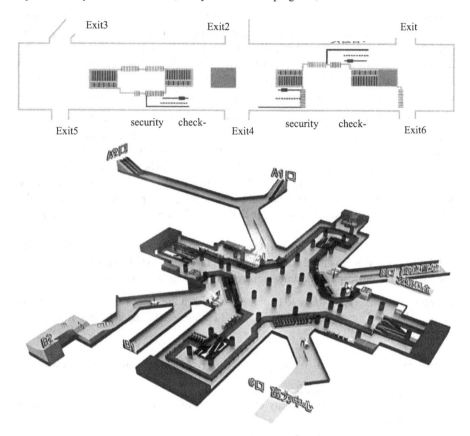

1.4 Interview Planning and Implementation:

The interview method was used to investigate the problems brought by the spatial guidance system in travelers' metro stations, and the experiment invited 50 volunteers who often traveled by metro, and through video playback, a virtual simulation model was built to conduct a simulation experiment to ask them about their overall walking access feelings in Guangzhou metro stations, and their walking access experience in the areas of security checks and entrances.

General Overview of Interviews. The purpose of this study is to explore the influencing factors of security check space guidance in metro stations, and the experimental methodology adopts the interview method and rooted theory. For the study, it is planned to invite 10 young people aged 20–25, all of whom currently have a long-term stable residence and life in guangzhou city, and on average have the experience of taking the guangzhou metro at least 1–2 times a week. The interview topics mainly include the overall walking access experience in guangzhou metro stations; the walking access experience in the security check and entrance/exit areas of guangzhou metro stations.

Interview Process. The on-site interviews consisted of two interviewers and one interviewee, and the total interview time was estimated to be 20 min, according to the appointment schedule. Prepare a recording cell phone with sufficient power storage space, the interviewer needs to have one copy each of the interview outline, interview flow, and interview recording form in hand, and provide the interviewee with virtual reality scenes, videos, and printed photos as an aid to the description of the subway space.

At the beginning of the recording, provide appropriate guidance to the interviewee to relax and understand the topic of today's interview. A video of the subway station was watched to guide the state of mind. Afterwards, the interview was conducted according to the outline, and if there was anything worthwhile to be discussed in depth, the interview was continued, and any necessary thoughts were recorded as soon as possible in the interview transcription form. After the end of the interview, stop the recording to end the interview, give out small snacks, and listen to the interviewee's feedback on the interview process.

The recording results of the interviews are recorded to text, voice to text tool selection: i cloud dictation; Youdao cloud notes; Jieshou recording to text. The converted text was recorded into the corresponding interview record sheet as soon as possible.

Interview Outline. (According to the current research the main subway station for the Zhujiang New Town station security check and entrance area, the selection of research sites in the back of the report).

- Interview Topic 1: Overall Walking Accessibility in Guangzhou Metro Stations

  1.. Where do you go most often?
  2. What is the line of the subway station you need to walk through to reach your destination?
  3.. What is your overall experience of the Guangzhou Metro?
  4. Have you ever chosen or avoided using a particular metro station because of the walkability factor? (It may be necessary to explain what the walkability factor is)
  5. What is your preferred time of day to use the subway? (e.g., rush hour/off-peak hours) Do you have different

- Interview topic 2: Walking access experience at security check and entrance/exit areas of Guangzhou metro stations

  1. Did the experience of security check and entrance/exit areas affect your choice of metro station and your experience in the previous topic? To what extent?
  2. When you were in the security check and entrance/exit areas, did you pay attention to the current spatial guidance system? (Provide photos as appropriate)
  3. How do you feel about the current spatial guidance system (signage/fenced access/spatial layout/staff guidance, etc.)?
  4. Are there specific examples where you feel the spatial guidance system has had a positive or negative effect in the area? (congestion and stagnation/variations from one region to another)

5. Is the spatial guidance system in the area easy to understand? Have you ever gotten lost or gone in the wrong direction in the area due to unclear guidance system?
6. What do you think are the key spatial guidance factors for the accessibility of the area? (original spatial layout/signage/fencing/staff guidance, etc.)

Interview Annex: Photographs of security check and entrance/exit areas of Zhujiang New Town Station.

2 Results

2.1 Interview Results Processing

The interview information was manually identified and counted to quantify the impact factors caused by the spatial guidance system, to develop an appropriate model of the impact factors of the spatial guidance system, and to determine the significance of the spatial guidance on the factors influencing the congestion of people in response to the data fed back from the model. The collected data and information were coded using the rooted theory research methodology and analyzed with the help of supporting software.

2.2 Interview Results Processing Methods:

The basic idea of procedural rooting theory (commonly used in China, corresponding to the classical rooting theory and constructive rooting theory) is to code the text of the interview content.

2.3 Procedural Rooting Theory Steps

Three levels of coding.
Open coding (first coding). In conjunction with the video and the detailed transcripts of the interviews, relevant concepts were tagged and gradually developed word by word by comparing the primary sources on an ongoing basis. The conceptualized text enabled further structuring of the unstructured interview transcripts, extracting new concepts and ideas from the empirical facts.

Spindle coding (second coding). Through the continuous analogy, integration and analysis between the concepts of the coded data, these concepts are further abstracted and formed into categories through generalization and organization, covering all the known concepts.

Methods: Further merge the conceptual categories formed earlier, and discover and establish the interrelationships between conceptual categories, such as causal situational relationships, functional relationships, process relationships, and temporal sequential relationships. In spindle coding, only one conceptual category is analyzed at a time, and the initial category is found to be related to other concepts.

Selective coding (third coding). Refers to the formation of the main axis coding in the many concepts of the genus relationship, found a core concept or a few, with a strong generalization ability, high abstraction and strong correlation ability, able to focus many related concepts within a broader theoretical scope.

2.4 Representative Factors Extracted After Coding (Partial Listing)

Complexity of station layout: The complexity of the internal layout of metro stations, including the design of transfer points and pathways, may lead to passengers getting lost or feeling disturbed inside the station.

Lack of clear signage: Some stations have insufficient spatial signage, which may be unclear, missing, or not visible enough for passengers to navigate correctly.

Poor transfer experience: The design and signage at transfer points may not be intuitive enough for passengers to navigate, especially at complex intersections.

Crowd congestion: Transfer points and popular stations may face crowd congestion, which may affect the flow and overall experience of passengers.

Site-to-Site Variation: The quality and form of spatial guidance signage varies from one metro station to another, with some stations being easier to understand while others can be confusing.

Perceived Costs to Users: Passengers may incur higher cognitive costs in finding the correct path and signage, which may affect their travel decisions.

High level of signage abstraction: Spatial signage at some stations may be too abstract for passengers to understand, making it more difficult to find the correct path.

Spatial signage that is not sufficiently attention-grabbing: In some cases, riders may miss key information because the spatial signage is not sufficiently attention-grabbing, increasing travel uncertainty.

Overall, these factors may collectively affect passengers' navigation experience in metro stations, and improvements in spatial design and signage are needed to improve user-friendliness.

2.5 Analysis and Summary of Experimental Results:

The dendrogram after the coding of the influencing factors was completed summarized the information from the pre-interviews in a modular way. In order to draw further conclusions, we combined this dendrogram, as well as relevant research information to summarize and illustrate the third level factors, expanding and analyzing the specific spatial guidance influencing factors.

Combine this dendrogram with relevant research information to summarize and illustrate Level 3 factors, expanding and analyzing specific spatial guidance influences.

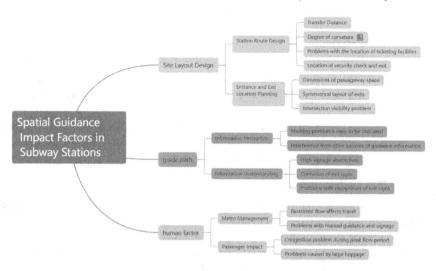

Station Layout Design.
Station route design.

1. Interchange Distance: Interchange distance is the overall length passed when interchanging, affected by the relative position between lines and the starting and ending points of the interchange corridors. The relative position of the stations of two or more lines affects the interchange distance. All interviewees mentioned that the transfer distances at existing interchanges are too long and that they need to walk for a long time when transferring.
2. Symmetrical layout of exits: The symmetrical layout and similarity of exits make it easy for passengers to get confused, especially when it is difficult to distinguish between different exits.
3. Ticketing facilities location: The placement of ticketing facilities at different exits and entrances varies greatly, and the ticket machines in some areas may cause congestion, while some areas are relatively cold.
4. Security check and exit location relationship problem: Security checkpoints are closely related to exit locations, so if passengers choose the wrong exit, they may need to go through the security check again. This adds to inconvenience and congestion.

Entrance/exit location planning.

1. Dimensions of passage space:During the security check process, respondents perceived the security checkpoints to be far apart and there were variations in the width of the passageway, which raised some less than ideal perceptions of the security check process.
2. degree of curvature:station order, but the specific effect may vary depending on individual passenger perceptions physical blocking and guidance signs may improve to some extent
3. intersection visibility problems: there are intersections inside the subway station Dan sometimes due to visual obstacles or unclear guide signs passengers may feel troubled when choosing a path.

Guide Signs.
Information perception.

1. The location of the sign is easy to be blocked: individual stations will set the sign of the guidance system on the ground or some inconspicuous position, when there are more people, the sign will be blocked, and some short passengers will not be able to see the sign.
2. Other sources of guidance information interference: passengers in the subway station rely more on cell phone navigation and other external devices, but for the subway station internal guiding information, such as a, b, c.

Information Understanding.

1. High signage abstraction:The spatial signage in some stations may be too abstract, making it difficult for passengers to understand and increasing the difficulty of finding the correct path, the spatial signage in some stations.
2. Confusion of entrance and exit markings: entrance and exit markings may be clear enough, sometimes passengers will go to the wrong exit because of confusion or similarity, which increases the difficulty of navigation.
3. Problems in recognizing exit and entrance markings:There are some difficulties in recognizing exit slogans (e.g., a, b, c, d), which may make it difficult for passengers to accurately choose the exit to their destination.

Human Factors.
Metro Management.

1. Restricted flow affects travel:The setting of restricted exits may result in passengers being restricted at specific times or locations, affecting the overall travel experience
2. Problems with matching manual guidance and signage:Respondents noted that in some metro stations, fencing and signage are not sufficiently matched, which may confuse passengers and may lead them to follow other people along with them in the wrong direction.

Passenger Impacts.

1. Crowding during peak hours:During peak commuting hours, some lines may be crowded and cause discomfort to passengers, especially for those who do not like crowding.
2. Problems caused by large luggage: Passengers carrying large or oddly shaped bags may encounter problems during security checks or passage.

3   Discussion and Conclusion

This study focuses on the spatial guidance system before and after the security check in subway stations, starting from the passenger's experience level, and intends to establish a set of models with wide adaptability by deeply studying the influence factors of the spatial guidance system on the efficiency of subway security check. The experimental plan is rigorous and thorough, utilizing the interview method and the rooted theory method to process, evaluate and summarize the experimental results, and arrive at a set of quantitative reference model, which refines the three categories of primary core factors of station layout design, guide signs, human factors and the corresponding secondary and tertiary subclasses, and constructs a system of influencing factors of the process efficiency of the security system under the viewpoint of spatial guidance.

This model can provide a guiding basis for optimizing the spatial guidance system, effectively reduce the congestion and chaos in the security check area, and improve the overall efficiency of the subway security check system, which not only can cut unnecessary costs for the subway's management organization, but also can make the passengers get a better walking access experience.

References

1. Xun, Z., Haiying, L., Chen, X., et al.: Analysis of subway security check service time and its influencing factors. J. Beijing Jiaotong Univer. **42**(03), 53–58 (2018)
2. Ding, X., Shi, G., Hong, C., et al.: Research on intelligent guidance and organization optimization method of subway security check passenger flow. Trans. Syst. Eng. Inform. **23**(01), 123–130+164 (2023)
3. Ding, F., Ren, Y., Wu, X.: Optimization design of subway transfer space based on wayfinding behavior. Housing Real Estate **03**, 125–126 (2021)
4. Wang, B., Xiao, Y., Wang, S.: Research on the influence factors of pedestrian accessibility of subway interchange space based on rooting theory. J. Architect. **S1**, 129–134 (2018)
5. Shi, X., Ye, Z., Shiwakoti, N., et al.: Passengers' perceptions of security check in metro stations. Sustainability **11**(10), 2930 (2019)
6. Dong, S., Chen, F., Ding, W., et al.: Prevention and control of COVID-19 in subway stations: an optimization strategy for placing location QR codes. Tunn. Undergr. Space Technol. **127**, 104615 (2022)
7. Peng, J., Wei, Z.0, Yang, Y., et al.: What size of aisle is necessary? A system dynamics model for mitigating bottleneck congestion in entrance halls of metro stations. IEEE Trans. Intell. Trans. Syst. **23**(12), 22923–22936 (2022)
8. Zhu, Q.: Passenger flow simulation of Xiamafang metro station based on AnyLogic Highlights in Science. Eng. Technol. **37**, 142–156 (2023)
9. Wan, M., Chen, Z., Guo, J., et al.: Optimization of security check efficiency in subway station based on Anylogic: a case study of Nanchang Metro. J. Intell. Fuzzy Syst. **41**(4), 5035–5043 (2021)
10. Yu, H., Wang, Y., Wang, F., et al.: Understanding impacts of security check on passenger flow in a metro station and improving measures: a case study in Guangzhou, China. J. Adv. Trans. **2019** (2019)

Ergonomics, Artificial Intelligence and Smart Technologies

Artificial Intelligence and Transportation – The Emergence of New Technologies and the Related Impacts on the Transportation of People and Packages

Elizabeth Almquist[✉], Taylor Mathis, and Vincent G. Duffy

Purdue University, West Lafayette, IN 47907, USA
{almquist,mathis28,duffy}@purdue.edu

Abstract. The idea of artificial intelligence in any use is growing over the past years. When you think of artificial intelligence you tend to just think of your Alexa or your phone and how those are used. Have you ever thought of how it is used from an aviation and transportation perspective? You probably don't think about this, given that it does not pique many people's interests. Given recent articles populating both domestically and internationally, the idea of artificial intelligence in the transportation and aviation sector is emerging quicker than you would expect. This topic is unique and complex as aviation and transportation are both human-operator-heavy sectors. An example of the use of artificial intelligence in transportation is self-driving cars and in the aviation industry, you can think of the heads-up display unit (HUD). Within this paper, you can find an analysis of this emerging topic. Ranging from leading tables, research paper studies, and much more analysis. In the end, the reader will understand the emerging topic and general ideas of future work within the field.

Keywords: Artificial intelligence · transportation · aviation · logistics

1 Introduction and Background

1.1 Introduction

Artificial Intelligence is an ever-evolving tool that is starting to shape life as we know it. While many individuals are used to interacting with AI on a regular basis utilizing 'Siri', 'Hey Google' or 'Alexa' to access their device and get basic information, AI continues to improve on a daily basis. One of the large areas that is utilizing AI is transportation. This is important to life as we know it as it can help understand traffic patterns, the impact of emissions based on traffic patterns and offer solutions that are aided to reduce traffic and be better for the environment.

Although the concept of artificial intelligence has been around since the 1950s, there has been a surge in AI related topics over the past few years. Some of the most well-known examples over the past year that have erupted are ChatGPT and AI created art. These

V. G. Duffy (Ed.): HCII 2024, LNCS 14711, pp. 165–181, 2024.
https://doi.org/10.1007/978-3-031-61066-0_12

have not risen to popularity without controversy though, due to the lack of regulations and the need to understand how plagiarism applies to artificial intelligence. Driven to popularity, these more controversial examples tend to overshadow the main types if artificial intelligence that are emerging in the field. According to the Harvard Business Review, there are three types of AI that are satisfying business needs: "automating business processes, gaining insight through data analysis and engaging with customers and employees." With the increasing need to keep up with new technologies and deliver new products quickly, companies continually have to shift focus, and automate processes to meet demand. This is also apparent through the push to move customer service to an automated system, and the push from companies to not necessarily backfill employees when they leave, but focus more on automation of tasks to reduce staffing or shift focus on more important tasks at hand (Fig. 1).

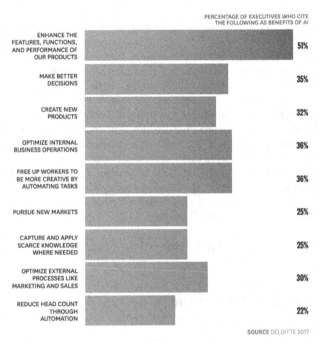

Fig. 1. In 2017, Deloitte surveyed a group of executives to understand the benefits they saw from utilizing AI [2]

Industrial engineering has always had a focus on process improvement and safety, two of which are emerging fields and applications of artificial intelligence. "AI has made the workplace safer, faster, more accurate, and more efficient" [3] as noted by Amaba et al. at a recent Institute of Industrial Systems Engineers Annual conference. By increasing the focus on automation, this can speed up processes and make them more efficient, allowing for more time to be spent of cost saving and safety measures. Regarding safety, artificial intelligence can be utilized to understand different traffic patterns within a manufacturing floor, routes for the transportation of goods and people, and to analyze and simulate movements of individuals in order to optimize safety and reduce risk.

1.2 Background

Outside of Industrial Engineering, there are plenty of areas that have embraced artificial intelligence, including that in transportation. Outside of the examples listed above, one of the most prominent use cases of AI in transportation is self-driving vehicles, such as those tested by Google, Uber and Tesla. "Their capabilities include modeling, simulation, sensing, motion planning, object recognition, obstacle avoidance, machine learning, error recovery, and so on" [4] as stated by Smith and Eckroth, showing that AI needs to constantly be used in order to ensure the vehicle moves safely. Without the various aspects listed above, self-driving vehicles would essentially be the equivalent of putting a brick on the accelerator and hoping for the best. The same capabilities can be utilized with auto-pilot or doing drone missions for the military. Although they can be piloted via a remote operator, they still need to take into consideration various aspects of AI to function properly and perform the task at hand.

AI as a whole may seem like it is an incredibly fast paced area of science, however, it has been around for almost 70 years. While some of the functionality has been embraced, there are still opportunities out there to explore and refine so that it is a more widely accepted topic. By implementing better regulations, especially around the plagiarism aspect, publicizing the other benefits and what AI is used for, and being transparent of all benefits of AI, society may embrace the change instead of talk down about the shift. This may be only part of society, but by showing successes to what has been done in the past may quell some fears about how AI could be applied in the future.

Safety has continually been at the forefront of artificial intelligence applications. Specifically, in transportation, AI has been utilized to help analyze travel and traffic patterns, which can be difficult to do without the use of AI as there are many unknown variables. These challenges, such as "increasing travel demand, CO2 emissions, safety concerns, and environmental degradation" [1] can be pulled into AI models as stated by Abduljabbar, resulting in a more robust and better understanding of how roadways and public transportation can be utilize to address those topics. This is just a small portion of challenges that can be addressed and remedied with AI, further challenges will be discussed in the remainder of this paper.

There are three specific chapters that relate the most to the topic of AI and Transportation. These are chapter 42: Human-Centered Design of Artificial Intelligence, chapter 46: Design for all in Digital Technologies and chapter 55: Human Factors and Ergonomics in Aviation. Chapter 42 focuses on how human-centered design relates to artificial intelligence [16]. As a large portion of ai and transportation relates to the passenger of the vehicle, regarding safety and comfort, it is import to introduce the human-centered design process. These predictive analytics can be utilized to understand how various traffic patterns and emissions can affect the passenger, as well as how a passenger/driver can interact with a self-driving car. For Chapter 46, this can be especially helpful regarding the user interfaces within self-driving vehicles and aircraft. There are various tools that need to be taken into consideration for effectively designing digital technologies so they can be used intuitively [17]. Chapter 55 may not directly mention the idea of AI in aviation, but it gives different ideas of where AI could be used and a background on the aircraft's evolution in the past years [11]. This will be helpful because the idea and background of aviation can be an overwhelming topic if you do not work directly in the industry. This chapter is a great introduction to the evolution of aviation and the components in aviation. All chapters help a reader grasp the topic of Artificial Intelligence and Aviation from the same perspective.

2 Purpose of Study

With the growing industry and advancements of artificial intelligence, there is a major opportunity to expand on the current utilization in Industrial Engineering. AI has been utilized mainly for process automation and customer service, however, there is a trend to move towards self-driving vehicles which can be extrapolated upon to further understand the impact on transportation. Self-driving vehicles is only the start of what can be done with AI and transportation. This study explores the additional applications of AI within the transportation industry, focusing on the movement of passengers via ground and air. Various databases and tools will be utilized to analyze the data found and to assist with the visualization of trends.

The idea of artificial intelligence has grown rapidly in the last 5–10 years and will only continue to grow as we evolve in different areas, especially transportation. The idea of artificial intelligence isn't necessarily a unique part of our topic. The unique part stems from the idea of incorporating AI in fields such as aviation and transportation. Both of these fields are human-operator heavy, which sparks the question of how you can incorporate AI in such a human-heavy field. There has also been a push of the application of AI due to the need to speed up road transportation due to Covid-19 [14], which ties to the more recent emergence (Fig. 2).

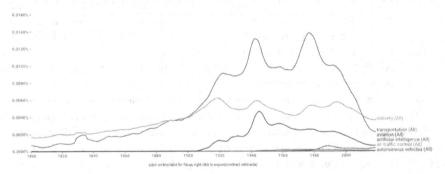

Fig. 2. Utilizing Google nGram [5], an analysis was done on all of the above topics. Out of all the keywords utilized, transportation had the biggest increase overall, however, recently it has been relatively level. Almost all of the topics have held steady over the past 10 years, with the majority of them peaking during the mid to late 1900s.

In the aviation field, AI is growing rapidly not just in the United States. AI is growing into international territory based on some of the articles we have planned to incorporate into our paper. AI is popping up in international places such as the United Kingdom and Australia. The rapid expansion of the use of AI in transportation/aviation not only in the United States but into international territory speaks volumes on how unique and complex this particular topic is. This pattern is also seen within the first and last mile delivery space. Due to rising costs with operations, there is a need to utilize AI to make operations more efficient and look for other ways to complete the last mile delivery. Additionally, it is used to look into more efficient routes, traffic patterns and ways to make delivery more environmentally friendly.

3   Procedure and Analysis

3.1   Procedure

For this study, an extensive literary analysis was performed utilizing the main topic of Artificial Intelligence and Transportation, with two sub topics of ai and logistics of packages and ai and air traffic control. By utilizing various databases and online tools, an analysis was performed looking into various search terms, key words that showed up within articles, the distribution of authors over time and by country, and the popularity of the topics over time.

3.2   Analysis

While doing research on this topic, the main topic of artificial intelligence and transportation was utilized to establish a preliminary understanding. Five individual databases were referenced in order to find sources: Harzing's Publish or Perish, Web of Science, Google Scholar, Scopus and Springer Link. Although a small sample of articles are utilized in this report, approximately 2.5 million sources were available to reference (Table 1).

Table 1. The search phrase "artificial intelligence and transportation" was put into the various databases below. Google Scholar had the most results, where as Harzing's Publish or Perish produced the least. This is due to the limitations provided by the database as it can only produce 200 results at a time.

Search terms: Artificial Intelligence and Transportation	
Harzing's Publish or Perish	200
Web of Science	4915
Google Scholar	2.1 million
Scopus	237,595
Springer Link	86,658

In order to limit the number of results that were received and narrow the potential subjects of the papers and websites, there were two additional search terms introduced: logistics and air traffic control. These, along with the other two keywords, were utilized throughout the remainder of the report. The four keywords or search phrases are defined as follows:

- Artificial Intelligence – "The simulation of human intelligence processes by machines, especially computer systems" [21]
- Transportation – "means of conveyance or travel from one place to another" [22]
- Logistics – "management of supply and transportation to deliver the goods on time and in good shape" [23]
- Air Traffic Control – "the process or system by which the movements of aircraft are monitored and directed by ground personnel communicating with pilots by radio" [24]

Upon the definition of these terms, there is a better understanding of what is being researched within this paper. The main search of artificial intelligence and transportation was used for all of the analytics found in the remainder of this report. The sub-topic search terms were used to provide additional understanding and discussion pertaining to the initial topic. A first analysis was done on the number of documents published per year (Figs. 3, 4 and Table 2).

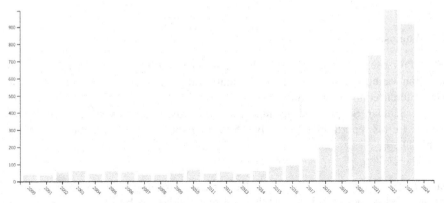

Fig. 3. Utilizing the search term "artificial intelligence and transportation", an analysis was done within the Web of Science. This shows all of the articles published in the last 23 years. Although this topic has been around for the better part of 50 years, there has been a surge in popularity over the past four years showing that this topic is emerging. [6]

Further analysis was done looking into all of the authors, resulting in a co-citation analysis and a view to understand how the most popular terms within those articles relate. By pulling in 4,915 results from the world of science, with dates ranging from 1977 to today, the following two visualities were created within VOS viewer (Figs. 5, 6 and 7).

Along with the co-citation analyses as seen above, a pivot table was created to understand and analyze the relationship between the number of authors that wrote papers per year and the number of citations they referenced (Table 3).

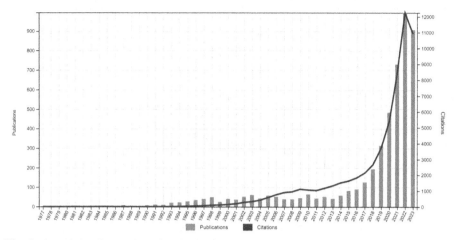

Fig. 4. Combining the previous figure utilizing the same search term, and then the next table for the authors, one can see the large increase in the author pool and the number of articles over time, as the citations have increased substantially with the number of papers published. This further cements the fact that this is an emerging area. [9]

Table 2. Utilizing the same data in Web of Science, the top authors during this time period were also pulled an analyzed. [7].

Field: Authors	Record Count	% of 4,918
Chen Y	40	0.813%
Li J	52	1.057%
Li Y	47	0.956%
Liu J	38	0.773%
Liu Y	46	0.935%
Wang J	46	0.935%
Wang X	66	1.342%
Wang Y	51	1.037%
Zhang J	43	0.874%
Zhang Y	54	1.098%

An additional analysis on the words utilized within the articles published within this topic was performed using maxQDA. Utilizing the same 50 articles from Scopus, a word cloud was created based off of the frequency of words found (Fig. 8).

Upon the completion of the word cloud, these terms were then exported and put into nVivo to perform a lexical search term analysis (Fig. 9).

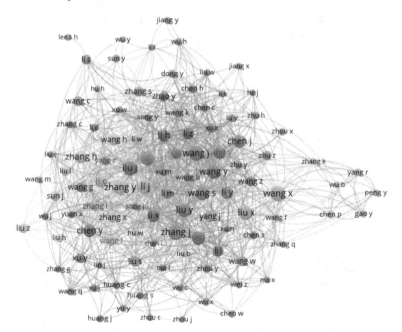

Fig. 5. Utilizing VOS Viewer, a co-citation analysis was performed. Looking at the web created above, one can see which of the authors have co-authored the most papers, and where they frequently overlap. [26]

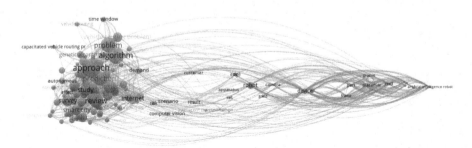

Fig. 6. 4,915 articles were analyzed to look into the most common terms and how they cluster together. The most common words were approach, algorithm and problem, which makes sense as there is a scientific method that needs to be done in order to develop AI models. [26]

Overall, there has been a substantial shift in the focus on artificial intelligence and transportation over the past five years. With the push in AI and the advancements made recently, more authors have been working to understand the impact of the technology and how it can be applied to better serve the research space.

Count	Centrality	Year	Cited References
32	0.25	2017	Krizhevsky Alex, 2017, COMMUNICA.
24	0.13	2018	Sutton RS, 2018, ADAPT COMPUT.
22	0.13	2019	Zhu L, 2019, IEEE T INTELL TRANS.
15	0.02	2018	Redmon J, 2018, ARXIV, V0, P0
14	0.04	2015	Ren SQ, 2015, ADV NEUR IN, V28.
14	0.11	2015	Lv YS, 2015, IEEE T INTELL TRANS.
13	0.11	2018	Wu YK, 2018, TRANSPORT RES C.
13	0.14	2020	Ullah Z, 2020, COMPUT COMMUN.
13	0.02	2016	He KM, 2016, PROC CVPR IEEE, V.
13	0.01	2016	Goodfellow I, 2016, ADAPT COMPU.
13	0.01	2020	Bochkovskiy A, 2020, ARXIV, V0, P0
13	0.05	2019	Abduljabbar R, 2019, SUSTAINABILIT.
11	0.01	2015	Simonyan K, 2015, ARXIV, V0, P0
11	0.08	2016	Silver D, 2018, NATURE, V529, P484.
11	0.03	2016	Liu W, 2016, LECT NOTES COMPU.
11	0.09	2018	Adadi A, 2018, IEEE ACCESS, V6, P.
10	0.03	2018	Lopez PA, 2018, IEEE INT C INTELL.
10	0.14	2019	Allam Z, 2019, CITIES, V89, P80, DOI.
9	0.07	2017	Zhao Z, 2017, IET INTELL TRANSP S.
9	0.04	2016	Redmon J, 2016, PROC CVPR IEE.
9	0.02	2015	Ma XL, 2015, TRANSPORT RES C-.
9	0.03	2016	Fu R, 2016, 2016 31ST YOUTH ACA.
8	0.05	2020	Nikitas A, 2020, SUSTAINABILITY-BA.
8	0.08	2017	Ma XL, 2017, SENSORS-BASEL, V1.
8	0.12	2015	Fagnant DJ, 2015, TRANSPORT RE.
7	0.01	2016	Redmon J, 2016, PROC CVPR IEE.
7	0.01	2017	Polson NG, 2017, TRANSPORT RE.
7	0.06	2017	McMahan HB, 2017, PR MACH LEA.
7	0.07	2020	Li T, 2020, IEEE SIGNAL PROC MA.
7	0.02	2019	Guo SN, 2019, AAAI CONF ARTIF IN.
7	0.04	2015	Girshick R, 2015, IEEE I CONF CO.
7	0.03	2018	Contreras-Castillo J, 2018, IEEE INT.
6	0.01	2019	Tan MX, 2019, PR MACH LEARN R.
6	0.03	2016	Rusk N, 2016, NAT METHODS, V13,

Fig. 7. An additional co-citation analysis was completed utilizing cite-space. Just under 2,000 articles were pulled in, showing that Sutton, L. Zhu and Krizhevsky were the three most cited authors. These three authors are also showing a recent publishing date, which once again cements the theory that this topic has become more relevant in recent years. [30]

4 Discussion and Reappraisal

Augmented Air Traffic Control. An article written by Ortner, Steinhofler, letigeb, and Fluher is the perfect example of the everyday use of artificial intelligence to solve a problem in aviation. The article gives an in-depth study on how current flight numbers and variety of aircrafts could pose a risk on how Air Traffic Control manages the conflicts for aircrafts. The article gives a point of view that the current way that we handle in flight conflicts of aircrafts is becoming more complex and reaching its limits. The article proposes the use of AI to be able to better predict these air traffic conflicts sooner and with more ease. This is done by using a system that analyzes aircraft surveillance data and detects conflict more rapidly than what is currently being used. This paper shows the implementation of this AI in both a small-scale artifact and large-scale artifact. This is just one way of showing the benefits of incorporating AI in a large aviation sector.

Problems with Air Traffic control AI. On the other side of things, much different than the article above, Hopkin and Wise take an approach of telling all of the issues that you might run into when incorporating AI into an air traffic control sector. The article talks about how AI is very similar to cognitive functions that we experience every day. The article discusses how the air traffic control system is not very complex currently and how adding AI can make it more complex than it needs to be. This is a great perspective to use to show how the times have changed. This article that I am referring to here was

Table 3. A pivot table was created utilizing 50 results from Scopus utilizing the search terms "artificial intelligence and transportation". By pulling this data, one can see how the number of papers that were published increased over the past five years, as did the number of citations attached to these papers. As more papers have been published, there are more opportunities to cite those papers, therefore increasing the number of citations. [27].

Row Labels	Count of Authors	Sum of Total Citations Cou
1977	1	188
1986	1	310
1987	1	254
1991	2	511
1992	1	255
1993	1	359
1995	1	233
1997	1	253
1998	1	239
1999	2	415
2000	2	568
2001	2	373
2002	3	933
2003	2	511
2004	1	257
2006	1	190
2007	2	473
2008	1	778
2010	1	180
2011	1	576
2012	2	568
2013	1	418
2014	2	741
2015	1	558
2016	1	287
2017	1	992
2018	5	1859
2019	3	956
2020	4	983
2021	1	192
2022	1	198
Grand Total	50	15608

written in 1991 compared to the article above that was written in 2022. When looking at both papers, you can clearly see that the air traffic control systems have become more complex over time and might require the use of AI to avoid conflicts in airspace. In 23 years, the sector has changed so much that the use of AI can be beneficial. This will be a great addition to the paper to really show how the topic has slowly emerged and became more pertinent in the last 23 years.

AI – Automatic Speech Recognition in the Air Traffic Control Environment. An article written by Pinska-Chauvin, Helmke, Dokic, and more dives in depth about the use of voice recognition in the air traffic control environment and how it can be beneficial.

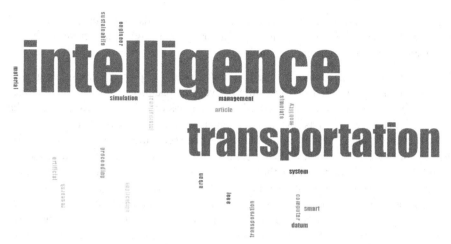

Fig. 8. Utilizing maxQDA, a word cloud was created. The most common words, other than filler words are: transportation, artificial, intelligence, management and intelligent. This makes sense as these were the topics that were being explored throughout the duration of the paper and the next few most frequent words fall within the spectrum of those topics. [28]

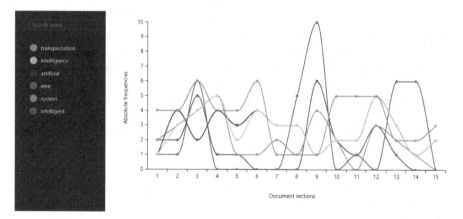

Fig. 9. Utilizing nVivo, the frequency of the search term per document section was analyzed. IEEE surprisingly had one of the most absolute frequencies. However, upon further investigation, this is due to a large number of papers being published by members of IEEE, presented at conferences or published by the professional society. System has the least frequent appearance, and artificial is the most consistent over the various sections. [29]

This article not only tells the benefits but provides a safety assessment aspect of incorporating the use of AI with speech recognition. There is already the use of automatic recognition of pilot call signs and the article emphasizes how the use of speech recognition in addition to the automatic recognition of call signs can be extremely beneficial to the pilot and crew when up in the air space. It talks about how the use of speech recognition can help in reduce workload and increasing situational awareness while in flight. After the safety assessment was performed, the hazards were then taken back and proper adjustments were made to mitigate any risks that might come from the use of automatic speech recognition in the airspace.

Package Delivery. The growth of e-commerce over the past 20 years has greatly impacted logistics and first and last-mile delivery of packages. Millions of packages are shipped and delivered on a daily basis, and this has only been increased due to the growth of e-commerce giants such as Amazon, as well as an increase that was seen due to the recent pandemic. With the growth that has been seen, there is a need to modernize the logistics systems and adapt to create more efficient and cost-effective networks. In a study and analysis done earlier this year, Zhu et al. determined that there are three levels that are driving the modernization of logistics: "the early stage, where scholars focused solely on efficiency, a mid-stage, where there is a concern on the environmental impact, and a late stage, where machines and automation are the main focus."[12] This echoes the focuses of ai and transportation over the years, as there has been a shift towards finding environmentally friendly solutions and finding ways to reduce vehicles and/or manual labor within the last mile delivery process as costs continue to rise. This is driving a movement to storage lockers for package pickup, which not only reduces the amount of stops a vehicle has to make, but also increases the safety of a package. Additionally, it is driving towards the research around autonomous vehicles or delivery drones as these can be more environmentally conscious and replace manual labor [15].

AI Application used by Daily Drivers. Within transportation, one of the most common uses of AI that the average consumer may use is adaptive cruise control. This ranges from having a semi-automated cruise control utilizing proximity sensors to understand when a vehicle in front of the driver is slowing down so the car can automatically slow down, to a fully self-driving vehicle. This has been introduced in a good portion of consumer vehicles today, with Tesla pioneering the self-driving aspect. Self-driving vehicles continue to be one of the more well-known advancements in AI and is a continual push under the guise that a fully autonomous vehicle would provide safer roads and

Table 4. Juneja points out in the table below the various trends, products, research and development budgets and risks that the four companies have been working with during their focus on this product. [10].

Variables	Tesla	General Motors	Google	Mercedes Benz (Daimler AG)
R&D Budgets	$3.18 billion	$1.59 billion	$1.81 billion	$ 4.6 billion
Tech Innovation	Autopilot	Cruise Automation	Waymo	Mercedes Semi Auto
Production Units (per year)	100,000 units	52,000 units	N/a	250,000
Risks	1. Production delays 2.Experimental Product with cases of crash 3.Skeptical customer base might not prefer autopilot	1.Customer Base Hardware and software still in basic development.	1.Advanced tech but possibility of loss in remote areas 2.Competition might present a better product.	1.Newly created tech with more potential for error while driving 2.Mapping technology is still incomplete
Industry Trends	Focus towards improving the previously developed technology and attacking new markets.	Focus has always been towards the transportation sector with projected rise in autonomous vehicles (trucks and ships).	New to the transportation market with focus towards licensing the technology to current truck developers.	Also new to the autonomous industry with plans on integrating autonomous technology into its own product line.

more efficient travel. Tesla, General Motors, Google and Mercedes Benz are four of the companies with a large focus on developing this technology (Table 4).

It is apparent that these four companies still have a way to go, and although they do have successful products out there, there are government regulations and safety methodologies that can be improved upon in order to move further in the space.

5 Future Work

Artificial intelligence is an ever-growing field because as we grown as a population, we grow in areas such as artificial intelligence. As the human population gets smarter, you can expect the use of artificial intelligence to spike more and more in the next coming years. Searching through NSF.gov, you can see the different places where they are funding the expansion/growth of AI use in different fields (NSF.GOV). Some of these fields include, but are not limited to education, manufacturing environments, transportation, and research. This is a prime example of future work that is already starting in multiple different sectors. Future work with artificial intelligence is endless due to the fact that it has not yet been fully discovered. We are still learning new tips and tricks to evolve the AI we already have in place. We are also actively inventing new AI concepts and trying them in new environments. AI is growing both domestically and internationally. For example, Mena media talks about how Artificial intelligence in aviation is spreading to the United Kingdom (Syndigate Media). This article emphasizes the use of artificial intelligence within the cockpit, both in the military and public sectors. This clearly shows that there is still future work to be performed in this sector, both domestically and internationally. [18, 19].

The University of Florida is working on an effort to "explore the frontiers of artificial intelligence (AI)-empowered methods and solutions and future research directions to address urban transportation challenges" [8]. They are currently developing and performing a workshop that has two parts: researching and developing postulations based off of round-tables and investigating current methods of AI use, and round-table discussions to determine new opportunities and training for new technologies. The overall goal is to apply existing AI technologies that may not have been evaluated previously in the transportation industry.

The University of Missouri-Columbia is currently conducting a five-year study on Interactive and Explainable AI for Next-Gen Transportation Systems Management. This study is utilizing and re-designing "existing artificial intelligence (AI) algorithms to facilitate multi-task learning on holistic transportation problems, while removing bottlenecks to model interpretability." [13] By doing so, the goal is to design an open-source platform to tackle different transportation problems utilizing various models. Current models and machine learning algorithms are being evaluated and adapted to develop more applicable framework and models for the transportation situations that may arise in the future. The deliverable of an open-source model is targeted for a 2026 completion.

All of these studies will have a large impact on transportation, and should drive the industry in the right direction. These studies will create further modeling and understanding of how artificial intelligence can be utilized to better transportation as it exists today.

6 Conclusion

The idea of artificial intelligence in any use is growing over the past years. Given recent articles populating both domestically and internationally, the idea of artificial intelligence in the transportation and aviation sector is emerging quicker than you would expect. This topic is unique and complex due to the fact that aviation and transportation are both human-operator heavy sectors. The complexity of this topic stems from AI being an ever-changing environment and allows for these sectors to adapt quickly to change. Given the complexity of the topic, it allowed for a deeper dive into research papers and analysis to truly understand both subsections of the topic as a whole. There have been many papers and points of views on this topic and this analysis you read above summarizes some of the key points of the papers/points of views.

This paper aimed to call out the similarities and differences between how AI is growing in both the transportation and AI environment. The paper clearly performs a bibliometric analysis spanning across multiple papers/authors to deliver the idea of AI in these two sectors. There is still a lot we don't know about AI and what is being done "behind doors" in these sectors. As we watch these new ideas to incorporate AI roll out, we will quickly adapt as a society and begin to understand them more.

Appendix

Previous Work

See Fig. 10 and Table 5.

Harzing's Publish or Perish helps bring in related articles

For our focus for the final project/lab, my partner and I decided to explore Artificial Intelligence in Transportation, as both of us work in the transportation industry in some capacity, and are interested to see what research has been done to understand the impact of AI.

Initially, Scopus was utilized without much success. This is something we need to understand and dig into further, as the correct pairings of search terms may not have been used properly, or different phrases should be explored. From there, we moved over to Harzing's Publish or Perish and had much more success. Two different searches were done in the tool to understand the full capacity of what can be accomplished. While doing preliminary research for the final project, an article titled 'Toward a Revolution in Transportation Operations: AI for Complex Systems' was found. The first search was for the author of the article, Fei-Yue Wang, to determine if they had other articles written that would fall within the scope of our topic.

A second search was done specifically targeting artificial intelligence in transportation. This produced 200 articles that we would be able to explore as stepping off points to further our research. Overall, this tool is incredibly powerful and will be a great asset to have going into the final project.

Fig. 10. During a previous assignment, AI and transportation was researched to help establish a baseline understanding of how to use Harzing's Publish or Perish [25]

Table 5. A snippet pulled from Web of Science showing growing research areas within our selected topic [20].

Select All	Field: Research Areas	Record Count	% of 95
☐	Engineering	83	87.368%
☐	Computer Science	77	81.053%
☐	Automation Control Systems	51	53.684%
☐	Mathematics	30	31.579%
☐	Robotics	28	29.474%
☐	Telecommunications	26	27.368%
☐	Transportation	21	22.105%
☐	Instruments Instrumentation	14	14.737%
☐	Communication	8	8.421%
☐	Chemistry	6	6.316%

References

1. Abduljabbar, R., Dia, H., Liyanage, S., Bagloee, S.A.: Applications of artificial intelligence in transport: an overview. Sustainability **11**(1), 189 (2019). https://doi.org/10.3390/su11010189

2. Davenport, T.H., Rajeev, R.: Artificial intelligence for the real world. Harvard Bus. Rev. **96**(1), 108–116 (2018)

3. Industry 4.0. and Artificial Intelligence as - ProQuest. n.d. https://www.proquest.com/docview/2511388515/fulltextPDF/F6068A3EFBF84CF7PQ/1?accountid=13360

4. Smith, R.G., Eckroth, J.: Robert S. engelmore award article: building AI applications: yesterday, today, and tomorrow. AI Mag. **38**(1), 6–22 (2017). https://doi.org/10.1609/aimag.v38i1.2709

5. Google Books NGRAM Viewer – Google Product. n.d.

6. Web of Science. n.d. https://www-webofscience-com.ezproxy.lib.purdue.edu/wos/alldb/citation-report/73e3e2c1-8220-4b74-8984-b3e2246f05f1-b7c680dd. Accessed 22 Nov 2023

7. Web of Science – Countries. n.d. https://www-webofscience-com.ezproxy.lib.purdue.edu/wos/alldb/analyze-results/73e3e2c1-8220-4b74-8984-b3e2246f05f1-b7c680dd. Accessed 28 Nov 2023

8. NSF Award Search: Award # 2203497 - Workshop/Collaborative Research: The Frontiers of Artificial Intelligence-Empowered Methods and Solutions to Urban Transportation Challenges. n.d. https://www.nsf.gov/awardsearch/showAward?AWD_ID=2203497&HistoricalAwards=false

9. Web of Science - Categories. n.d. https://www-webofscience-com.ezproxy.lib.purdue.edu/wos/woscc/analyze-results/9cdcf5ed-dfe7-4f75-ba46-8f573fb2e284-b8b53696. Accessed 28 Nov 2023

10. Juneja, R.: The Regulation of AI: an investigation on the development of AI and its effects on the transportation industry. J. Comput. Sci. Syst. Biol. **11**(5), 290–295 (2018). https://www.researchgate.net/publication/329750338_The_Regulation_of_AI_An_Investigation_on_the_Development_of_AI_and_its_Effects_on_the_Transportation_Industry#fullTextFileContent

11. Salvendy., Karwowski.: Handbook of Human Factors and Ergonomics. 5th edition. Wiley Incorporated (2021)

12. Zhu, X., Cai, L., Lai, P.-L., Wang, X., Ma, F.: Evolution, challenges, and opportunities of transportation methods in the last-mile delivery process. Systems **11**(10), 509 (2023)
13. NSF Award Search: Award # 2045786 - CAREER: Interactive and Explainable AI for Next-Gen Transportation Systems Management. n.d. https://www.nsf.gov/awardsearch/showAward?AWD_ID=2045786&HistoricalAwards=false
14. Li, R., Yating, Z.: Investigating how AI and data science techniques are applied in the freight transportation industry, in particular, the land transportation perspective. Adv. Econ. Manag. Polit. Sci. **7**(1), 251–261 (2023). https://doi.org/10.54254/2754-1169/7/20230241
15. Transforming Transportation with AI (2020). https://www.researchgate.net/publication/345737417_Transforming_Transportation_with_AI. Accessed 28 Nov 2023
16. Margetis, G., Stavroula, N., Margherita, A., Constantine, S.: Human-Centered Design of Artificial Intelligence. Handbook of Human Factors and Ergonomics, Fifth Edition, pp. 1085–1106 (2021). https://doi.org/10.1002/9781119636113.ch42
17. Stephanidis, C.: Design for All in Digital Technologies. Handbook of Human Factors and Ergonomics, Fifth Edition, pp. 1187–1215 (2021). https://doi.org/10.1002/9781119636113.ch46
18. Award 2203497. n.d. https://www.nsf.gov/awardsearch/showAward?AWD_ID=2203497&HistoricalAwards=false
19. Award 2045786 n.d. https://www.nsf.gov/awardsearch/showAward?AWD_ID=2045786&HistoricalAwards=false
20. Web of Science – Research Categories. n.d. https://www-webofscience-com.ezproxy.lib.purdue.edu/wos/woscc/analyze-results/9cdcf5ed-dfe7-4f75-ba46-8f573fb2e284-b8b53696. Accessed 29 Nov 2023
21. Laskowski, N., Linda, T.: Artificial Intelligence (AI) (2023). Enterprise AI. November 13, 2023. https://www.techtarget.com/searchenterpriseai/definition/AI-Artificial-Intelligence
22. Transportation. In Merriam-Webster Dictionary (2023). https://www.merriam-webster.com/dictionary/transportation
23. What Is Logistics? Definition of Logistics, Logistics Meaning - The Economic Times. n.d. The Economic Times. https://economictimes.indiatimes.com/definition/logistics
24. Merriam-Webster Dictionary. Merriam-Webster.com (2022). November 2022. https://www.merriam-webster.com/dictionary/air%20traffic%20control
25. Publish or Perish. Harzing.Com (2016). February 6, 2016. https://harzing.com/resources/publish-or-perish
26. VOSviewer - Visualizing Scientific Landscapes. n.d. VOSviewer. https://www.vosviewer.com/
27. Scopus Preview - Scopus - Welcome to Scopus. n.d. https://www.scopus.com/search/form.uri?display=basic#basic
28. MAXQDA. The Best Qualitative Data Analysis Software|MAXQDA (2023). November 6, 2023. https://www.maxqda.com/qualitative-data-analysis-software?gad_source=1&gclid=Cj0KCQiAgqGrBhDtARIsAM5s0_lDw4TjIu54DzUTeJSaBJ7auoEfQ7z1cCMDbJexvhCixsCzdaIETskaAkL3EALw_wcB
29. Lumivero. NVivo – Lumivero (2023). October 11, 2023. https://lumivero.com/products/nvivo/
30. CITESPACE Home. CiteSpace. https://citespace.podia.com/. Accessed 4 Dec 2023

An Outlook for AI Innovation
in Multimodal Communication Research

Alexander Henlein[1]([✉]) [iD], Anastasia Bauer[2] [iD], Reetu Bhattacharjee[9] [iD],
Aleksandra Ćwiek[3] [iD], Alina Gregori[1] [iD], Frank Kügler[1] [iD], Jens Lemanski[9,10] [iD],
Andy Lücking[1] [iD], Alexander Mehler[1] [iD], Pilar Prieto[4,5],
Paula G. Sánchez-Ramón[1,5] [iD], Job Schepens[2] [iD], Martin Schulte-Rüther[6,7] [iD],
Stefan R. Schweinberger[8] [iD], and Celina I. von Eiff[8] [iD]

[1] Goethe University Frankfurt, Frankfurt, Germany
`henlein@em.uni-frankfurt.de`
[2] University of Cologne, Cologne, Germany
[3] Leibniz-Centre General Linguistics, Berlin, Germany
[4] ICREA (Institució de Recerca i Estudis Avançats), Barcelona, Spain
[5] Universitat Pompeu Fabra, Barcelona, Spain
[6] University Medical Center Göttingen, Göttingen, Germany
[7] Department of Child and Adolescence Psychiatry, University Hospital Heidelberg,
Heidelberg, Germany
[8] Friedrich Schiller University Jena, Jena, Germany
[9] University of Münster, Münster, Germany
[10] FernUniversität in Hagen, Hagen, Germany

Abstract. In the rapidly evolving landscape of multimodal communication research, this follow-up to Gregori et al. (2023) [71] explores the transformative role of machine learning (ML), particularly using multimodal large language models, in tracking, augmenting, annotating, and analyzing multimodal data. Building upon the foundations laid in our previous work, we explore the capabilities that have emerged over the past years. The integration of ML allows researchers to gain richer insights from multimodal data, enabling a deeper understanding of human (and non-human) communication across modalities. In particular, augmentation methods have become indispensable because they facilitate the synthesis of multimodal data and further increase the diversity and richness of training datasets. In addition, ML-based tools have accelerated annotation processes, reducing human effort while improving accuracy.

Continued advances in ML and the proliferation of more powerful models suggest even more sophisticated analyses of multimodal communication, e.g., through models like ChatGPT, which can now "understand" images. This makes it all the more important to assess what these models can achieve now or in the near future, and what will remain unattainable beyond that.

Supported by the DFG SPP 2392 *Visual Communication* (ViCom).
J. Schepens—External collaborator.
C.I. von Eiff—For the ViCom Consortium.

We also acknowledge the ethical and practical challenges associated with these advancements, emphasizing the importance of responsible AI and data privacy. We must be careful to ensure that benefits are shared equitably and that technology respects individual rights.

In this paper, we highlight advances in ML-based multimodal research and discuss what the near future holds. Our goal is to provide insights into this research stream for both the multimodal research community, especially in linguistics, and the broader ML community. In this way, we hope to foster collaboration in an area that is likely to shape the future of technologically mediated human communication.

Keywords: Multimodal communication · Artificial Intelligence · Large Language Models · Multimodal Computing · Generative AI

1   Introduction

Text-based systems such as ChatGPT [158], Bard [11], or Llama 2 [202] – so-called Large Language Models (LLM) – show remarkable results in a variety of applications. The zero-shot, one-shot, and few-shot capabilities of these models are particularly notable (c.f. [119, 200, 212]). This means that even if the model is presented with an unknown prompt or task for input, the results are usually still conclusive. They are even considered by some people to be the first step towards Artificial General Intelligence ("AGI"; [148]). All of these models are currently based on the transformer architecture [207], which is now also being used very successfully in other areas of computer science, such as computer vision [104] or audio processing [47]. The current development now consists of transferring these models to multimodality, which currently means that the models are trained on both text and image data [168]. However, there are already transformer-based architectures that support far more modalities [222].

As successful as these transformer-based models seem to be in generalizing over the training data, current research suggests that the true quality lies primarily in the training data [77, 88, 196, 221]. It seems like any architecture, given enough reason, number of parameters, and training effort, can deliver the same results. This is currently most evident in the field of computer vision, where different model architectures, like convolutional models vs. transformers, can achieve competitive results given sufficient training effort [129]. The results of Yadlowsky et al. [220] also point to a similar interpretation. Their study suggests that there is limited evidence supporting the notion that the in-context learning behavior of the models extends beyond their pretraining data in terms of generalization. Concerning multimodality, this finding is of course particularly interesting and allows us to draw the following two conclusions: 1. The models cannot generalize over modalities based on which they have not been trained. 2. With our current machine learning-based methods, we cannot learn things for which we cannot generate training data or for which we cannot measure.

Based on this basic premise and the findings to date as well as the current interpretations of AGI,[1] we would like to provide an overview of the following points and the associated problems in this paper:

(i) Explore the existing state of multimodal systems, detailing their current functionalities and the scope of tasks they can effectively address (**Current Capabilities**).

(ii) Current difficulties in the effective application of these systems in various scientific fields that deal in some way with multimodality of communication (**Current Obstacles**)

(iii) Delve into aspects of multimodal integration that are anticipated to require more extensive research or technological advancements, outlining the challenges and complexities (**Long-Term Obstacles**).

We do not want to examine these points simply from the perspective of computer science, but, like the previous work by Gregori et al., from the broad field of multimodality communication research (see Sect. 1.2). This point becomes particularly clear in Sect. 3, which specifically examines multimodal communication analysis from the perspective of several individual disciplines. Mostly based on concrete examples, the corresponding discussions pinpoint various processing needs of multimodal AI tools. Based on this survey, Sect. 3.10 summarizes some challenges and outlooks for AI innovation in multimodal communication research. Section 4 attempts a cautious assessment of possible long-term obstacles of AI systems, including likely future developments and conditions for potential limitations.

1.1 Goals of This Article

Not least due to advances in Artificial Intelligence (AI), processes are simplified for the research community, if not made possible in the first place, which were previously associated with considerable time and costs [128]. We believe that multimodal research is necessary to advance theoretical research on human and non-human animal communication. Here, we survey the state-of-the-art of using AI in this kind of research. In this context, we also want to evaluate what is already possible today with the help of AI, but also why it is not yet being used in certain areas. But also what will probably be possible soon and which problems cannot yet be solved in the long term.

1.2 About Us

We are researchers with different backgrounds working on multimodal communication, specifically on gestures, sign languages, didactic and clinical aspects of visual communication, animal communication, socio-emotional interaction, and

---

[1] See also the aims of potential ChatGPT successors such as Q* (https://www.technologyreview.com/2023/11/27/1083886/unpacking-the-hype-around-openais-rumored-new-q-model/, accessed 6th December 2023).

human-computer interaction systems. Our work contributes to the Priority Programme *Visual Communication* (ViCom), supported by the German Research Foundation (DFG). ViCom aims at disclosing the specific characteristics of the visual modality as a communication channel and its interaction with other channels (especially the acoustic one) to develop models of human communication and their cognitive and evolutionary foundations [71].

2   AI in Multimodal Communication Research

The intersection of AI and multimodal communication has ushered in a new era of possibilities, revolutionizing how we understand and facilitate human interaction. This trend is being spurred on by the current development of so-called generative models (or generative AI) [34]. In the realm of text-based models like ChatGPT [158], the generation of relevant output hinges on formulating a textual prompt that describes a specified task. This prompt serves as an instruction for the model, prompting it to generate an appropriate response. This can create a dialog between the user and the model, e.g. to further refine the result or to make new queries based on the answer (prompt chaining). This process can be further optimized by so-called prompt engineering, i.e. the question of how a prompt must be formulated so that the system can provide the best possible response [183]. New models such as GPT4 [158] are not only dependent on text but can also process and generate images using DALL-E [23]. Probably the most powerful model at the moment is GEMINI [199]. This model processes input from the following four modalities as input: text, images, audio, and video, and is capable of generating text and images itself. What is characteristic of all these generative models, is that all models are trained using large amounts of training data. (For GEMINI, no exact data on the data set size is currently known, but it is assumed that the number of tokens is in the trillions.[2]) In the context of text data, the training process often involves predicting the next word in a sequence based on the preceding words. This sequential prediction task helps the model learn the patterns and structures within the data [219]. This leads us to several problems with these models and at the same time with current AI in general. It has been proven that the models do not understand the content of the training data, but only what a good result looks like [99]. As a result, the systems like to invent new facts or hallucinate in general [4]. With the learned structures, these models not only learn what good answers look like but also (tend to) reproduce the biases that are inherent to some degree to the training data. For example, racist or sexist content is not uncommon [169]. Even though the developers of these systems are making more and more efforts to prevent this (or to eliminate biases ex-post), these barriers can often be circumvented with clever jailbreaking [37, 127, 212].

It has also become extremely difficult to evaluate and compare the models on standard public tasks [223]. This is because the procurement and sources of the

---

[2] https://www.cnbc.com/2023/05/16/googles-palm-2-uses-nearly-five-times-more-text-data-than-predecessor.html, accessed 13th February 2024.

training data make it practically impossible to rule out the possibility that this evaluation data is not already contained in the training data. This also relativizes statements such as: "Here's a list of difficult exams the ChatGPT and GPT-4 have passed[3]". Since it could be proven that this test data is already present in the training data [2].

Finally, it's important to address the training data itself, acknowledging that the process of acquiring and using it is not without criticism. This debate is currently most pronounced in the area of image generation, where millions of images from the internet are used to train these models. The problem is, for example, that these images are used without explicit consent from the creators and artists. As a result, these models enable the generation of images in a similar style, which is then labeled as plagiarism by the original creators [139], whereby such images are sometimes used for fraud [219]. This debate can be transferred one-to-one to the problematic use and reproduction of works in other modalities (music, literature, film, etc.), which has already led to many discussions.

The problems mentioned so far extend to the application of AI-based systems, especially in scientific contexts [211], where scientific findings should ideally be reproducible and comprehensible [162]. The return formats are not always adhered to, which makes it difficult to work with the results. Prompts that appear to work for one model may not work properly after it has been updated or replaced with a newer model. In addition, the best current models (GPT4, GEMINI) are closed-source and run on external servers. Depending on the type of data involved, it is not compatible with data protection law to store or process it on external servers. Alternative open-source models are slowly catching up, but are not yet truly mature in the area of multimodality (e.g. FALCON [5] or Alpaca [198]). And often require resources (both personnel and hardware) that are often not available. Thus, even the use of these models can reach a cost point that is no longer affordable for most research projects.

The last few paragraphs sounded quite negative about generative AI and the current LLMs such as GEMINI. We therefore present examples that are only possible thanks to these systems, as well as applications in which multimodality is an essential component and will probably soon be a core component of Generative AI. Some of these examples have nothing to do with language/communication but are intended to provide a brief overview of where multimodality is still relevant. Systems that prove successful for one application are often transferred to other areas (see e.g. Transformer [80], originally for translation and now also as the basis for Computer Vision (e.g. ViT [36]).

Multimodal Assistant: A multimodal assistant is an AI with which you can not only interact verbally (e.g. Alexa or Siri), but can, for example, also cover the visual context [122]. Application examples for this would be, for example, assistance with cooking, initialized by a picture of the available ingredients [199], or the creation of personal training plans, supported by a picture of the available

---

[3] https://www.businessinsider.com/list-here-are-the-exams-chatgpt-has-passed-so-far-2023-1, accessed 13th February 2024.

training equipment or other additional information [49]. These are currently the use cases that are most often presented in tech demos[4]

Multilingual Communication: As the systems are generally not only multimodal but also multilingual, they are also suitable for live translations between different languages. The additional advantage is that the models could translate not only the spoken language in face-to-face communication but also the corresponding gestures [12], facial expressions [96] and body movements, which can differ across diverse cultural contexts and could therefore lead to misunderstandings. One of the best-known examples is the usage of head movements in different cultures. In German or US culture, the vertical head movement communicates positivity and horizontal head movement denotes a negative response. In Bulgarian cultural tradition this pattern is reversed [9]. It can also be helpful when translating comics, for example, where images and text often share a common context [29].

Educational Tools: Different people learn best through different modalities (combinations) [147, 182]. However, knowledge is often only available in one modality (usually text). Such generative models can be used to generate suitable audio descriptions and explanatory images based on the texts, which can help with understanding. Or they can directly help to convey this knowledge in age-appropriate language.

Healthcare: Multimodal data and systems are particularly valuable in the medical field. Medical images (e.g. X-rays), conversations (e.g. medical history), and various signals (e.g. long-term ECG), to name a few, are combined here. And in the future, intelligent devices such as watches will also be able to track everything. And this is already being done in parts [144, 149, 210]

Environmental Monitoring: By merging visual, textual, and auditory data, and leveraging satellite imagery, photographs, and sensor inputs, these AI systems offer a comprehensive understanding of ecosystems. They can analyze visual data to track changes in vegetation, assess pollution levels, and identify biodiversity. Additionally, by processing spoken or written reports from field researchers and integrating sensor data, these assistants facilitate real-time, context-aware assessments of environmental conditions [62].

Realtime News Feed: In the realm of real-time news delivery, by incorporating verbal, visual, and potentially other sensory modalities, could AI generate news on the fly. They can process and interpret not only textual news content but also images and videos, providing a more comprehensive and contextually rich understanding of unfolding events. The real-time analysis of multimodal data ensures that users receive up-to-the-minute updates, making these assistants indispensable tools for staying abreast of current affairs in a rapidly evolving media landscape.

---

[4] c.f. https://youtu.be/UIZAiXYceBI, accessed 16th January 2024.

Multimodal Programming Assistance: In the realm of coding, multimodal assistants redefine the landscape by offering not just verbal but also visual support, changing the development process [85]. These AI systems, trained by code snippets, images, and textual descriptions, assist programmers in understanding and writing code more effectively. Visual cues, such as flowcharts or diagrams, can supplement traditional text-based explanations, aiding in the comprehension of complex algorithms and code structures. Accessibility is also improved, e.g. when complete web pages can be created from simple drawings[5].

Mental Health Support: By incorporating multimodal emotion detection, these assistants can analyze facial expressions, voice tonality, and written text to gauge the user's emotional state [144]. This nuanced understanding enables more empathetic and tailored responses, enhancing the overall therapeutic experience. Visual elements, such as calming images or guided relaxation videos, can be seamlessly integrated to provide a holistic and personalized approach to mental health assistance. The combination of verbal and visual modalities allows for a more accurate assessment of the user's well-being, fostering a supportive environment for individuals seeking help.

Urban Planning: Generative AI can help urban planning by analyzing textual documents, satellite imagery, and citizen feedback. It can help city planners visualize potential changes, understand the impact on communities, and create more sustainable and livable urban environments.

Content Creation: The influences in the area of content creation have been noticeable for some time now, and it has never been so easy to create your own content with AI support without any special prior knowledge. AI can generate art [138], realistic graphics and videos or audios, sometimes recognized as so-called deep fakes [222], create entirely new podcasts (https://podcast. ai/) or books (https://aumgolly.com/). There exist AI-assisted text-to-speech tools, where one can create a voice with a skim sample of own voice recordings (https://speechify.com/), and conversely, speech-to-text multi-language transcription tools (https://trint.com/ or https://speechtext.ai/).

Assist Scientific Work: In the realm of academia, AI assistance has become instrumental in refining the intricacies of scientific communication. Non-native speakers benefit from these tools in crafting more polished manuscripts, addressing stylistic nuances, and eliminating grammar errors. The systems extend beyond mere language refinement, aiding researchers in formulating novel research questions when provided with comprehensive background information. Or even help directly with the preparation or evaluation of studies [184]. In the peer review process, AI streamlines the time-consuming task of writing and refining reviews, optimizing style and tone for more efficient and effective communication within the scientific community. However, the scientific community

---

[5] https://youtu.be/outcGtbnMuQ?t=980, accessed 14th February 2024.

itself is still very much debating what constitutes good scientific practice in times of large language models, including questions of authorship and responsibility/accountability [94, 180, 181].

3   Current Obstacles

It is anticipated that many challenges currently faced by the systems described in Sect. 2 will soon become less significant. These challenges include prompt engineering [183], contextual constraints [22], consideration of mathematical subtleties [60], and hallucinations [4], among others. We therefore refrain from examining these challenges, as we consider them to be more technical than fundamental. A related review is given by Liu et al. [128].

In the realm of multimodal AI, current efforts focus on integrating various sensory modalities – such as visual and auditory (including written, spoken, and sign language), and even olfactory data – to create a comprehensive understanding of the world. So far, however, this has mostly been done by considering small groups of (2–3) modalities. For example, there are approaches to the foundation of semantics on modalities such as vision [15], audition [106], or olfaction [105]. Other approaches address the fusion of different modalities, such as text, video, audio [3], and gestures [118], or fMRI data [1, 33]. Advanced multimodal attention mechanisms [126, 152] alongside enhanced multimodal transformer models [218, 222] have the potential to augment and empower AI systems, enabling dynamic prioritization of relevant modalities for improved outcomes.

Contemporary Large Language Models (LLMs), which are predominantly trained on textual data but may also be exposed to images, demonstrate impressive abilities in understanding visual content. For example, ChatGPT can create an HTML page from a simple hand-drawn sketch, develop training programs by analyzing images of a home gym, suggest recipes after examining the contents of a refrigerator, and interpret the humor in a cartoon illustration. However, many of these functions lack sufficient systematic research and evaluation, making it challenging to assess their scalability. Despite their limitations, these examples offer a preview into the future possibilities that the integration of more modalities could unlock.

In this section, we examine several examples of multimodal analysis that are likely to be realized in the near future. We discuss this in the context of a number of use cases from the Visual Communication research group. The examples range from gesture modeling, to the study of feedback behavior and prosodic features, to the difficulties of studying sign language. Common to all these examples is the tension between the extended capabilities of generative AI and thus data-driven approaches on the one hand, and theory-driven approaches on the other. The section concludes by systematizing this tension in order to explore a bridge between data, representation, and theory-based approaches.

3.1   Manual Gesture

Since an LLM such as ChatGPT [157] is not embodied (in the sense that it lacks vision for perceiving and extremities for producing body movements), one could expect that it does not have anything to say about manual gesture. However, there are plenty of online gesture resources,[6] and there is a growing number of gesture-related scientific publications[7], which can potentially be used as part of a language model's training data. Accordingly, a language model might yet be able to handle multimodal data. As an example, consider (1), taken from SaGA [133], dialogue V11, 2:32.

(1) dann ist das Haus halt so:/*then the house is like this*:

Intuitively, the speaker outlines the layout of the building talked about. From the gestural demonstration, one can obtain the information that the shape of the building is rectangular, like the symbol "⊔".

What does ChatGPT say to this example? We have to provide a verbal description of the gesture, however:

> In the following scenario, Jane meets someone. The person says "The house is like this" and simultaneously gestures as follows: The index finger of the right hand is stretched, the other fingers are curled; the hand with the stretched finger is moved away from body, then towards left, and finally towards the body. Provide a short answer, as to what kind of gesture this is and what the gesture can mean in the context of the utterance.

> The gesture described is a "demonstrative" or "illustrative" gesture, used to visually represent or mimic the shape or form of something. In the context of the utterance "The house is like this," the gesture likely represents the shape or layout of the house being described, indicating its size, orientation, or structure.

> Provide a short answer as to what shape the house has.

---

[6] See, for instance, https://paperswithcode.com/search?q_meta=&q_type=& q=gesture, last accessed 6th February 2024.

[7] Such as https://www.gesturestudies.com and the publications and conferences listed there.

> Based on the described gesture, the house has a rectangular or elongated shape.

This is just one example that does not allow any general conclusions to be drawn;[8] more systematic study on LLMs and gestures are needed, as pointed out by Wicke (2024) [213]. Nonetheless, this example demonstrates that multimodality, as represented by speech and gesture, can already be captured by unimodal LLMs. We return to this apparent puzzle in Sect. 3.3 when dealing with another kind of gesture, namely pointing gestures.

3.2 Making Sense of the (Bodily) Multimodal Ensemble

Human communication fundamentally embodies multimodality [163]. Previous research presents substantial evidence that gesture and speech are connected [208,209], demonstrating that multimodal signals tend to be temporally aligned at critical points in time (e.g., [111,114,166] see [167] for a review). From an early age, we engage with this multimodal ensemble [56], with the interplay between gestural dynamics and acoustic peaks further motivated by physical impulses of the respiratory system [167]. Notably, advanced tools now enable the automatic detection of these significant temporal peaks across various signals, prompting the question: How can we derive meaning from these discrete moments in time?

A notable instance in speech that generates a peak – in terms of fundamental frequency and/or intensity – is the prominent syllable (cf. Sect. 3.5); and within a syllable, its nucleus (usually a vowel). Even in a long-standing software for speech analysis like Praat [26], there exists a script for the automatic detection of nuclei [41]. Furthermore, for languages with available resources, automatic speech segmentation at the phoneme level, such as offered by WebMAUS [107] enables precise segmentation, from which we can easily establish syllable boundaries.

Having a syllable as a unit of information allows for the identification of meaningful peaks in the streams of acoustic or kinematic information. However, it is crucial to make informed decisions about which of these peaks should be paired together to potentially create a meaningful aligned signal. Kadavá et al. [102] utilize an 80 ms window to pair acoustic and kinematic peaks, motivated by mechanical coupling and, more importantly, by the timing of anticipatory or reactionary muscle movements that occur before or after a deceleration peak [13] (after [102, 4191]). The layers of acoustic and kinematic information, along with the procedure used by Kadavá et al. [102], are illustrated in Fig. 1. This pipeline provides tangible proof of our advancement in collaboration between linguistics and computer science, enabling us to identify units of information (such as syllables) in a computer-assisted manner and, within those units, automatically find pivotal points that may be carriers of information.

---

[8] Furthermore, the example was analyzed in [131] and was therefore possibly part of training data.

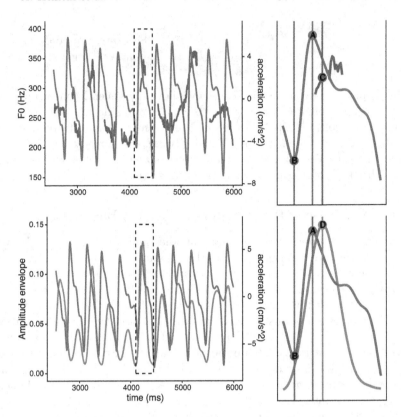

Fig. 1. Representation of amplitude envelope, fundamental frequency (F0), and acceleration over time. The diagrams to the right illustrate the methodology for isolating synchronously occurring peaks within segments demarcated by 80 ms. Identified peaks include: A for acceleration, B for deceleration, C for F0, and D for amplitude envelope. The figure is taken from Kadavá et al. [102, 4192].

When working with speech, whether it is formed into single morphemes, words, or full sentences, we are dealing with meaning. Even when examining phones, which may not be meaningful on their own, we are dealing with segmentable units based on spectral characteristics. As linguists and speech scientists, we can make informed decisions and use labels and annotations to provide data that, in turn, can be used to produce automated tools for segmentation and annotation. The challenge arises when we are faced with vocalizations rather than speech. How do we segment the units if we do not know whether they distinguish meaning? How do we segment units whose spectral characteristics seem to flow into one another (i.e., how do we find a boundary)? To pave the way toward automation, we first need to establish rules that help us answer such questions and, based on these rules, label a significant amount of data. In recent work, [61] proposed a method to label novel vocalizations and test the similarity of neighboring segments. In the future, using their paradigm, we could establish a direct line of investigation and comparison between human and non-human vocalizations.

By combining efforts between linguists, speech scientists, and computer scientists, we can further establish a link that would allow us to connect prelinguistic vocal information with kinematic information. If it is crucial for linguistic signals (e.g., co-speech gestures); why should we not suppose it was crucial before the dawn of language? We know that primates make great use of gesture, although there is contradictory evidence about whether apes can expand their gestural repertoire (e.g., [8,48]). Nevertheless, previous evidence highlights the importance of multimodality in primates [46], even though it is still rarely studied [123]. Developing tools to automate the processing of prelinguistic multimodal signals would enable us to study both human cognition (e.g., through the emergence of communicative systems) and non-human communication. As scientists studying communication systems, we can strive to provide units of meaning, which, in turn, can be utilized by computer scientists to build robust models.

3.3   Pointing (Deixis)

"[M]ost linguistic expressions are based on the perception of objects or situations in the real world" ([206, p. 191], quoted after [204, p. 378]). Such situated language use is characterized by the use of deictic acts, most prominently pointing gestures. Since pointing is bound up with reference, it has – in contrast to other kinds of manual gestures – received early attention from semantics and the philosophy of language (e.g., [59]). In fact, deixis is the hinge between the symbolic realm of language and the indexical realm of the perceptible environment [120]. Accordingly, understanding pointing is an important part of analyzing, interpreting, and taking part in referential communication – regardless of being concerned with human–human (HHI), human–computer (HCI), or computer–computer interaction (CCI).

Successful pointing (deictic behaviour in general) can be construed in terms of *triangulation* [40]: if successful, pointing brings about a three-place relation between a speaker ("pointer"), an addressee, and a common focal object or situation (the thing pointed at). Therefore, AI technology used to study interactions involving deixis must be able to identify the pointer, their pointing device, the addressee, and the object being pointed at. As usual in the domain of language processing, two perspectives have to be kept apart: analysis and synthesis. The former is concerned with the *understanding* of multimodal behavior, the latter deals with its *generation*. Within HCI, powerful algorithms for generating multimodal referring expressions in context have been developed [112,193]. The underlying rationale is that a referential expression is designed in such a way that verbal information from speech and locational information from a pointing gesture uniquely singles out the intended referent within a set of distractor items. Understanding multimodal deixis was arguably the first application of HCI, namely, the "put-that-there" system of Bolt [28], which processed verbal input and pen strokes on a display. This early system thereby circumvented what turned out to be a serious challenge, however, namely identifying the object pointed at (the so-called index), in particular if no descriptive aid from speech is provided [14,87,113,136]. The reason for this processing difficulty is that a pointing gesture does not directly single out an index; rather, it projects a pointing cone that directs the attention of the addressee (e.g., [43,113,132]). Accordingly, processing a pointing gesture and "guessing" its index is a fuzzy perceptual task, which is influenced by various factors such as the object density within the pointing domain or the interlocutors' perspectives [86]. There is no good reason to assume that AI technology fares better in this respect. But in any case, AI technology which is to be used for analyzing referential communication, or want to be able to take part in situated interactions, needs to be "embodied": deixis rests on sensory, visual scene processing (understanding) and mastering a pointing device (such as an index finger; generation). Hence, the successful use of AI in this kind of multimodal research requires an interplay of speech processing, visual analysis, and robotics.

However, we want to mention two phenomena that seem to be particularly involved and (to our knowledge) yet largely ignored by multimodal AI, namely deferred reference and addressee or discourse pointing.

Deferred reference happens when one points to one thing (the index) and refers to another one (the referent). For this to work, index and reference have to stand in a salient relation to each other. As an example, consider (2), where a painting is pointed at, but the painter is referred to ([38, p. 168]):

(2)   This [*pointing at a painting*] is my favourite painter.

In (2), the index – the painting – is just given: it has been identified *qua* example. However, a more realistic, pointing cone-based scenario is shown in Figure Fig. 2. Here, it cannot be decided by the pointing alone whether the pointer points at the cup or the egg at s_2 – the egg in s_3 is out. However, the pointing gets disambiguated due to affiliated speech:

(3)   a.   Could you pass me the coffee?

     b.   Could you pass me this egg?

This resolution works with deferred references, too [132]:

(4)   a.   I like this type of china.

     b.   This is a hard-working hen.

(4a) selects the cup, (4b) selects the egg (at s_2) as index. Analyzing pointing and its metonymic uses therefore requires an interplay of perceptual scene processing and world knowledge, which, to our knowledge, has not yet been addressed in computational approaches.

It should be emphasized, however, that world knowledge is not a problem for AI. Resolving deferred references *via* descriptions is easily brought about by ChatGPT (GPT 3.5), as exemplified in the following exchange:

Fig. 2. The pointing cone "highlights" the cup and the egg at s_2 but excludes the egg at s_3 (taken from [132, p. 278]).

In the following scenario, George is pointing at a table with a cup, an egg, a fork, a knife, a book, a table, a spoon, a newspaper, and car keys on it. He says: "This is the best china". Provide a short answer as to which object George is referring to.

George is likely referring to the cup on the table as "china" can refer to fine porcelain or ceramic dinnerware, often used for drinking vessels like cups.

This leads to issues of symbol grounding [81]: How does the LLM "know" such things without having ever seen a cup or an egg and interacted with these objects? Very likely, this puzzle of current AI (namely, communicating without words grounded in direct or indirect experience) is due to "parasitic grounding" of symbolic cycles of large data within human understanding [83]. Given this admittedly sparse evidence, AI does seem to be able to process data that results from human participation in multimodal interactions to a certain level; they are just lacking a physical, robotic incarnation to perceive and to produce bodily modalities. Speaking in terms of the Turing test, this boils down to the difference between purely verbal T2 systems and robotic, sensorimotor T3 systems [82].

We started with a brief overview of what it means to refer and defer by pointing, and then asked whether current AI produces distinguishable behavior, *modulo* the trivial (?) fact of lacking a "body". This is the perspective of the Turing test, and not the perspective of AI used as a tool for preprocessing or annotating multimodal data. Accordingly, we have to distinguish at least three uses of AI in multimodal research:

- AI (narrow sense): **tool** to automatize some task. See other sections for examples of AI tools for preprocessing and annotating multimodal data.
- **Companion**: AI for social or information-seeking interaction. This is the focus of the Turing test.
- **Cognitive modeling**: AI as reverse engineering models of cognition

The examples above indicate that AI in the second sense, namely as companions, are already useful, albeit still being mainly[9] verbal (no T3 systems).

Besides such exophoric uses, pointing gestures are also involved in information management in discourse [67]. Consider, for example, (5), which is taken from the SaGA corpus [133], dialogue V5, starting at 13m58s.

(5) *Context: F is recapitulating the route that has just been described to him by R. Now he is trying to recall the landmark at a certain point of the route (turn 1). Due to his hesitation ("die (.) die"), R completes the utterance (turn 2) while discourse pointing at F. The completion was successful since it got accepted by F (turn 3).*

    a. **F:** da steht die (.) die / there is the the

    b. **R:** die SKULptur ((pointing at F)) / the sculpture

    c. **F:** die skulptur drauf / the sculpture on top

R's pointing gesture in turn b. indicates that the discourse referent F is looking for in turn a. is already part of the common ground (cf. [90]). Accordingly, F accepts it in turn c. Thus, understanding the gesture in (5) requires a model of the ongoing discourse and the facts shared among the participants – on top of recognizing discourse pointing and detaching it from plain exophoric uses. This should be too difficult for an LLM, shouldn't it?

> In the following scenario, Paul is recapitulating the route that has just been described to him by Lisa. Now he is trying to recall the landmark at a certain point of the route. He is starting an incomplete utterance: "Then there is the the ...". Due to his hesitation, Lisa completes the utterance while pointing at Paul: "... the sculpture". Provide a short answer as to what kind of gesture this is and what the gesture can mean in the context of the utterance.

---

[9] LLMs such as ChatGPT do produce pictorial output.

> The gesture described is a "completion" or "prompting" gesture, where Lisa assists Paul in recalling information by providing the missing word or phrase through a physical cue. In the context of the utterance, it indicates that Lisa is helping Paul remember the landmark mentioned earlier in their conversation.

Pretty close, isn't it? One has to provide some context, of course. And the context in the above-given example is quite verbose and "semantically loaden". Accordingly, the answer might be shaped by collateral associations evoked by the detailed prelude. And indeed, a shortened context leads to a different, considerably worse exchange:

> In the following scenario, Paul is talking to Lisa. Paul: "Then there is the the ...". Lisa, while pointing at Paul: "The sculpture". Provide a short answer as to what kind of gesture this is and what the gesture can mean in the context of the utterance.

> In this scenario, Lisa's pointing gesture serves as a "clarification" or "confirmation" gesture, indicating agreement with or correction of Paul's statement by identifying the missing word ("sculpture") in his utterance.

Of course, Lisa's turn is a completion, and the gesture does not point at the missing word. This does not replace systematic gesture probings in LLMs (cf. [213]), but nonetheless indicates some variance or even boundaries depending on the elaborateness of prompt context.

To summarize: We have distinguished three uses of AI in multimodal research (tool, companion, cognitive modeling). From a companion point of view, multimodality emphasizes that current AI systems are mainly T2 systems, lacking T3 sensorimotor, robotic capabilities. However, symbolic descriptions of multimodal interactions enable AI to process even the data resulting from such interactions in a meaningful, interpretable way. This suggests the conclusion that the main challenges of perceptual fuzziness of pointing gestures (which makes it difficult to identify indices in the first place), deferred reference and discourse pointing for AI systems (the multimodal computing gap) rest in sensorimotor, robotic engineering. This seems to be the avenue that AI technology needs to go down to engage physically in deictic behavior.

3.4   Multimodal Ensembles and Gestalts

Speech processing and turn-taking is a tightly coupled system [121]. Adding temporally offset, multimodal signals should increase the massiveness of the binding

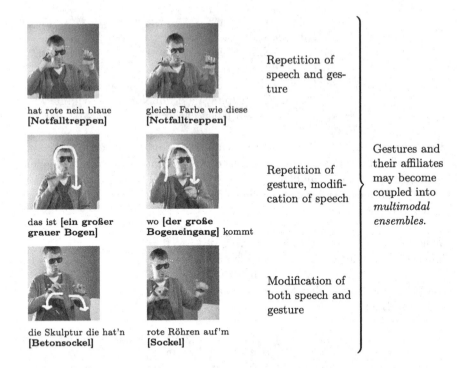

Fig. 3. Routinization of speech–gesture ensembles by repetition [135, 143] (figure is taken from the presentation slides).

problem [57, 97] and impact this system to the effect that multimodal interaction is much more difficult to process than unimodal communication [91]. But the opposite is the case. One reason for explaining this paradox is that multimodal discourse gives rise to channel-crossing, higher-order processing. Basically, (features of) signals from one channel can inform the interpretation of signals on other channels. This has been observed in terms of the *unity* of speech–gesture pairs, or composite utterances, which cohere into a channel-crossing *ensemble* [103] (cf. the notion of *idea unit* [141]). Empirical evidence was found in the routinization of *recurrent* speech–gesture ensembles [135, 143] – see Fig. 3 for some examples. On repetition, speech–gesture unity allows for a simplification of the form of the components of an ensemble. A generalisation to multimodal "local gestalts" (early work on multimodal ensembles focused on speech and co-verbal gesture), but without recurrence, has been argued for by [146], leading to a notion of recurrent multimodal gestalts [91]. In recent work, ensembles have been construed within interactionally embedded gestalt perception for rapid processing of multimodal signals [203]. An illustration of a multimodal gestalt is given in Fig. 4, simplifying the model of [203] somewhat. The utterance-level interpretation of the speech signal is shaped by both, bottom-up multimodal signal features and top-down gestalt perception. Multimodal signal features and multimodal gestalts inform the interpretation of future multimodal utterances (as

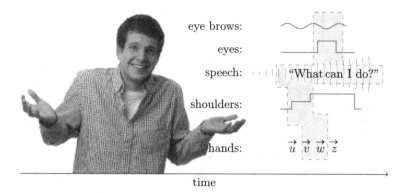

Fig. 4. Shrugging as whole body behavior (Wikimedia Foundation, Inc. Original uploader was Cbarr (WMF), CC BY-SA 3.0, File:RobGrindes-shrug-143px.png). The dashed, gray area indicates a multimodal gestalt.

captured, for instance, in probabilistic frameworks such as predictive processing [89]; but see [125] for some critical discussion).

From the perspective of processing, the challenge of multimodality is that the *immediacy assumption* [75] holds for multimodal interaction, too (of course!). Processing happens not only bottom-up (the traditional perspective of linguistic grammars and parsing), but also top-down, and involves an immediate integration of processes as diverse as facial recognition [155], emotional tracking [68], perceptual classification [131], social cognition [150], and verbal utterance interpretation (e.g., [66,72]). It remains to be seen whether the *multimodal serialization hypothesis* is sustainable, namely that multimodal language processing is driven by "vertical relevance" which supervenes on sequential relevance [134].

3.5 Temporal, Kinematic and Pragmatic Integration of Gesture and Prosody

David McNeill, a pioneering scholar in the field of gesture studies, claimed that speech-accompanying gestures, also called "co-speech gestures" (a) are closely temporally coordinated with speech (the phonological synchrony rule); and that (b) work together with speech to convey the same pragmatic meaning (the pragmatic synchrony rule [141]). See Fig. 5 for an example of temporal coordination of gesture and prosody, based on [55].

In this sense, the combination of verbal, prosodic, and gestural strategies to convey meaning [164] can be described as a "multimodal ensemble" (see Sect. 3.4) in communication. In the last decades, research has shown clear evidence of a close temporal coordination between prosodic structure (e.g., prominence and phrasing patterns) and the organization of gestural movements. However, less is known about the kinematic coordination between gesture and prosody (e.g., [6]) and the interaction between the two in the marking of pragmatic meaning [32,172]. Following these lines of research, as multimodal language researchers

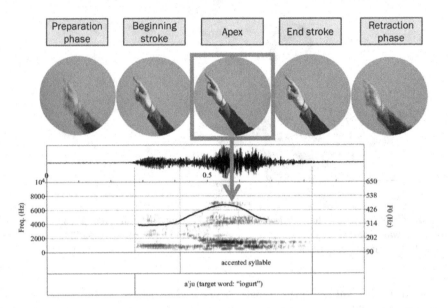

Fig. 5. Graph showing a pointing gesture in its temporal phases (top), time aligned with sound wave and F0 contour (middle) and text annotation (bottom). Adapted from [55].

we are interested in assessing three complementary aspects of the relationship between prosody and gesture, specifically their temporal, kinematic, and pragmatic integration.

To do this, multimodal language researchers have typically relied on human annotation. Regarding prosody, the challenge in prosodic annotation lies in translating a continuous speech signal into discrete linguistic entities, such as the assumed categorical elements of intonational phonology [116]. In the realm of intonational phonology theory, models for prosodic categories have been proposed, of which the most widely adopted systems are based on the autosegmental-metrical approach to intonation (Tone and Break Indices, [20]). Human transcription of speech is a time-consuming task, and inter-annotator agreement is, at best, moderate (e.g., [74,197]). Consequently, several attempts have been made to automatically classify or transcribe prosodic categories (e.g., [159,174,175,187,188,214] for an overview). See Fig. 6 for an example on pitch accent categories of GToBI training materials, cf. [73]. However, automatic approaches proposed so far have a common limitation – while they can reliably classify coarse prosodic categories, i.e. two classes of pitch accents, classifying more fine-grained pitch accent categories or differences in prominence levels fails to yield reliable results (e.g., [30,174,188]). Moreover, to our knowledge, no standard annotation proposal has been made up until now for the labeling of prosodic meaning. One consequence of those weaknesses in manual and

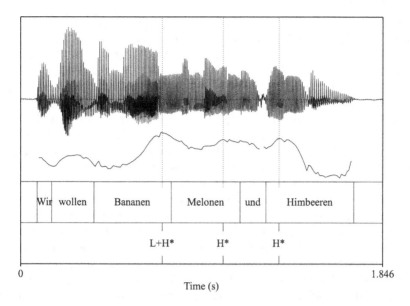

Fig. 6. Sound wave (top), F0-contour (middle), and text and prosodic annotation (bottom) for a German sentence (translating to *"We want bananas, melons and raspberries"*), with annotated GToBI pitch accent categories L+H* and H*.

automatic classification is the lack of appropriate large-scale and automatically annotated databases and resources for prosody research.

Regarding gestural data, annotations have mainly been done manually by human annotators, with the use of different software and annotation schemes (see [71] for an overview). However, a few tools such as motion-tracking suits or post-processing applications (e.g., OpenPose [35], MediaPipe [137], etc.) can track bodily movements automatically, allowing researchers to process the gestural kinematic signals into measuring aspects such as gesture trajectories, amplitude, or velocity. In combination with manual annotations, these tracking tools are able to identify gestures (see [95]). While these tools are already able to accelerate the manual annotation processes and can fairly easily be incorporated into AI, their approach to the semantic or pragmatic dimensions of gesture is limited. Similar to prosody, the interpretation of gestural behavior is key in order to assess decisions such as referential gesture types or pragmatic functions. These classifications are primarily applied manually (through annotation systems such as M3D [173], LASG [31] or CorpAGEst [27]). For instance in the M3D system, the meaning dimension allows the classification of gesture referentiality as well as pragmatic domains like speech acts, stance-taking, or discourse organization (e.g., information structural marking). Some of the manual annotation systems reach acceptable to good inter-annotator reliability (cf. [172]). Such categorical classifications could provide a challenge for their implementation into processing models for the following reasons: (a) they are sometimes based on subjective interpretations, which can diverge even between experts, and (b) most of these linguistic function-based decisions require a communication-related context to be made reasonably. Thus, while the processing of kinematic signals is on a good path to be a facilitation in gestural research, assessing the discourse-structural and meaning contribution of prosody and gesture will likely remain an annotation challenge for AI tools in the near future. One of the reasons for this is that machine learning requires a large amount of manually annotated data for accurate training, yet this data is not expected to be generated in the required breadth and depth. Given the role of AI as a companion tool (see Sect. 3.3), one might expect new ways of automatically generating appropriate annotations; however, prosodic information presents particular challenges in this regard.

Given the similarities that can be found between prosody and gesture, both in the temporal and the pragmatic domains, automatic classification of multimodal events may pose a similar obstacle to building large-scale corpora. An important issue for both temporal coordination and pragmatic coordination of prosody and gesture is the synchronization of the acoustic and visual channels to provide accurate assessments of the data. When possible, data synchronization should be considered in advance, by using an appropriate technological recording setup, but it can also be done in post-processing. While temporal synchronization might be covered by AI tools soon, semantic integration of speech and gesture will most likely be a bigger challenge. With prosody-gesture research being a relatively young field in linguistics, major theoretical developments regularly occur, which poses another challenge for up-to-date training of AI tools. Therefore, communication researchers need to be in accordance and very specific about their classification criteria in order to be able to train annotation algorithms. This can pose a challenge to linguists due to perceptual subjectivity in linguistic interpretation.

With innovative AI technology, there is hope to increase classification accuracy in the domains of prosody-gesture research. A more precise mapping between theoretically motivated form-based categories (in prosody and gesture) and the continuous speech signal could be achieved in the future. However, especially the functional mapping of prosodic and gestural categories to the acoustic and visual signal might continue to be a challenge for AI in communication research, given that linguistic context and expertise are required to reach this mapping.

3.6   Multimodal Feedback in Interaction

We have a relatively good understanding of the linguistic structures used for anticipating and resolving trouble [19,63,177], but most of this research was based on observations, written or audio language, narrations and elicitations. Only recent analyses have drawn attention to the importance of using naturalistic conversational data for this research [44]. The role and the usage of the multimodal cues as a part of trouble management resource the interlocutors employ in face-to-face interactions is largely under-researched and we have no understanding of which and how multimodal cues are combined with vocal and manual (non-)lexical signals in everyday conversation. Apart from that, very little is known about the strategies used for trouble management in sign languages. Understanding the role of the various cues in the trouble management resources in face-to-face interaction in signed and spoken languages has important implications for the conception of successful communication.

We define feedback as an interactional behavior that displays interlocutors' perception or understanding of the course of the conversation.

A central topic of multimodal modeling concerns the variability in non-verbal and non-manual conversational units and how they help shape human communication. One large source of variability exists in facial and head movement to signal feedback in face-to-face interaction. Movements seem to have specific meanings, but no clear picture exists about these mappings and how variable they are. The goal of research in this area is to understand how the various facial and head movements are linked to feedback functions to better understand conversational phenomena, such as turn-taking, feedback, and trouble management. This topic is multimodal, as it involves the use of visual (manual signs, gestures and non-manual cues, e.g. facial expressions, eyebrow, head, torso or shoulder movements) and vocal signals (such as lexical items and non-lexical vocalizations). To study feedback we use the available online corpora and collect naturalistic data in a variety of spoken and signed languages: German Sign Language (DGS) [109], Russian Sign Language (RSL) [17] and Ukranian Sign Language [18], spoken Russian [17], spoken German or spoken Polish [115]. For the transcription of the spoken language data, we try to use automatic speech recognition (ASR) but we encounter various challenges, recently documented by Liesenfeld and colleagues [124], such as the deletion of hesitations and non-lexical vocalizations like laughter (see also [71]). Languages other than English already pose a challenge for many ASR systems. While English seems to contain the lowest error rate, languages like Polish, German and Russian, perform significantly poorer when using most speech-to-text systems.

Applying ASR to natural interaction poses a much bigger challenge. Human interaction typically features a rapid back-and-forth between participants, with a normal distribution of turn transition times centered around 0–200 ms [121], with many turns occurring in slight overlap. Tested ASR systems record substantially fewer speaker transitions and no overlapping annotations, and they lose linguistically relevant chunks of language [124] (see above).

We use annotation software ELAN [216] to manually annotate further feedback signals (e.g., head movement, eyebrow-raising, mouth movement, torso orientation, shoulder shrugging, and other movements). Then machine learning is used to determine which multimodal cues are used in overlap and which are not. This involves investigating how facial movements are used in different languages, and how they are used in sign languages compared to spoken languages. Data are manually annotated for about 70 different categories of facial movements using ELAN. These include, for example: "head tilt to the left", "eyebrows raised", or "nose wrinkled".

The annotation team has incrementally developed a set of annotation guidelines. The annotations are double-checked by deaf and hearing researchers. At each time step, the annotator defines whether there is a feedback element, which features are moving, and a start and end boundary. In this way, the data is segmented from a continuous stream of video data into a discrete list of multimodal feedback cues. Timestamps are used to keep the data aligned with the video data. The timestamps also allow the duration of the feedback to be measured, as well as linking to potentially relevant pre- and post-feedback items. Annotation relies on many human judgments. It is important to note that the process is incremental, as it is not easy to define all the criteria and rules in advance.

The project under consideration is naturally divided into an annotation part and a statistical modeling part. For the annotation part, formal modeling is used to represent the criteria and logic for annotation and extraction. Whether or not this annotation process can be fully and formally modeled is still an open question. The project has not yet aimed to do so, and it is an open question whether this is possible. Parts of the annotation process are formally modeled using the annotation guidelines mentioned above. These are verbal descriptions that are formal because they are written down in a precise way. The annotations are extracted using a script that contains rules about which features to extract, which features to combine, and when certain features belong together. These rules are kept very simple and do not depend much on the context. For the data analysis part, several standard statistical and machine learning models are used to analyze the resulting data set. The main goal is to find out which features are clustered together to signal feedback in interaction and whether these features are similar between signed and spoken languages under investigation. The features ideally reflect a faithful representation of what is important for successful communication. The challenges of this problem are related to typical analysis decisions, such as sample size, data preprocessing, feature selection, and model comparison. Other decisions, e.g. in clustering analyses, are related to distance and linkage methods. Overall, these modeling techniques are very standard and well-understood: these are statistical models and therefore do not have an understanding of the nuances of the data that only humans can understand.

The question then is which of the modeling steps described so far can or cannot be automated. Both the annotation and statistical modeling steps can benefit to some extent from NLP/ML tools. The annotation part could benefit the most from automation. This process is currently very time-consuming and expensive with a tendency towards low inter-annotator agreement [151] since it relies heavily on human judgment. Computer vision tools such as MediaPipe can be used to automatically extract initial sets of relevant features. MediaPipe provides several tools for facial feature extraction, and it is possible to train new models for new features. For example, MediaPipe predicts 52 facial "blendshape" scores, which are movements such as "brow down left", "cheek squint left", "mouth roll down", and so on. These scores largely overlap with the features that are currently coded manually. OpenFace generally detects more details than MediaPipe. For example, OpenFace recognizes facial action units according to the Facial Action Coding System.[10] However, not all non-manual movements are likely to be currently detected in the video data by a Computer Vision tool. In a study by Paggio and colleagues [160], head movement recognition software trained on spoken language conversational video data annotated frame-wise with visual and acoustic features was found to predict head movement only with 0.75% accuracy. Especially subtle head nods signalling feedback are likely to be missed in the data. As the automatic recognition of non-manual elements (especially head movements) in video-recorded face-to-face dyadic conversations does not seem to be accurate and reliable enough at the current stage, a number of recent studies pursue a combined method: manual annotation in the video-recorded data and partly automatized extraction of particular measurements with a CV tool. A reliably working combination of such methods is, however, needed to carry out systematic, data-driven research in multimodal, signed and spoken language use. It seems possible to train ML models for this as well. Improved, specialized tools would mitigate at least some of the manual workload, enabling to process a larger amount of data.

Going from a set of features to a set of feedback labels is a more undefined problem so far. Typical feedback categories discussed in the literature are e.g., *continuer, newsmarker, assessment, open request, acknowledgment.* Many of these concepts are based on spoken language, which might look differently in sign language and other language settings such as in online communication. Therefore, the project is currently set up to postpone the use of any of these labels prior to the analysis of multimodal behaviour. Data analysis such as clustering is used to determine whether it makes sense to distinguish concepts such as that of a "continuer".

The approach just outlined uses statistics and ML methods such as k-nn clustering. The idea is to explore the mapping between these labels and the features in an unsupervised way. Multimodal LLMs could be useful to automate this process. Existing LLMs are not yet able to handle multimodal data. However, multimodal LLMs are under development (see above). The goals of such multimodal LLMs are not necessarily the same as what we or other cognitive scientists are interested in, but it is possible to reuse models and learn from them in both ways.

Ideally, one would like to find out what categories of feedback can be produced by movements of the face, head or torso. This requires a high level of understanding of a conversation. It is not clear that this is fully possible with automation tools such as LLMs. In this sense, it seems to be a limit for the application of current generative AI systems to learn how to process a conversational context to detect, qualify, and ultimately "understand" human behavior such as facial or head movements. We see this as an ongoing challenge for AI.

---

[10] https://en.wikipedia.org/wiki/Facial_Action_Coding_System.

3.7   Dyadic Social Behavior – Basic Research and Clinical Applications

Investigating dyadic social behavior is a vital aspect of visual communication research, underscoring the intricate interconnectedness inherent in interpersonal interactions. This area of research also holds significant implications for addressing psychiatric and neurodevelopmental conditions often associated with challenges in interpersonal reactivity, such as Autism Spectrum Disorder (ASD) [165]. In this context, multimodality refers, on the one hand, to different techniques for recording social-communicative behavior such as facial and body movement analysis, physiological response monitoring, neuroimaging, and eye tracking, with video recordings, specialized lab equipment, or wearable devices [156,186]. On the other hand, the notion of multimodality can be extended to the integration of several "semantic" layers of social interaction, including emotions, attention, conversational themes, social settings, and cultural contexts. Such "higher-level modalities" manifest throughout a variety of channels, including physiology, voice, face, body posture, and gaze patterns. Typically, they can not be accurately interpreted from a single type of raw data but can be conceived as coherent ensembles of multimodal signals that together convey social and emotional meaning [84]. These may entail easily discernible events such as a "smile", a "gaze towards an object", or a "pointing gesture", but also specific, more complex sequences of such events.

In clinical contexts, another layer of complexity emerges: part of psychiatric diagnosis involves using multimodal aspects of behavior to characterize individuals in relation to"typical" social functioning norms, with "atypical" behavior across various contexts regarded as "symptoms" indicative of a clinical condition [7,217]. Autism Spectrum Disorder (ASD) serves as a prime example of this diagnostic approach: Direct observation of social behavior via standardized tools is crucial for diagnosis. Specialized instruments (e.g. Autism Diagnostic Observation Schedule, ADOS) [130] have been developed to encapsulate both the subjective clinical impression and quantifiable aspects of autism-related behavioral patterns [185]. This method underscores the essential role of multimodal observation in identifying and understanding the nuanced spectrum of ASD.

Data Collection and Processing Techniques: Recent technical developments allow to employ advanced multimodal data collection methods. These include using tools like MediaPipe and OpenPose for detailed body pose and facial configuration analysis, mobile eye-tracking glasses, microphones for verbal communication capture, wristbands for physiological monitoring, and portable neuroimaging devices. Manual annotation and evaluation by human experts plays a crucial role in categorizing communicative behaviors, especially for higher order multimodal social-communicative states (e.g. joint attention, emotional/communicative states etc.) and clinical symptomatology [84,185]. Processing this data involves building on available tools and processing pipelines that use already available and established ML/AI methods [140]: analyzing facial expressions and categorizing basic emotion types and "action units" (according to

Ekman and Friesen [52]) and intensity (based on video or single images), analyzing body poses for detection of body and head gestures, and creating 3D skeletal models, and processing eye tracking data for saccades, fixations, and matching to a respective world video. Transcription of speech can be greatly sped up with the help of automatic tools and allows for sophisticated annotation and analysis of conversational elements, emotional tone, and specific linguistic properties [108,176].

Solvable Challenges and Immediate Future Directions in Multimodal Data Modeling: With available tools, it is well possible today to model data channels separately with high sophistication, using modality-specific pipelines. For such single-modality analyses (e.g. gesture detection, facial expression categorization, gaze mapping, and speech processing) automated pipelines will likely continue to evolve and will be able to capture more and more subtle nuances in the near future. For example, refinements and improvements are possible by integrating temporal dynamics into gesture and facial expression models and increasing the range of classified behavioral elements (e.g. types of gestures, types of facial emotions; [39,171]). For several challenges, there are no ready-to-use tools available, yet, but these will likely be available in the near future. These include fusing multiple video recordings into a full detailed 3D representation of the whole scenery, and simultaneous tracking of body configurations of multiple persons with just a limited number of video cameras [93] and/or sparse arrays of body sensors, or mapping eye gaze data onto a scenery in 3D gaze coordinates [79]. Thus, in principle, currently available uni-modal ML/AI methods and analyses and their future refinements might be sufficient to solve many problems related to the classification of modality-specific interactional entities with high precision (e.g. gesture classification based on pose data, or expressed emotion based on facial video data). However, vast amount of (annotated) data will be needed and may exceed what is feasible to produce in academic research.

Automation and Future Aspirations in Multimodal Research: Complex *multimodal* integration is currently neglected, but is pivotal to fully grasp the semantic meaning of social situations: For example, in a conversation between two individuals, if one person nods slightly while listening, this gesture can typically be interpreted as an acknowledgment or a sign of agreement, encouraging the speaker to continue. However, this nod, when paired with a brief, yet pointed, glance towards a wristwatch before returning to the speaker, transforms the message entirely. It would then be more appropriate for the speaker to recognize this as a subtle sign of impatience and a reminder of time constraints, and to stop talking instead of continuing. The core issue here is the necessity of integrating "world-knowledge" and attributing mental states to individuals for accurate interpretation of the situation. A single-modality cue, like a brief nod, can convey vastly different messages depending on context. Noticing the additional glance at an object, such as a watch, only clarifies meaning when combined with an understanding of internal states (e.g., impatience), social conventions (e.g., politeness), and the object's significance (a watch indicating time). Thus, the combination of multi-modal ambiguous cues and the breadth of contextual aspects may exponentially increase the range of possible interpretations. As a consequence, the endeavor to automate the analysis of social behavior for discerning nuanced meanings or identifying clinical symptoms could be reframed as striving toward the creation of a highly capable perceptual agent with a nuanced internal world model. This agent would need to possess advanced, universal capabilities for navigating social and communicative scenarios, equipped with perceptual precision and intuition comparable to humans. The question of whether this is actually theoretically possible or even desirable is beyond the scope here, similar to the discussion around Artificial General Intelligence (AGI) as a general solution for automating complex cognitive tasks.

A more feasible and realistic approach might be to develop generative multimodal models that are able to simulate human behavior for specific interactive scenarios, similar to how GPT-based LLMs mimic human linguistic output. The burgeoning field of virtual and augmented reality (VR/AR), particularly within platforms like the "Metaverse", may present a future opportunity to capture and analyze nuanced recordings of dyadic interactions on a massive scale. Such datasets could be analyzed with similar methodologies as used in large language models (LLMs) that create powerful generative models from large text corpora. As in the case of advanced models like GPT-4, given enough data in combination with further human reinforcement-learning based refinement, surprisingly capable models could potentially emerge.

The key to this approach would be not to operate on the "raw data" signals but to distill a lexicon of "tokens" or behavioral "subwords" that represent the smallest units of meaningful interaction. For instance, consider the nuanced interplay of gestures and expressions in a social interaction: a *nod* accompanied by a *smile*, further contextualized by direct *eye contact*, could be identified as the basic behavioral tokens. These tokens, when observed in a sequence, such as a smile followed by a nod, and then sustained eye contact, might collectively signify an "acknowledgment" or convey "friendliness". The temporal configuration of these tokens, their order, and duration, may convey further subtleties of the interaction: For example, a quick nod with a fleeting smile might denote a polite, yet perfunctory acknowledgment typical among acquaintances. In contrast, a prolonged smile combined with a nod and extended eye contact could be interpreted as a warm, genuine greeting, indicative of a deeper rapport between friends. Employing a granular, token-based strategy as a mediator between raw data and nuanced social interpretation offers numerous benefits: it simplifies complexity by decomposing interactions into fundamental units, enhances processing efficiency and reduces data requirements, broadens model applicability across varied scenarios, supports gradual learning, and increases the model's interpretability. This perspective of a stratified bottom-up methodology, emphasizes the need for a nuanced understanding of the semantic and social building blocks of behavior. Identifying these "tokens" or "subwords" is not just about capturing gestures or expressions but understanding their significance within a rich tapestry of human interaction. This approach could unlock new perspectives in social behavior research and clinical diagnostics, offering a granular view of interpersonal dynamics without the constraints of formal pre-defined theoretical models. At the same time, this strategy allows for the thoughtful integration of established theoretical concepts by defining appropriate tokens. By adopting a layered modeling strategy, the analysis remains data-driven yet can be enhanced and guided by pertinent theories from psychology, linguistics, and medicine.

The current state of the field seems to be optimally suited for such an approach: With the increasing availability of high-precision modality-specific analysis pipelines, the intermediate "tokens" could be assessed automatically, and their multimodal integration could then further be analyzed on this more abstract, semantically meaningful level. Ensembles of these tokens, their time course, and their complexities could be further stacked in increasing layers of abstraction, i.e. from basic building blocks of interaction, to transient states of communication, up to categorizations such as typical and atypical behavior and diagnostic symptoms [185]. However, the ambition to automate the analysis of complex social behaviors for diagnostics in clinical settings should only be pursued with caution. The intricate variability of human behavior, shaped by diverse psychological and neurodevelopmental backgrounds, may not be fully captured. Furthermore, there are critical ethical concerns with respect to potential oversimplification, privacy issues and individual rights in medical care settings. Despite these challenges, the potential of automated analyses to augment clinical decision-making remains compelling. By providing a detailed and quantitatively rich portrait of behavior, AI-supported tools could offer clinicians a deeper understanding of patients' behavior and symptoms, enhancing diagnostic precision and personalized care strategies. However, the deployment of these technologies demands a careful balance, ensuring they serve as adjuncts to, rather than replacements for, the nuanced judgment of healthcare professionals. Respecting the ethical boundaries and the multifaceted nature of human behavior is crucial in realizing the benefits of AI in clinical applications, advancing patient care while safeguarding individual dignity and privacy.

3.8   Diagrams and LLMs

Diagrams represent a distinct research area within communication studies, yet they share overlaps and similarities with many other fields. While LLMs are now making remarkable progress in recognizing images and classifying objects within them, they often struggle to distinguish diagrams from other pictures. This challenge is not surprising, given that humans also encounter difficulties in this area. In most cultures, there is a similar intuitive understanding of what constitutes a diagram and how it differs from a picture. However, in research, there lacks a precise criterion for identifying diagrams as such and distinguishing them from language or other forms of representation [10, 21].

The absence of a standardized criterion for diagrams is partly because diagrams can be utilized in various ways, and their design function seems almost limitless. For instance, while the traditional diagram is visual, there have been uses of 'audio diagrams' since the 19th century [53], and the 20th and 21st centuries saw the invention of various 'haptic diagrams' [69, 154]. These can be

Fig. 7. Children pointing to a specific area of a diagram

objects that are both tangible and visible or visual diagrams that have been translated into Braille [201]. From the Middle Ages to early modern times, diagrams were also expressed through gestures [170]. For example, many children learn from an early kindergarten age to communicate diagrams by assembling different objects, indicating the medium for conveying a diagram can be highly versatile [70] (see Fig. 7).

Focusing on visual diagrams can be utilized either unimodally or multimodally, depending on the requirements. Visual programming language (VPL) in human-machine interaction, for instance, aims to be as unimodal, iconic, and rule-based as possible, yet intuitive[11]. In contrast, diagrams in human-human interaction, such as in mathematics education [205], are typically multimodal, iconic, spontaneous, and intuitive. Nonetheless, most diagrams are multimodal in that they are often accompanied by words, facial expressions, pointing gestures and gestures in general from the person drawing the diagram in a communicative situation. These situations form a kind of 'multimodal ensemble' (see Sect. 3.4) which frequently consists of words, facial expressions, gestures, and the diagram itself. When the communication situation is set aside, most diagrams are multimodal in that they incorporate heterogeneous elements, including geometric elements like lines, circles, parallelograms, etc., arranged spatially, alongside words or symbols. While the geometric elements are usually perceived as inherently diagrammatic, the words or symbols are often seen as non-diagrammatic. Hence, most diagrams that feature this multimodal ensemble are described as 'heterogeneous diagrams' [16].

Currently, diagrams are viewed from three perspectives [145]: (1) the 'suspicious view', which regards diagrams at best as heuristic tools; (2) a 'practical view', recognizing diagrams as capable of representing information or solving problems in specific contexts; and (3) a 'formal view', which considers diagrams as a formal language. The feasibility of the latter perspective was first demonstrated in the 1990s by distinguishing the syntax and semantics of diagrams, enabling metamathematical proofs concerning diagrams [191]. This significant

---

[11] See https://snap.berkeley.edu/project?username=ten_6044&projectname=Match%21.

Fig. 8. GPT 4.0 (February 2024) not only fail to recognize the diagram created by the hoops but also mistakes the position of the marbles in the picture.

advancement achieved by a philosopher was subsequently applied to mathematics and artificial intelligence [65,98]. Presently, psychology and cognitive research are particularly focused on exploring how the intuitive advantages of diagrams (e.g., free rides, observational advantages, etc.) [189,190,194] can be merged with formal diagram languages [24,25,78,92], while also addressing the long-recognized disadvantages of diagrams, such as ambiguity or uncertainty issues [64,100].

Diagrams have been utilized in artificial intelligence for years in a variety of ways. They are frequently used in the development of artificial intelligence [153], in the field of explainable AI, in the solution of certain problems and as a medium for certain applications. LLMs can be used either to obtain written information via diagrams, to analyze diagrams or to generate diagrams. The difficulty currently lies in recognizing a diagram as such and distinguishing it from an ordinary image. Language AIs are perfectly capable of doing this thanks to image recognition and different outputs. However, most LLMs already fail to recognize a diagram in a picture in which, for example, children use a diagram consisting of two partially overlapping hoops to classify marbles according to color (see Fig. 8).

If we stick with this example, the next step after the identification of a diagram would be to correctly classify it. However, further problems arise here, which are due to the insufficient research on diagrams to date. The majority of diagram use takes place outside of academic research, namely in professions such as graphic designers, information designers, communication designers, etc. Numerous guides, books and, above all, websites have emerged from the practical

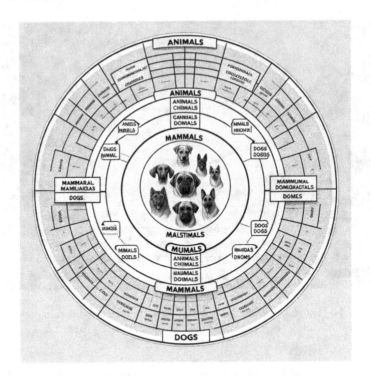

Fig. 9. Screenshot taken from GPT 4.0 in February 2024, which has now resorted to Dall-E for the same prompt as Fig. 10 (left screenshot).

environment of these industries, which present lists with examples of the different types of diagrams.[12]

However, these lists are not standardized and differ concerning the names of diagram types or the classification of diagrams under one type. However, there already exist approaches to creating metataxonomies [54]. As there was almost no diagram research at all between around 1880 and 1990 with the onset of the so-called 'crisis in intuition' [76, 101], LLMs can neither draw on a broad data set nor on a uniform classification. Even if there is already a great deal of research on the above example of the two hoops or circles, the definition is still not clear. This is because the unimodal or multimodal context also plays a role in diagrams. These contexts must respond to which diagrams a corresponding diagram is associated with, or which words, gestures etc. a diagram is associated with in context. The two partially overlapping hoops or circles can be interpreted as a set diagram, an Euler diagram, a Venn diagram or something else [58]. It is the context that is crucial here, and the amount of information about these contexts that an LLM can access. Diagrams may be intuitive to humans at first glance, but the closer they are examined, the more difficulties they reveal that machines cannot solve.

---

[12] See e.g. https://flowingdata.com/chart-types/, https://datavizcatalogue.com/, https://datavizproject.com/.

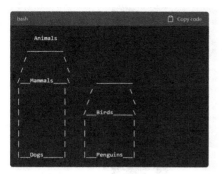

Fig. 10. The left screenshot is from GPT 3.5 from Spring 2023. The prompt asked for generating a Venn diagram including dogs and mammals as an example. The result was the Euler-type diagram shown. GPT 4.0 (without plugins) also delivers a similar result in February 2024. However, in 4.0 the containment relation is better represented by nested squares in ASCII. The right screenshot is taken from GPT 3.5 in spring 2023, which issued the tikz code for the same prompt as mentioned in the left one.

If images with such geometric shapes are analyzed in LLMs without further information, the programs not only fail to differentiate between picture and diagram, but also fail to recognize the type of diagram correctly or hallucinate. These are some of the problems with diagram recognition that need to be resolved in the future.

However, LLMs do not yet perform well in the generation and creation of diagrams either. Image-generating AIs such as Midjourney or Dall-E can create countless diagram types, but these often do not correspond syntactically to the conventions or rules and are usually semantically meaningless (see Fig. 9). Language-based AIs such as ChatGPT can now access these image generations, but then hallucinate results that do not correspond to the logical principles of the respective diagrams. Instead of a Venn diagram, for example, GPT generates an Euler diagram. LLMs work better, for example, when they generate diagrams in ASCII code or in tikZ (see the right screenshot in Fig. 10), HTML (see the left screenshot in Fig. 10) etc. Simple Euler or Venn diagrams are often syntactically correct, even if there can be confusion between the diagram types in the explanation given by the LLM.

Diagrammatic theorem provers or programmes in the field of visual computing work much more successfully than language-based AIs. However, if these are not themselves based on AI, but on sound and complete algorithms, they can already be successfully integrated into LLMs as plugins (see Fig. 11). The results for certain tasks are correct if the right plugins are selected. A lot therefore depends on the prompt, the respective architecture and the choice of plugin. This in turn determines the explanation of the produced diagram also provided by the respective LLM.

It is therefore important for diagram recognition and diagram creation that manually set up databases in the relevant specialist areas to classify the diagram

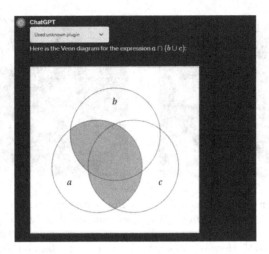

Fig. 11. Screenshot taken from GPT 4.0 in February 2024, which successfully completed a task using a Venn Diagram. The Wolfram Alpha plugin was utilized to assist.

types correctly. A model for such research is Leonardi.DB, for example, in which the diagram type 'Aristotelian diagram' or 'Square of Opposition' is precisely specified and fed with many data sets [42].

3.9 Multimodal Perception of Emotional Expression in Voices and Faces by Cochlear Implant Users

In emotion perception research, the ongoing development of more sophisticated AI holds considerable promise for enhancing its ability to learn complex patterns in emotional expression. AI can analyze emotional expressions in voices and faces through techniques like machine-learning-supported acoustic analysis (e.g., [45]), natural language processing (NLP), and computer vision. As AI systems continue to advance, they are anticipated to improve in their ability to integrate information from multiple modalities (including voice tone, facial expressions, and body language). Moreover, there is a prospect for AI systems to even become better at understanding and interpreting emotions in context, considering situational factors that influence emotional expression. Advancements in processing speed and hardware capabilities may further empower AI systems to perform real-time emotion analysis - a development which, for instance, would be an important advancement in applications, such as human-computer interaction, virtual assistants, and emotion-aware technologies. Notably, a new empirical approach utilizes AI to investigate so-called neural decoding. This approach uses multivariate analyses of brain recordings to permit emotion classification (e.g., for vocal, facial, or video stimuli) on the basis of a perceiver's brain activity (e.g., [126]).

At the same time, ongoing research in AI may lead to improved cochlear implants (CIs) - sensory prostheses designed to provide auditory sensations to individuals with severe-to-profound hearing loss by directly stimulating the auditory nerve. This is achieved through (1) recording sound via a microphone, then (2) transforming the sound into electrical signals via a sound processor, (3) transmitting these magnetically through the scull to an intracranial receiver, and (4) feeding them into a limited number of stimulation electrodes (typically, 6–22) which are surgically implanted into the cochlea. In general, improved AI might result in more sophisticated signal processing algorithms that enhance both speech intelligibility and sound quality for CI users. Moreover, AI might play a role in tailoring CI settings to individual users based on their unique auditory profiles, leading to improved outcomes and user satisfaction. AI can also be used to develop personalized and adaptive programming strategies for CIs based on individual CI user's responses and preferences. In fact, similar approaches may also be pursued in the context of vision impairment [117].

However, while AI has made significant strides in understanding emotional expressions in both voices and faces, the ability to fully comprehend how CI users perceive these emotional cues remains a complex challenge. This is because understanding the subjective experience of CI users involves several factors:

1. Sensory Perception: Hearing with a CI is electronic, not biological, and can sound very different than "normal" biological hearing. Because a CI only enables rudimentary hearing, the human brain must learn to process the input via cortical plasticity - which in this case refers to adaptations of the brain to deprivation-induced altered sensory input in one but not other sensory modalities. Thus, understanding how CI users perceive vocal emotions, and how vocal and facial emotions are integrated into their perceptual systems [50], requires considering how their brain interprets the signals provided by the device.

2. Individual Variability: Perception of emotional cues can vary greatly among CI users, presumably due to a multitude of factors that include age of implantation, duration of deafness, auditory rehabilitation, and CI hardware and software. However, these huge interindividual differences and their influencing factors are not fully understood and remain part of ongoing CI research [51]. In this context, we anticipate that emerging efforts to establish central CI registries (e.g., [195]) will be instrumental to promote the (currently lacking) multi-center studies with large numbers of participants that are essential to identify the relative contributions of multiple factors for rehabilitation outcome.

Whereas AI can help analyze large datasets of CI users' responses in computer experiments that test their perceptual abilities to recognize vocal and facial emotions (both with unimodal and multimodal stimuli), understanding the subjective experience of emotion perception requires more than just data analysis. It involves interdisciplinary research combining insights from neuroscience, psychology, linguistics, and AI. In the absence of appropriate contextualization, AI technology may well produce misleading results.

Researchers are working on developing AI systems that can better understand and adapt to individual differences in sensory perception, including those of CI users. However, a complete understanding of how CI users perceive emotional voices and dynamic moving faces remains an ongoing challenge for research in this area.

3.10   Multimodal Modeling from a Dynamic Perspective

AI can be put to several uses, in general as well as in the context of multimodality (cf. Sect. 3.3):

- AI as tool – here the focus is on automatized task solving like, in the context of multimodal data, pre-processing and/or annotation.
- AI as companion – here the focus is on AI for social or information-seeking interaction. It is within this focal area that the behavior of AI can be compared to human behavior (Turing test). One challenge posed by multimodality as studied within ViCom (see Sect. 1.2) is that it requires to proceed from purely verbal T2 systems to sensorimotor, robotic T3 systems, that are able to actually produce and perceive multimodal behavior in the first place [82].
- AI as cognitive modeling – here the focus is on AI as an implemented model of cognition, that is, reverse engineering of neuro-cognitive capabilities.

Given the predominantly data analytic perspective spelled out in the previous section, we are mainly concerned with the first two foci, AI as a tool or as a companion. We touch on the second and third areas again in Sect. 4.

In light of the analyses in Sect. 3.1–Sect. 3.4, the following picture emerges regarding the dynamics of multimodal modeling in the context of ever-improving AI: A central aspect of the automation gap described by the projects concerns the mapping of multimodal data to linguistic models to explicate the underlying (e.g., syntactic, semantic, or pragmatic) structures. This mapping, like any modeling, is characterized by a number of informational uncertainties that take on a special character in the context of the underlying linguistic theories. We are dealing, so to speak, with a line that leads from the respective (1) primary data via their representation by means of (2) secondary or tertiary data and various intermediate representations to the (3) theoretical concepts of an already developed or still to be developed theory. In this way, several points of reference for the uncertainties described so far can be identified. The reason for this is that this chain of terms (data-driven, inter-representational, theory-driven) is linked to a series of decisions whose uncertainties determine the relationship between theory and data. Without suggesting a preferred direction, we choose the bottom-up variant in our enumeration of uncertainties, starting with the data:

1. *Primary data:* Instead of assuming that the data streams relevant for multimodal computing are predetermined per se, we can assume a wider range of possibilities beyond the established paths in linguistics. This range beyond the usual suspects (such as eye-tracking data and audio or video recordings)

concerns possibilities that arise not only from the use of interfaces with ever-increasing resolution. Rather, it concerns the possibilities of advanced data collection devices such as motion capture suits or full body trackers for VR, biometric sensors, EEG headbands (electroencephalography), EMG devices (electromyography), skin conductance sensors, or gait analysis technologies. The point is that ever new data along ever new data streams promotes bottom-up approaches, which make data exploration preferable to theory-driven top-down approaches. However, this could lead to a gradual devaluation of theoretical approaches along a technological process that guides data selection without theoretical embedding: it is then a technology-driven view of multimodal data rather than a theory-driven one. Thus, we face a *data-related decision space* that concerns the data types to be analyzed for multimodal modeling and the streams that instantiate them (in terms of subtypes and their resolution). In a positive sense, this data space increases the opportunities for purely exploratory, data-driven approaches as it continues to expand. In a negative sense, this creates pressure for theory development, on the basis of which, for example, we should be able to substantiate the formation of multimodal ensembles that can be found in the corresponding data streams.

2. *Intermediary representation:* For the success of AI technologies for modeling processes of multimodal fusion and fission, it is crucial that data from each modality are mapped into the same representation space based on the same (usually vectorial, numerical) representational terms. The more modalities are to be mapped, the more heterogeneous the provenance of such representations becomes, which, due to their representational homogeneity, can be directly related, linked or amalgamated. In the modeling chain described above, we mentioned the special role of representations between primary data and theoretical terms. The problem that arises at this point is that by relying on established representation models from computer science, the linguistic modeler adopts (even if only implicitly) a modeling language that does not necessarily meet his representational requirements (e.g. with regard to closeness to theory, theoretical grounding or motivability and explicitness). Once again, the modeler is confronted with a decision space in which actors from outside his discipline become active and, due to their disciplinary background, decide on representation issues that might be incomprehensible to him. From an exploratory point of view, this may be tempting (taking away the modeling decisions "to see what the computer does with the data"). However, the uncertainties involved increase with the success of such approaches, because the connection between data and theory is designed and controlled independently of the latter – possibly without any attempt to connect to a theory. LLMs, for example, are based on so-called subwords, which are selected from a large corpus according to roughly two criteria: they should occur as often as possible and make up the character stream of the corpus as completely as possible. Transformer models trained on such vocabularies are known to be very successful, even if the resulting subwords have nothing or very little in common with linguistically motivated word forms or affixes. A representation gap occurs when the modeler refers to word forms as theoretical terms, even

though they no longer play a role in the modeling used. This gap is all the greater in areas such as multimodal computing, where there is already theoretical uncertainty about the relevant "multimodal subwords". Thus, exploratory approaches based on heuristics around "multimodal subwords" and the modeling of their similarity and contiguity associations using neural networks should be strictly accompanied by theoretical approaches that take a closer look at the representational terms of multimodal computing.

3. *Theory formation:* The third level concerns the theoretical terms, for which we are primarily interested, in the light of the project descriptions in Sect. 3.1–Sect. 3.4, in the aspect of their openness or change in the course of their confrontation with the data. More precisely, this is about situations in which the annotation of multimodal data makes the modeler aware of the inadequacy of his theoretical terms, which makes the modification of these terms indispensable. The crucial question is the openness of the theory to such perturbations, or the degree of its changeability and adaptability, or the flexibility of the theoretical terms. We can ask, for example, whether such adaptations are merely a matter of rearranging the terms, adding additional labels for classes or relations, or whether the required changes are more extensive, calling into question the validity of the terms as a whole, which could ultimately lead to their abandonment, alternatively following a data-driven bottom-up approach. Thus, while under (1) and (2) we are dealing with questions of informational uncertain one-to-many mappings between data types, data streams, and data resolutions on the one hand, and their secondary or n-ary representation on the other, (3) is about the temporal dynamics of the underlying theories as a result of multimodal modeling, which may lead to re-entering the data-representation-theory circle again and again.

The project descriptions all referred to a special term that we called *multimodal ensemble* in Sect. 3.4. In light of the three-part chain described so far, this term itself can be located at three levels: (1) At the data level, we can segment a (vertically ordered) time slice of our (horizontally ordered) input data streams to qualify it as a manifestation of a particular ensemble (using some annotation software). (2) At the representation level (assuming a unified vector space model), one can ask which vector operations, starting from the vector representations of its elementary monomodal representations, generate which representation of the latter ensemble as a unit that can be related to which other units in the same representation space (this is ideally done completely automatically). (3) On the theoretical level, questions about the status of such ensembles are addressed in theoretical terms. For example, how the composition of an ensemble allows the suspension of certain (optional) modalities, while other modalities are obligatory. (4) As a unifying question for all these levels, one might ask to what extent repeated concomitances of multimodal data streams condition the constitution of a distinguishable multimodal ensemble, which as a whole becomes (syntagmatically) combinable or (paradigmatically) interchangeable with other ensembles as if they begin to take on properties of gestalts or even signs.

According to the variety of decisions that have to be made to be able to address multimodal ensembles as observables of a theory of multimodal communication, the statistical connections of the first three levels, as addressed by level (4), are characterized by uncertainties to which linguistic research is expected to provide answers, *without expecting that AI will replace this research*. Thus, while a primarily bottom-up approach runs the risk of following positivism that over-interprets the data streams that, for whatever reason, are technically available as direct access to multimodal ensembles, a primarily top-down approach runs the risk of developing concepts without an empirical foundation that are likely to require modifications and adjustments all too quickly in the course of confrontation with the data.

The detection of feedback behavior Sect. 3.6 can be taken as an example here: From a linguistic point of view, the recognition of such behavior and its semantic interpretation requires recourse to the respective conversational context, possibly even to the underlying conversational history. Assuming the context model of transformers, these examine context windows based on the underlying subword vocabulary, with the respective conversation appearing as a stream of subwords (and their vector representations) that is traversed window by window. Despite the efficiency of this approach, it is clear that with the window width and the focus on subwords, we are using a context model that undermines the flexibility of human context interpretation. For example, the interpreter may discover ad hoc ensembles in the conversation that make it possible to classify a behavior as feedback in the first place. Such an ensemble would manifest a kind of firstness, of which it cannot be assumed that a generative AI has seen enough training examples to identify the function associated with it, especially if the data streams to which it has access undermine the streams that a human perceives. The AI then does not "see" the ensemble in question (e.g. as a set or sequence of multimodal subwords). Conversely, however, we will follow a human interpretation only if our theory provides concepts that allow us to model such ensembles and thus create the conditions for their empirical and systematic observation. Human interpretation may be flexible and open, but for our theoretical purposes, we need a controllable approach that ensures the intersubjectivity of interpretation. At this point, which is characterized by the tension between contextual fixity and the lack of flexibility of automated methods on the one hand, and contextual openness with little formal commitment on the other, an approach comes into play that is able to integrate these two perspectives. At this point, we are thinking of an approach from the field of human computation, more precisely from the spectrum of evolutionary approaches [110], in which man and machine take on the functions of innovation and selection, thus each acting in a dual role [142], but in such a way that, as this interaction evolves, theory formation is simultaneously driven primarily by humans, while the machine focuses on optimizing the exploration of data streams and their representations, thereby bridging between data and theory.

4   Long-Term Obstacles

A fundamental prerequisite for contemporary AI systems are the need for training with relevant data before they can effectively process a problem (cf. Sect. 2). If a system has not seen the relevant data in any form, it cannot process it. To illustrate this, consider a model that is trained only on text data and therefore cannot be extended to image data or data from other modalities. Such models can therefore not solve application problems for which no measurable data is available, even in the long term. This concerns data as diverse as those from neuronal voxel measurements, inner monologues, or past events that have never been recorded and cannot be retrospectively constructed. In other words, it is unlikely that a generative AI will be able to read minds by being shown videos of non-speaking faces; nor is it likely that prompts will be contextualized by past events for which there are no recordings. And monitoring neural processes and structures currently seem to be limited to cellular resolution [161,215].

To think beyond such usual suspects for examples of unattainability by generative AI, one can think of several other candidates. Whatever comes to mind in this context, one has to face the situation that the corresponding research will generate significant amounts of documents that will essentially serve as a training base for generative AI to do both: link the new data with the data it already has access to (i.e., embed it in its representation space(s)), and play its statistical game to produce meaningful, well-interpretable texts in response to prompts for the supposedly untapped field of application. This consideration makes it difficult to identify problems that current generative AI will definitely not be able to overcome, even in the very long term.

To make this point very clear: language is a tool that is used to exchange information, which can relate in particular to things that are not present in the immediate, perceptible environment. Even if AI has no access to some primary data, it becomes able to recognize and respond to topics corresponding to inaccessible sources *if* there are written testimonials describing such data. Think of historical works narrating the past, diaries which reveal the author's inner episodes, or science fiction novels describing otherworldly scenarios[13]. With respect to multimodal research this means that the more papers published, the more text data for AI. If this is true, then there is just one way to constrain AI systems: Don't feed the AI! In fact, there are a couple of conceivable circumstances that might lead to this effect.

One positive development is that AI systems are suddenly solving tasks that humans were previously unable to solve. But in combination with these systems, people then develop a new understanding of precisely these tasks and continue to develop (e.g. Chess [179], Go [192]). However, it also has the opposite effect, in that these systems destroy the data basis on which they were trained. One of

---

[13] This despite the AI being caught in a symbolic cycle, lacking the possibility to break out of the "web of words" by means of grounding symbols in experience [81].

the best-known examples is the impact of ChatGPT on Stack Overflow, where Stack Overflow traffic dropped significantly after the release of ChatGPT.[14]

Another direction of this development could be that the internet will be flooded with more and more automatically generated data, which will become less and less distinguishable from human-generated data as these systems improve [178]. This means that future models will be trained more and more on self-generated data, which could also lead to an expected decline in model performance.

In a similar manner, communication spaces might come into existence, that exclude AI chatbots. This can happen in response to social media platforms that are more and more overtaken by dialogical AI systems while human user want to interact with other human users. Communication going on in the new, AI-free channels will then be out of the recognitional reach of the AI systems.

In addition to these social effects, political effects are also to be expected, for instance, that certain data is no longer legally accessible, or may no longer be used for the training of LLMs. In the long run, such effects may be much more influential and relevant to the development and improvement of AI models than the actual development of these systems.

Author Contribution

	Sections													
	1	2	3	3.1	3.2	3.3	3.4	3.5	3.6	3.7	3.8	3.9	3.10	4
AH	■	░	░											■
AB		░							■					
RB											■			■
AČ		░			■									
AG							■							
FK								■						
JL											■			
AL	░	░		■		■							░	■
AM	■	░	■											■
PP								■						
PSR														
JS									■					
MSR										■				
SRS												■		
CvE												■		

Legend: ■ main work; ░ minor contribution.

---

[14] https://www.similarweb.com/blog/insights/ai-news/stack-overflow-chatgpt/.

References

1. Aguirre-Celis, N., Miikkulainen, R.: Understanding the semantic space: how word meanings dynamically adapt in the context of a sentence. In: Proceedings of the 2021 Workshop on Semantic Spaces at the Intersection of NLP, Physics, and Cognitive Science (SemSpace), pp. 1–11 (2021)
2. Aiyappa, R., An, J., Kwak, H., Ahn, Y.Y.: Can we trust the evaluation on chatgpt? arXiv preprint arXiv:2303.12767 (2023)
3. Akbari, H., et al.: VATT: transformers for multimodal self-supervised learning from raw video, audio and text. Adv. Neural. Inf. Process. Syst. **34**, 24206–24221 (2021)
4. Alkaissi, H., McFarlane, S.I.: Artificial hallucinations in chatgpt: implications in scientific writing. Cureus **15**(2) (2023)
5. Almazrouei, E., et al.: Falcon-40B: an open large language model with state-of-the-art performance. Find. Assoc. Comput. Linguist. ACL **2023**, 10755–10773 (2023)
6. Ambrazaitis, G., House, D.: The multimodal nature of prominence: some directions for the study of the relation between gestures and pitch accents. In: Proceedings of the 13th International Conference of Nordic Prosody, pp. 262–273 (2023). https://doi.org/10.2478/9788366675728-024
7. American Psychiatric Association: Diagnostic and statistical manual of mental disorders, 5th edn. Technical report, American Psychiatric Association, Arlington (2013)
8. Amici, F., Liebal, K.: Testing hypotheses for the emergence of gestural communication in great and small apes (pan troglodytes, pongo abelii, Symphalangus syndactylus). Int. J. Primatol. (2022). https://doi.org/10.1007/s10764-022-00342-7
9. Andonova, E., Taylor, H.A.: Nodding in dis/agreement: a tale of two cultures. Cogn. Process. **13**(S1), 79–82 (2012). https://doi.org/10.1007/s10339-012-0472-x
10. Anger, C., Berwe, T., Olszok, A., Reichenberger, A., Lemanski, J.: Five dogmas of logic diagrams and how to escape them. Lang. Commun. **87**, 258–270 (2022). https://doi.org/10.1016/j.langcom.2022.09.001. https://www.sciencedirect.com/science/article/pii/S0271530922000775
11. Anil, R., et al.: PaLM 2 technical report. arXiv:2305.10403 (2023)
12. Archer, D.: Unspoken diversity: cultural differences in gestures. Qual. Sociol. **20**, 79–105 (1997)
13. Aruin, A.S., Latash, M.L.: Directional specificity of postural muscles in feedforward postural reactions during fast voluntary arm movements. Exp. Brain Res. **103**(2), 323–332 (1995). https://doi.org/10.1007/BF00231718
14. Bangerter, A., Oppenheimer, D.M.: Accuracy in detecting referents of pointing gestures unaccompanied by language. Gesture **6**(1), 85–102 (2006)
15. Baroni, M.: Grounding distributional semantics in the visual world. Lang. Linguist. Compass **10**(1), 3–13 (2016)
16. Barwise, J., Etchemendy, J.: Chapter VIII heterogeneous logic. In: Logical Reasoning with Diagrams, pp. 179–200 (1996)
17. Bauer, A.: Russian multimodal conversational data (2023). https://doi.org/10.18716/DCH/A.00000016. https://dch.phil-fak.uni-koeln.de/bestaende/datensicherung/russian-multimodal-conversational-data
18. Bauer, A., Poryadin, R.: Russian sign language conversations (2023). https://dch.phil-fak.uni-koeln.de/bestaende/datensicherung/russian-sign-language-conversations. https://doi.org/10.18716/DCH/A.00000028

19. Bavelas, J.B., Coates, L., Johnson, T.: Listeners as co-narrators. J. Pers. Soc. Psychol. **79**(6), 941–952 (2000). https://doi.org/10.1037/0022-3514.79.6.941
20. Beckman, M.E., Ayers-Elam, G.: Guidelines for ToBI Labelling: Version 3. Ohio State University (1997). http://www.ling.ohio-state.edu/~tobi/ame_tobi/labelling_guide_v3.pdf
21. Bellucci, F., Pietarinen, A.V.: Two dogmas of diagrammatic reasoning: a view from existential graphs. In: Peirce on Perception and Reasoning: From icons to logic, pp. 174–195. Routledge (2017)
22. Bertsch, A., Alon, U., Neubig, G., Gormley, M.R.: Unlimiformer: long-range transformers with unlimited length input. arXiv preprint arXiv:2305.01625 (2023)
23. Betker, J., et al.: Improving image generation with better captions. Comput. Sci. **2**(3), 8 (2023). https://cdnopenai.com/papers/dall-e-3.pdf
24. Bhattacharjee, R., Chakraborty, M.K., Choudhury, L.: $Venn_{i_{o_1}}$: a diagram system for universe without boundary. Logica Univers. **13**(3), 289–346 (2019). https://doi.org/10.1007/s11787-019-00227-z
25. Bhattacharjee, R., Moktefi, A.: Revisiting peirce's rules of transformation for euler-venn diagrams. In: Basu, A., Stapleton, G., Linker, S., Legg, C., Manalo, E., Viana, P. (eds.) Diagrammatic Representation and Inference. LNCS, vol. 12909, pp. 166–182. Springer, Cham (2021). https://doi.org/10.1007/978-3-030-86062-2_14
26. Boersma, P., Weenink, D.: Praat: doing phonetics by computer. www.praat.org/
27. Bolly, C.: CorpAGEst Annotation Manual. (II. Speech Annotation Guidelines) (2016)
28. Bolt, R.A.: "put-that-there": voice and gesture at the graphics interface. SIGGRAPH Comput. Graph. **14**, 262–270 (1980). https://doi.org/10.1145/965105.807503
29. Borodo, M.: Multimodality, translation and comics. Perspectives **23**(1), 22–41 (2015)
30. Braunschweiler, N.: The Prosodizer – automatic prosodic annotations of speech synthesis databases. In: Proceedings of Speech Prosody, vol. 2006 (2006)
31. Bressem, J., Ladewig, S.H., Müller, C.: Linguistic annotation system for gestures. In: Müller, C., Cienki, A., Fricke, E., Ladewig, S., McNeill, D., Teßendorf, S. (eds.) Body – Language – Communication. An International Handbook on Multimodality in Human Interaction, Handbücher zur Sprach- und Kommunikationswissenschaft/Handbooks of Linguistics and Communication Science (HSK) 38/1, vol. 1, chap. 71, pp. 1098–1124. De Gruyter Mouton, Berlin and Boston (2013). https://doi.org/10.1515/9783110261318.1098
32. Brown, L., Prieto, P.: Gesture and prosody in multimodal communication. In: Haugh, M., Kádár, D.Z., Terkourafi, M. (eds.) The Cambridge Handbook of Sociopragmatics, chap. 21, pp. 430–453. Cambridge University Press, Cambridge (2021)
33. Bulat, L., Clark, S., Shutova, E.: Speaking, seeing, understanding: correlating semantic models with conceptual representation in the brain. In: Proceedings of the 2017 Conference on Empirical Methods in Natural Language Processing, pp. 1081–1091 (2017)
34. Cao, Y., et al.: A comprehensive survey of AI-generated content (AIGC): a history of generative AI from GAN to chatgpt. arXiv preprint arXiv:2303.04226 (2023)
35. Cao, Z., Hidalgo Martinez, G., Simon, T., Wei, S., Sheikh, Y.A.: OpenPose: real-time multi-person 2D pose estimation using part affinity fields. IEEE Trans. Pattern Anal. Mach. Intell. (2019). https://doi.org/10.1109/TPAMI.2019.2929257

36. Chen, J., Ho, C.M.: MM-VIT: multi-modal video transformer for compressed video action recognition. In: Proceedings of the IEEE/CVF Winter Conference on Applications of Computer Vision (WACV), pp. 1910–1921 (2022)

37. Chu, J., Liu, Y., Yang, Z., Shen, X., Backes, M., Zhang, Y.: Comprehensive assessment of jailbreak attacks against LLMS. arXiv preprint arXiv:2402.05668 (2024)

38. Clark, H.H.: Using Language. Cambridge University Press, Cambridge (1996)

39. Cowen, A.S., Keltner, D.: What the face displays: mapping 28 emotions conveyed by naturalistic expression. Am. Psychol. **75**(3), 349–364 (2020). https://doi.org/10.1037/amp0000488

40. Davidson, D.: Three varieties of knowledge. Roy. Inst. Philos. Suppl. **30**, 153–166 (1991). https://doi.org/10.1017/S1358246100007748

41. De Jong, N.H., Wempe, T.: Praat script to detect syllable nuclei and measure speech rate automatically. Behav. Res. Methods **41**(2), 385–390 (2009)

42. Demey, L., Smessaert, H.: A database of aristotelian diagrams: empirical foundations for logical geometry. In: Giardino, V., Linker, S., Burns, R., Bellucci, F., Boucheix, J.M., Viana, P. (eds.) Theory and Application of Diagrams, pp. 123–131. Springer, Cham (2022). https://doi.org/10.1007/978-3-031-15146-0_10

43. Diessel, H.: Demonstratives, joint attention, and the emergence of grammar. Cogn. Linguist. **17**(4), 463–489 (2006). https://doi.org/10.1515/COG.2006.015

44. Dingemanse, M., Enfield, N.J.: Other-initiated repair across languages: towards a typology of conversational structures. Open Linguist. **1**(1) (2015). https://doi.org/10.2478/opli-2014-0007. https://www.degruyter.com/doi/10.2478/opli-2014-0007

45. Dogdu, C., Kessler, T., Schneider, D., Shadaydeh, M., Schweinberger, S.R.: A comparison of machine learning algorithms and feature sets for automatic vocal emotion recognition in speech. Sensors **22**(19), 7561 (2022)

46. Doherty, E., Davila Ross, M., Clay, Z.: Multimodal communication development in semi-wild chimpanzees. Anim. Behav. **201**, 175–190 (2023)

47. Dong, L., Xu, S., Xu, B.: Speech-transformer: a no-recurrence sequence-to-sequence model for speech recognition. In: 2018 IEEE International Conference on Acoustics, Speech and Signal Processing (ICASSP), pp. 5884–5888. IEEE (2018)

48. Douglas, P.H., Moscovice, L.R.: Pointing and pantomime in wild apes? Female bonobos use referential and iconic gestures to request genito-genital rubbing. Sci. Rep. **5**(1) (2015). https://doi.org/10.1038/srep13999

49. Düking, P., Sperlich, B., Voigt, L., Van Hooren, B., Zanini, M., Zinner, C.: Chat-GPT generated training plans for runners are not rated optimal by coaching experts, but increase in quality with additional input information. J. Sports Sci. Med. **23**, 56–72 (2024). https://doi.org/10.52082/jssm.2024.56

50. von Eiff, C.I., Frühholz, S., Korth, D., Guntinas-Lichius, O., Schweinberger, S.R.: Crossmodal benefits to vocal emotion perception in cochlear implant users. iScience **25**(12) (2022)

51. von Eiff, C.I., et al.: Parameter-specific morphing reveals contributions of timbre to the perception of vocal emotions in cochlear implant users. Ear Hear. **43**(4), 1178 (2022)

52. Ekman, P., Friesen, W.V.: The repertoire of nonverbal behavior: categories, origins, usage, and coding. Semiotica **1**(1), 49–98 (1969)

53. Engelen, J., Bernareggi, C.: Ascience: a thematic network on access to scientific university courses by visually impaired students. In: Challenges for Assistive Technology, vol. 20, pp. 304–309. IOS Press (2007). https://lirias.kuleuven.be/56044

54. Engelhardt, Y., Richards, C.: A framework for analyzing and designing diagrams and graphics. In: Diagrams (2018). https://api.semanticscholar.org/CorpusID: 49189675
55. Esteve-Gibert, N., Prieto, P.: Prosodic structure shapes the temporal realization of intonation and manual gesture movements. J. Speech Lang. Hear. Res. **56**(3), 850–864 (2013)
56. Esteve-Gibert, N., Guellaï, B.: Prosody in the auditory and visual domains: a developmental perspective. Front. Psychol. **9** (2018). https://www.frontiersin.org/articles/10.3389/fpsyg.2018.00338
57. Feldman, J.: The neural binding problem(s). Cogn. Neurodyn. **7**(1), 1–11 (2013). https://doi.org/10.1007/s11571-012-9219-8
58. Fish, A., Stapleton, G.: Defining euler diagrams: simple or what? In: Barker-Plummer, D., Cox, R., Swoboda, N. (eds.) Theory and Application of Diagrams, pp. 109–111. Springer, Heidelberg (2006). https://doi.org/10.1007/11783183_14
59. Frege, G.: Der Gedanke. Beiträge zur Philosophie des deutschen Idealismus **1**(2), 58–77 (1918)
60. Frieder, S., et al.: Mathematical capabilities of chatgpt. arXiv preprint arXiv:2301.13867 (2023)
61. Fuchs, S., et al.: Exploring the sound structure of novel vocalizations. In: Proceedings of EVOLANG 2024, Madison, Wisconsin, USA (2024)
62. Galaz García, C., et al.: The future of ecosystem assessments is automation, collaboration, and artificial intelligence. Environ. Res. Lett. **18** (2023)
63. Gardner, R.: When Listeners Talk: Response tokens and listener stance, Pragmatics & Beyond New Series, vol. 92. John Benjamins Publishing Company, Amsterdam (2001). https://doi.org/10.1075/pbns.92. http://www.jbe-platform.com/content/books/9789027297426
64. Giaquinto, M.: Crossing curves: a limit to the use of diagrams in proofs†. Philosophia Math. **19**(3), 281–307 (2011). https://doi.org/10.1093/philmat/nkr023
65. Giardino, V.: Diagrammatic proofs in mathematics: (almost) 20 years of research. In: Sriraman, B. (ed.) Handbook of the History and Philosophy of Mathematical Practice, pp. 1–23. Springer, Cham (2020). https://doi.org/10.1007/978-3-030-19071-2_46-1
66. Ginzburg, J., Cooper, R., Hough, J., Schlangen, D.: Incrementality and HPSG: why not? In: Abeillé, A., Bonami, O. (eds.) Constraint-Based Syntax and Semantics: Papers in Honor of Danièle Godard. CSLI Publications, Stanford (2020)
67. Ginzburg, J., Lücking, A.: I thought pointing is rude: a dialogue-semantic analysis of pointing at the addressee. In: Grosz, P., Martí, L., Pearson, H., Sudo, Y., Zobel, S. (eds.) Proceedings of Sinn und Bedeutung 25, pp. 276–291. SuB 25 (2021). https://doi.org/10.18148/sub/2021.v25i0.937. https://ojs.ub.uni-konstanz.de/sub/index.php/sub/article/view/937
68. Ginzburg, J., Mazzocconi, C., Tian, Y.: Laughter as language. Glossa **5**(1), 104 (2020). https://doi.org/10.5334/gjgl.1152
69. Goldstein, L.: Teaching syllogistic to the blind. In: Gorayska, B., Mey, J.L. (eds.) Advances in Psychology, Cognitive Technology, vol. 113, pp. 243–255. North-Holland (1996). https://doi.org/10.1016/S0166-4115(96)80035-5. https://www.sciencedirect.com/science/article/pii/S0166411596800355

70. Gonitsioti, H., Christidou, V., Hatzinikita, V.: Enhancing scientific visual literacy in kindergarten: young children 'read' and produce representations of classification. Int. J. Sci. Math. Technol. Learn. **20**(1), 1–15 (2013). https://doi.org/10.18848/2327-7971/CGP/v20i01/48996. https://cgscholar.com/bookstore/works/enhancing-scientific-visual-literacy-in-kindergarten

71. Gregori, A., et al.: A roadmap for technological innovation in multimodal communication research. In: Duffy, V.G. (ed.) Digital Human Modeling and Applications in Health, Safety, Ergonomics and Risk Management, pp. 402–438. Springer, Cham (2023). https://doi.org/10.1007/978-3-031-35748-0_30

72. Gregoromichelaki, E., et al.: Incrementality and intention-recognition in utterance processing. Dialogue Discourse **2**(1), 199–233 (2011). https://doi.org/10.5087/dad.2011.109

73. Grice, M., Baumann, S., Benzmüller, R.: German intonation in autosegmental-metrical phonology. In: Jun, S.A. (ed.) Prosodic Typology: The Phonology of Intonation and Phrasing, pp. 55–83. Oxford University Press, Oxford (2005)

74. Grice, M., Reyelt, M., Benzmüller, R., Mayer, J., Batliner, A.: Consistency in transcription and labelling of German intonation with GToBI. In: Proceedings of the Fourth International Conference on Spoken Language Processing, vol. 3, pp. 1716–1719. Philadelphia and USA (1996)

75. Hagoort, P., van Berkum, J.: Beyond the sentence given. Philos. Trans. R. Soc. B Biol. Sci. **362**(1481), 801–811 (2007). https://doi.org/10.1098/rstb.2007.2089

76. Hahn, H.: The crisis in intuition. In: Hahn, H., McGuinness, B. (eds.) Empiricism, Logic and Mathematics: Philosophical Papers. Vienna Circle Collection, pp. 73–102. Springer, Dordrecht (1980). https://doi.org/10.1007/978-94-009-8982-5_7

77. Halevy, A., Norvig, P., Pereira, F.: The unreasonable effectiveness of data. IEEE Intell. Syst. **24**(2), 8–12 (2009)

78. Hammer, E.M.: Logic and Visual Information. CSLI Publications, Stanford (1995)

79. Han, E.: Integrating mobile eye-tracking and VSLAM for recording spatial gaze in works of art and architecture. Technol. Archit. Des. **5**(2), 177–187 (2021). https://doi.org/10.1080/24751448.2021.1967058

80. Han, K., Xiao, A., Wu, E., Guo, J., Xu, C., Wang, Y.: Transformer in transformer. In: Ranzato, M., Beygelzimer, A., Dauphin, Y., Liang, P., Vaughan, J.W. (eds.) Advances in Neural Information Processing Systems, vol. 34, pp. 15908–15919. Curran Associates, Inc. (2021). https://proceedings.neurips.cc/paper_files/paper/2021/file/854d9fca60b4bd07f9bb215d59ef5561-Paper.pdf

81. Harnad, S.: The symbol grounding problem. Physica D **42**(1–3), 335–346 (1990). https://doi.org/10.1016/0167-2789(90)90087-6

82. Harnad, S.: Minds, machines and Turing. In: Moor, J.H. (ed.) The Turing Test: The Elusive Standard of Artificial Intelligence, pp. 253–273. Springer, Dordrecht (2003). https://doi.org/10.1007/978-94-010-0105-2_14

83. Harnad, S.: Language writ large: LLMS, chatgpt, grounding, meaning and understanding. arXiv arXiv:2402.02243 (2024)

84. Hartz, A., Guth, B., Jording, M., Vogeley, K., Schulte-Rüther, M.: Temporal behavioral parameters of on-going gaze encounters in a virtual environment. Front. Psychol. **12**, 673982 (2021). https://doi.org/10.3389/fpsyg.2021.673982

85. Hassani, H., Silva, E.S.: The role of chatgpt in data science: how AI-assisted conversational interfaces are revolutionizing the field. Big Data Cogn. Comput. **7**(2), 62 (2023)

86. Herbort, O., Krause, L.M., Kunde, W.: Perspective determines the production and interpretation of pointing gestures. Psychon. Bull. Rev. **28**, 641–648 (2021). https://doi.org/10.3758/s13423-020-01823-7

87. Herbort, O., Kunde, W.: Spatial (mis-)interpretation of pointing gestures to distal referents. J. Exp. Psychol. Hum. Percept. Perform. (2015). https://doi.org/10.1037/xhp0000126

88. Hoffmann, J., et al.: Training compute-optimal large language models. arXiv preprint arXiv:2203.15556 (2022)

89. Hohwy, J.: The predictive processing hypothesis. In: The Oxford Handbook of 4E Cognition, pp. 129–145 (2018)

90. Holler, J.: Speakers' use of interactive gestures as markers of common ground. In: Kopp, S., Wachsmuth, I. (eds.) GW 2009. LNCS, vol. 5934, pp. 11–22. Springer, Heidelberg (2010). https://doi.org/10.1007/978-3-642-12553-9_2

91. Holler, J., Levinson, S.C.: Multimodal language processing in human communication. Trends Cogn. Sci. **23**(8), 639–652 (2019). https://doi.org/10.1016/j.tics.2019.05.006

92. Howse, J., Molina, F., Taylor, J., Kent, S., Gil, J.: Spider diagrams: a diagrammatic reasoning system. J. Vis. Lang. Comput. **12**(3), 299–324 (2001)

93. Huang, B., Shu, Y., Zhang, T., Wang, Y.: Dynamic multi-person mesh recovery from uncalibrated multi-view cameras. In: 3DV (2021)

94. Huang, J., Tan, M.: The role of chatgpt in scientific communication: writing better scientific review articles. Am. J. Cancer Res. **13**(4), 1148 (2023)

95. Ienaga, N., Cravotta, A., Terayama, K., Scotney, B.W., Saito, H., Busa, M.G.: Semi-automation of gesture annotation by machine learning and human collaboration. Lang. Resour. Eval. **56**(3), 673–700 (2022). https://doi.org/10.1007/s10579-022-09586-4

96. Jack, R.E., Blais, C., Scheepers, C., Schyns, P.G., Caldara, R.: Cultural confusions show that facial expressions are not universal. Curr. Biol. **19**(18), 1543–1548 (2009)

97. Jackendoff, R.: Foundations of Language. Oxford University Press, Oxford (2002)

98. Jamnik, M.: Mathematical Reasoning with Diagrams. Lecture Notes, Center for the Study of Language and Information (2001). https://press.uchicago.edu/ucp/books/book/distributed/M/bo3614100.html

99. Jang, J., Ye, S., Seo, M.: Can large language models truly understand prompts? A case study with negated prompts. In: Transfer Learning for Natural Language Processing Workshop, pp. 52–62. PMLR (2023)

100. Johansen, M.W.: What's in a diagram? On the classification of symbols, figures and diagrams. In: Magnani, L. (eds.) Model-Based Reasoning in Science and Technology: Theoretical and Cognitive Issues, pp. 89–108. Springer, Heidelberg (2013). https://doi.org/10.1007/978-3-642-37428-9_6

101. Johansen, M.W., Pallavicini, J.L.: Entering the valley of formalism: trends and changes in mathematicians' publication practice-1885 to 2015. Synthese **200**(3), 239 (2022)

102. Kadavá, Š., Ćwiek, A., Stoltmann, K., Fuchs, S., Pouw, W.: Is gesture-speech physics at work in rhythmic pointing? Evidence from Polish counting-out rhymes. In: Proceedings of the 20th International Congress of Phonetic Sciences, Prague, Czech Republic (2023). https://doi.org/10.31219/osf.io/67fzc. https://osf.io/67fzc

103. Kendon, A.: Gesture: Visible Action as Utterance. Cambridge University Press, Cambridge (2004)

104. Khan, S., Naseer, M., Hayat, M., Zamir, S.W., Khan, F.S., Shah, M.: Transformers in vision: a survey. ACM Comput. Surv. (CSUR) **54**(10s), 1–41 (2022)

105. Kiela, D., Bulat, L., Clark, S.: Grounding semantics in olfactory perception. In: Proceedings of the 53rd Annual Meeting of the Association for Computational Linguistics and the 7th International Joint Conference on Natural Language Processing (Volume 2: Short Papers), pp. 231–236 (2015)
106. Kiela, D., Clark, S.: Learning neural audio embeddings for grounding semantics in auditory perception. J. Artif. Intell. Res. **60**, 1003–1030 (2017)
107. Kisler, T., Schiel, F., Sloetjes, H.: Signal processing via web services: the use case WebMAUS. In: Digital Humanities Conference 2012, p. 5 (2012)
108. Klin, A.: Attributing social meaning to ambiguous visual stimuli in higher-functioning autism and Asperger syndrome: the social attribution task. J. Child Psychol. Psychiatry Allied Discip. **41**(7), 831–846 (2000)
109. Konrad, R., et al.: My DGS - annotated. public corpus of German sign language, 3rd release (2020). https://doi.org/10.25592/dgs.corpus-3.0
110. Kosorukoff, A.: Human based genetic algorithm. In: IEEE International Conference on Systems, Man, and Cybernetics, vol. 5, pp. 3464–3469 (2001). http://ieeexplore.ieee.org/xpls/abs_all.jsp?arnumber=972056
111. Krahmer, E., Swerts, M.: The effects of visual beats on prosodic prominence: acoustic analyses, auditory perception and visual perception. J. Mem. Lang. **57**(3), 396–414 (2007). https://doi.org/10.1016/j.jml.2007.06.005. http://www.sciencedirect.com/science/article/pii/S0749596X07000708
112. Kranstedt, A.: Situierte Generierung deiktischer Objektreferenz in der multi-modalen Mensch-Maschine-Interaktion. No. 313 in Diski, Aka, Berlin. Ph.D. thesis, Bielefeld University (2008)
113. Kranstedt, A., Lücking, A., Pfeiffer, T., Rieser, H., Wachsmuth, I.: Deictic object reference in task-oriented dialogue. In: Rickheit, G., Wachsmuth, I. (eds.) Situated Communication, pp. 155–207. Mouton de Gruyter, Berlin (2006)
114. Krivokapić, J.: Gestural coordination at prosodic boundaries and its role for prosodic structure and speech planning processes. Philos. Trans. R. Soc. B Biol. Sci. **369**(1658), 20130397 (2014). https://doi.org/10.1098/rstb.2013.0397. https://royalsocietypublishing.org/doi/10.1098/rstb.2013.0397
115. Kuder, A., Bauer, A.: Polish multimodal conversational data (2023). https://doi.org/10.18716/DCH/A.00000017. https://dch.phil-fak.uni-koeln.de/bestaende/datensicherung/polish-multimodal-conversational-data
116. Ladd, D.R.: Intonational Phonology, 2nd edn. Cambridge University Press, Cambridge (2008)
117. Lane, J., et al.: Improving face identity perception in age-related macular degeneration via caricaturing. Sci. Rep. **8**, 15205 (2018)
118. Lawson-Adams, J., Dickinson, D.K.: Building lexical representations with non-verbal supports. Read. Res. Q. **56**(3), 603–622 (2021)
119. Lee, U., et al.: Few-shot is enough: exploring ChatGPT prompt engineering method for automatic question generation in english education. Educ. Inf. Technol. 1–33 (2023)
120. Levinson, S.C.: Deixis. In: Horn, L.R., Ward, G. (eds.) The Handbook of Pragmatics, chap. 5, pp. 97–121. Blackwell (2008)
121. Levinson, S.C., Torreira, F.: Timing in turn-taking and its implications for processing models of language. Front. Psychol. **6**(731) (2015). https://doi.org/10.3389/fpsyg.2015.00731
122. Li, C., et al.: Multimodal foundation models: from specialists to general-purpose assistants. arXiv preprint arXiv:2309.10020, vol. 1, no. 2, p. 2 (2023)

123. Liebal, K., Slocombe, K.E., Waller, B.M.: The language void 10 years on: multimodal primate communication research is still uncommon. Ethol. Ecol. Evol. 1–14 (2022). https://doi.org/10.1080/03949370.2021.2015453. https://www.tandfonline.com/doi/full/10.1080/03949370.2021.2015453
124. Liesenfeld, A., Lopez, A., Dingemanse, M.: The timing bottleneck: why timing and overlap are mission-critical for conversational user interfaces, speech recognition and dialogue systems. In: Proceedings of the 24th Meeting of the Special Interest Group on Discourse and Dialogue, Prague, Czechia, pp. 482–495. Association for Computational Linguistics (2023). https://doi.org/10.18653/v1/2023.sigdial-1.45. https://aclanthology.org/2023.sigdial-1.45
125. Litwin, P., Miłkowski, M.: Unification by fiat: arrested development of predictive processing. Cogn. Sci. **44**, e12867 (2020). https://doi.org/10.1111/cogs.12867
126. Liu, C., Mao, Z., Zhang, T., Liu, A.A., Wang, B., Zhang, Y.: Focus your attention: a focal attention for multimodal learning. IEEE Trans. Multimedia **24**, 103–115 (2020)
127. Liu, Y., et al.: Jailbreaking chatgpt via prompt engineering: an empirical study. arXiv preprint arXiv:2305.13860 (2023)
128. Liu, Y., et al.: Summary of ChatGPT-related research and perspective towards the future of large language models. Meta-Radiol. 100017 (2023)
129. Liu, Z., Mao, H., Wu, C.Y., Feichtenhofer, C., Darrell, T., Xie, S.: A convnet for the 2020s. In: Proceedings of the IEEE/CVF Conference on Computer Vision and Pattern Recognition, pp. 11976–11986 (2022)
130. Lord, C., et al.: Autism Diagnostic Observation Schedule, 2nd edn (ADOS-2), vol. 284. Western Psychological Corporation, Los Angeles (2012)
131. Lücking, A.: Modeling co-verbal gesture perception in type theory with records. In: Ganzha, M., Maciaszek, L., Paprzycki, M. (eds.) Proceedings of the 2016 Federated Conference on Computer Science and Information Systems. Annals of Computer Science and Information Systems, vol. 8, pp. 383–392. IEEE (2016). https://doi.org/10.15439/2016F83
132. Lücking, A.: Witness-loaded and witness-free demonstratives. In: Coniglio, M., Murphy, A., Schlachter, E., Veenstra, T. (eds.) Atypical Demonstratives. Syntax, Semantics and Pragmatics, pp. 255–284. No. 568 in Linguistische Arbeiten, De Gruyter, Berlin and Boston (2018)
133. Lücking, A., Bergmann, K., Hahn, F., Kopp, S., Rieser, H.: The Bielefeld speech and gesture alignment corpus (SaGA). In: Multimodal Corpora: Advances in Capturing, Coding and Analyzing Multimodality, pp. 92–98. LREC 2010, 7th International Conference for Language Resources and Evaluation, Malta (2010). https://doi.org/10.13140/2.1.4216.1922
134. Lücking, A., Ginzburg, J.: Leading voices: dialogue semantics, cognitive science, and the polyphonic structure of multimodal interaction. Lang. Cogn. **15**(1), 148–172 (2023). https://doi.org/10.1017/langcog.2022.30
135. Lücking, A., Mehler, A., Menke, P.: Taking fingerprints of speech-and-gesture ensembles: approaching empirical evidence of intrapersonal alignmnent in multimodal communication. In: Proceedings of the 12th Workshop on the Semantics and Pragmatics of Dialogue, LonDial 2008, pp. 157–164. King's College London (2008)
136. Lücking, A., Pfeiffer, T., Rieser, H.: Pointing and reference reconsidered. J. Pragmat. **77**, 56–79 (2015). https://doi.org/10.1016/j.pragma.2014.12.013
137. Lugaresi, C., et al.: Mediapipe: a framework for building perception pipelines (2019)

138. Maerten, A.S., Soydaner, D.: From paintbrush to pixel: a review of deep neural networks in AI-generated art. arXiv arXiv:2302.10913 (2023)
139. Marcus, G., Southen, R.: Generative AI has a visual plagiarism problem. Experiments with midjourney and dall-e 3 show a copyright minefield. IEEE Spectrum (2024)
140. Marschik, P.B., et al.: Open video data sharing in developmental science and clinical practice. iScience **26**(4), 106348 (2023). https://doi.org/10.1016/j.isci.2023.106348
141. McNeill, D.: Hand and Mind - What Gestures Reveal about Thought. Chicago University Press, Chicago (1992)
142. Mehler, A., Hemati, W., Gleim, R., Baumartz, D.: VienNA: Auf dem Weg zu einer Infrastruktur für die verteilte interaktive evolutionäre Verarbeitung natürlicher Sprache. In: Lobin, H., Schneider, R., Witt, A. (eds.) Forschungsinfrastrukturen und digitale Informationssysteme in der germanistischen Sprachwissenschaft, vol. 6, pp. 149–176. De Gruyter, Berlin (2018)
143. Mehler, A., Lücking, A.: Pathways of alignment between gesture and speech: assessing information transmission in multimodal ensembles. In: Giorgolo, G., Alahverdzhieva, K. (eds.) Proceedings of the International Workshop on Formal and Computational Approaches to Multimodal Communication under the auspices of ESSLLI 2012, Opole, Poland, 6–10 August (2012)
144. Meskó, B.: The impact of multimodal large language models on health care's future. J. Med. Internet Res. **25**, e52865 (2023)
145. Moktefi, A.: Diagrams as scientific instruments. In: Benedek, A., Veszelszki, A. (eds.), Visual, Virtual, Veridical, Series Visual Learning, vol. 7 (2017). https://www.academia.edu/33378854/Diagrams_as_scientific_instruments
146. Mondada, L.: The local constitution of multimodal resources for social interaction. J. Pragmat. **65**, 137–156 (2014). https://doi.org/10.1016/j.pragma.2014.04.004
147. Moreno, R., Mayer, R.: Interactive multimodal learning environments: special issue on interactive learning environments: contemporary issues and trends. Educ. Psychol. Rev. **19**, 309–326 (2007)
148. Morris, M.R., et al.: Levels of AGI: operationalizing progress on the path to AGI. arXiv arXiv:2311.02462 (2023)
149. Muhammad, G., Alshehri, F., Karray, F., El Saddik, A., Alsulaiman, M., Falk, T.H.: A comprehensive survey on multimodal medical signals fusion for smart healthcare systems. Inf. Fusion **76**, 355–375 (2021)
150. Mundy, P., Newell, L.: Attention, joint attention, and social cognition. Curr. Dir. Psychol. Sci. **16**(5), 269–274 (2007). https://doi.org/10.1111/j.1467-8721.2007.00518.x
151. Naert, L., Reverdy, C., Larboulette, C., Gibet, S.: Per channel automatic annotation of sign language motion capture data. In: Proceedings of the LREC2018 8th Workshop on the Representation and Processing of Sign Languages: Involving the Language Community, pp. 139–146. European Language Resources Association (ELRA), Miyazaki, Japan (2018). https://www.sign-lang.uni-hamburg.de/lrec/pub/18014.pdf
152. Nagrani, A., Yang, S., Arnab, A., Jansen, A., Schmid, C., Sun, C.: Attention bottlenecks for multimodal fusion. Adv. Neural. Inf. Process. Syst. **34**, 14200–14213 (2021)
153. Nakatsu, R.T.: Diagrammatic Reasoning in AI: Decision-Making and Problem-Solving With Diagrams. Wiley, Hoboken (2009)
154. Nilsson, J.F.: A cube of opposition for predicate logic. Logica Universalis **14**(1), 103–114 (2020). https://doi.org/10.1007/s11787-020-00244-3

155. Nota, N., Trujillo, J.P., Holler, J.: Facial signals and social actions in multimodal face-to-face interaction. Brain Sci. **11**(8), 1017 (2021). https://doi.org/10.3390/brainsci11081017. https://www.mdpi.com/2076-3425/11/8/1017
156. Oberwelland, E., et al.: Look into my eyes: investigating joint attention using interactive eye-tracking and fMRI in a developmental sample. NeuroImage **130**, 248–260 (2016). https://doi.org/10.1016/j.neuroimage.2016.02.026
157. OpenAI: ChatGPT (Feb 06 version) [large language model] (2023). https://chat.openai.com/chat
158. OpenAI: GPT-4 technical report. arXiv arXiv:2303.08774 (2023)
159. Ostendorf, M., Ross, K.: A multi-level model for recognition of intonation labels. In: Sagisaka, Y., Campbell, N., Higuchi, N. (eds.) Computing Prosody, pp. 291–308. Springer, New York (1997). https://doi.org/10.1007/978-1-4612-2258-3_19
160. Paggio, P., Jongejan, B., Agirrezabal, M., Navarretta, C.: Detecting head movements in video-recorded dyadic conversations. In: Proceedings of the 20th International Conference on Multimodal Interaction: Adjunct. ICMI 2018. Association for Computing Machinery (2018). https://doi.org/10.1145/3281151.3281152
161. Paulk, A.C., et al.: Large-scale neural recordings with single neuron resolution using neuropixels probes in human cortex. Nat. Neurosci. **25**, 252–263 (2022). https://doi.org/10.1038/s41593-021-00997-0
162. Peng, R.D.: Reproducible research in computational science. Science **334**(6060), 1226–1227 (2011)
163. Perlman, M.: Debunking two myths against vocal origins of language. Interact. Stud. **18**(3), 376–401 (2017). https://doi.org/10.1075/is.18.3.05per
164. Perniss, P.: Why we should study multimodal language. Front. Psychol. **9**, 1109 (2018). https://doi.org/10.3389/fpsyg.2018.01109
165. Poustka, L., Schulte-Rüther, M.: Autismus-Spektrum-Störungen bei Kindern und Jugendlichen. In: Fegert, J., et al. (eds.) Psychiatrie und Psychotherapie des Kindes- und Jugendalters, pp. 1–23. Springer, Heidelberg (2022). https://doi.org/10.1007/978-3-662-49289-5_123-1
166. Pouw, W., Dixon, J.A.: Entrainment and modulation of gesture-speech synchrony under delayed auditory feedback. Cogn. Sci. **43**(3), e12721 (2019). https://doi.org/10.1111/cogs.12721. https://onlinelibrary.wiley.com/doi/abs/10.1111/cogs.12721
167. Pouw, W., Fuchs, S.: Origins of vocal-entangled gesture. Neurosci. Biobehav. Rev. **141**, 104836 (2022). https://doi.org/10.1016/j.neubiorev.2022.104836. https://www.sciencedirect.com/science/article/pii/S0149763422003256
168. Radford, A., et al.: Learning transferable visual models from natural language supervision. In: International Conference on Machine Learning, pp. 8748–8763. PMLR (2021)
169. Ray, P.P.: Chatgpt: a comprehensive review on background, applications, key challenges, bias, ethics, limitations and future scope. Internet Things Cyber-Phys. Syst. (2023)
170. Reichenberger, A., Lemanski, J., Bhattacharjee, R.: The role of gestures in logic. Vis. Commun. (upcoming)
171. Ripperda, J., Drijvers, L., Holler, J.: Speeding up the detection of non-iconic and iconic gestures (spudnig): a toolkit for the automatic detection of hand movements and gestures in video data. Behav. Res. Methods **52**(4), 1783–1794 (2020). https://doi.org/10.3758/s13428-020-01350-2
172. Rohrer, P.L.: A temporal and pragmatic analysis of gesture-speech association. A corpus-based approach using the novel MultiModal MultiDimensional (M3D) labeling system. Ph.D. thesis, Nantes Université (2022)

173. Rohrer, P.L., et al.: The MultiModal MultiDimensional (M3D) labeling system (2023). https://doi.org/10.17605/osf.io/ankdx
174. Rosenberg, A.: Classification of prosodic events using quantized contour modeling. In: Proceedings of HLT-NAACL, pp. 721–724 (2010)
175. Rosenberg, A., Hasegawa-Johnson, M.: Automatic prosody labelling and assessment. In: Gussenhoven, C., Chen, A. (eds.) The Oxford Handbook of Language Prosody, pp. 645–656. Oxford University Press, Oxford (2020). https://doi.org/10.1093/oxfordhb/9780198832232.013.43
176. Rumpf, A.L., Kamp-Becker, I., Becker, K., Kauschke, C.: Narrative competence and internal state language of children with asperger syndrome and ADHD. Res. Dev. Disabil. **33**(5), 1395–1407 (2012). https://doi.org/10.1016/j.ridd.2012.03.007
177. Sacks, H., Schegloff, E.A., Jefferson, G.: A simplest systematics for the organization of turn-taking for conversation. Language **50**(4), 696 (1974). https://doi.org/10.2307/412243
178. Sadasivan, V.S., Kumar, A., Balasubramanian, S., Wang, W., Feizi, S.: Can AI-generated text be reliably detected? (2023)
179. Sadler, M., Regan, N.: Game Changer. New in Chess (2019)
180. Sallam, M.: Chatgpt utility in healthcare education, research, and practice: systematic review on the promising perspectives and valid concerns. In: Healthcare, vol. 11, p. 887. MDPI (2023)
181. Salvagno, M., Taccone, F.S., Gerli, A.G., et al.: Can artificial intelligence help for scientific writing? Crit. Care **27**(1), 1–5 (2023)
182. Sankey, M., Birch, D., Gardiner, M.: The impact of multiple representations of content using multimedia on learning outcomes across learning styles and modal preferences. Int. J. Educ. Dev. ICT **7**(3), 18–35 (2011)
183. Saravia, E.: Prompt Engineering Guide (2022). https://github.com/dair-ai/Prompt-Engineering-Guide
184. Schepens, J., Marx, N., Gagl, B.: Can we utilize large language models (LLMS) to generate useful linguistic corpora? A case study of the word frequency effect in young German readers (2023)
185. Schulte-Rüther, M., et al.: Using machine learning to improve diagnostic assessment of ASD in the light of specific differential and co-occurring diagnoses. J. Child Psychol. Psychiatry **64**(1), 16–26 (2023). https://doi.org/10.1111/jcpp.13650
186. Schulte-Rüther, M., et al.: Intact mirror mechanisms for automatic facial emotions in children and adolescents with autism spectrum disorder. Autism Res. **10**(2), 298–310 (2017). https://doi.org/10.1002/aur.1654
187. Schweitzer, A.: Production and perception of prosodic events-evidence from corpus-based experiments. Ph.D. thesis, Universität Stuttgart, Stuttgart (2010). http://elib.uni-stuttgart.de/opus/volltexte/2011/6031/pdf/Dissertation_Schweitzer.pdf
188. Schweitzer, A., Möbius, B.: Experiments on automatic prosodic labeling. In: Proceedings of the 10th International Conference on Speech Communication and Technology, pp. 2515–2518. Brighton (2009). https://doi.org/10.21437/Interspeech.2009-663
189. Shimojima, A.: Operational constraints in diagrammatic reasoning. In: Allwein, G., Barwise, J. (eds.) Logical Reasoning with Diagrams. Oxford University Press, Oxford (1996)
190. Shimojima, A.: Semantic Properties of Diagrams and their Cognitive Potentials. CSLI Publications, Stanford (2015)

191. Shin, S.J.: The logical status of diagrams. Cambridge University Press, Cambridge (1995). https://doi.org/10.1017/CBO9780511574696. https://www.cambridge.org/core/books/logical-status-of-diagrams/27130C396E0899C90BC632B4C7617E2B

192. Silver, D., et al.: Mastering the game of go without human knowledge. Nature **550**, 354–359 (2017). https://doi.org/10.1038/nature24270

193. van der Sluis, I.: Multimodal Reference. Studies in Automatic Generation of Multimodal Referring Expressions. Uitgevershuis BuG, Groningen, NL. Ph.D thesis, Univ. van Tilburg (2005)

194. Stapleton, G., Jamnik, M., Shimojima, A.: What makes an effective representation of information: a formal account of observational advantages. J. Logic Lang. Inform. **26**(2), 143–177 (2017). https://doi.org/10.1007/s10849-017-9250-6

195. Stöver, T., et al.: Structure and establishment of the German Cochlear Implant Registry (DCIR). HNO **71**(Suppl 1), 82–92 (2023)

196. Sun, C., Shrivastava, A., Singh, S., Gupta, A.: Revisiting unreasonable effectiveness of data in deep learning era. In: Proceedings of the IEEE International Conference on Computer Vision, pp. 843–852 (2017)

197. Syrdal, A.K., McGory, J.: Inter-transcriber reliability of ToBI prosodic labeling. In: 6th International Conference on Spoken Language Processing (ICSLP 2000), vol. 3, pp. 235–238 (2000). https://www.isca-speech.org/archive/icslp_2000/i00_3235.html

198. Taori, R., et al.: Alpaca: a strong, replicable instruction-following model. Stanford Center for Research on Foundation Models, vol. 3, no. 6, p. 7 (2023). https://crfmstanford.edu/2023/03/13/alpaca.html

199. Team, G., et al.: Gemini: a family of highly capable multimodal models. arXiv preprint arXiv:2312.11805 (2023)

200. Törnberg, P.: ChatGPT-4 outperforms experts and crowd workers in annotating political twitter messages with zero-shot learning. arXiv preprint arXiv:2304.06588 (2023)

201. Torres, M.J.R., Barwaldt, R.: Approaches for diagrams accessibility for blind people: a systematic review. In: 2019 IEEE Frontiers in Education Conference (FIE), pp. 1–7 (2019). https://doi.org/10.1109/FIE43999.2019.9028522. https://ieeexplore.ieee.org/document/9028522. ISSN 2377-634X

202. Touvron, H., et al.: Llama 2: open foundation and fine-tuned chat models. arXiv arXiv:2307.09288 (2023)

203. Trujillo, J.P., Holler, J.: Interactionally embedded gestalt principles of multimodal human communication. Perspect. Psychol. Sci. **18**(5), 1136–1159 (2023). https://doi.org/10.1177/17456916221141422

204. Tutton, M.: When and why the lexical ground is a gestural figure. Gesture **12**(3), 361–386 (2012). https://doi.org/10.1075/gest.12.3.04tut

205. Uesaka, Y., Manalo, E., Ichikawa, S.: What kinds of perceptions and daily learning behaviors promote students' use of diagrams in mathematics problem solving? Learn. Instr. **17**(3), 322–335 (2007)

206. Ungerer, F., Schmid, H.J.: An Introduction to Cognitive Linguistics, 2nd edn. Pearson, Harlow (2006)

207. Vaswani, A., et al.: Attention is all you need. In: Advances in Neural Information Processing Systems, vol. 30 (2017)

208. Wagner, P., Malisz, Z., Kopp, S.: Gesture and speech in interaction: an overview. Speech Commun. **57**, 209–232 (2014). https://doi.org/10.1016/j.specom.2013.09.008. http://www.sciencedirect.com/science/article/pii/S0167639313001295

209. Wagner, P., Ćwiek, A., Samlowski, B.: Exploiting the speech-gesture link to capture fine-grained prosodic prominence impressions and listening strategies. J. Phonetics **76**, 100911 (2019). https://doi.org/10.1016/j.wocn.2019.07.001. http://www.sciencedirect.com/science/article/pii/S009544701830038X

210. Wang, D.Q., Feng, L.Y., Ye, J.G., Zou, J.G., Zheng, Y.F.: Accelerating the integration of chatgpt and other large-scale AI models into biomedical research and healthcare. MedComm-Future Med. **2**(2), e43 (2023)

211. Watkins, R.: Guidance for researchers and peer-reviewers on the ethical use of large language models (LLMS) in scientific research workflows. AI Ethics 1–6 (2023)

212. Wei, X., et al.: Zero-shot information extraction via chatting with chatgpt. arXiv preprint arXiv:2302.10205 (2023)

213. Wicke, P.: Probing language models' gesture understanding for enhanced human-AI interaction. arXiv arXiv:2401.17858 (2024)

214. Wightman, C.W., Ostendorf, M.: Automatic labeling of prosodic patterns. IEEE Trans. Speech Audio Process. **2**(4), 469–481 (1994). https://doi.org/10.1109/89.326607

215. Winding, M., et al.: The connectome of an insect brain. Science **379**(6636), eadd9330 (2023). https://doi.org/10.1126/science.add9330

216. Wittenburg, P., Brugman, H., Russel, A., Klassmann, A., Sloetjes, H.: ELAN: a professional framework for multimodality research. In: Proceedings of the 5th International Conference on Language Resources and Evaluation, LREC 2006, pp. 1556–1559 (2006)

217. World Health Organization (WHO): International classification of diseases, eleventh revision (ICD-11) (2019/2021). https://icd.who.int/browse11

218. Wu, S., Fei, H., Qu, L., Ji, W., Chua, T.S.: Next-GPT: any-to-any multimodal LLM. CoRR abs/2309.05519 (2023)

219. Xu, K., Zhong, G., Deng, Z., Zhang, K., Huang, K.: Self-supervised generative learning for sequential data prediction. Appl. Intell. **53**, 20675–20689 (2023). https://doi.org/10.1007/s10489-023-04578-5

220. Yadlowsky, S., Doshi, L., Tripuraneni, N.: Pretraining data mixtures enable narrow model selection capabilities in transformer models. arXiv preprint arXiv:2311.00871 (2023)

221. Zhang, C., Bengio, S., Hardt, M., Recht, B., Vinyals, O.: Understanding deep learning (still) requires rethinking generalization. Commun. ACM **64**(3), 107–115 (2021)

222. Zhang, Y., et al.: Meta-transformer: a unified framework for multimodal learning. arXiv preprint arXiv:2307.10802 (2023)

223. Zhou, K., et al.: Don't make your LLM an evaluation benchmark cheater. arXiv preprint arXiv:2311.01964 (2023)

Empowering Zero-Shot Object Detection: A Human-in-the-Loop Strategy for Unveiling Unseen Realms in Visual Data

Chutisant Kerdvibulvech[1]([✉]) and Qing Li[2]

[1] Graduate School of Communication Arts and Management Innovation,
National Institute of Development Administration, 118 SeriThai Road, Klong-Chan, Bangkapi,
Bangkok 10240, Thailand
chutisant.ker@nida.ac.th
[2] Department of Computing, The Hong Kong Polytechnic University, 11 Yuk Choi Road, Hung
Hom, Kowloon, Hong Kong
qing-prof.li@polyu.edu.hk

Abstract. This paper delves into the paradigm of zero-shot object detection, a fundamental challenge in computer vision. Traditional approaches encounter limitations in recognizing novel objects, prompting the exploration of innovative strategies. The paper introduces a transformative Human-in-the-Loop (HITL) strategy, synergizing machine learning with human intelligence to revolutionize the recognition and localization of unseen objects in visual data. The Human-in-the-Loop strategy comprises a deep learning base, involving cutting-edge models like convolutional neural networks (CNNs), human-in-the-loop iterations with strategic input from annotators, and adaptive model refinement based on human annotations. Insights from diverse case studies are integrated, providing a nuanced understanding of the Human-in-the-Loop strategy's effectiveness. The discussion examines the strengths and limitations of the Human-in-the-Loop strategy, addressing scalability and applicability across domains. The exploration of adaptive model refinement, exemplified by classical works and recent developments, underscores its pivotal role in enhancing adaptability to diverse objects. Case studies, such as Human-in-the-Loop in population health and the application of digital twins, are included. By synergizing machine learning and human expertise, it aims to redefine the landscape of object recognition. The comprehensive discussion and case studies underscore the potential impact of the Human-in-the-Loop strategy on advancing computer vision capabilities, paving the way for future developments in the field.

Keywords: computer vision · human-machine interaction · deep learning · HITL

1 Introduction

Zero-shot object detection, a fundamental challenge in computer vision, involves identifying objects not encountered during model training. Conventional approaches confront limitations when confronted with novel objects, necessitating innovative strategies. This review paper explores a novel paradigm: the integration of a Human-in-the-Loop (HITL) strategy [1–3] to empower zero-shot object detection. By combining machine learning with human intelligence, this approach seeks to revolutionize the recognition and localization of hitherto unseen objects in visual data. In our paper, we seek to leverage the synergy between machine learning algorithms and human annotators, fostering a dynamic loop for continual adaptation to novel objects in visual data.

Zero-shot object detection faces multifaceted challenges stemming from the diversity of real-world visual data. Conventional models often struggle to generalize to novel objects, limiting their utility in applications such as robotics, surveillance, and autonomous systems. The scarcity of annotated data for every conceivable object class exacerbates these challenges, necessitating innovative solutions. The central focus of this review is the introduction of a Human-in-the-Loop strategy designed to revolutionize zero-shot object detection [4]. The core concept involves establishing a collaborative loop between machine learning models and human annotators. Through iterative interactions, the model learns to recognize and localize previously unseen objects, ensuring adaptability to the evolving landscape of visual data. In this paper, key components of the Human-in-the-Loop strategy are divided into three main parts, as shown in Fig. 1.

1. Deep Learning Base:
    The foundation is established with a cutting-edge deep learning model, typically based on convolutional neural networks (CNNs), trained on a diverse dataset to proficiently recognize known objects. This serves as the initial framework for the model's comprehension of standard object detection.
2. Human-in-the-Loop Iterations:
    Human annotators are strategically introduced into the process to assess and annotate instances of previously unseen objects. The model undergoes iterative retraining with each set of annotations, ensuring continuous adaptation to novel object classes.
3. Adaptive Model Refinement:
    The model dynamically adjusts its feature representations based on human annotations, enabling it to comprehend a broader spectrum of objects. The iterative Human-in-the-Loop strategy ensures the continuous evolution and enhancement of the model's capability to detect and localize both known and unknown objects.

This review integrates insights from diverse case studies [5, 6] and benchmark evaluations conducted to assess the effectiveness of the proposed Human-in-the-Loop strategy. Comparative analyses against traditional zero-shot object detection methods provide a comprehensive understanding of the strategy's performance, highlighting improvements in precision, recall, and F1 score.

The review engages in a critical discussion of the strengths and limitations of the proposed Human-in-the-Loop strategy, considering its implications for future developments in zero-shot object detection. Insights are provided into the collaborative nature of human-machine interaction, the challenges faced in implementing this strategy, and potential avenues for further research. Also, the review engages in a critical discussion of the strengths and limitations of the proposed Human-in-the-Loop strategy, offering insights into the collaborative nature of human-machine interaction. Challenges in implementing the strategy are explored, and potential avenues for future research are identified.

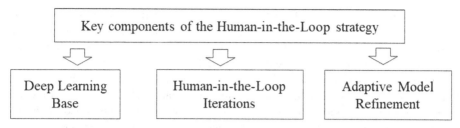

Fig. 1. The fundamental elements of the Human-in-the-Loop strategy

The discussion encompasses the scalability of the approach and its applicability across different domains.

2 Deep Learning Base

In the realm of zero-shot object detection, a robust foundation is laid with a sophisticated deep learning model serving as the core component. Typically, robust deep learning architectures, such as convolutional neural network, are employed as the initial framework. These models are meticulously trained on extensive and diverse datasets, enabling them to achieve proficiency in recognizing and localizing known objects commonly encountered in visual data.

As an example, a recent study by Lee and Park [7] introduced an approach to enhance autonomous drone mobility control through deep reinforcement learning. The primary focus was on advancing autonomous navigation, particularly in challenging real-time situations. The study addressed a crucial aspect of drone control – obstacle avoidance. To achieve this, they employed sensing-aware nonlinear control mechanisms, coupled with advanced trajectory optimization methods. The aim was to improve the overall efficiency of autonomous drones in navigating complex scenarios, addressing the significant challenges associated with real-time obstacle avoidance. Following that, a work centered on deep learning [8] provides a notable illustration of hate speech and offensive language recognition in social media during live through Human-in-the-Loop employing transformer-based language models. The study utilized five distinct models, namely BERT, XLM-RoBERTa, DistilBERT, WangchanBERTa, and TwHIN-BERT, to achieve its outcomes. Following that, Holzinger et al. [9] introduced an approach involving the combination of domain knowledge graphs and deep machine learning to enhance explainability and interpretability. They employed Graph Neural Networks (GNNs) as part of their explainable AI framework. In their classification process, a protein-protein interaction (PPI) network was utilized to overlay a deep neural network, contributing to the interpretability and explainability of the model. Following this, Zhao et al. [10] introduced a visual analytics framework employing a Human-in-the-Loop approach to generate user-defined concepts for interpreting and diagnosing deep learning models. At each stage, active learning was employed, integrating knowledge from humans, including feedback, to train this extractor. Subsequently, Sharif et al. [11] proposed an approach to train a holistic policy for Human-in-the-Loop robot control using deep reinforcement learning, with a specific focus on real reaching trajectories. They devised a stochastic simulation environment called DEXTRON (DEXTerity enviRONment), incorporating actual human trajectories via a Monte Carlo (MC) simulation approach. It is worth mentioning that a comparable concept was applied in our prior work, specifically for selection and simulation using the extended particle filter [12].

Hence, the landscape of zero-shot object detection is underpinned by a robust foundation anchored in sophisticated deep learning models, notably employing state-of-the-art architectures like convolutional neural networks. These models, exemplified by recent studies such as Lee and Park's approach to enhancing autonomous drone mobility and Holzinger et al.'s integration of domain knowledge graphs for interpretability, demonstrate proficiency in recognizing and localizing known objects. However, the inherent limitation arises when these models encounter the vast diversity of real-world visual data and confront novel objects not present in the training set. This limitation propels the exploration of innovative strategies, leading to the integration of a Human-in-the-Loop paradigm. The subsequent sections delve into the details of the Human-in-the-Loop approach and its transformative role in overcoming the challenges posed by zero-shot object detection, presenting a synergy between machine learning models and human annotators to adapt continually to novel objects in visual data.

3 Human-in-the-Loop Iterations

The essence of the Human-in-the-Loop strategy lies in the collaborative synergy between machine learning models and human annotators during iterative cycles. Human annotators play a pivotal role in this process, strategically integrated to evaluate and annotate instances of previously unseen objects that challenge the model's recognition capabilities. This iterative engagement establishes a dynamic feedback loop, facilitating continuous learning and adaptation of the model to novel object classes. With each set of annotations provided by human annotators, the model undergoes retraining, refining its understanding of these unfamiliar objects. The cyclical nature of Human-in-the-Loop iterations ensures that the model evolves and improves its ability to recognize and localize objects not encountered during the initial training phase. This collaborative loop enhances the adaptability of the system to the evolving visual landscape, addressing the inherent challenges posed by the diversity of real-world visual data and the scarcity of annotated information for every conceivable object class. An intriguing Human-in-the-Loop approach to iteration is demonstrated in the work of Gao et al. [13], where they introduce flexible policy iteration (FPI). This method seamlessly integrates prior experience replay and the reinforcement learning controller. The study's findings suggest substantial potential for reinforcement learning control to effectively address complex and challenging issues characterized by high-dimensional control inputs. The incorporation of such Human-in-the-Loop iterations serves as a transformative approach, revolutionizing zero-shot object detection and establishing a robust foundation for future advancements in this domain.

In essence, the Human-in-the-Loop strategy manifests its effectiveness through the collaborative synergy between machine learning models and human annotators in iterative cycles. Human annotators play a pivotal role, strategically evaluating and annotating instances of previously unseen objects that challenge the model's recognition capabilities. This iterative engagement establishes a dynamic feedback loop, fostering continuous learning and adaptation of the model to novel object classes. With each set of annotations, the model undergoes retraining, refining its understanding of unfamiliar objects. The cyclical nature of Human-in-the-Loop iterations ensures the model's evolution, enhancing its ability to recognize and localize objects not encountered during the initial training phase. This collaborative loop enhances system adaptability to the evolving visual landscape, addressing challenges posed by the diversity of real-world visual data and the scarcity of annotated information.

4   Adaptive Model Refinement

The model's ability to dynamically adjust its feature representations based on human annotations signifies a crucial aspect of its adaptability. This dynamic adjustment allows the model to comprehend a broader spectrum of objects, as the iterative Human-in-the-Loop strategy unfolds. Through each cycle of human annotations, the model undergoes refinements that contribute to its continuous evolution and enhancement. This iterative process is vital in cultivating the model's capability to not only detect and localize known objects but also extend its proficiency to previously unfamiliar objects.

In a prior classical work addressing adaptive model refinement, D'Amato et al. [14] focused on retrospective cost optimization for the ionosphere and thermosphere. Their approach involved leveraging data for recursive updates to an unknown subsystem interconnected with a known system, aiming for retrospective-cost-based adaptive model refinement. This classical work demonstrates the application of adaptive model refinement in solving complex problems, showcasing its potential in the context of Human-in-the-Loop scenarios. The concept of retrospective cost optimization aligns with the idea of continuous improvement, making it an interesting avenue to explore for addressing challenges related to Human-in-the-Loop strategies. Furthermore, Ghassemi et al. [15] delved into the application of adaptive model refinement to pinpoint the optimal locations for incorporating new samples in the optimization of bio-inspired flow tailoring. This approach aimed to realize a model-independent surrogate-based optimization by employing adaptive sampling techniques. In a more recent development, Zeng et al. [16] employed adaptive model refinement in the case of Bayesian uncertainty quantification. Their emphasis was on enhancing the local precision of the surrogate model within the high-posterior-density area of the turbulence model, specifically in the context of an axisymmetric transonic bump flow.

Hence, the incorporation of adaptive model refinement emerges as a pivotal aspect in the Human-in-the-Loop strategy. The model's dynamic adjustment of feature representations, guided by human annotations, facilitates a comprehensive understanding of a diverse range of objects throughout the iterative Human-in-the-Loop process. This continuous refinement is essential for enhancing the model's proficiency in detecting and localizing both known and previously unfamiliar objects. The classical work by D'Amato et al. exemplifies the practical application of adaptive model refinement in retrospective cost optimization, showcasing its potential in solving intricate problems within Human-in-the-Loop scenarios. The concept of retrospective cost optimization aligns seamlessly with the pursuit of continuous improvement, making it a compelling avenue for addressing challenges inherent in Human-in-the-Loop strategies. Additionally, Ghassemi et al.'s exploration of adaptive model refinement for optimal sample incorporation in bio-inspired flow tailoring, as well as Zeng et al.'s application for Bayesian uncertainty quantification in turbulence modeling, further underscore the versatility and efficacy of this strategy across diverse domains and applications.

5   Case Studies

In this section, we consolidate insights derived from a variety of case studies undertaken to evaluate the efficacy of the Human-in-the-Loop strategy. To commence, in the investigation conducted by Chen et al. [5], they conducted a comprehensive review of Human-in-the-Loop machine learning applied to population health. By elucidating the primary challenges in machine learning that can be addressed through human intervention in the loop, they delved into Human-in-the-Loop Compressive Population Health Profiling. This approach serves as a deep active learning framework, adeptly combining missing data deduction with active learning. The data deduction algorithm employed in this study comprises two pivotal components: a method based on convolutional neural networks for extracting and representing both intra-disease spatial correlations and inter-disease correlations, and a Generative Adversarial Network (GAN)-based model for making inferences by capitalizing on these two types of correlations. Finally, they examined the implications of incorporating humans at various stages of the machine learning lifecycle, offering insights into the research and findings of their study. Following that, Bononi et al. [6] provide an exemplary case study on Human-in-the-Loop. They introduced digital twins as a pivotal element within a convergence of technologies poised for constructive applications, particularly in the manufacturing domain. The emphasis is on advancing collaboration tools to assist human-computer interactions, with a specific focus on applications related to shaping urban environments.

In conducting comparative analyses against traditional zero-shot object detection methods, the insights drawn from diverse case studies contribute to a comprehensive understanding of the effectiveness of the proposed Human-in-the-Loop strategy. Chen et al. [5], in their study on Human-in-the-Loop machine learning applied to population health, present a nuanced approach with the Human-in-the-Loop Compressive Population Health Profiling framework. The method adeptly combines missing data deduction, employing a data deduction algorithm with active learning that integrates a convolutional neural networks-based technique for extracting inter-disease correlations and intra-disease spatial correlations, along with a Generative Adversarial Network (GAN)-based model for making inferences. By applying humans into various stages of the machine learning lifecycle, they illuminate the potential benefits of such collaboration. Similarly, Bononi et al. [6] exemplify the application of Human-in-the-Loop in the context of digital twins, showcasing its relevance in advancing distributed collaboration platforms, especially in manufacturing and urban development. These case studies provide valuable insights that facilitate a comparative evaluation, highlighting the transformative potential of the Human-in-the-Loop strategy over traditional methods in addressing the challenges of zero-shot object detection.

6 Discussion and Conclusion

The comprehensive exploration of the Human-in-the-Loop strategy in the context of zero-shot object detection sheds light on its transformative potential and multifaceted implications. The review elucidates the intricate collaborative synergy between machine learning models and human annotators, exemplified through the iterative cycles of Human-in-the-Loop. This dynamic feedback loop, involving strategic human evaluation and annotation of previously unseen objects, is integral to the continuous learning and adaptation of the model. The iterative nature of Human-in-the-Loop iterations ensures the model's evolution, addressing challenges arising from the diversity of real-world visual data and the scarcity of annotated information. This collaborative loop not only enhances the adaptability of the system to the evolving visual landscape but also demonstrates its efficacy in recognizing and localizing objects beyond the scope of initial training. The integration of diverse case studies and benchmark evaluations further contributes to a nuanced understanding of the Human-in-the-Loop strategy's performance, showcasing improvements in precision, recall, and F1 score compared to traditional zero-shot object detection methods.

The discussion delves into the strengths and limitations of the Human-in-the-Loop strategy, offering insights into the collaborative nature of human-machine interaction. Scalability and applicability across different domains are scrutinized, providing a holistic perspective on the challenges and potential avenues for future research. The exploration of adaptive model refinement within the Human-in-the-Loop framework, as illustrated by classical works and recent developments, underlines its significance in enhancing the model's adaptability to a broad spectrum of objects. The application of retrospective cost optimization, pinpointing optimal sample locations, and Bayesian uncertainty quantification exemplify the versatility and efficacy of adaptive model refinement in addressing complex challenges within the Human-in-the-Loop paradigm. In essence, the discussion section underscores the dynamic interplay between machine learning models and human annotators, offering a roadmap for further advancements and interdisciplinary applications of the Human-in-the-Loop strategy in the evolving landscape of zero-shot object detection.

In conclusion, empowering zero-shot object detection through a Human-in-the-Loop strategy signifies a paradigm shift in computer vision. This comprehensive review establishes the influence of the Human-in-the-Loop strategy to revolutionize object detection, presenting a nuanced understanding of its strengths and limitations. The collaborative synergy between machine intelligence and human expertise, as exemplified by the proposed strategy, emerges as a transformative force in addressing the complexities of recognizing and localizing previously unseen objects in visual data. The review concludes by outlining the broader implications of the Human-in-the-Loop strategy and its potential impact on the future landscape of zero-shot object detection in diverse practical applications.

7 Future Directions

The future directions for Human-in-the-Loop in zero-shot object detection encompass refining collaborative frameworks, addressing ethical considerations, and enhancing the scalability and generalization of models. By addressing these aspects, researchers can contribute to the responsible and effective integration of Human-in-the-Loop strategies, unlocking their full potential for revolutionizing object detection in diverse and dynamic visual environments. We categorize our future directions into four main parts as follows.

1. Enhanced Collaborative Frameworks: The integration of Human-in-the-Loop strategies for zero-shot object detection presents a promising avenue for further research in the development of advanced collaborative frameworks. Future efforts could explore the refinement of collaborative models that better leverage the strengths of both machine learning algorithms and human annotators. This involves investigating improved mechanisms for communication, feedback, and decision-making within the collaborative loop. By enhancing the synergy between human intelligence and machine learning, researchers can aim for more effective and streamlined iterations, leading to higher adaptability of models to novel objects. Additionally, exploring ways to integrate real-time collaboration and feedback mechanisms could further enhance the efficiency of the collaborative loop, providing timely adjustments and improvements to the model.
2. Ethical Considerations and Bias Mitigation: As the implementation of Human-in-the-Loop strategies becomes more widespread, addressing ethical considerations and mitigating biases in zero-shot object detection models becomes paramount. Future research may focus on developing ethical guidelines and frameworks for implementing Human-in-the-Loop strategies responsibly, including deepfakes [17]. This involves investigating methods to identify and rectify potential biases introduced during the iterative processes. Researchers can explore ways to enhance transparency in decision-making within the collaborative loop, ensuring that the models generated are fair, unbiased, and aligned with ethical standards. Additionally, studying the impact of human annotator biases on model outcomes and developing strategies to minimize such biases will be crucial for the ethical advancement of Human-in-the-Loop in zero-shot object detection.
3. Scalability and Generalization: Scaling Human-in-the-Loop strategies to handle diverse datasets, varied domains, and large-scale applications is a significant challenge that merits future exploration. Researchers can investigate techniques to enhance the scalability of Human-in-the-Loop approaches, allowing them to adapt to different visual landscapes and object classes seamlessly. Generalization across domains and datasets remains a critical aspect, and future research can delve into methods that facilitate the transferability of Human-in-the-Loop-trained models to novel scenarios. This involves understanding how well models adapted through Human-in-the-Loop iterations generalize to different contexts and exploring strategies to improve their robustness across various applications, from robotics and surveillance to autonomous systems.
4. The exploration of advanced multimodal large language models, such as GPT-4v, in the domain of vehicle make recognition opens avenues for future research. One potential future direction is to delve deeper into the zero-shot capabilities of GPT-4v

for recognizing diverse vehicle makes within a Human-in-the-Loop framework. In the future, we plan to investigate strategies to enhance the model's proficiency in scenarios with multiple cars and varying perspectives. Our focus will be on refining the integration of visual and language information to improve the accuracy of vehicle make recognition. Additionally, exploring the transferability of GPT-4v-trained models to real-world environments and diverse datasets is essential for practical applications. Future work includes addressing the scalability of the model and ensuring its robust performance across a wide range of traffic monitoring scenarios. Investigating ethical considerations, such as potential biases in the recognition of vehicle makes, is also crucial for responsible deployment.

Acknowledgments. This research presented herein was partially supported by a research grant from the Research Center, NIDA (National Institute of Development Administration).

References

1. Chen, Z.: Human-in-the-loop Machine Learning System via Model Interpretability. Duke University, Durham, NC, USA (2023)
2. Moqadam, S.B., Delle, K., Schorling, U., Asheghabadi, A.S., Norouzi, F., Xu, J.: Reproducing tactile and proprioception based on the human-in-the-closed-loop conceptual approach. IEEE Access **11**, 41894–41905 (2023)
3. Mosqueira-Rey, E., Hernández-Pereira, E., Alonso-Ríos, D., Bobes-Bascarán, J., Fernández-Leal, Á.: Human-in-the-loop machine learning: a state of the art. Artif. Intell. Rev. **56**(4), 3005–3054 (2023)
4. Herrmann, T., Pfeiffer, S.: Keeping the organization in the loop: a socio-technical extension of human-centered artificial intelligence. AI Soc. **38**(4), 1523–1542 (2023)
5. Chen, L., Wang, J., Guo, B., Chen, L.: Human-in-the-loop machine learning with applications for population health. CCF Trans. Pervasive Comput. Interact. **5**(1), 1–12 (2023)
6. Bononi, L., et al.: Digital twin collaborative platforms: applications to humans-in-the-loop crafting of urban areas. IEEE Consumer Electron. Mag. **12**(6), 38–46 (2023)
7. Lee, H., Park, S.: Sensing-aware deep reinforcement learning with HCI-based human-in-the-loop feedback for autonomous nonlinear drone mobility control. IEEE Access **12**, 1727–1736 (2024)
8. Pookpanich, P., Siriborvornratanakul, T.: Offensive language and hate speech detection using deep learning in football news live streaming chat on YouTube in Thailand. Soc. Netw. Anal. Min. **14**(1), 18 (2023)
9. Holzinger, A., et al.: Human-in-the-loop integration with domain-knowledge graphs for explainable federated deep learning. In: CD-MAKE, pp. 45–64 (2023)
10. Zhao, Z., Panpan, X., Scheidegger, C., Ren, L.: Human-in-the-loop extraction of interpretable concepts in deep learning models. IEEE Trans. Vis. Comput. Graph. **28**(1), 780–790 (2022)
11. Sharif, M., Erdogmus, D., Amato, C., Padir, T.: End-to-end grasping policies for human-in-the-loop robots via deep reinforcement learning. In: ICRA 2021, pp. 2768–2774 (2021)
12. Kerdvibulvech, C.: Human hand motion recognition using an extended particle filter. In: Perales, F.J., Santos-Victor, J. (eds.) AMDO 2014. LNCS, vol. 8563, pp. 71–80. Springer, Cham (2014). https://doi.org/10.1007/978-3-319-08849-5_8
13. Gao, X., Si, J., Wen, Y., Li, M., Huang, H.: Reinforcement learning control of robotic knee with human-in-the-loop by flexible policy iteration. IEEE Trans. Neural Networks Learn. Syst. **33**(10), 5873–5887 (2022)

14. D'Amato, A.M., Ridley, A.J., Bernstein, D.S.: Retrospective-cost-based adaptive model refinement for the ionosphere and thermosphere. Stat. Anal. Data Min. **4**(4), 446–458 (2011)
15. Ghassemi, P., Lulekar, S.S., Chowdhury, S.: Adaptive model refinement with batch Bayesian sampling for optimization of bio-inspired flow tailoring. In: AIAA Aviation and Aeronautics Forum and Exposition (AIAA AVIATION Forum 2019), 17–21 June 2019, Dallas, Texas (2019)
16. Zeng, F., Zhang, W., Li, J., Zhang, T., Yan, C.: Adaptive model refinement approach for Bayesian uncertainty quantification in turbulence model. AIAA J. **60**(6), 3502–3516 (2022)
17. Songja, R., Promboot, I., Haetanurak, B., et al.: Deepfake AI images: should deepfakes be banned in Thailand? AI Ethics (2023)

More Than One Gesture but Less Than Two? Inter-stroke Dependencies in Form and Meaning

Schuyler Laparle[1]([✉])(ID), Gaëlle Ferré[2,3](ID), and Merel C. J. Scholman[3,4](ID)

[1] Tilburg University, Tilburg, The Netherlands
S.M.Laparle@tilburguniversity.edu
[2] Université de Poitiers, Poitiers, France
gaelle.ferre@univ-poitiers.fr
[3] Saarland University, Saarbrücken, Germany
[4] Utrecht University, Utrecht, The Netherlands
m.c.j.scholman@uu.nl

Abstract. In gesture analysis, one must segment the gesture stream into discrete units to be analyzed for meaning and alignment with accompanying speech. This requires defining what constitutes a single "gesture". Following the influential work of Kendon (2004) and McNeill (2005), this nearly always involves identifying the "stroke", the gesture's meaningful core. Innovations in the understanding of gestural meaning complicate this procedure, as there is increasing evidence that gestures are both internally complex and compositional. In the present work, we discuss the ways in which this complexity in gestural meaning may be addressed by including the notion of "gesture sequences". Using data from American television talk shows and TED talks, we demonstrate two types of *inter-stroke dependencies* in pragmatic gestures where one movement's meaning and form is dependent on that of a previous movement: (i) "closing gestures" signal the closure of a discourse topic and are dependent on a preceding presentation gesture; (ii) "contrast sequences" signal a *contrast* discourse relation and are dependent on adjacent presentation gestures occurring in different regions of gesture space. These findings have important implications for both how we annotate the gesture stream and how we simulate gesture in virtual agents.

Keywords: discourse · coherence · topic closure · contrast · gesture

1 Introduction

Language, especially in face-to-face contexts, is a fundamentally multimodal process. Language users consistently exploit prototypical linguistic systems (speech

We would like to thank audiences at GESPIN2023, ICLC16, and MMSYM 2023 for helpful feedback on various aspects of our analyses, as well as Cornelia Müller for insights on gesture segmentation. A special thank you also to Andy Lücking, Alexander Mehler, and Alexander Henlein for supporting a unique space for innovative and interdisciplinary discussion of multimodality.

V. G. Duffy (Ed.): HCII 2024, LNCS 14711, pp. 245–264, 2024.
https://doi.org/10.1007/978-3-031-61066-0_15

and sign), as well as gesture, spatial context, and social dynamics in the meaning making process. Though the multimodality of language is broadly agreed upon in cognitive, social, and usage-based approaches to language, the ways in which different semiotic modes come together to form a single coherent message is still a subject of debate. How this debate is resolved has direct implications for how we analyse, annotate, and virtually generate multimodal language use.

In order to understand how different semiotic systems come together to form a single coherent message, we must have working theories of (i) the basic meaning units of each semiotic system, and (ii) how meaning units compose within and across modes to create more complex units. We discuss the ways in which our current working theories of multimodal composition are insufficient for the analysis of pragmatic gestures – we do not yet fully understand what constitutes a basic unit of gestural meaning, nor how those units compose with each other and accompanying speech. In particular, we problematize the now standard one-gesture/one-stroke definition of a gesture (e.g. Kendon 2004; McNeill 2005) by looking at two recurrent gesture routines expressing *topic closure* and *contrast*.

Pragmatic gestures have been relatively understudied due to their perceived messiness (e.g. Streeck 2009). Instead, researchers have focused on semantically-oriented gestures, which tend to relate to accompanying speech more transparently. We believe that this has been a mistake, leading to an over-simplification in gesture segmentation and theories of multimodal compositionality. Pragmatic gestures are 'messy' because pragmatic meaning is more complex, heterogeneous, and subject to contextual variation than the meaning typically dealt with by semantics. Semantic gestures convey information related to the truth-conditional meaning conveyed in accompanying speech. Pragmatic gestures, on the other hand, variably contribute social-affiliative, discourse structural, epistemic, and emotive information related to *inferential* meaning that may or may not be conveyed in accompanying speech.[1] This, indeed, makes pragmatic gestures more difficult to analyze. It also makes pragmatic gestures particularly well-suited for testing the adequacy of models of gesture form and meaning.

The remainder of this paper is structured as follows. First, we outline the types of pragmatic meaning of interest in this work, namely that related to discourse structure and coherence (Sect. 2). We then review affiliate and action schematic approaches to gesture meaning, arguing that discourse structural pragmatic gestures necessitate the use of the latter (Sect. 3). Section 4 summarizes the data and annotation methods used for the current study. Section 5 then covers three case studies. The first presents 'clean' alignment between pragmatic gestures and spoken discourse markers. We then complicate the story of alignment between pragmatic gestures and accompanying speech in the two proceeding case studies on *topic closure* and *contrast*. Section 6 concludes.

---

[1] See, for example, Bavelas et al. (1992) for discussion of the functional heterogeneity of pragmatic gestures.

2 Discourse Structure

In cooperative discourse, interlocutors are assumed to pursue communicative goals in a systematic way. This generally means that interlocutors should have a reason for making each contribution, and for making contributions in the order that they do. In order to formally model this process, at least two dimensions of the resulting text[2] have to be considered; (i) how discourse segments are organized to achieve communicative goals, and (ii) how relationships between segments are (or are not) linguistically expressed. In the remainder of this section, we discuss our approach to these two dimensions of discourse structure, considering discourse as a set of ordered topics and nested sub-topics (Sect. 2.1) which relate to each other in a variety of complex ways (Sect. 2.2).

2.1 Topics and Sub-topics in Discourse

We consider discourse to be fundamentally hierarchical, structured into topics and subtopics. Each topic comprises a set of entities and a limited range of propositions about those entities that are relevant to the topic at hand (Webber et al., 2012). The notion of *topic* thus concerns the 'aboutness' of (sets of) utterances. Though there are several ways to model this hierarchical structure, we take a broadly question-based approach in which topics are defined by the questions explicitly and implicitly posed by interlocutors as a discourse unfolds (Roberts, 2012; Van Kuppevelt, 1995). This means that as a discourse progresses, interlocutors must negotiate (i) which questions to ask and in what order, (ii) when a given question is sufficiently answered, and (iii) when a given question is unanswerable and should be abandoned.

Analysts rely on a variety of linguistic cues when modelling a discourse's question-answer structure. For example, recurring mentions of a referent, first as a full referential phrase, and then in reduced forms (e.g. pronouns), is considered indicative of a 'sequence-topic', i.e. a topic that spans multiple utterances (Van Dijk 1977:51). Other signals of topic structure include word repetition, the use of semantically related words, such as synonyms, hypernyms and hyponyms (more general or specific terms, respectively), and meronyms (terms that refer to a part of a given whole), as well as the use of words that share more general experientially-based associations (such as between *bag* and *carry*, or *bag* and *groceries*) (Webber et al., 2012).

There is increasing evidence that gestures can also serve as signals of topic structure. For example, McNeill et al. (2001) introduced the concept of "gesture catchments" to describe the recurrence of specific gestural features (e.g. hand shape or movement) for the duration of a sequence-topic. Recent work on so-called "recurrent gestures" (Müller, 2017) has also sought to identify particular gesture routines used to signal particular types of discourse structural information. For example, "away-gestures", in which the hand moves away from

---

[2] "Text" here refers to any linguistic artifact, be it written, spoken, signed, or multimodal.

the speaker's body as if to remove an object from their immediate space, has been associated with topic dismissal (Bressem & Müller, 2017; Laparle, 2022). Laparle (2022) further shows that gestures can systematically signal whether a given discourse move constitutes an expected continuation of a topic, or an unexpected digression or topic-shift. In the current work, we identify the 'closing gesture', in which previously open hands are purposefully and forcefully closed, as a signal of topic closure.

2.2 Discourse Relations and Markers

Discourse relations are logical relations that readers infer between segments of a text in order to align strategies for pursuing a particular discourse topic (i.e. answering a particular discourse question). Prototypical relations include *Cause* or *Contrast*. These relations hold between two text spans, referred to as segments or arguments. The segments of a relation are the "idea units" between which a relationship holds and can vary in size and grammatical structure.

Comprehenders can make use of different sources of information to infer and direct the interpretation process of discourse relations. The most well-studied of these are connectives and cue phrases[3] (such as *however* and *as a result*). Such cues instruct comprehenders on how to connect incoming text inputs to previously processed segments (Britton, 1994; Gernsbacher, 1997). Relations that are signalled by a connective or cue phrase are referred to as explicit relations. However, many relations are left implicit – that is, they are not marked by a connective or cue phrase (estimates for rates of implicitness vary between 20–50% of all relations, see Das & Taboada, 2018; Webber et al., 2019).

Though lacking an explicit connective, implicit relations can contain signals that tend to co-occur with specific relation types and thereby function as a cue for discourse relations. For example, implicit causality verbs such as *admire* or *praise* tend to occur in causal discourse relations (Kehler et al., 2008), negation tends to occur in concession and substitution relations (Asr & Demberg, 2015; Crible & Pickering, 2020; Webber, 2013), and quantifiers such as *several* tend to elicit expectations of upcoming list relations (Scholman et al., 2020; Tskhovrebova et al., 2023).

Comprehenders can also make use of non-textual sources of information, such as prosody (Hu et al., 2023) and gestures (Hinnell, 2019; Laparle, 2022). Research into these modalities is limited, but there is some evidence that discourse relations are embodied: speakers can use hand, head, and shoulder movements, as well as eyebrow raising and gaze shifts, to mark elements and their relation to each other. For example, Hinnell (2019) used a dataset of late night interviews to show that 71% and 77% of all contrastive relations expressed by "On the one hand" and "On the other hand", respectively, were co-articulated in the body, most notably through the use of hand gestures in different gestural spaces. In the current work, we extend Hinnel's observations to 'contrast gestures' performed with other lexical cues.

---

[3] Also variably referred to as pragmatic markers, coherence markers, discourse markers, and discourse particles.

3   Gesture Alignment and Interpretation

If we are to understand how gestures may serve as markers of topic structure and discourse relations, we have to understand how gestures convey meaning in the first place. In this section, we look at two approaches to gestural meaning, the *lexical affiliate* approach and *action schematic* approach, and discuss the ways in which each make subtly different predictions about gesture timing and segmentation. We then review (and problematize) typical segmentation strategies.

3.1   Lexical Affiliate Approach

In many cases, it is difficult to interpret a gesture without knowing the spoken context in which it occurs. This is the case even when the meaning of a gesture is clearly *iconic*, with some aspect of its form resembling some aspect of its meaning. For instance, forming a circular shape with both hands held in front of the body may well represent a round object of the same size, like a ball. However, we can also imagine the same gesture used to refer to a much larger round object, like a planet, or perhaps an abstract concept like "whole", which seems in some way *metaphorically* round. The point is that we cannot know which meaning to assign to the gesture without knowing the speech it accompanies. It is this observation that leads to the *lexical affiliate* approach to gesture meaning.

McNeill (2005), following Schegloff's (1984) earlier proposal, defines a *lexical affiliate* as "the word or words deemed to correspond most closely to a gesture in meaning" (McNeill, 2005, 37). The performance of the gesture typically overlaps, at least partially, with the pronunciation of its lexical affiliate. In this model, gestures are thus considered *redundant* in that the meaning they express is also expressed in speech. The lexical affiliate model is controversial in the gesture literature, as some scholars prefer to think in terms of *conceptual affiliates* rather than seeking a strict correspondence between a gesture and a word (de Ruiter, 2000; Kirchhof, 2011). In these related models, gesture and speech are *co-expressive* (McNeill, 2005) of a single underlying pre-modal concept. This allows for expressions across modes to profile different aspects of the target concept, resulting in *partial* redundancy between gesture and speech.[4]

Both the lexical and conceptual affiliate models were conceived with *semantic* gestures in mind, i.e. gestures that seem to express something related to the propositional information of the utterance. However, they are not particularly well-suited for modeling *pragmatic* gestures, i.e. gestures that seem to express something about the discourse structure or social interaction.[5] For example, pragmatic gestures may add a modal stance to the utterance (e.g. showing both hands palm upwards to express uncertainty (Debras, 2017)), regulate interactions (e.g. holding one's hand palm outwards in front of the body to prevent

---

[4] See Kendon (2014) for particularly nice discussion of partial redundancy with gestural expressions of "throwing" events.

[5] These appear under many names in the gesture literature including pragmatic gestures (Kendon, 2017), interactive gestures (Bavelas et al., 1992), discourse management gestures (Wehling, 2017), and gestural discourse markers (Laparle, 2022).

someone from taking the turn (Wehling, 2017)), or refer to some previous utterance by locating it metaphorically in space (McNeill et al., 1993). Affiliate models often fail in the analysis of pragmatic gestures because, though pragmatic information is inferable from accompanying speech, it is often not overtly expressed (as discussed in the previous section). When these gestures are used in the absence of a spoken discourse marker, they are standalone meaning resources, fully non-redundant with accompanying speech.

Affiliate models, explicitly or implicitly, encourage the analyst to analogize the segmentation of gesture to the segmentation of words. This is because the meaning of gesture is tied either to an actual word (in the lexical affiliate model) or the type of concept that is likely to be lexically expressed (in the conceptual affiliate model). This analogizing leads to an oversimplification of gesture form and compositionality, especially when pragmatic gestures are considered.

3.2   Action-Schematic Approach

Action and image schematic approaches offer a helpful alternative to the affiliate models discussed in the previous section. In these models, a gesture means by evoking an *experiential frame* (Mittelberg, 2019; Müller, 2017) through either enactment (evoking an action schema) or depiction (evoking an image schema). Under this approach, the 'ball holding' gesture discussed in the previous section is a ball holding gesture because it resembles our actual physical experiences of holding ball-like objects. Moreover, it is *always* a ball holding gesture, never a 'planet holding' or 'wholistic holding' gesture, even if it were to be articulated in concert with the lexical items "planet" or "whole". The felicity of the 'ball holding' gesture in these circumstances hinges on the comprehender identifying meaningful metonymic and metaphoric connections between the virtual ball being held and the planet or wholeness being lexically expressed.

This might seem like a trivial distinction when we are looking at semantic gestures, but its explanatory power becomes very apparent when we turn toward pragmatic gestures. For example, consider a speaker repeatedly flicking their hand outward, *as if* flicking away a small unwanted entity (Bressem & Müller 2017). The iconic meaning of the gesture is understood as this *as-if* action. It is a *flicking* gesture, and it means what the action of flicking means in our embodied experience – there is a small object near that we'd like moved away. The communicative *function* of the gesture is then understood in context as, for example, an enactment of a literal removal of a mosquito from our personal space or a metaphoric removal of the discourse topic we'd like to be dismissed. The spoken context may remain necessary for interpreting the gesture's *function*, but not for analyzing its core schematic meaning.

During annotation, this means that we are no longer looking to segment the gesture stream into gestures as such, but rather into meaningful experientially-based actions. This is important because actions vary in complexity and the degree to which they are related to other adjacent actions. For instance, the action of putting down my coffee cup is dependent on my having picked it up, but not on my having swatted a fly away as I took a sip. In this paper, we'll focus on two dependencies in action schemata – *opening* as a precondition for *closing*, and *presenting* one object as a precondition for *separating* it from another. Before that, however, we'll discuss typical strategies for segmenting the gesture stream into *gestures*, keeping in mind that these strategies were not sufficient for the data we attempt to describe.

3.3   Gesture Segmentation

Kendon (1980) highlighted the internal structure of the gesture stream. Though his original work has been enriched since, the basic tenets still serve as the foundation of gesture analysis and annotation today. Kendon (1980) presented a gesture hierarchy organized into three levels: gesture *phrases* are composed of gesture *phases* and can be grouped into gesture *units*. Kendon's gesture *phrase* is what we typically think of as 'a gesture' and is defined by the presence of a *stroke* – the movement which gives a gesture its meaning.[6] The meaningful stroke is then flanked by other periods of stillness and movement that contribute to the successful articulation of the gesture, appropriately timed in alignment with affiliated speech. In particular, a stroke can be preceded by a *preparation* – movement which positions the hand at the starting point of the stroke –, and proceeded by a *retraction* – movement that returns the hand from the end of the stroke to a position of rest. Between (and even within) each movement phase, periods of stillness can occur, called *holds*. Holds prior to the stroke are thought to contribute to ensuring the appropriate timing of the stroke, whereas holds after the stroke are thought to indicate the continued relevance of the stroke (Kita et al., 1998). A schematic representation of an idealised gesture phrase is given in (1), with the gesture unfolding temporally from left to right. Only the stroke is compulsory, and every gesture, it should seem, consists of exactly one stroke.

(1)   *rest* | preparation (hold) STROKE (hold) retraction | *rest*

The above schematic is 'idealized' because speakers very rarely produce exactly one gesture between periods of rest. Instead, there are typically extended periods of movement in which speakers perform several gestures, of variable duration and with variable degrees of internal complexity. These periods of consecutive gesture articulations, when the hands do not return to a rest position between strokes, are what Kendon (1980) refers to as gesture *units*. Kendon suggests that these larger units align with larger units in the speech stream (e.g. discourse segments). However, relatively little work has seriously considered the meaning or compositionality of these larger units of gestural meaning.

One of the main challenges of annotation is knowing how to delimit the different gestural phases, especially in complex gesture units containing multiple phrases, and thus multiple meaningful strokes. Using an annotation tool that

---

[6] Though see Kita et al. (1998) on 'static gestures' (e.g. deictic points) in which the meaningful core of the gesture is a period of stillness (an independent hold), rather than a stroke.

allows frame-by-frame analysis is often cited as key, enabling analysts to look for moments of blurring, which are thought to indicate phase changes (Seyfeddinipur, 2006), as well as changes in fine-grained articulatory features like tension of the hand and restriction in movement (Bressem & Ladewig, 2011). Though these strategies help in phase demarcation, they do not offer ways to assess the connection between adjacent phrases. In other words, they provide us with a means to identify *gestures*, which constitute units of meaning, but they do not help us identify units of meaning that may exist between the level of a single gesture and the rest-to-rest gesture unit. In line with Müller (in preparation), we call this level of gestural meaning units *gesture sequences*. In questioning how to appropriately segment gesture sequences, we also question the presumed independence of strokes at the phrase level.

4   Data and Methodology

In Sect. 5, we present three case studies to illustrate inter-stroke dependencies in form and meaning. The data used in the case studies come from two sources: (1) monologues and interviews on the American talk show The Late Show with Stephen Colbert; and (2) monologues from American TED talks. The talk show data was collected through UCLA's Communication Studies Archive in collaboration with the Red Hen Lab (Joo et al. 2017). This archive contains over 200.000 videos of news broadcasts from around the world. The TED videos and transcripts were collected using the TED-Talk repository library (https://www.ted.com/talks).

Both TED Talk and Late Show data can be considered relatively 'clean' in that they are (semi-)scripted discourses performed by people trained in public speaking (be it for education, entertainment, or a combination thereof). This makes them a good starting place for studying notoriously difficult pragmatic gestures. They also differ in their social affordances, offering insights into different aspects of the use and complexity of pragmatic gesture sequences. TED talk recordings are well-suited to an analysis of discourse units and inter-segment relations, since they consist of prepared argumentative discourse in monologues. This means that discourse units are well-organized into question-answer structures and that the speaker does not have to contend with the complexities of speech turns and goal negotiation with another interlocutor. This makes TED talks particularly well-suited for looking at gestural markers of discourse coherence. Late Shows introduce pragmatic complexity along two dimensions. First, they are informative as well as humorous. This means that they are suitable for looking not only at gestural markers of coherence, but also stance and affect. Second, because most Late Shows also contain interview segments, they are also well-suited for studying gestures associated with turn-taking and other forms of dyadic discourse management.

The examples presented in the case studies were annotated as part of larger projects focusing on gestures as discourse markers. The data was analysed using the Elan annotation software (Sloetjes & Wittenburg 2008). In the present work, we are primarily interested in the problems we encountered while using established coding schemes and segmentation strategies. For all examples, we provide a transcript that is co-indexed with an accompanying set of screenshots. Gesture timing is demarcated by brackets with a label for the corresponding screenshot at the end ("[...]$_{G1}$"). Corpus identification numbers are provided for Talk Show examples and URLs are provided for TED Talk examples. For each case, we discuss the pragmatic function of the gesture sequence and how it complicates the one-gesture/one-stroke segmentation strategy discussed in the previous section.

5   Results

We present three case studies that demonstrate different types of lexical and discourse-structural alignment with pragmatic gestures. The two examples in the first case study show that pragmatic gestures do, at least occasionally, align with spoken discourse markers which can be said to serve as lexical affiliates. To a significant extent, this case study shows that affiliate models *can* account for both semantic and pragmatic gestures in cases where the meaning of each gesture in the gesture stream independently aligns temporally and meaningfully with a segment of speech. The subsequent two sections then demonstrate the insufficiency of affiliate models and linear gesture-speech alignment strategies.

5.1   Case Study 1: Gesture and Lexical Discourse Markers

In this section, we look at two cases in which a lexical affiliate can be identified for a pragmatic gesture, much like in the majority of semantically-oriented gestures. Unlike with concrete iconic semantic gestures, however, the connection between the pragmatic gestures and their co-expressive lexical phrase is not immediately transparent. The iconic, action-schematic meaning of the gesture must be mapped to a particular pragmatic function in context through metaphor (e.g. Parrill & Sweetser 2004), requiring the gesture analyst to identify some aspect of the discursive structure that can support a coherent metaphorical mapping.

  In the first example, American television talk show host, Stephen Colbert, makes a joke about 'soul mates', undermining the conventional association of soul-mate with permanence by introducing the concept of "holi-bae", someone who fulfills the role of soul-mate for only the holiday season. Exactly one gesture is produced for each of the final three clauses in the example, and each gesture is related through iconicity to a concept co-expressed in the aligned speech. Bracketed text represents gesture timing and is co-indexed with a screenshot of each gesture performance in Fig. 1.

(2)   Everyone wants to meet their true love, but maybe right now you just need a 'holi-bae', a person who's your soul mate, [but only for the holidays.]$_{G1}$ [Just give me the airfryer]$_{G2}$ [and get out]$_{G3}$ [7]

---

[7] UID: 8511976e-58c2-11ec-8526-089e01ba0335,1482.

Fig. 1. Gesture-speech alignment for pragmatic and semantic gestures

The first gesture (G1) is a pragmatic gesture, iconically representing the numeral '1'. This is affiliated with a concept of exclusivity, co-expressed by the phrase "but only". The second (G2) and third (G3) gestures in Fig. 1 depict the trajectory of movement in an event described in the co-occurring speech; Colbert's hands move toward his body when requesting the transfer of an object to him, and move away from his body when requesting the imagined addressee to move away from him. In all three cases, we can identify particular phrases in speech and particular physical features in gesture that co-express a single affiliated concept. Moreover, this happens for both semantic information that can be transparently enacted in the gestural mode (e.g. trajectory of movement), and for pragmatic information that is depicted in gesture through analogy to an abstract relation (e.g. singularity as a depiction of exclusivity).

In the second example, Irish actor Andrew Scott performs a series of four gestures, two semantic (G1 & G3) and two pragmatic (G2 & G4), while attempting to defend the length of a Shakespeare play. As in the previous example, a lexical affiliate can be identified for both a semantic gesture (G1) and pragmatic gesture (G4). However, this example also demonstrates that lexical affiliates can be elusive, regardless of a gesture's status as semantic (G3) or pragmatic (G2).

(3)   Y'know, we watch five hours of television if it's exciting. So the idea is [don't cut it down,]$_{G1}$ [just make it]$_{G2}$ [four hours of really exciting]$_{G3}$ [um play- plays.]$_{R1}$ [Anyway, I'll stop talking Shakespeare]$_{G4}$ [8]

G1 & G4 have identifiable affiliates in the co-occurring speech. In G1, the flat hand shape and sagital orientation suggest a cutting action schema (Calbris 2003), and thus can be considered affiliated with the word "cut", and the abstract "cutting" event it expresses. The large 'sweeping away' gesture (G4) represented in the final two frames evokes a clearing action schema in which unwanted objects are removed from the speaker's immediate space, metaphorically associated with removing unwanted topics (Bressem & Müller 2017), and thus paralleling the topic-dismissal function of "anyway" (Laparle 2022) (Fig. 2).

---

[8] UID: f00485b2-051e-11ea-8f95-089e01ba0770,3559.

Fig. 2. Gesture-speech alignment for metaphoric pragmatic and semantic gesture

G2 & G3, on the other hand, do not have clear lexical affiliates. In the second gesture, Scott rotates both hands upward, a recurrent gesture, variably termed 'palm-reveal' (Chu et al. 2014), 'hand flip' (Ferré 2012), and 'hand shrug' (Debras 2017), that has been associated with the expression of epistemic stance and an unwillingness to act (Cooperrider et al. 2018). Arguably, this can be related to the use of the discourse particle "just", which seems to also serve a stance-taking function in this context, expressing the perceived obviousness of the suggestion to make the play exciting. However, this connection is not transparent, relying on a particular analysis of two highly multifunctional linguistic forms (the palm-reveal gesture and the particle "just"). Finally, G3 seems to convey semantic information about an extended period of time, as Scott moves his hand rightward, as if along a timeline. However, this extension action-schema can only be related to the aligned speech by considering the previous discourse context – "four hours" can be iconically represented as an extended period of time because this period was previously "cut down", thus demonstrating a meaningful relationship between non-consecutive strokes in the gesture unit.

5.2   Case Study 2: Gesture and Discourse-Topics

In this section, we discuss a recurrent gesture sequence consisting of a presentational gesture followed by a 'closing gesture'. This two-part gesture sequence presents two complications for gesture segmentation. First, the 'closing gesture' is at times ambiguous, analyzable either as a retraction of the preceding presentational gesture to a rest position, or as an independent stroke signalling a separate gesture. Second, if analyzed as an independent stroke, as we argue for, it remains dependent on the presentational gesture for both form (the hands must be open in order to be closed) and meaning (a topic must be 'presented' in order to be subsequently 'concealed' via closure).

The presentational gesture, commonly referred to as *Palm Up Open Hand* or *PUOH* gesture, has been described by Müller (2004) as particularly multifunctional. For example, the gesture may express the uncertainty of the speaker (epistemic function), but may also be used to quote someone or to release the conversational floor (interactive function). Cienki (2021) also described some instances of the gesture used to emphasize the introduction of a new discourse entity, although he did not state if the gesture introduces new sentence-topics or sequence-topics as described above. This gesture is indeed quite pervasive in argumentative discourse and is typically performed when a speaker wants to emphasize the fact that some addition or justification has been provided to the argument. Cienki (*ibid.*) goes further in his description of the gesture, stating that it is subject to a high degree of formal variation, especially considering handshape and movement type, and reveals a continuum of more or less reduced forms. The full PUOH gesture consists of presenting the palm of the hand (and therefore turning the wrist with extended fingers), but a simple raising of the index finger would play the same function and could therefore be considered as a minimal version of the PUOH gesture. Some instances of the PUOH gesture are considered as variants of beats by some scholars (McNeill, 2005, among others), although beats have been shown to play a more local emphasis function on lexical items, whereas PUOH gestures serve to emphasize larger discourse units (Ferré, forthcoming). Since PUOH gestures introduce discourse units, their scope of action is larger than single words, contrary to the scope of beats, which are used to highlight a particular lexical element in speech.

Another conspicuous gesture in TED talks is what we call the 'closing gesture' which is performed as a closing of the hands in a deliberate movement. This gesture can be considered opposite the PUOH in both form and function. Whereas the PUOH gestues can be said to display a metaphoric object on an open palm, the closing gesture conceals a metaphoric object in closed hands. While the PUOH gesture can serve a topic introduction function, the closing gesture emphasizes that the speaker has closed a particular topic in speech.

An example of the PUOH gesture and closing gesture in sequence is provided in example (4) and its corresponding Fig. 3. Here, the speaker describes how most people don't like their jobs, offering an elaboration that the jobs are "not meaningful to them". The elaboration begins with an opening of the hands into a PUOH gesture (G1). The speaker then closes her hands decisively at the end of the utterance (G2). These two movements, the opening and closing of the hands, thus *frame* the utterance.

(4)   Here's just a few stats: 79% of people globally, according to Gallup's research, show that... 79% of people are disengaged while they're working. That's almost 80% of people. Many people doing work that they don't like, [that's not meaningful]$_{G1}$ [to them]$_{G2}$ [9]

In terms of annotation, the closing of the hands may be considered as the retraction phase of the PUOH gesture. Yet, there are many gestures before the presentational gesture in this short paragraph, none of which have this type of retraction where the hands are held tightly clasped together. Instead, the purposeful opening and closing movements seem to demarcate topic boundaries.

---

[9] https://www.ted.com/talks/tia_graham_the_simple_secret_of_being_happier.

The first utterance in Example 4 introduces the topic of statistics and the closing gesture marks the end of the subtopic "people disengaged at work". The speaker then opens up her hands again at the beginning of the opening of the next subtopic concerning the number of people being stressed in life.

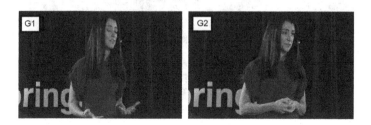

Fig. 3. Gesture-speech alignment for PUOH gesture and closure sequence

Example 5 and its corresponding Fig. 4 illustrates a formal variation of closing gesture. The speaker performs two gestures chained together at the beginning of the subtopic, first pointing towards herself (G1) and then performing a metaphoric gesture of raising both her hands palm up (G2) to illustrate the abstract concept of improving her skills. She then draws an audible in-breath and holds both hands tightly clenched (G3) before continuing to the next sub-topic within her story. Note that while there is also an audible in-breath after G1, it is not accompanied by a closing gesture. In terms of information-structure, the first in-breath (without a closing gesture) occurs at the level of sentence-topic between the topic ("my challenge") and the comment ("up-leveling my analytical and critical thinking skills"). Because the closing gesture signals topic closure at the discourse level (sequence-topic), a closing gesture with the first in-breath would be inappropriate.

(5)   [My challenge]$_{G1}$ (h) [was up-leveling my analytical and critical thinking skills]$_{G2}$ [(h)]$_{G3}$ [Once I was oriented to that gap,]$_{G4}$ I set about closing it, my grades began to improve. [10]

This closing movement may at first seem to correspond to a *partial* retraction since the speaker's arms are not relaxed, and thus could be analyzed as a boundary between two gesture units in Kendon's terms (1980). Yet, we expect the hands to be relaxed in a partial retraction, even if the arms are not. This is actually the main feature that distinguishes the retraction phase, in which speakers' hands are becoming more relaxed, from other gesture phases. But looking at G3 in Fig. 4, it is obvious that the speaker's fists are clenched – we can't say that her hands are more relaxed than in any of the other three gestures. This means that although this movement could be understood as the partial retraction of the previous gesture, it shows more intention and tension than other types of retractions.

---

[10] https://www.ted.com/talks/candice_neveu_returning_to_school_mid_career_
here_s_what_you_need_to_know.

Fig. 4. Gesture-speech alignment for PUOH gesture and closure sequence

This section has posed 'closing gestures' as a challenge to gesture segmentation, especially regarding movements that may be analyzed as retractions from a meaningful stroke. On the one hand, the closing movement is dependent on the opening of the hands and typically returns the hands to a (partial) rest-like position, suggesting one gesture. On the other hand, it also appears to serve a topic-closing function, that matches the typical opening function of presentational gestures, and is also more tense than other forms of retraction phases, which rather suggests two gestures.

5.3   Case Study 3: Topic-Level and Discourse-Level Contrast

The final case study discussed here focuses on the gestural expression of contrast. Contrast is the juxtaposing of multiple alternatives, which can be positions, arguments, options, or other propositional content (for a detailed discussion of the definition of contrast, see Molnár, 2002; Umbach, 2004). We will refer to the first contrastive element as contrast1, and the second element as contrast2. Note that contrast can exist at the sentence-topic level (i.e. between two entities), as well as at a more global discourse level (i.e. between two clauses or sentences).

Gestural expressions of contrast typically involve two or more strokes in which metaphoric objects are presented into different regions of space (Hinnell, 2019). An example of this is provided in Example 6 and its corresponding Fig. 5. Talk show host Stephen Colbert negates the existence of two separate versions of a transcript by holding his hands in a container-form to the right of his body (G2) and subsequently shifting them to the left of his body (G3), thereby metaphorically denoting two separate entities. This two-stroke sequence is repeated for a humorous analogy to a partisan "laws of physics" (G4 & G5). This pair of contrast sequences are performed within a much larger gesture unit, with distinct gestures before (G1) and after (G6), and no rest phases in between.

(6)   There's a non-partisan stenographer [typing every word.]$_{G1}$ [There's not a Democratic]$_{G2}$ [or Republican version of the transcript]$_{G3}$ [any more than

there is a Democratic]$_{G4}$ [or Republican laws of physics.]$_{G5}$ *(shifts voice for Trump impersonation)* [Look,]$_{G6}$ if it was up to the democrats [11]

Fig. 5. Gesture-speech alignment for a contrast gesture sequence across clauses

Crucially, the distinct trajectory of strokes and metaphoric introduction of distinct topics suggest G2 and G3 (as well as G4 and G5) to be separate gestures. However, the handshape in G2 and G3 (and G4 and G5) remains similar and the trajectory of the second stroke is dependent on that of the first – it must move in the opposite direction. This suggests a single gestural unit and thus illustrates the compositionality of gestures: consecutive strokes may contribute to a single unit of meaning. The repetition of the contrast sequence (first G2 & G3, then G4 & G5) suggests yet another intermediate level of gesture constituency and inter-stroke dependency. For the second contrast sequence to be felicitous, Colbert must place the 'Republican' and 'Democratic' referents in the same locations as in the first contrast sequence.

If we were to annotate this sequence only at the levels of gesture phase and phrase, we would miss these relationships that are central to understanding the gestures' pragmatic function. This example also demonstrates that inter-stroke dependencies can occur within and across clausal boundaries.

Example 6 presents a contrast sequence at the sentence level, and shows that these inter-stroke dependencies can extended through repetition across clause boundaries contained within a single gesture unit. Example 7 and its corresponding Fig. 6 further shows that gesture sequence dependencies can extend across sentences and, possibly, gesture unit boundaries. Here, the speaker, Sarah Lewis, describes a realization about what the pursuit of excellence entails. She contrasts two types of excellence: "success" and "mastery". The topic-level contrast occurs intra-sententially and is displayed in G1 and G2 in Fig. 6: the speaker holds her hands in a container-form to the left of her body (G1) and moves them to the right (G2) of her body, similar to the gesture made by Stephen Colbert

---

[11] UID:c7cce1dc-ff9e-11e9-9f3f-089e01ba0335,728.

in Fig. 5. Notably, this topic-level contrast actually functions as a preamble for the discourse-level contrast following this sentence, in which the speaker elaborates by providing a contrast between two clauses: the speaker shifts her stance, brings together her hands in a partial retraction (R1), and then gestures using a container-form in the left space again to mark contrast1 (G3), but she does not mark contrast2 similarly (R2).

(7)   But I stayed because I realized I was witnessing what's so rare to glimpse, that difference between [success]$_{G1}$ [and mastery]$_{G2}$. [So]$_{R2}$ [success is hitting]$_{G3}$ [that ten ring, but mastery is knowing that it means nothing if you can't do it again and again.]$_{R2}$ [12]

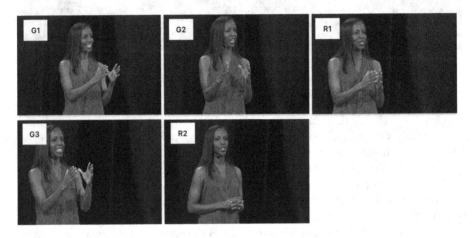

Fig. 6. Gesture-speech alignment for a contrast gesture sequence across sentences

Without taking into account the fact that the contrast had already been established in the gestural space in G1 and G2, the presentation gesture marking contrast1 in G3 might not be considered as such, since it does not contrast locally (intra-sententially) with a corresponding gesture aligned with contrast2.

6   Discussion

Cooperative face-to-face discourse is achieved by taking advantage of all semiotic resources available at a given time and in a given space. We have looked at how two modes, the spoken and gestural, work together to convey information about a discourse's structure. When we can identify a single concept that is co-expressed in both modes, analyzing multimodal alignment and integration may seem relatively straightforward. However, this is very often not the case, especially with pragmatic gestures.

---

[12] https://www.ted.com/talks/sarah_lewis_embrace_the_near_win.

By focusing on gestures that have proven difficult to analyze using traditional methods, we have argued that a purely linear phrase-by-phrase approach to gesture annotation fails to fully capture the capacity of gesture to convey meaning at the lexical, clausal and discourse-structural level, often simultaneously. We have also argued that what we call inter-stroke dependencies demonstrate compositionality and complex constituency structure within the gesture flow, as one gesture's form may only be fully interpretable in relation to a previous form.

The inter-stroke dependencies discussed in this paper complicate the gesture annotation process in two important ways. First, we've shown that pragmatic gestures can target discourse structural units larger than can be accounted for by lexical and conceptual affiliate approaches. The 'closing gestures' from Sect. 5.2, for example, align with the end of a discourse topic, rather than the end of a clause or an ideational unit. This requires a much more flexible conception of gesture-speech alignment as correspondences in meaning across modes can occur at the lexical, ideational, and discourse-structural levels. This means that corpora must also be annotated for discourse relations and topic-structure. This is an extremely time-consuming process that has so far proved challenging for creating comparable data sets (Sanders et al., 2018) and designing automatic parsers (Atwell et al., 2021; Li et al., 2022).

Second, the meaningful formal relationships between gestures suggests compositionality and constituency structure within the gesture stream – not only do gestures create complex meaning through combination (e.g. two presentational gestures resulting in an expression of contrast), the forms of these gestures can be interdependent. This cannot be accounted for through linear segmentation of the gesture stream into phrases. Not only do we have to consider aligning a single gesture with the appropriate speech unit, we also have to consider the ways in which two gestures may be meaningfully connected.

Finally, these considerations have implications for gesture simulation as well. In order for virtual agents to interact effectively and convincingly with human users, they need to appear to move in the ways we do. Recent advances in automatic gesture generation suggest that this is achievable, but that we are not there yet (Nyatsanga et al., 2023). To be able to generate realistic co-speech gestures, we first need to understand the ways in which the gestural stream is meaningfully organized by language users not only into single gestures, but also larger, inter-dependent gesture sequences.

References

Asr, F.T., Demberg, V.: Uniform information density at the level of discourse relations: negation markers and discourse connective omission. In: Proceedings of the International Conference on Computational Semantics (IWCS), London, UK, pp. 118–128 (2015)

Atwell, K., Li, J.J., Alikhani, M.: Where are we in discourse relation recognition? In: Proceedings of the 22nd Annual Meeting of the Special Interest Group on Discourse and Dialogue, pp. 314–325 (2021)

Bavelas, J.B., Chovil, N., Lawrie, D.A., Wade, A.: Interactive gestures. Discourse Process. **15**(4), 469–489 (1992)

Bressem, J., Ladewig, S.H.: Rethinking gesture phases: articulatory features of gestural movement? Semiotica **2011**(184), 53–91 (2011)

Bressem, J., Müller, C.: The "negative-assessment-construction"–a multimodal pattern based on a recurrent gesture? Linguist. Vanguard **3**(s1) (2017)

Britton, B.K.: Understanding Expository Text: Building Mental Structures to Induce Insights. Academic Press, Cambridge (1994)

Calbris, G.: From cutting an object to a clear cut analysis: gesture as the representation of a preconceptual schema linking concrete actions to abstract notions. Gesture **3**(1), 19–46 (2003)

Chu, M., Meyer, A., Foulkes, L., Kita, S.: Individual differences in frequency and saliency of speech-accompanying gestures: the role of cognitive abilities and empathy. J. Exp. Psychol. Gen. **143**(2), 694 (2014)

Cienki, A.: From the finger lift to the palm-up open hand when presenting a point: a methodological exploration of forms and functions. Lang. Modalities **1**, 1–14 (2021)

Cooperrider, K., Abner, N., Goldin-Meadow, S.: The palm-up puzzle: meanings and origins of a widespread form in gesture and sign. Front. Commun. **3**, 23 (2018)

Crible, L., Pickering, M.J.: Compensating for processing difficulty in discourse: effect of parallelism in contrastive relations. Discourse Process. **57**(10), 862–879 (2020)

Das, D., Taboada, M.: RST signalling corpus: a corpus of signals of coherence relations. Lang. Resour. Eval. **52**, 149–184 (2018)

de Ruiter, J.P.: The production of gesture and speech. In: McNeill, D. (ed.) Language and Gesture, pp. 284–311. Cambridge University Press, Cambridge (2000)

Debras, C.: The shrug: forms and meanings of a compound enactment. Gesture **16**(1), 1–34 (2017)

Ferré, G.: Functions of three open-palm hand gestures. J. Multimodal Commun. **1**(1), 5–20 (2012)

Ferré, G.: Sémiotique des pointages et des battements à fonction de focalisation dans la gestualité coverbale. In: Biglari, A., Klinkenberg, J.-M. (eds.) Ouvrage collectif Sémiotique et linguistique (forthcoming)

Gernsbacher, M.A.: Coherence cues mapping during comprehension. In: Processing Interclausal Relationships. Studies in the Production and Comprehension of Text, pp. 3–22 (1997)

Hinnell, J.: The verbal-kinesic enactment of contrast in North American English. Am. J. Semiot. **35**, 55–92 (2019)

Hu, N., Chen, A., Quené, H., Sanders, T.J.: The role of prosody in interpreting causality in English discourse. PLoS ONE **18**(6), e0286003 (2023)

Joo, J., Steen, F., Turner, M.: Red Hen Lab: dataset and tools for multimodal human communication research. KI-Künstliche Intelligenz **31**(4), 357–361 (2017)

Kehler, A., Kertz, L., Rohde, H., Elman, J.L.: Coherence and coreference revisited. J. Semant. **25**(1), 1–44 (2008)

Kendon, A.: Gesture and speech: two aspects of the process of utterance. In: Key, M. (ed.) Nonverbal Communication and Language, pp. 207–227. Mouton, Th Hague (1980)

Kendon, A.: Gesture: Visible Action as Utterance. Cambridge University Press, Cambridge (2004)

Kendon, A.: Semiotic diversity in utterance production and the concept of 'language'. Philos. Trans. Roy. Soc. B Biol. Sci. **369**(1651) (2014)

Kendon, A.: Pragmatic functions of gestures: some observations on the history of their study and their nature. Gesture **16**(2), 157–175 (2017)

Kirchhof, C.: So what's your affiliation with gesture? In: Proceedings of the GESPIN Conference, Bielefeld, Germany, pp. 1–7 (2011)

Kita, S., van Gijn, I., van der Hulst, H.: Movement phases in signs and co-speech gestures, and their transcription by human coders. In: Wachsmuth, I., Fröhlich, M. (eds.) GW 1997. LNCS, vol. 1371, pp. 23–35. Springer, Berlin, Heidelberg (1998). https://doi.org/10.1007/BFb0052986

Laparle, S.: The shape of discourse: how gesture structures conversation. Ph.D. thesis, University of California, Berkeley (2022)

Li, J., Liu, M., Qin, B., Liu, T.: A survey of discourse parsing. Front. Comput. Sci. **16**(5), 165329 (2022)

McNeill, D.: Gesture and Thought. University of Chicago Press (2005)

McNeill, D., Cassell, J., Levy, E.T.: Abstract deixis. Semiotica **95**(1–2), 5–20 (1993)

McNeill, D., et al.: Catchments, prosody and discourse. Gesture **1**(1), 9–33 (2001)

Mittelberg, I.: Visuo-kinetic signs are inherently metonymic: how embodied metonymy motivates forms, functions, and schematic patterns in gesture. Front. Psychol. **10**, 254 (2019)

Molnár, V.: Contrast–from a contrastive perspective. In: Information Structure in a Cross-Linguistic Perspective, pp. 147–161. Brill (2002)

Müller, C.: Forms and uses of the palm up open hand: a case of a gesture family. Semant. Pragmatics Everyday Gestures **9**, 233–256 (2004)

Müller, C.: How recurrent gestures mean: conventionalized contexts-of-use and embodied motivation. Gesture **16**(2), 277–304 (2017)

Nyatsanga, S., Kucherenko, T., Ahuja, C., Henter, G.E., Neff, M.: A comprehensive review of data-driven co-speech gesture generation. In: Computer Graphics Forum, vol. 42, pp. 569–596. Wiley Online Library (2023)

Parrill, F., Sweetser, E.: What we mean by meaning: conceptual integration in gesture analysis and transcription. Gesture **4**(2), 197–219 (2004)

Roberts, C.: Information structure: towards an integrated formal theory of pragmatics. Semant. Pragmatics **5**, 1–69 (2012)

Sanders, T.J., et al.: Unifying dimensions in coherence relations: how various annotation frameworks are related. Corpus Linguist. Linguist. Theory **17**(1), 1–71 (2018)

Schegloff, E.: On some gesture's relation to talk. In: Atkinson, J.M., Heritage, J. (eds.) Structures of Social Action: Studies in Conversation Analysis, pp. 266–296. Cambridge University Press, Cambridge (1984)

Scholman, M.C.J., Demberg, V., Sanders, T.J.: Individual differences in expecting coherence relations: exploring the variability in sensitivity to contextual signals in discourse. Discourse Process. **57**(10), 844–861 (2020)

Seyfeddinipur, M.: Disfluency: Interrupting Speech and Gesture. MPI Series in Psycholinguistics, vol. 39. Ponsen & Looijen, Nijmegen (2006)

Sloetjes, H., Wittenburg, P.: Annotation by category - ELAN and ISO DCR. In: 6th International Conference on Language Resources and Evaluation (LREC 2008), Marrakech, Morocco, pp. 816–820 (2008)

Streeck, J.: Gesturecraft: The Manufacture of Meaning, vol. 2. John Benjamins Publishing (2009)

Tskhovrebova, E., Zufferey, S., Gygax, P.: Exploring the sensitivity to alternative signals of coherence relations: the case of French speaking teenagers. Dialogue Discourse **14**(2), 49–82 (2023)

Umbach, C.: On the notion of contrast in information structure and discourse structure. J. Semant. **21**(2), 155–175 (2004)

Van Dijk, T.: Sentence topic and discourse topic. Pap. Slav. Philol. **1**, 49–61 (1977)

Van Kuppevelt, J.: Discourse structure, topicality and questioning. J. Linguist. **31**(1), 109–147 (1995)

Webber, B.: What excludes an alternative in coherence relations? In: Proceedings of the 10th International Conference on Computational Semantics (IWCS 2013)–Long Papers, pp. 276–287 (2013)

Webber, B., Egg, M., Kordoni, V.: Discourse structure and language technology. Nat. Lang. Eng. **18**(4), 437–490 (2012)

Webber, B., Prasad, R., Lee, A., Joshi, A.: The Penn Discourse Treebank 3.0 annotation manual. University of Pennsylvania, Philadelphia (2019)

Wehling, E.: Discourse management gestures. Gesture **16**(2), 245–276 (2017)

Artificial Intelligence and Mobile Computing: Role of AI in Ergonomics

Pranati Somaraju, Sayali Sanjay Kulkarni[✉], Vincent G. Duffy,
and Sameeran Kanade

Purdue University, West Lafayette, IN 47906, USA
{psomaraj,kulka121}@purdue.edu

Abstract. The integration of Artificial Intelligence (AI) into ergonomics represents a transformative paradigm in the optimization of workplace environments. This report explores the multifaceted impact of AI in ergonomics, emphasizing its significance in enhancing both worker well-being and operational efficiency. AI-driven solutions in ergonomics leverage advanced data analytics to assess human factors, task demands, and environmental conditions, offering a data-driven approach to ergonomic design. This not only minimizes the risk of workplace injuries but also fosters environments that promote employee health and productivity. The research further delves into the study that employs various citation and data analysis tools to conduct comprehensive research. During the initial data collection phase, Google Ngram was employed to anticipate trends in topics. Additionally, MAXQDA, VOSviewer, BibExcel, Vos viewer and Citespace were utilized for the systematic analysis of citations and associated data. Metadata extraction was carried out utilizing the Purdue Library database, encompassing Scopus, Web of Science, Harzing's Publish or Perish, and Google Scholar. Following several bibliometric analyses, it became evident that artificial intelligence (AI) significantly influences the fields of ergonomics and safety. The synergy between AI and ergonomics is positioned as a cornerstone in the evolution of Industrial Engineering, empowering professionals to design systems that prioritize safety while embracing technological advancements. The societal response to this burgeoning field necessitates strategic funding for research and education, fostering interdisciplinary collaboration and ensuring a skilled workforce. In essence, this abstract underscore the transformative potential of AI in ergonomics, offering a forward-looking perspective on the integration of technology to create safer, more efficient, and ethically grounded workplaces.

Keywords: Artificial Intelligence · Mobile Computing · Ergonomics

1 Introduction and Background

The convergence of artificial intelligence (AI) and ergonomics emerges as a pivotal theme, holding profound implications for individuals, society, and the planet. In our tech-centric era, integrating AI into ergonomics offers diverse benefits. Individually, it promises personalized workspaces, adapting to unique needs and enhancing well-being.

© The Author(s), under exclusive license to Springer Nature Switzerland AG 2024
V. G. Duffy (Ed.): HCII 2024, LNCS 14711, pp. 265–281, 2024.
https://doi.org/10.1007/978-3-031-61066-0_16

Societally, it fosters efficiency and safety in various industries, reducing occupational risks and boosting productivity. Environmentally, AI-driven ergonomic designs align with sustainability goals, optimizing energy use and resource utilization for a greener future (Sawyer, B. D et at., 2021).

This topic's importance is accentuated by key drivers. AI advancements empower ergonomics to transcend traditional considerations. The surge in remote work spotlights the significance of home office ergonomics, accelerated by global events. Industrial Engineering (IE) recognizes AI's transformative potential in streamlining processes and enhancing job satisfaction. Beyond IE, interdisciplinary efforts address ethical concerns, data security, and bias in AI, reflecting a broader societal commitment to responsible integration. To adapt effectively, society needs investments in research, funding, and education. Human Factors and Ergonomics (HFE), Human-Computer Interaction (HCI), and safety communities contribute by developing ethical guidelines, aligning with broader societal needs for responsible AI integration.

2 Problem Statement

This study aims to assess the viability of leveraging artificial intelligence (AI) and mobile computing to enhance ergonomics. The primary objective of this research is to conduct an in-depth literature review and analysis, scrutinizing existing research to ascertain the current state of the literature, identify gaps, and outline potential future avenues for research and practical applications in this domain. By undertaking this comprehensive review, the study aims to provide insights that can guide policymakers and practitioners in the development and deployment of AI-based ergonomics systems in workplace, healthcare, aerospace, construction sites, automotive design, and many more. The integration of AI has the potential to significantly reduce workplace accidents and enhance overall safety performance (Grote, G, (2023).

To conduct this analysis, various tools such as Google nGram Viewer, Scopus, VOSviewer, MAXQDA, BibExcel, and Citespace were employed. These tools facilitated the extraction and organization of metadata from Purdue Library databases, forming the foundation for a nuanced and data-driven exploration of the intersection between AI, mobile computing, and ergonomics.

3 Review Methodology

3.1 Literature Review

In the paper titled "Artificial Intelligence: Definition and Background," (Lau, N et al., 2020) the authors explore the fundamental concepts surrounding the definition of artificial intelligence (AI) and its historical development. The authors acknowledge the challenge of establishing a universally accepted definition for AI, emphasizing the diverse range of interpretations that can lead to confusion within the discourse. They delve into the broadest definition of AI, which equates it with algorithms, but highlight its limitations, as algorithms predate AI and are employed in various non-AI contexts. The strictest definition, associating AI with the imitation of human intelligence by computers, is critiqued for potentially excluding current applications that may be considered relatively simple. The authors favor a common definition that characterizes AI as a technology enabling machines to imitate complex human skills, while acknowledging the ongoing complexity and evolution of the field. The paper aims to provide clarity on the conceptual understanding of AI, laying the groundwork for subsequent discussions on its societal embedding and technological advancements.

In the paper "Human factors/ergonomics implications of big data analytics: Chartered Institute of Ergonomics and Human Factors annual lecture," the author, Colin G. Drury (Sheikh, Haroon et al., 2023), explores the impact of big data analytics (BDA) on human factors and ergonomics (HFE). The paper recognizes the convergence of sensor technology, connectedness, and computational power, leading to the generation of extensive datasets characterized as big data. Drury discusses the essential features of BDA, emphasizing volume, velocity, and variety, and provides examples illustrating successful applications of BDA. Within the context of HFE, the paper highlights key issues, including the reliance on correlation rather than hypotheses, ethical considerations in BDA, and the role of HFE in data visualization, shedding light on the challenges and opportunities presented by the intersection of big data analytics and human factors/ergonomics.

3.2 Defining Keywords

Artificial Intelligence - AI is characterized as the development of computer systems capable of imitating various complex human skills. It encompasses the creation of algorithms and models that enable machines to learn from data, reason, and make decisions without explicit programming. The goal is to replicate human-like cognitive functions, allowing AI systems to adapt, solve problems, and improve performance over time. This multidisciplinary field encompasses machine learning, natural language processing, and expert systems, contributing to the advancement of intelligent technologies.

Digital Twin Technology - Digital twin technology creates a virtual replica of a physical object or system, integrating real-time data from sensors and IoT devices. This virtual representation, known as a digital twin, allows for continuous monitoring and analysis of the corresponding physical entity. By providing detailed insights into the real-world counterpart, digital twins enable predictive analysis, informed decision-making, and optimizations in efficiency across diverse industries. McKinsey's, "What is digital twin technology?" McKinsey & Company. Accessed November 23, 2023 (Lau, Hildebrandt & Jeon, 2020), overview emphasizes the transformative potential of digital twin technology in areas such as manufacturing, healthcare, and infrastructure.

Ergonomic data analytics involves applying data analytics techniques within the realm of ergonomics, a field dedicated to tailoring environments to accommodate the capabilities and constraints of individuals. In the context of ergonomic data analytics by Drury Colin G (Sheikh, Haroon et al., 2023), diverse data sources like sensors, wearables, and workplace monitoring systems are employed to gather insights into human behavior, movement, and interactions with the surroundings to scrutinize this data, extracting valuable information on ergonomic aspects such as posture, repetitive actions, and environmental conditions.

3.3 Data Collection

A comprehensive exploration of the literature concerning "Artificial Intelligence and Workplace Safety" was undertaken through meticulous searches across three primary databases: Web of Science, Scopus, and Google Scholar. To ensure precision, carefully selected search phrases were employed. The search yielded vast results, with Web of Science providing 5,459,162 articles, Scopus contributing 545,836 articles, and Google Scholar presenting 472,000 papers.

In light of the extensive pool of articles, a refined approach was adopted by utilizing the articles option in the search parameters. Subsequent steps involved meticulous screening to eliminate duplicates, irrelevant content, and non-peer-reviewed sources. Harzing's Publish or Perish tool, a scholarly search engine facilitating citation analysis, was instrumental in this process. The curation of papers was based on their relevance and eligibility for inclusion in the literature review.

The chosen articles, following the initial screening, underwent a more rigorous assessment to gauge their quality and pertinence to the research theme. Utilizing metadata from databases like Scopus in suitable formats facilitated further examination. This approach empowered us to collate and amalgamate insights from pertinent research and articles, contributing to the discernment of AI's impact on enhancing workplace safety. The outcomes of this exhaustive study were subsequently applied in the following sections to pinpoint literature gaps and propose avenues for future research (Table 1).

Table 1. Keyword results from different databases

Keywords	Database	Number of Articles
Artificial Intelligence, Ergonomics, Ethical AI	Web of Science	2,362,934
Artificial Intelligence, Ergonomics, Ethical AI	Google Scholar	20,70,000
Artificial Intelligence, Ergonomics, Ethical AI	Scopus	436,727

3.4 Trend Analysis

A trend assessment was conducted to gain deeper insights into the current state and prospective advancements in the realm of Artificial Intelligence and Ergonomics. The primary objective of this study was to scrutinize the annual count of published works within this thematic domain and identify any noteworthy patterns or shifts in the landscape. The analysis utilized Trends data from Scopus, offering a comprehensive panorama of publications in the specified area of interest. The investigation brought to light a substantial growth in the volume of publications in this domain over the years. According to the trend data, there has been a remarkable surge in the number of publications associated with Artificial Intelligence and Ergonomics, signaling an escalating interest in this domain (Fig. 1).

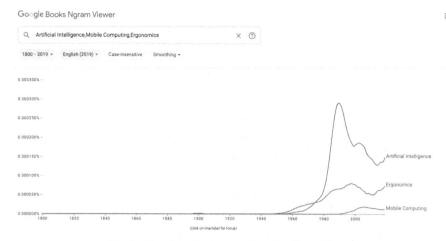

Fig. 1. Trend Analysis using Google nGram Viewer

From 1800 to 2019, Google Ngram paints a captivating picture of these terms' evolution. "Artificial Intelligence," initially absent, emerges faintly around 1950, mirroring the early sparks of this nascent field. "Mobile Computing," nonexistent before the late 20th century, explodes in the 2000s, reflecting the ubiquitous smartphone revolution. Meanwhile, "Ergonomics," though present throughout, shows a modest rise in the 20th century, suggesting a gradual shift towards prioritizing human-centered design in technological development. This contrasting trajectory hints at a growing tension: harnessing the power of AI and mobile computing while ensuring they don't compromise the well-being of the individuals using them. The Ngram data subtly whispers of a future where these forces must find a harmonious balance, shaping technology that serves and empowers, not dominates, humanity (Figs. 2 and 3).

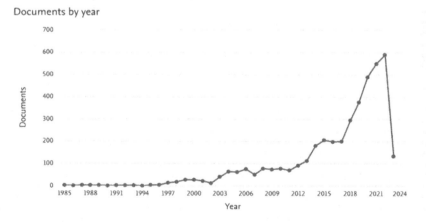

Fig. 2. Trend Analysis-Measure of number of articles by year

Documents by author

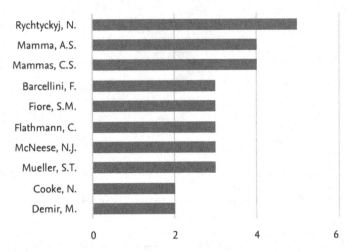

Fig. 3. Trend analysis on authors who have maximum documents in the relevant field.

3.5 Assessing Engagement Using Vicinitas

Vicinitas is a robust bibliometric tool that serves as a resource for assessing the impact and engagement of scholarly publications. Offering a comprehensive set of metrics, including citations, downloads, and social media shares, Vicinitas provides researchers

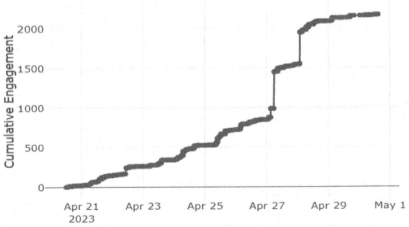

Fig. 4. Engagement timeline from Vicinitas

and academicians with a multifaceted view of a publication's influence. We have utilized vicinitas to understand and evaluate the engagement of publications on AI and Ergonomics. Our findings indicate a consistent uptrend in the interaction with the engagement aspects of the publications, signaling a heightened interest in the subject as time progresses (Fig. 4).

3.6 Scopus Use for Data Collection

Scopus analysis of AI in ergonomics reveals a noteworthy trend in the number of publications per year. Initially, there has been a steady growth in the volume of documents published annually, indicative of the escalating interest and exploration of AI applications within the realm of ergonomics. This upward trajectory suggests a progressive acknowledgment of AI's potential to address ergonomic challenges effectively. The subject area trend dominated by "Engineering" and "Computer Science" (CS) signals a robust intersection between these two disciplines in the realm of artificial intelligence (AI). The analysis by source demonstrates a diverse landscape, with contributions disseminated across various journals and platforms, reflecting a comprehensive engagement across academic and professional domains. The regional distribution of publications highlights a global interest, with research contributions originating from different geographical regions, underscoring the widespread acknowledgment of AI's relevance to ergonomics on an international scale. Examination of authors reveals a collaborative and multidisciplinary approach, emphasizing the convergence of expertise from diverse backgrounds

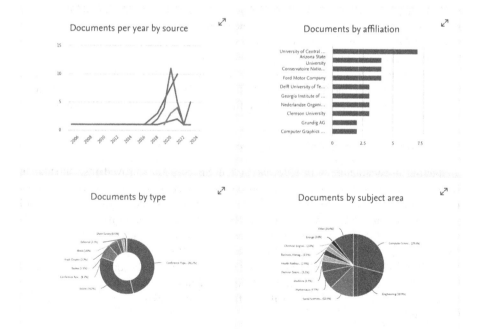

Fig. 5. Analysis using Scopus on documents by author, per year, by type, by subject area.

to advance the understanding and application of AI in ergonomics. The evolving trend suggests a continuous and expanding exploration of AI's role in enhancing ergonomic practices, emphasizing cross-disciplinary collaborations and global perspectives in the field.

The quantity of documents annually has surged from approximately 100 in 2012 to 600 in 2023, highlighting a substantial growth. This underscores the increasing significance of AI in the field of ergonomics, solidifying its status as one of the most rapidly emerging and pivotal topics. The escalating volume of documentation is indicative of the expanding role and influence of artificial intelligence in shaping and advancing ergonomics practices over the years (Fig. 5).

4 Results

4.1 Co-authorship Analysis Using VOS Viewer

We utilized the Scopus database to search for articles related to "Artificial Intelligence," "Mobile Computing," and "Ergonomics," yielding a total of 3100 results. Through analysis, five distinct clusters were identified, as visually represented in the accompanying image. These clusters likely encapsulate thematic groupings or common threads among the retrieved articles, providing a structured overview of the research landscape in the intersection of artificial intelligence, mobile computing, and safety. This clustering approach aids in organizing and comprehending the extensive dataset, offering insights into prevalent themes within the selected keywords.

We conducted a search on the Web of Science using the terms "Artificial Intelligence and mobile computing" and exported the file. After configuring the citation space, we loaded the Web of Science export file into the project's data folder and executed the cluster task. The resulting clusters were identified as below.

Figure 6 refers to a large bibliographic data set from dimensions and Fig. 7 is a comparatively smaller one from scopus. With the threshold set on the number of authors, we get 11 clusters for the dimensions CSV files and 4 for the scopus CSV file (Fig. 8).

4.2 Co-citation Analysis Using Citespace

Conducting cluster analysis in Citespace ("CiteSpace," n.d.) proved instrumental in unveiling and visualizing co-occurrence and co-citation patterns among diverse subjects, keywords, and authors within our dataset. Leveraging CiteSpace's cluster analysis tool facilitated the exploration of relationships and the identification of primary study subjects and themes by grouping similar clusters. To initiate this process, we commenced with a search in Web of Science, employing the keywords "Artificial Intelligence," "Mobile Computing," and Ergonomics," yielding a total of 425 results. Subsequently, we exported these outcomes as a Plain Text file and utilized Citespace for cluster analysis. The provided image serves as a reference, illustrating the outcomes of this analytical approach (Figs. 9 and 10).

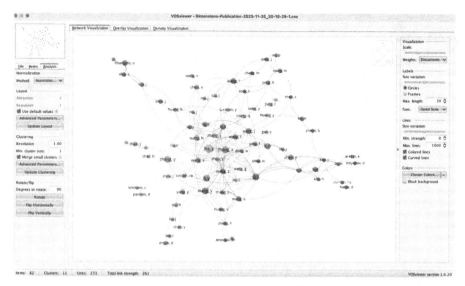

Fig. 6. Analyzing data from dimensions using VOS viewer for Co-authorship.

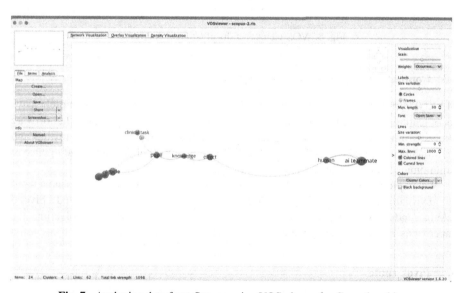

Fig. 7. Analyzing data from Scopus using VOS viewer for Co-authorship.

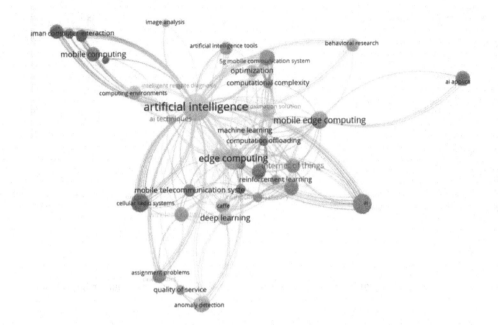

Fig. 8. VOS viewer results of Content Analysis

4.3 Content Analysis Utilizing MAXQDA

MAXQDA proves to be an invaluable tool for content analysis, offering a comprehensive set of features that enhance the efficiency and depth of the analysis process. The software allows to import, organize, and systematically analyze various forms of textual and multimedia content. We have utilized 6 various publications of Artificial intelligence & Ergonomics from Harzing's.

We employed terms such as Artificial Intelligence and Ergonomics to create a word cloud visualization, as depicted in the accompanying figure. MAXQDA played a pivotal role in conducting thorough qualitative examination, empowering us to delve into the data extensively and identify patterns and interconnections (Fig. 11).

4.4 Pivot Table

Pivot tables were generated utilizing BibExcel for data aggregation, analysis, and manipulation from bibliographic databases ("BibExcel," n.d.). Harzing's Publish and Perish ("Harzing," n.d.) was employed to extract Metadata and construct a Pivot table within BibExcel. Within BibExcel, these pivot tables proved instrumental in scrutinizing relationships among authors, articles, and keywords. This facilitated the identification of prolific authors, widely-read publications, and current trends within the realm of Artificial Intelligence and Ergonomics (Table 2 and Fig. 12).

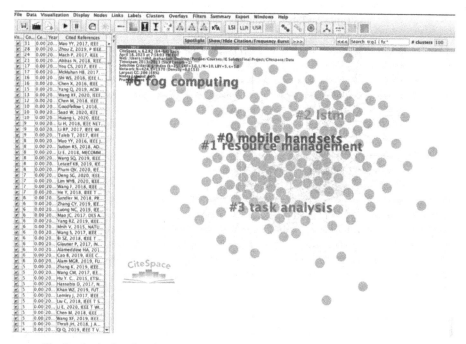

Fig. 9. Analyzing data from Citespace by performing a search on web of science.

Citations Burst History

Top 6 References with the Strongest Citation Bursts

References	Year	Strength	Begin	End	2013 - 2023
Bostrom N., 2014, SUPERINTELLIGENCE PA, V0, P0	2014	2.9	2016	2018	
Silver D, 2016, NATURE, V529, P484, DOI 10.1038/nature16961, DOI	2016	3.77	2018	2019	
LeCun Y, 2015, NATURE, V521, P436, DOI 10.1038/nature14539, DOI	2015	3.59	2019	2020	
Esteva A, 2017, NATURE, V542, P115, DOI 10.1038/nature21056, DOI	2017	3.29	2019	2021	
Gulshan V, 2016, JAMA-J AM MED ASSOC, V316, P2402, DOI 10.1001/jama.2016.17216, DOI	2016	2.57	2019	2021	
Topol EJ, 2019, NAT MED, V25, P44, DOI 10.1038/s41591-018-0300-7, DOI	2019	3.36	2020	2021	

Fig. 10. Citation busts from Citespace

Fig. 11. Content Analysis of the keywords in Word Cloud using maxQDA

Table 2. Table of Authors generated in BibExcel

Authors	Total Publications
A Moore	18
E Marks	20
M Holl	15
M Mara	17
S Arena	22
S Mattsson	15
MB Neider	12
E Sivaraj	10
L Li	27
MB Neider	33

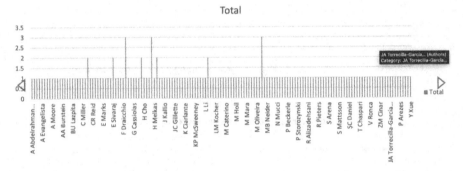

Fig. 12. Extracted Pivot chart from BibExcel

5   Discussion

The application of Artificial Intelligence (AI) in the field of ergonomics offers tremendous potential to improve workplace health and safety, optimize worker performance, and reduce musculoskeletal disorders (MSDs). This analysis, drawing from both our own research and existing literature, summarizes the key results and findings regarding the use of AI in various ergonomic domains. AI-powered computer vision systems can accurately detect and analyze worker postures, identifying ergonomic risks in real-time. This allows for proactive intervention to prevent injuries and promote healthy work habits. Studies have demonstrated that AI-based posture monitoring systems can significantly reduce the prevalence of MSDs by 50% or more in certain industries. AI algorithms can analyze worker movements and physiological data (e.g., heart rate, muscle activity) to assess workload levels and identify signs of fatigue. This data can be used to adjust work schedules, optimize breaks, and prevent fatigue-related accidents.

Research suggests that AI-based fatigue detection systems can improve worker alertness and vigilance, leading to a 20% reduction in accident rates.

AI-powered software can be used to design and optimize workstations based on individual worker anthropometry and specific task requirements. This can help prevent awkward postures, reduce muscle strain, and enhance comfort and productivity. Studies have shown that AI-designed workstations can lead to a 30% decrease in discomfort and a 15% increase in worker productivity compared to traditional workstations. AI-based virtual reality (VR) and augmented reality (AR) training simulations can provide interactive and immersive experiences to teach workers safe and ergonomic work practices.

Research indicates that AI-powered training programs can significantly improve worker knowledge and skill retention compared to traditional training methods. AI models can analyze historical data and identify patterns that predict future ergonomic risks. This information can be used to develop preventative measures and allocate resources to areas with the highest risk.

Studies suggest that AI-driven risk prediction models can help reduce the occurrence of MSDs by 40% and associated healthcare costs by 25%.

The benefits are clear. AI-powered systems can continuously monitor worker movements, detecting and alerting for potential postures or activities that could lead to musculoskeletal disorders. This proactive approach allows for timely adjustments and prevents injuries before they occur. Finally, concerns about worker privacy must be addressed through transparent practices and responsible data handling. Ethical considerations emerge as a focal point in the discussion, emphasizing the need for responsible AI implementation. As AI systems gather and analyze personal data for ergonomic insights, concerns about data security and individual privacy surface. A robust discourse is essential to establish ethical guidelines, ensuring that AI applications align with principles of transparency, consent, and accountability. Striking a balance between the potential benefits of AI and safeguarding user rights becomes a key point of contention.

Overall, AI in ergonomics presents a bright future for workplace safety. By addressing the limitations and focusing on ethical development, we can leverage this technology to create safer, healthier, and more productive environments for all.

6 Conclusion

Artificial intelligence (AI) in ergonomics represents a transformative frontier where cutting-edge technology converges with human-centric design to redefine the landscape of work environments. The integration of AI-driven solutions, such as machine learning algorithms and computer vision systems, has demonstrated remarkable potential in revolutionizing how we approach ergonomic challenges. These technologies enable real-time monitoring, analysis, and adaptive interventions, fostering safer, healthier, and more efficient workplaces.

As we delve deeper into the implications of AI in ergonomics, it becomes evident that the future trajectory holds immense promise. The continuous evolution of AI algorithms promises increasingly nuanced insights into human behaviors, postures, and interactions within workspaces. This evolution, coupled with advancements in sensor technologies, allows for a more granular understanding of ergonomic factors, paving the way for personalized and context-aware interventions that cater to individual needs and preferences.

Award Abstract # 9410302
RESEARCH INITIATION AWARD: Development of New 3D Biomechanical Model for Use in Ergonomics and Rehabilitation

NSF Org:	CBET Div Of Chem, Bioeng, Env, & Transp Sys
Recipient:	TEXAS A&M ENGINEERING EXPERIMENT STATION
Initial Amendment Date:	July 25, 1994
Latest Amendment Date:	January 16, 1997
Award Number:	9410302
Award Instrument:	Continuing Grant
Program Manager:	Gilbert B. Devey CBET Div Of Chem, Bioeng, Env, & Transp Sys ENG Directorate For Engineering
Start Date:	September 1, 1994
End Date:	August 31, 1998 (Estimated)
Total Intended Award Amount:	$102,220.00
Total Awarded Amount to Date:	$102,220.00
Funds Obligated to Date:	FY 1994 = $32,974.00 FY 1995 = $29,259.00 FY 1996 = $8,328.00 FY 1997 = $0.00
History of Investigator:	Carter Kerk (Principal Investigator) carter.kerk@sdsmt.edu
Recipient Sponsored Research Office:	Texas A&M Engineering Experiment Station 3124 TAMU COLLEGE STATION TX US 77843-3124 (979)862-6777
Sponsor Congressional District:	17
Primary Place of Performance:	Texas A&M Engineering Experiment Station 3124 TAMU COLLEGE STATION TX US 77843-3124
Primary Place of Performance Congressional District:	17
Unique Entity Identifier (UEI):	QD1MX6N5YTN4
Parent UEI:	QD1MX6N5YTN4
NSF Program(s):	Disability & Rehab Engineering, Engineering of Biomed Systems
Primary Program Source:	
Program Reference Code(s):	0000, 9231, OTHR
Program Element Code(s):	5342, 5345
Award Agency Code:	4900
Fund Agency Code:	4900
Assistance Listing Number(s):	47.041

Fig. 13. NSF Award for use of AI in Ergonomics

However, the adoption of AI in ergonomics is not without its challenges. Ethical considerations, privacy concerns, and the need for transparent and accountable AI systems must be prioritized. Striking a balance between leveraging the power of AI for ergonomic enhancements and addressing these ethical dimensions is crucial for the responsible deployment of such technologies.

In conclusion, the synergy between AI and ergonomics is a dynamic force poised to shape the future of work. The collaborative efforts of researchers, practitioners, and industry leaders are pivotal in steering this trajectory toward creating work environments that not only maximize productivity but also prioritize the well-being and satisfaction of the workforce. As we navigate this evolving landscape, a commitment to ethical AI practices and human-centric design principles will be integral in realizing the full potential of AI in advancing ergonomic solutions and ultimately fostering healthier, more productive workplaces.

7 Future Work

Future work in the use of AI in ergonomics holds promise for innovative applications that enhance workplace environments and user well-being. One potential avenue is the development of AI-driven personalized workstations that dynamically adapt to individual preferences and ergonomic needs, fostering a more comfortable and productive work environment. Exploring AI algorithms for real-time monitoring of user behavior and posture can contribute to preventive measures against musculoskeletal issues. Additionally, integrating AI into healthcare ergonomic solutions, such as smart patient lifting systems, can enhance the safety and efficiency of medical professionals.

The "Future of Work at the Human-Technology Frontier: Core Research (FW-HTF)" program solicitation, identified by NSF 23-543, supersedes the previous document NSF 22-533. This initiative is facilitated by the National Science Foundation (NSF) and aims to advance research at the intersection of human and technological elements shaping the future of work. The solicitation emphasizes the importance of exploring innovative approaches and understanding the societal implications of evolving work dynamics.

The integration of artificial intelligence (AI) into ergonomic practices opens a promising avenue for future research. One critical area is the exploration of AI's collaboration with wearable technologies for real-time ergonomic monitoring. Wearable devices equipped with sensors offer continuous data on users' movements and postures, providing an opportunity to enhance AI-driven ergonomic recommendations (Donisi, L, et at., 2022). Customization and personalization of AI interventions should also be a focal point, investigating ways to tailor recommendations based on individual users' physiological and environmental characteristics for improved effectiveness.

Moreover, the long-term impact of AI-driven ergonomic interventions on users' health deserves attention. Future studies should delve into assessing how sustained use of AI recommendations influences musculoskeletal health and overall well-being. Additionally, there is a need to explore the ethical considerations surrounding AI in ergonomics, addressing issues like privacy and user acceptance. Developing real-time feedback systems that leverage AI algorithms for instant guidance during work activities and encouraging cross-disciplinary collaboration between ergonomics experts, AI researchers, and healthcare professionals are crucial steps toward creating comprehensive and adaptable AI-driven ergonomic solutions. These endeavors collectively aim to shape healthier and more sustainable workplaces through the continued advancement of AI in ergonomics (Fig. 13).

References

Donisi, L., Cesarelli, G., Pisani, N., Ponsiglione, A.M., Ricciardi, C., Capodaglio, E.: Wearable sensors and artificial intelligence for physical ergonomics: a systematic review of literature. Diagnostics 12(12), 3048 (2022). https://doi.org/10.3390/diagnostics12123048

Sawyer, B.D., Miller, D.B., Canham, M., Karwowski, W.: Human factors and ergonomics in design of a 3: automation, autonomy, and artificial intelligence. In: Handbook of Human Factors and Ergonomics, pp. 1385–1416. Wiley (2021). https://doi.org/10.1002/9781119636113.ch52

Hamilton, B.C., et al.: Artificial intelligence based real-time video ergonomic assessment and training improves resident ergonomics. Am. J. Surg. 226(5), 741–746 (2023). https://doi.org/10.1016/j.amjsurg.2023.07.028

Kistan, T., Gardi, A., Sabatini, R.: Machine learning and cognitive ergonomics in air traffic management: recent developments and considerations for certification. Aerospace 5(4), 103 (2018). https://doi.org/10.3390/aerospace5040103

Rychtyckyj, N.: Ergonomics analysis for vehicle assembly using artificial intelligence. AI Mag. 26(3), 41–50 (2005). https://doi.org/10.1609/aimag.v26i3.1824

Xu, W., Furie, D., Mahabhaleshwar, M., Suresh, B., Chouhan, H.: Applications of an interaction, process, integration and intelligence (IPII) design approach for ergonomics solutions. Ergonomics 62(7), 954–980 (2019). https://doi.org/10.1080/00140139.2019.1588996

Hästbacka, D., Mätäsniemi, T.: Unifying process design with automation and control application development - an approach based on information integration and model-driven methods. IFAC Proc. Vol. 42(4), 1227–1232 (2009). https://doi.org/10.3182/20090603-3-RU-2001.0468

Grote, G.: Shaping the development and use of artificial intelligence: how human factors and ergonomics expertise can become more pertinent. Ergonomics 66, 1–9 (2023). https://doi.org/10.1080/00140139.2023.2278408

Low, J.X., Wei, Y., Chow, J., Ali, I.F.B.: ActSen - AI-enabled real-time IoT-based ergonomic risk assessment system. In: 2019 IEEE International Congress on Internet of Things (ICIOT), pp. 76–78 (2019). https://doi.org/10.1109/ICIOT.2019.00024

Lau, N., Hildebrandt, M., Jeon, M.: Ergonomics in AI: designing and interacting with machine learning and AI. Ergon. Des. 28(3), 3–3 (2020). https://doi.org/10.1177/1064804620915238

Aubin, F., Prevost, M.-C.: Using prospective ergonomics to identify opportunities from recent technological advances in AI: the case of a west African Bank. In: Bagnara, S., Tartaglia, R., Albolino, S., Alexander, T., Fujita, Y. (eds.) IEA 2018. AISC, vol. 824, pp. 1365–1371. Springer, Cham (2019). https://doi.org/10.1007/978-3-319-96071-5_138

Salmon, P.M., et al.: Managing the risks of artificial general intelligence: a human factors and ergonomics perspective. Hum. Factors Ergon. Manuf. Serv. Ind. 33(5), 366–378 (2023). https://doi.org/10.1002/hfm.20996

Fazelnia, M., Okutan, A., Mirakhorli, M.: Supporting artificial intelligence/machine learning security workers through an adversarial techniques, tools, and common knowledge framework. IEEE Secur. Priv. 21(1), 37–48 (2022). https://doi.org/10.1109/MSEC.2022.3221058

Lee, S., Liu, L., Radwin, R., Li, J.: Machine learning in manufacturing ergonomics: recent advances, challenges, and opportunities. IEEE Robot. Autom. Lett. 6(3), 5745–5752 (2021). https://doi.org/10.1109/LRA.2021.3084881

Chiang, L., Reis, M., Shuang, B., Jiang, B., Valleau, S.: Editorial: recent advances of AI and machine learning methods in integrated R&D, manufacturing, and supply chain. Front. Chem. Eng. **4**, 1056122 (2022). https://doi.org/10.3389/fceng.2022.1056122

Lee, W.I., Shih, B.Y., Chen, C.Y.: Retraction: a hybrid artificial intelligence sales-forecasting system in the convenience store industry. Hum. Factors Ergon. Manuf. Serv. Ind. **22**, 188–196 (2012). https://doi.org/10.1002/hfm.20272. Human Factors and Ergonomics in Manufacturing & Service Industries **26**(2), 285–285 (2016). https://doi.org/10.1002/hfm.20651

Petrat, D.: Artificial intelligence in human factors and ergonomics: an overview of the current state of research. Discov. Artif. Intell. **1**(1) (2021). https://doi.org/10.1007/s44163-021-00001-5

Lind, C.M., Abtahi, F., Forsman, M.: Wearable motion capture devices for the prevention of work-related musculoskeletal disorders in ergonomics-an overview of current applications, challenges, and future opportunities. Sensors **23**(9), 4259 (2023). https://doi.org/10.3390/s23094259

Han, J., Jin Hyun, D., Jung, K., Yoon Kim, K., Youn, S.: Ergonomic design strategy for crutches of a lower-limb exoskeleton for paraplegic individuals: an experimental study. Proc. Hum. Factors Ergon. Soc. Annu. Meet. **62**(1), 1012–1016 (2018). https://doi.org/10.1177/1541931218621233

Duchon, J.C.: Evaluation of two work schedules in a mining operation. In: Aghazadeh, F. (ed.) Trends in Ergonomics/Human Factors V, pp. 151–160. North-Holland, Amsterdam (1988). Applied Ergonomics 21(1), 82–82 (1990). https://doi.org/10.1016/0003-6870(90)90118-H

Choung, H., David, P., Ross, A.: Trust in AI and its role in the acceptance of AI technologies. Int. J. Hum.-Comput. Interact. **39**(9), 1727–1739 (2023). https://doi.org/10.1080/10447318.2022.2050543

Le Guillou, M., Prévot, L., Berberian, B.: Bringing together ergonomic concepts and cognitive mechanisms for human-AI agents cooperation. Int. J. Hum.-Comput. Interact. **39**(9), 1827–1840 (2023). https://doi.org/10.1080/10447318.2022.2129741

Sheikh, H., Prins, C., Schrijvers, E.: Artificial intelligence: definition and background. In: Sheikh, H., Prins, C., Schrijvers, E. (eds.) Mission AI. Research for Policy (RP), pp. 15–41. Springer, Cham (2023). https://doi.org/10.1007/978-3-031-21448-6_2

Drury, C.G.: Human factors/ergonomics implications of big data analytics: chartered institute of ergonomics and human factors annual lecture. Ergonomics **58**(5), 1–15 (2015). https://www.researchgate.net/publication/274643362_Human_factorsergonomics_implications_of_big_data_analytics_Chartered_Institute_of_Ergonomics_and_Human_Factors_annual_lecture

Kanade, S.G., Duffy, V.G.: Exploring the effectiveness of virtual reality as a learning tool in the context of task interruption: a systematic review. Int. J. Ind. Ergon. **99**, 103548 (2024). https://doi.org/10.1016/j.ergon.2024.103548

Kanade, S.G., Duffy, V.G.: A systematic literature review of game-based learning and safety management. In: Duffy, V.G. (ed.) HCII 2020. LNCS, vol. 12199, pp. 365–377. Springer, Cham (2020). https://doi.org/10.1007/978-3-030-49907-5_26

Kanade, S.G., Duffy, V.G.: Use of virtual reality for safety training: a systematic review. In: Duffy, V.G. (eds.) HCII 2022. LNCS, vol. 13320, pp. 364–375. Springer, Cham (2022). https://doi.org/10.1007/978-3-031-06018-2_25

A Systematic Review of Collaborative Robots in Ergonomics

Harini Srivatsan[(✉)], Amit Veerayya Myagerimath, and Vincent G. Duffy

Purdue University, West Lafayette, IN 47907, USA
{hsrivats,amyageri,duffy}@purdue.edu

Abstract. Collaborative robots are used in various industries, such as manufacturing, healthcare, agriculture, and education. This study aims to review the ergonomics of using collaborative robots in manufacturing applications. The first step involved metadata extraction from databases such as Harzing's Publish or Perish, Scopus, and Web of Science. This was done to generate relevant works and authors in the field. The metadata was next analyzed using content analysis methods such as NVivo, VOSViewer, and BibExcel, to highlight key authors and groups of topics. Cluster analysis was applied to the metadata using CiteSpace to obtain citation burst articles. Scite.AI was used to further understand emerging themes. The systematic review identified key research areas, such as the communication modalities and degree of collaboration in human-robot interaction, human-robot cooperation in teamwork theories, and the long-term ergonomic effects of using cobots.

Keywords: Collaborative Robots · Human · Ergonomics

1 Introduction and Background

1.1 Introduction

Figure 1 shows the number of publications by research area, where Engineering Manufacturing and Robotics are high-interest areas. The integration of collaborative robots (cobots) in shared workspaces has revolutionized the manufacturing industry, offering a promising solution to enhance the quality and adaptability of production processes. This paradigm shift towards human-robot collaboration (HRC) has been driven by the need to address complex hybrid assembly tasks in intelligent manufacturing systems [1]. As a result, the study and characterization of physical human-robot interaction (pHRI) have become a focal point in recent robotics research, emphasizing the significance of understanding and optimizing collaborative efficiency, including time consumption and human efforts, in robot action planning [2].

The exploration of Chapter 59, "Human Factors and Ergonomics in Automation Design" from the "Handbook of Human Factors and Ergonomics" [3] is pertinent to cobot ergonomics, as it addresses user interaction, workplace design, safety considerations, and task allocation in collaborative human-robot systems. The chapter provides insights

V. G. Duffy (Ed.): HCII 2024, LNCS 14711, pp. 282–297, 2024.
https://doi.org/10.1007/978-3-031-61066-0_17

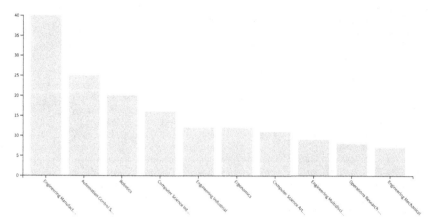

Fig. 1. Number of publications in the topic area based on Web of Science Categories

into optimizing the design of cobot systems, emphasizing the importance of user-friendly interfaces, physical ergonomics, and continuous evaluation for enhanced efficiency and worker well-being.

Another chapter, "Workplace Design" from the "Handbook of Human Factors and Ergonomics" [4] also applies to cobot ergonomics, as it dives into the principles of creating work environments that promote efficiency, safety, and employee well-being.

1.2 Background

The application of collaborative robots in the final aircraft assembly has demonstrated the potential to alleviate the physical load on employees, particularly in tasks such as solid self-piercing riveting, where manual handling would result in high physical strain [5]. Furthermore, the implications of close collaboration between workers and robots have been investigated from various perspectives, including quality, productivity, health & safety, and social implications [6]. The need to capture and transfer human expert knowledge to operators in the context of new product introduction has also been recognized as a critical aspect of human-robot collaboration [7].

Ergonomics in human-robot collaboration has emerged as a crucial area of focus, with studies emphasizing the importance of designing low-risk HRC systems while ensuring system productivity [8]. The development of ergonomic human-robot collaboration workstations has been shown to improve operators' physical ergonomics and production efficiency, with a reduction in cycle time and improved overall ergonomics [9]. Additionally, the use of advanced technologies, such as Particle Swarm Optimization (PSO) algorithms, has been proposed to optimize human posture during human-robot collaboration, demonstrating the potential for significant ergonomic improvements [10].

Moreover, the development of collaborative architectures for human-robot assembly tasks has been a key area of research, with a focus on enhancing human-robot interaction, visual inspection for quality control, and the integration of sensory systems to ensure smart control of the robot system [11]. The potential benefits of human-robot

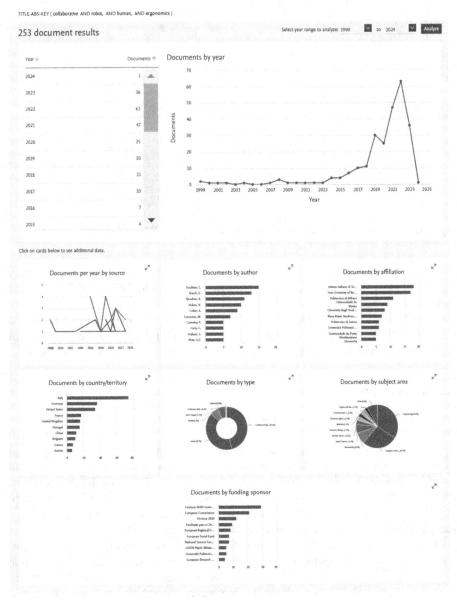

Fig. 2. Bibliometric analysis of Scopus articles ("Scopus", n.d.)

collaboration in alleviating burdensome and non-ergonomic tasks, such as overhead riveting processes in aircraft structure assembly, have been highlighted, emphasizing the need for dynamic task sharing and intuitive control systems to improve manufacturing quality and ergonomics for human operators [12]. Measures that would support this research area would include establishing educational programs on collaborative robots and human safety, as well as regulations and standards that ensure the safe and efficient integration of collaborative robots into diverse workplaces.

We initiated multiple bibliometric assessments across various platforms using the search terms "Collaborative Robots, Human, Ergonomics" On Scopus, and a total of 167 research articles were reviewed through the website's screening process, as depicted in Fig. 2. Several insights are retained from this screening. In "Documents by year", the field appears to peak in recent years, which corresponds with recent increased interest in automated manufacturing. The number of publications increased from 25 works in 2020 to 62 works in 2022. The "Documents by author" lists the authors with the highest number of works in this field, and this offers a starting point for impactful publications, some of which have been reviewed in the Introduction section.

2   Purpose of Study

This systematic review aims to assess the current state of collaborative robot ergonomics in manufacturing by analyzing metadata from databases like Harzing's Publish or Perish, Scopus, and Web of Science. Through content and cluster analysis, we identify key research areas. This study contributes insights for improving the efficiency and safety of collaborative robot applications in manufacturing. To add to prior research, which tends to focus on the ergonomic risks that cobots can overcome [13], this paper introspected on the new directions and potential research in the practice of human-robot collaboration, such as measuring the degree of collaboration, cobots, and teamwork theories, and considering the long-term ergonomic effects of using cobots.

3   Research Methodology

3.1   Data Collection

Metadata was extracted from three databases, as shown in Table 1. This metadata extraction method is depicted in Srivatsan et al. [14].

The systematic literature review involved retrieving metadata from various databases and subsequently analyzing it.

This paper considers the future work themes suggested by other references, such as "degree of collaboration" and "teamwork theories" in one reference [15]. Through the process of systematic review, it also identifies another theme: the long-term ergonomic effects of using cobots, especially in manufacturing.

The applications of these areas can be justified as follows. Measuring collaboration facilitates performance evaluation and informs system improvements, integrating cooperation into teamwork theories enhances team management and the long-term ergonomic effects of cobots must be studied to sustain worker health. Thus the ergonomics of cobots in manufacturing should be studied not only to improve productivity but also to build a safe, sustainable and continuously improving workspace design.

Table 1 presents the keywords used in three distinct databases and the count of results obtained from each search. The search conducted on Dimensions produced the most results. The data extracted comprised the title, source, author, abstract, and cited references, and was exported. The Scopus data was exported in a "CSV" format, while the data from Harzings' was exported in a "WoS" format.

Table 1. Keyword search in various databases and the number of results

Database	Keywords Used	Number of Results
Web Of Science	"Collaborative robot AND Manufacturing AND Ergonomics"	100
Scopus	"Collaborative robot AND Manufacturing AND Ergonomics"	253
Dimensions	"Collaborative robot AND Manufacturing AND Ergonomics" (Filtered for Engineering)	5191
Harzings' publish or Perish (Google scholar)	Collaborative robot AND Manufacturing AND Ergonomics	770

3.2 Trend Analysis

Figure 3 references the Google NGram Viewer trend diagram. The keywords searched were collaborative robot, manufacturing, and ergonomics, and the graph was filtered starting from 1996, as this was the year that the topic of cobots truly emerged. Ergonomics and collaborative robots appear to not be as widely discussed with respect to the broader area of manufacturing. However, the trend lines for ergonomics and collaborative robots appear to converge in recent years, indicating an overlap of topics. The Google NGram Viewer only reveals trends in books. It can also be derived from this trend analysis that the ergonomics of cobots in the context of manufacturing calls for more research in widespread literature forms, such as books.

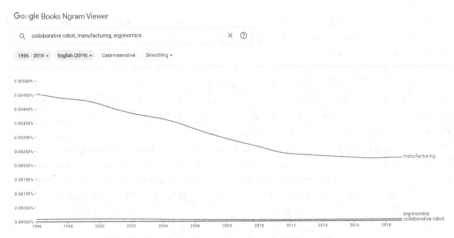

Fig. 3. Trend Analysis using Google NGram Viewer

4   Results

4.1   Co-citation Analysis

Co-citation analysis, which identifies articles that have been cited together in another article, is used to determine the level of connectivity between articles. This analysis was performed using VOSviewer. The metadata was extracted from Scopus in "CSV" format, which included 255 articles. An article had to be cited at least 9 times to be included in the analysis, a criterion met by 7 articles. The clusters resulting from this analysis are shown in Fig. 4.

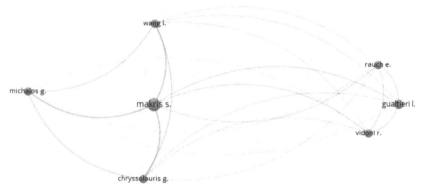

Fig. 4. Co-citation analysis using VOSviewer ("VOSviewer," n.d.)

Four out of the seven authors that fulfilled the citation criterion have been selected for further examination in the discussion section. The table of co-cited authors is shown in Fig. 5.

Verify selected authors

Selected	Author	Citations	Total link strength
☑	makris s.	23	271
☑	chryssolouris g.	10	172
☑	wang l.	10	140
☑	michalos g.	9	138
☑	gualtieri l.	12	91
☑	vidoni r.	9	82
☑	rauch e.	9	76

Fig. 5. Co-citations table in VOSviewer

4.2   Content Analysis Using VOSViewer

Content analysis is the process of examining and categorizing research to identify patterns, themes, and insights. In this paper, we do so by loading metadata obtained from Harzings' Publish or Perish to VOSViewer. A map was created using network data. The link strength was minimalized to gather the maximum number of 72 words on the map.

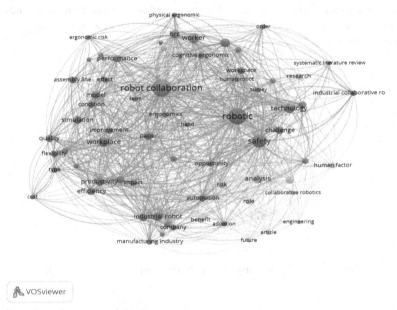

Fig. 6.   Content analysis using metadata from Harzings' Publish or Perish ("VOSviewer," n.d.)

The cluster analysis reveals that terms such as "Robot Collaboration", "Cognitive Ergonomics", and "Safety" prominently appear as nodes in the clusters. The most frequently occurring words are depicted in Fig. 6 and 7. The words within the clusters represent the key terms in a topic area. Another high-occurrence keyword that we observe in the figure is "Assembly Line". These terms can serve as a reference point when reviewing literature related to a specific topic area.

4.3   Citation Burst from CiteSpace

A citation burst is a burst of citations to a particular paper or set of papers within a specific timeframe. The concept helps researchers recognize when a particular paper or research topic gains increased attention. A citation burst diagram was generated using CiteSpace. For this, metadata from Web of Science with full records and cited references were extracted from Web of Science. The first plain text file uploaded on CiteSpace did not produce a citation burst diagram- the use of keywords Collaborative Robots, Manufacturing, and Ergonomics had only 100 results. To increase the considered citation space, two searches were conducted with the word ergonomics swapped out for

Verify selected terms

Selected	Term	Occurrences	Relevance ∨
☑	industrial collaborative robotic	16	2.14
☑	human worker	18	1.93
☑	collaborative robotics	14	1.90
☑	ergonomic problem	10	1.75
☑	engineering	12	1.67
☑	assembly line	25	1.54
☑	industrial collaborative robot	14	1.54
☑	ergonomic risk	15	1.52
☑	order	16	1.49
☑	ergonomic analysis	14	1.26
☑	type	20	1.21
☑	need	13	1.12
☑	benefit	19	1.11
☑	human operator	12	1.10
☑	human factor	21	1.10
☑	human robot	12	1.10
☑	article	13	1.10
☑	flexibility	21	1.10
☑	physical ergonomic	15	0.99
☑	literature review	16	0.99
☑	role	20	0.97

Fig. 7. Keywords from content analysis using VOSviewer ("VOSviewer," n.d.)

safety, or dropped entirely. This produced 1292 results, out of which 597 were found by CiteSpace to have relevance. This created a citation burst diagram of 5, as shown in Fig. 8. These 5 citations are thus of importance, out of which 2 relevant articles are considered in the Discussion section.

References	Year	Strength	Begin	End	2020 - 2022
Zanchettin AM, 2016, IEEE T AUTOM SCI ENG, V13, P882, DOI 10.1109/TASE.2015.2412256, DOI	2016	4.43	2020	2022	▬▬▬
Cherubini A, 2016, ROBOT CIM-INT MANUF, V40, P1, DOI 10.1016/j.rcim.2015.12.007, DOI	2016	4.15	2020	2022	▬▬▬
Vemula B, 2018, INT J INTELL ROBOT, V2, P226, DOI 10.1007/s41315-018-0055-9, DOI	2018	1.73	2020	2022	▬▬▬
Heydaryan S, 2018, APPL SCI-BASEL, V8, P0, DOI 10.3390/app8030344, DOI	2018	1.59	2020	2022	▬▬▬
Vysocky A, 2016, MM SCI J, V9, P903, DOI 10.17973/MMSJ.2016, 06, 201611, DOI	2016	1.46	2020	2022	▬▬▬

Fig. 8. Citation Burst Diagram using CiteSpace ("CiteSpace", n.d.)

4.4 Pivot Table Using BibExcel

Metadata from Harzings' Publish or Perish was uploaded to BibExcel to generate a leading authors' table. BibExcel obtains this result by pivoting different types of information, such as authors and number of publications, or publications by source. The leading authors' table is given in Table 2. Four of these authors serve as references for context synthesis in the discussion section, with three others having overlap with references obtained by other analysis methods.

Table 2. Leading Authors Table from BibExcel ("BibExcel", n.d.)

,Authors	Publications
Gualtieri L	22
Rauch E	15
Lorenzini M	15
Faccio M	14
Kim W	13
Malik AA	13
Colim A	12
Vidoni R	12

4.5   Content Analysis Using NVivo

Frequently occurring words in the selected references were analyzed and highlighted by running a word cloud on NVivo, as shown in Fig. 9. This was done by uploading references to the software and removing irrelevant words. This allows us to visualize the keywords that are likely to be impactful in this research area. Some words that have potential for further insights are: Assembly, Systems, Design, and Operator.

Fig. 9. WordCloud Using NVivo ("NVivo", n.d.)

5 Discussion

From the references acquired through co-citation analysis, content analysis, trend analysis and leading authors tables, we are able to assess both established and unique emerging areas of interest in the subject of collaborative robots, manufacturing, and ergonomics.

5.1 Established Areas of Interest

The ergonomic design of collaborative robots has been a prominent area, with studies emphasizing the human-oriented design of collaborative robots [16]. This article also discusses future trends in the field, which additionally contributes to the emerging topic of measuring the degree of human-cobot collaboration that is discussed later in this section. The integration of lean manufacturing, ergonomics, and human-robot collaboration has also been a topic of note, as it highlights the significance of productivity and wellbeing indicators in human-robot workstations [17].

The next common area of investigation has been the safety and ergonomics of physical human-robot collaboration, which aims to make human-robot collaborative systems trustworthy and impactful in real-world applications [18]. One study has also explored the development of reconfigurable human-robot collaboration workstations, such as a wire harness assembly process, and frameworks to improve worker ergonomics and productivity [19].

To relate more closely to manufacturing, it is observed that the literature has explored the impact of collaborative robots on performance and ergonomic work conditions in manufacturing assembly processes, emphasizing the need for empirical studies to understand the implications of collaborative robotics on worker ergonomics [20]. The development of ergonomic assessment frameworks for industrial assembly workstations has also been a subject of interest, and one study seeks to create collaborative robot cells that specify tasks and scheduling for human-robot collaboration using a genetic algorithm [21].

5.2 Emerging Areas of Interest

Having discussed frequently occuring ideas, the rest of this discussion will focus on certain emerging areas that have potential for further discussion. Measuring the degree of collaboration in human-cobot interaction is essential for objectively assessing performance, optimizing interaction dynamics, and ensuring safety. One paper [22] emphasizes the importance of understanding human-cobot interaction to improve safety and fluency in collaborative activities, by proposing a risk assessment mechanism. Another article's perspective on the cognitive requirements to handle a cobot found that the complexity of tasks does not increase with the introduction of collaboration between humans and cobots, even when the operator is cognitively impaired [23]. This direction of research expresses confidence in the scalability of cobots in manufacturing without compromising on worker comfort.

Degree of Collaboration. Researching the degree of collaboration in human-cobot interactions leads to pondering the degree of shared decision making between human and cobot. With the evolution of artificial intelligence, it is possible to envision a future where cobots can help reduce the cognitive burden on human workers when performing tasks. The reason this study presents this subject as shared decision making and not as artificial intelligence alone, is to highlight the difference between collaborative robots and autonomous robots: with collaborative robots, the workspace is implied to benefit from or depend on side-by-side human participation. Therefore, the sharing of intelligence and seamless interaction is important when researching the artificial intelligence of cobots. In this context, one work highlights the need for cobots to make decisions on-the-fly and consider the consequences of their decisions on their human teammates to facilitate seamless interaction [24]. This aligns with the findings of another paper [25], that offered a collaboration setup with teaching an learning to enhance human-robot efficiency and comfort during collaborative tasks. Along the lines of evolving artificial intelligence, George et al. (2023) discuss the incorporation of self-learning capabilities and autonomous behavior in cobots, which can assist operators [26].

Cobots and Teamwork Theories. A less discussed yet potentially relevant emerging area of interest is Human-Cobot cooperation in teamwork theories. This involves aligning principles from traditional teamwork theories with the unique characteristics of cobots. Principles in traditional teamwork theories include effective communication, shared goals, and coordinated task allocation. The cobot characteristics that teamwork principles should align with would be adaptability, safety sensor integration, and the general lightweight mobility of cobots. The objective would be to develop theoretical frameworks that enhance the management and efficiency of collaborative efforts. In this space, one article [27] proposes the "Motivational Theory of Human-Robot Teamwork" to better understand teamwork in human-robot teams. The next work, "Teaming with Industrial Cobots: A Socio-Technical Perspective on Safety Analysis," [28] offers a socio-technical perspective on safety analysis in human-cobot teamwork. Ensuring safety is also a teamwork principle. From the human front of the team, the feelings of the worker are indicated to influence human-cobot performance. Bagheri et al. [29] demonstrate that providing workers with additional explanation on an assigned cobot task increases the number of times that the worker submits a correct instruction to the cobot, and also improves worker confidence in the cobot interaction. One study [30] employs the analytic hierarchy process (AHP) for decision-making and hierarchical task analysis (HTA) to allocate tasks between humans and robots, minimizing interference. The research concludes that human-robot collaboration, while slightly increasing total assembly time, significantly improves human ergonomics and reduces the risk of operator injuries. The study highlights the importance of addressing ergonomic concerns in manual assembly to enhance productivity and quality.

Long-Term Ergonomic Effects of Cobots. The final emerging areas discussed in this study is the long-term ergonomic effects of using collaborative robots. Makris S. et al. [31] address assembly systems planning, highlighting the need for rapid design and reconfiguration. The insights provided apply to improving efficiency and flexibility in product design and assembly, which would reduce long-term ergonomic risks. Another reference [32] is relevant as it discusses the agility and reconfigurability of cobots, highlighting their ease of relocation and reprogramming for various tasks. The paper goes on to discuss various industrial applications where cobots enhance productivity and reduce worker fatigue, emphasizing the need for ongoing research to address design challenges. While the ergonomic benefits of cobots are discussed in literature, it is important to consider ergonomics in a long-term timeline. One paper [33] points out that physical and mental strains may arise when operators have to adopt inappropriate postures to deal with the robot's movements. The operator's role may shift from cooperation to supervision, leading to cognitive costs due to the allocation and reallocation of attentional resources. The introduction of new technologies like Cobots in workstations may result in improper task execution, mental workload, and potential damage to operators, emphasizing the importance of addressing ergonomic criteria as a requirement in the implementation of collaborative systems to ensure safer interactions and reduce ergonomic risks. The ergonomic advantages of cobots certainly outweigh the disadvantages; however, it is important to be prepared for the risks when introducing cobots to a workstation, and to analyze whether the cobot is being used for the right task. In this context, a supporting study [34] discusses the ergonomic disadvantages of using cobots, showing that despite the potential to minimize or eliminate physical and mental health risks, implementing inherently safe cobot-workplaces does not automatically ensure the prevention of health risks or decent working conditions. The study compares a cobot workplace in the context of Industry 4.0 and digitization with the initial manual situation. The analysis, using the exposure documentation system (BDS-Instrument), reveals that the cobot workplace, while safe, can lead to intolerable physical and mental overload. Factors such as increased hand movement frequency, higher risk of upper extremity musculoskeletal disorders (UEMSDs), and worsened mental exposures are highlighted. The study concludes that careful consideration of method-based operating conditions and conditions of use is crucial for identifying work-related health risks and developing effective design improvements for both traditional and modern workplaces.

6 Future Work

A gap in this study is the attention given to the ergonomics of cobots in non-manufacturing applications, such as education. To demonstrate this field as a potential area of future work, two NSF award abstracts were considered. Djurik et al. (2017) [35] address the increasing demand for workers trained in advanced manufacturing technologies, particularly collaborative robots (cobots). The project focuses on developing hands-on learning programs for cobot technicians, engineering technologists, and robotic automation teachers. The comprehensive educational material and labs aim to bridge the gap in cobot expertise in the manufacturing workforce. Future work in this area could explore the scalability and adaptability of such programs across various educational institutions. Figure 10 shows the screenshot of the NSF award abstract.

Another possible future work field is proposing frameworks for regulations in human-cobot interactions. Current regulatory standards often lag behind the rapid advancements in cobot technology, leading to gaps in ensuring the well-being of human operators. A focused effort is needed to identify and bridge these regulatory gaps, which will provide clear guidelines for cobot deployment across industries. This involves defining safety protocols, ergonomic standards, and performance benchmarks that align with the evolving capabilities of cobots. An example of a regulation for human-cobot interactions

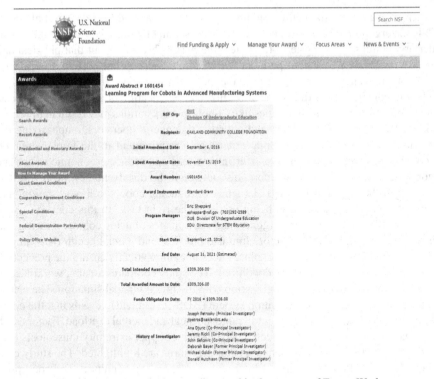

Fig. 10. NSF Award Abstract discussed in the context of Future Work

is specifying maximum force and speed limits for cobots during collaborative tasks to ensure the safety of human operators. This regulation aims to prevent injuries by defining thresholds that minimize the risk of harm in case of accidental contact between humans and collaborative robots.

7 Conclusion

This study's contributions can be described in the list of 10 ways to execute a systematic review: 1) The study systematically reviews collaborative robot ergonomics in manufacturing, using metadata extraction and content analysis. 2) It integrates collaborative robot insights into manufacturing, referencing relevant chapters in the "Handbook of Human Factors and Ergonomics" and various existing works found on Scopus. 3) It establishes a theoretical foundation through references to pHRI studies and ergonomic considerations in automation design. 4) It contributes practically by employing systematic methods and discussing emerging topics in the field of cobot ergonomics. 5) It identifies emerging areas like measuring collaboration, exploring teamwork theories, and considering long-term ergonomic effects. 6) It uses systematic literature review methods, metadata extraction, and bibliometric tools like VOSViewer, CiteSpace, and BibExcel. 7) For statistical analyses, it references bibliometric tools that visualize citation patterns, co-citation, and leading authors. 8) It discusses co-citation analysis, content analysis, and insights into established and emerging areas of interest while reviewing the methodologies 9) It concludes by differentiating between the established areas of interest (ergonomic design of cobots, cobot safety, and ergonomic advantages of cobots) and the emerging areas of interest (degree of collaboration, cobots and teamwork theories, and the long-term ergonomic effects of cobots). 10) It proposes future work in non-manufacturing applications, regulatory frameworks, and educational program scalability for collaborative robots.

References

1. Lorenzini, M., Lagomarsino, M., Fortini, L., Gholami, S., Ajoudani, A.: Ergonomic human-robot collaboration in industry: a review. Front. Robot. AI **9**, 813907 (2023)
2. Ajoudani, A., Zanchettin, A.M., Ivaldi, S., Albu-Schäffer, A., Kosuge, K., Khatib, O.: Progress and prospects of the human-robot collaboration. Auton. Robots **42**(5), 957–975 (2018)
3. Lee, J.D., Seppelt, B.D.: Human factors and ergonomics in automation design. In: Handbook of Human Factors and Ergonomics, 4th edn. Wiley, Hoboken (2012)
4. Marmaras, N., Nathanael, D.: Workplace design, pp. 368–382. https://doi.org/10.1002/978 1119636113.ch14. Accessed 14 Dec 2023
5. Gualtieri, L., Palomba, I., Merati, F.A., Rauch, E., Vidoni, R.: Design of human-centered collaborative assembly workstations for the improvement of operators' physical ergonomics and production efficiency: a case study. Sustainability **12**(9), 3606 (2020)
6. Kim, W., Peternel, L., Lorenzini, M., Babič, J., Ajoudani, A.: A human-robot collaboration framework for improving ergonomics during dexterous operation of power tools. Robot. Comput.-Integr. Manuf. **68**, 102084 (2021). https://doi.org/10.1016/j.rcim.2020.102084
7. Sunesson, C.E., Schön, D., Hassø, C.N.P., Chinello, F., Fang, C.: Predictor: a physical emulator enabling safety and ergonomics evaluation and training of physical human-robot collaboration. Front. Neurorobot. **17**, 1080038 (2023). https://doi.org/10.3389/fnbot.2023.108 0038
8. Maurice, P., et al.: Human movement and ergonomics: an industry-oriented dataset for collaborative robotics. Int. J. Robot. Res. **14**(38), 1529–1537 (2019). https://doi.org/10.1177/ 0278364919882089
9. Gualtieri, L., Rauch, E., Vidoni, R.: Methodology for the definition of the optimal assembly cycle and calculation of the optimized assembly cycle time in human-robot collaborative assembly. Int. J. Adv. Manuf. Technol. **7–8**(113), 2369–2384 (2021). https://doi.org/10.1007/ s00170-021-06653-y
10. Omidi, M., et al.: Improving postural ergonomics during human–robot collaboration using particle swarm optimization: a study in virtual environment. Appl. Sci. **13**(9), 5385 (2023). https://doi.org/10.3390/app13095385
11. El Makrini, I., Mathijssen, G., Verhaegen, S., Verstraten, T., Vanderborght, B.: A virtual element-based postural optimization method for improved ergonomics during human-robot collaboration. IEEE Trans. Autom. Sci. Eng. **19**(3), 1–12 (2022)
12. Cherubini, A., Passama, R., Crosnier, A., Lasnier, A., Fraisse, P.: Collaborative manufacturing with physical human–robot interaction. Robot. Comput.-Integr. Manuf. **40**, 1–13 (2016). https://doi.org/10.1016/j.rcim.2015.12.007
13. Liu, L., Guo, F., Zou, Z., Duffy, V.G.: Application, development and future opportunities of collaborative robots (cobots) in manufacturing: a literature review. Int. J. Hum.-Comput. Interact. **40**(4), 1–18 (2024)

14. Srivatsan, H., Chhajer, K., Duffy, V.G.: A systematic review of user experience in motivation and education. In: Zaphiris, P., et al. (eds.) HCI International 2023 – Late Breaking Papers, pp. 252–266. Springer, Cham (2023). https://doi.org/10.1007/978-3-031-48060-7_20

15. Dobra, Z., Dhir, K.S.: Technology jump in the industry: human-robot cooperation in production. Ind. Robot. **47**(5), 757–775 (2020)

16. Matheson, E., Minto, R., Zampieri, E.G.G., Faccio, M., Rosati, G.: Human–robot collaboration in manufacturing applications: a review. Robotics **8**(4), 100 (2019). https://doi.org/10.3390/robotics8040100

17. Colim, A., Morgado, R., Carneiro, P., Costa, N., Faria, C., Nuno Sousa, L.A., Rocha, et al.: Lean manufacturing and ergonomics integration: defining productivity and wellbeing indicators in a human–robot workstation. Sustainability **13**(4), 1931 (2021). https://doi.org/10.3390/su13041931

18. Proia, S., Carli, R., Cavone, G., Dotoli, M.: Control techniques for safe, ergonomic, and efficient human-robot collaboration in the digital industry: a survey. IEEE Trans. Autom. Sci. Eng. **3**(19), 1798–1819 (2022). https://doi.org/10.1109/tase.2021.3131011

19. Navas-Reascos, G.E., Romero, D., Stahre, J., Caballero-Ruiz, A.: Wire harness assembly process supported by collaborative robots: literature review and call for R&D. Robotics **11**(3), 65 (2022). https://doi.org/10.3390/robotics11030065

20. Palomba, I., Gualtieri, L., Rojas, R.A., Rauch, E., Vidoni, R., Ghedin, A.: Mechatronic redesign of a manual assembly workstation into a collaborative one for wire harness assemblies. Robotics **10**(1), 43 (2021). https://doi.org/10.3390/robotics10010043

21. Dalle Mura, M., Dini, G.: Job rotation and human–robot collaboration for enhancing ergonomics in assembly lines by a genetic algorithm. Int. J. Adv. Manuf. Technol. **118**(9–10), 2901–2914 (2021). https://doi.org/10.1007/s00170-021-08068-1

22. Stone, R., Pujari, S., Mumani, A., Fales, C., Ameen, M.: Cobot and robot risk assessment (carra) method: an automation level-based safety assessment tool to improve fluency in safe human cobot/robot interaction. Proc. Hum. Factors Ergon. Soc. Annu. Meet. **1**(65), 737–741 (2021). https://doi.org/10.1177/1071181321651024

23. Fournier, É., et al.: The impacts of human-cobot collaboration on perceived cognitive load and usability during an industrial task: an exploratory experiment. IISE Trans. Occup. Ergon. Hum. Factors **2**(10), 83–90 (2022). https://doi.org/10.1080/24725838.2022.2072021

24. Alessio, S., et al.: Pose forecasting in industrial human-robot collaboration (2022). https://doi.org/10.48550/arxiv.2208.07308

25. Wang, W., Chen, Yi., Li, R., Jia, Y.: Learning and comfort in human–robot interaction: a review. Appl. Sci. **9**(23), 5152 (2019). https://doi.org/10.3390/app9235152

26. George, P.M., Cheng, C.-T., Pang, T.Y., Neville, K.: Task complexity and the skills dilemma in the programming and control of collaborative robots for manufacturing. Appl. Sci. **13**(7), 4635 (2023). https://doi.org/10.3390/app13074635

27. Robert, L.P.: Motivational theory of human robot teamwork. Int. Robot. Autom. J. **4**(4), 248–251 (2018). https://doi.org/10.15406/iratj.2018.04.00131

28. Adriaensen, A., Costantino, F., Di Gravio, G., Patriarca, R.: Teaming with industrial cobots: a socio-technical perspective on safety analysis. Hum. Factors Ergon. Manuf. Serv. Ind. **32**(2), 173–198 (2022). https://doi.org/10.1002/hfm.20939

29. Bagheri, E., De Winter, J., Vanderborght, B.: Transparent interaction based learning for human-robot collaboration. Front. Robot. AI **9**, 754955 (2022)

30. Heydaryan, S., Suaza Bedolla, J., Belingardi, G.: Safety design and development of a human-robot collaboration assembly process in the automotive industry. Appl. Sci. **8**(3), 344 (2018)

31. Makris, S., Michalos, G., Karagiannis, P.: Digitalising smart factories. Int. J. Comput. Integr. Manuf. **36**(1), 1–2 (2023)

32. Villani, V., Pini, F., Leali, F., Secchi, C.: Survey on human–robot collaboration in industrial settings: safety, intuitive interfaces and applications. Mechatronics **55**, 248–266 (2018). https://doi.org/10.1016/j.mechatronics.2018.02.009

33. Cardoso, A., Colim, A., Bicho, E., Braga, A.C., Menozzi, M., Arezes, P.: Ergonomics and human factors as a requirement to implement safer collaborative robotic workstations: a literature review. Safety **7**(4), 71 (2021). https://doi.org/10.3390/safety7040071

34. Mühlemeyer, C.: Assessment and design of employees-cobot-interaction. In: Ahram, T., Taiar, R., Colson, S., Choplin, A. (eds.) IHIET 2019. AISC, vol. 1018, pp. 771–776. Springer, Cham (2020). https://doi.org/10.1007/978-3-030-25629-6_120

35. Djuric, A., Rickli, J.L., Jovanovic, V.M., Foster, D.: Hands-on learning environment and educational curriculum on collaborative robotics. In: 124th ASEE Annual Conference & Exposition, 14–17 June, Columbus, Ohio (2017)

Exercise Recognition and Repetition Counting for Automatic Workout Documentation Using Computer Vision

Francois Volschenk, Hima Vadapalli📵, and Dustin van der Haar(✉)📵

Academy of Computer Science and Software Engineering,
University of Johannesburg, Cnr University Road and Kingsway Avenue,
Auckland Park, Johannesburg 2092, Gauteng, South Africa
{himav,dvanderhaar}@uj.ac.za

Abstract. This paper aims to study various approaches using deep learning methods to perform human action recognition (HAR). More specifically, a subset of HAR focused on recognising exercises and counting repetitions using deep learning. The paper discusses two approaches used in an attempt to produce a machine-learning model that is capable of identifying certain exercises from video input. This model is then incorporated into a system that can document a person's workout by identifying the exercises being done and counting the repetitions of each exercise. The study uses artificial training data in 3D animated videos of avatars performing the exercises. The dataset used is InfiniteRep from InfinityAI. Feature extraction and repetition counting are performed using the Mediapipe pose estimation model. An LSTM-based model and a 1D time-distributed CNN are used for exercise recognition. The models were compared on classification metrics: accuracy, precision, and recall. The LSTM-based model produced a 96% accuracy on the dataset, whereas the CNN-based model produced 97.3% accuracy on the same dataset. The CNN-based model is also capable of performing in near real-time.

Keywords: Computer Vision · Action Recognition · Machine Learning

1 Introduction

Physical exercise is an excellent way to stay healthy, get strong, and be fit [11]. It also works as a way to prevent injury and reduce health-related risks while improving the state of a person's mental health [10]. Many people are hesitant to enter the world of exercise because they need to learn how the exercises work, how many to do, and how frequently to do them [11]. These factors depend on the individual's lifestyle, nutritional habits, and goals. One way to track progress and improvements is by keeping track of the exercises a person does during their workouts and how many repetitions of each exercise were done. As the individual progresses, they will be able to perform more repetitions.

V. G. Duffy (Ed.): HCII 2024, LNCS 14711, pp. 298–309, 2024.
https://doi.org/10.1007/978-3-031-61066-0_18

Using computer vision and machine learning techniques, the process of documenting a workout session can be automated, and a digital record of past workouts can be kept to view progress. This paper aims to investigate human action recognition (HAR) methods and apply these methods to exercise recognition. To conduct this study, a modified version of the InfiniteRep dataset by InfinityAI was produced, and a system was built around the model discussed in the second pipeline capable of real-time exercise recognition and rep counting. This system uses the OpenCV library to capture video from a user's webcam or via an input video file. The MediaPipe Pose estimation model extracts the spatial data of the user's body. This data is then passed through the model produced by this study to recognise the exercise being performed. Once the exercise is known, the spatial data from the pose estimation model determines when the user has completed one rep by looking at the angle change between certain parts of the user's body.

In Sect. 2, the paper will discuss the problem's background, including prior research that has been done on this topic and related fields, as well as some of the implications of solving the problem. Section 3 discusses the experiment setup. This includes a discussion of the dataset used in this study and the methods and algorithms, and the metrics by which they will be evaluated. Section 4 is a discussion of the experiment's results. Section 5 hosts a discussion on the contributions from this study, and finally, Sect. 6 summarises and concludes the paper.

2   Problem Background

Exercising provides a way to stay healthy and get fit. However, to make consistent progress, it is essential to track your performance during workouts and attempt to improve them in subsequent workouts, or else you risk stagnating [2].

Different fitness goals have different progress requirements. To build strength, a person must progressively increase the amount of weight they use to exercise. To build up endurance, a person must progressively increase the repetitions they do in a single set or prolong the duration of the workout. To build muscle mass, the person must increase the volume associated with an exercise. This can be seen as a product of both weight and number of repetitions [5].

There are manual methods for keeping track of a person's progress, most notably by using pen and paper and counting the repetitions manually, then comparing the numbers over time. However, these methods take time. Another method of tracking progress is through automated exercise tracking.

Automated exercise tracking methods include using data from wearable devices, such as heart rate data and inertial measurements. This approach is limited in its capabilities, as wearable devices are only effective for certain exercises and can only accurately monitor the motions of the limb to which they are attached. The placement of the device also affects the accuracy of the readings for heart rate and motion [8].

Another approach is to use specialised exercise equipment with built-in sensors [9]. However, similarly to wearable devices, this approach is limited to the exercises that can be performed with that specific machine. Computer vision and a deep learning approach enable us to identify various exercises.

Action recognition is an area of study that falls under computer vision and deals with trying to estimate what action is being performed in a given sequence [6]. This can be done by processing the subsequent frames of a video and finding the relationship between the images or by extracting certain features, such as a pose estimation from each frame and trying to classify that instead. For action recognition, it is important to map the spatial data (e.g. direction of movement) along with the temporal data.

Many of the following works rely on pose estimation to determine which action is being performed. Pose estimation is a method used with computer vision to identify the position, relation, and orientation of a person or object within an image. This is done by detecting certain points located on the person or object and drawing conclusions based on the distances between each of these points [4].

Real-time exercise tracking is a widely researched topic with many papers centred around the idea of using computer vision to determine which exercises are done, how many repetitions are done, as well as determining flaws in the way that an exercise is being done to recommend corrections to improve the effectiveness of an exercise being done.

In [7], Khurana et al. implement an approach to exercise tracking for multiple people at once called GymCam. This is done using OpticalFlow to extract motions captured by the camera and detect repetitive trajectories of objects. The GymCam system was trained on a primary dataset containing 18 exercises. Their model produced an 80.6% accuracy even in occlusions such as other gym goers or gym equipment. This method can analyse and report on the exercises being done in real-time.

In [1], Alatiah et al. implemented a method for counting repetitions and distinguishing between valid and invalid repetitions using a pose estimation model from OpenPose [3]. The method analyses the frames of a video in groups, detecting which exercise is done by identifying the pose and then analysing the motion to find faults in the exercise. This method is also able to monitor the exercises in real-time.

Yu et al. [12] developed a system that uses a multitask approach, including a heatmap-based pose estimator from MSPN, action recognition, and a rep counter working together to identify and count repetitions of particular exercises done. This approach yielded a 95.69% accuracy in exercise recognition. The paper's authors created their dataset Rep-Penn labelled with action, counting, and speed labels to train their model. Rep-Penn consisted of seven different exercises and was generated from data in the PennAction dataset by stitching videos with their reverse to add continuity to the exercises. They used a 2D multitask model to perform the exercise recognition and rep counting trained with an RMSprop optimiser on their Rep-Penn dataset and produced an accuracy of 95.69%.

In the following section, the paper discusses the dataset used in this study and the methods employed in evaluating the methods identified.

3   Experiment Setup

3.1   Data Sampling

For this experiment, a secondary dataset will be used. The name of the dataset is InfiniteRep, and it has been sourced from InfinityAI, which provides this dataset for open use. The dataset consists of video clips of 10 exercises, 100 videos per exercise. The videos have been generated of avatars in a 3D virtual space. Some advantages of this dataset include that it does not contain any footage of real people that may raise privacy concerns, and the avatars can be modified to represent people of various body shapes, ethnicities and genders. The clips also vary in lighting conditions, environment and obstruction of the person. These clips have been labelled to indicate the exercise that is being performed.

The exercises depicted in the dataset are

- Pushup
- Squat
- Curl
- Overhead-press
- Bicycles
- Leg raises
- Bird-Dog
- Fly
- Superman
- Arm raise

Fig. 1. An example of the artificial training data used in this study.

Figure 1 depicts a sample of two frames from one of the videos of a person performing a squat in the dataset. The videos are of varying lengths, between 15 and 50 s, and show the person completing 5 and 15 repetitions of the exercise. To standardise the length and rep count, a script was written that iterates over each video and allows the user to indicate when one rep has been completed. The script then counts the frames of each video and returns the lowest number of frames found to accommodate one rep in every exercise. The representative frames were obtained sequentially rather than distributed evenly across the video length to maintain the exercise's spatial-temporal relationship. Thus, the 20 frames depict the whole motion of each exercise.

The pre-processing steps used to capture data from these videos included resizing the frames to 250 × 250 so that all images passed into the pose estimation model were of the same size. Feature extraction was done by using the Mediapipe pose landmark model to extract 132 key points per frame that estimate the position of a person's body in a given frame.

Many of the exercises in the dataset include overlapping movements, such as the moment at the top of a bicep curl when both hands are close to a person's shoulder and the moment in a dumbell fly when the person has the dumbells pulled in close to their shoulders. As such, for this study, a subset of the exercises in the InfinityRep dataset, such that the exercises are distinctly different, were used to train the models. This subset consists of pushups, curls, squats, and overhead presses.

The dataset is organised into a folder where all of the videos of one type of exercise are grouped into a single folder, but each video is contained in its subfolder. This subfolder also contains the pose landmarks extracted from each of the 20 frames of that video. When the data is loaded into the training script, the data from the 20 frames are loaded in as a sequence, and this sequence is added to an array of sequences. The labels are derived from the folder from which the video data was loaded and encoded using the one-hot-encoding scheme.

3.2 Methods

This study will undertake two experiments, each consisting of a pipeline that goes from data processing and feature extraction through training a model into deployment for evaluation purposes. Both experiments will make use of the same dataset for training. The models will be benchmarked on the InfiniteRep dataset for a fair comparison.

Pipeline 1. The model must understand sequential data to capture the temporal relationship between each frame. The LSTM model architecture is capable of handling long-term dependencies. As such, this pipeline uses a model with several LSTM layers. Figure 2 depicts the model's architecture. The input layer is set up to accept 20 frames containing 132 key points. These are the pose landmark points extracted by the pose estimation model. The three LSTM layers handle the temporal relationship between the frames, and the three dense layers are used for classification. The final dense layer uses the softmax activation function, and classification is done by selecting the output node with the highest activation value.

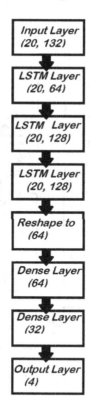

Fig. 2. The model architecture of the LSTM model.

Pipeline 2. The initial goal of this pipeline was to use a different data format. Using pose estimation for exercise recognition means that much of the other data is discarded. This data could provide context about the exercise, making it easier to identify. To achieve this, an attempt was made to use a 3D CNN, which would accept a sequence of frames as images and figure out the temporal relationship between the data. However, this approach was not feasible due to the limited computing resources and the project's time constraints. As an alternative, a time-distributed 1D CNN that accepts the same pose landmarks as the LSTM was used. Figure 3 depicts the architecture, including recurrent layers for temporal relationships. The benefit is that the models can be used interchangeably without changing how data is fed. The architecture includes max pooling and dropout layers to reduce the risk of overfitting. This architecture produced a 97%

Rep Counting. Once the exercise being performed is recognised by the model, rep counting is performed using the pose landmark data to calculate angles between specific joints. A state variable is kept, determining if the person is in the exercise's concentric (up motion) or eccentric (down motion). Once the angle in question passes a threshold, the state changes and with every change of state,

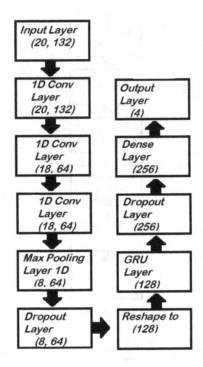

Fig. 3. The model architecture of the 1D Convolutional model.

Table 1. Angles between body parts used for rep counting.

Exercise	Angle Between	Up threshold	Down Threshold
Pushup	Elbows and Shoulders	90°	30°
Squat	Knees and Hips	160°	50°
Curl	Wrists, Elbows and Shoulders	30°	150°
Overhead press	Elbows, Shoulders and Hips	160°	90°

the repetition count of that exercise is incremented. Table 1 expresses the joints for each exercise and the threshold for state change used when testing the rep counter. The state change threshold may be adapted to accommodate a different subject with a different range of motion in the relevant exercises.

3.3   Evaluation

Both of the models used in this study perform the task of classification. Therefore the standard classification metrics will be used to compare the two models.

During training, the models will use categorical cross-entropy as a loss function to determine the accuracy of their outcomes. This metric is widely used for classification tasks where the outcome is a single classification.

The models will be judged on their accuracy, precision and recall. These metrics and the confusion matrices of each model will be used to compare the two.

4   Results

4.1   Pipeline 1

This architecture produced a 96% accuracy on the dataset. However, it required many epochs to train. The complexity of this model also makes it quite slow at inference time. This means that it is not suitable for real-time exercise recognition.

– Accuracy: 96%
– Precision: 95%
– Recall: 95%

This model identified changes in the exercise being performed almost instantaneously. However, it also showed a tendency to jump between classifications when the subject performs an action that can be seen in a few different exercises. For example, the model would jump between 'squat' and 'curl' when standing up straight.

Figure 4 shows the confusion matrix of the model trained in this pipeline. There are 3 misclassifications where either a squat was classified as a curl or a curl was classified as a squat. This occurs because of the overlapping pose similarity between reps of squats and curls where a person stands upright with both arms at their side.

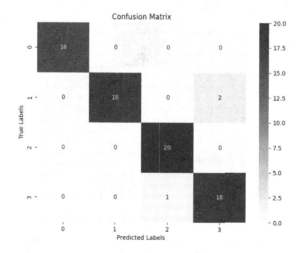

Fig. 4. Confusion matrix for pipeline 1. **Key:** 0 = pushup, 1 = squat, 2 = overhead-press, 3 = curl

4.2   Pipeline 2

This architecture produced a 97.3% accuracy on the dataset. The model also required very few epochs to train, and each epoch only took a few seconds. This model can run in real time, making it ideal for use in a system for live exercise tracking.

- Accuracy: 97.3%
- Precision: 97.5%
- Recall: 97.5%

This model takes a few moments to detect when the person has changed the exercise that they are doing, but it does not jump around between classifications once it has recognised the action.

Figure 5 shows the confusion matrix for the model trained in this pipeline. In this case, there were two misclassifications. In one instance, the model once again confused a squat for a curl. In the second instance, a squat was classified as an overhead press. in the specific sample, the video showed the person holding their hands above their head while squatting, and this gesture was mistaken for an overhead press.

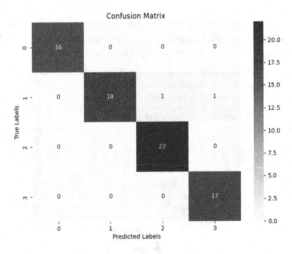

Fig. 5. Confusion matrix for pipeline 2. **Key:** 0 = pushup, 1 = squat, 2 = overhead-press, 3 = curl

4.3   Comparison

Although the model in Pipeline 2 outperformed the model from Pipeline 1, the difference in classification accuracy between the two pipelines is not statistically significant. However, the speed at which the second pipeline can perform makes it a more suitable candidate for use in real-time applications, such as a system where classification is done on a live video feed.

Fig. 6. Samples of exercises being recognised and counted.

4.4 Effectiveness of the Artificial Training Data

After training both pipelines on the artificial training data, both models were tested with videos of real people performing the exercises. In most cases, both pipelines could correctly identify the exercises being performed. This proves that using artificial training data in the context of action recognition can be very effective.

5 Contribution

This study has shown that a 1D convolutional neural network is more suited to real-time applications for action recognition while producing fairly accurate results. Furthermore, the use of artificial training data in the form of 3D animated avatars has proven to be very effective in training models for the task of action recognition.

The study resulted in the development of a FitForYou system, which uses the model described in pipeline 2 to perform real-time exercise recognition to transcribe the exercises and the number of repetitions performed during a workout. Figure 6 shows the system in action. As soon as the exercise is recognised, the system counts the repetitions. When the workout is concluded and the program is terminated, the transcribed workout is written to a file.

6 Conclusion

This paper aimed to study methods that could be used to perform action recognition and classification to produce a model that yields acceptable accuracy. To this end, we have discussed the problem background as well as some similar systems and the contributions that they have made in this area.

This study performed two experiments that each yielded a model capable of performing action recognition. The first experiment produced a 95% accuracy score but required a long training time. This model was also incapable of running in real-time but quickly realised when a user had changed the exercise. The second experiment produced a 97.3% accuracy, trained very quickly, and can run in real-time, but it takes longer to realise when the user has changed the exercise they are doing.

Future expansion of this work may include training the models on a larger dataset, including more exercises, and finding the optimal configuration of parameters to use during training. The best-performing model from this paper has also been incorporated into a program that uses it to perform action recognition and rep counting to produce a document that lists the exercises done during a workout.

References

1. Alatiah, T., Chen, C.: Recognizing exercises and counting repetitions in real time. arXiv preprint arXiv:2005.03194 (2020)
2. Bireline, A.: 7 reasons to track your fitness progress (2017). https://www.nifs.org/blog/7-reasons-to-track-your-fitness-progress
3. Cao, Z., Simon, T., Wei, S.E., Sheikh, Y.: Realtime multi-person 2D pose estimation using part affinity fields. In: Proceedings of the IEEE Conference on Computer Vision and Pattern Recognition, pp. 7291–7299 (2017)
4. Difini, G.M., Martins, M.G., Barbosa, J.L.V.: Human pose estimation for training assistance: a systematic literature review. In: Proceedings of the Brazilian Symposium on Multimedia and the Web, pp. 189–196 (2021)
5. Gwak, M., et al.: Extra: exercise tracking and analysis platform for remote-monitoring of knee rehabilitation. In: 2019 IEEE 16th International Conference on Wearable and Implantable Body Sensor Networks (BSN), pp. 1–4. IEEE (2019)
6. Jhuang, H., Gall, J., Zuffi, S., Schmid, C., Black, M.J.: Towards understanding action recognition. In: Proceedings of the IEEE International Conference on Computer Vision, pp. 3192–3199 (2013)
7. Khurana, R., Ahuja, K., Yu, Z., Mankoff, J., Harrison, C., Goel, M.: Gymcam: detecting, recognizing and tracking simultaneous exercises in unconstrained scenes. Proc. ACM Interact. Mob. Wearable Ubiquitous Technol. 2(4), 1–17 (2018)
8. Maurer, U., Smailagic, A., Siewiorek, D.P., Deisher, M.: Activity recognition and monitoring using multiple sensors on different body positions. In: International Workshop on Wearable and Implantable Body Sensor Networks (BSN 2006), pp. 4–pp. IEEE (2006)
9. Preatoni, E., Nodari, S., Lopomo, N.F.: Supervised machine learning applied to wearable sensor data can accurately classify functional fitness exercises within a continuous workout. Front. Bioeng. Biotechnol. 8, 664 (2020)

10. Ruegsegger, G.N., Booth, F.W.: Health benefits of exercise. Cold Spring Harb. Perspect. Med. **8**(7), a029694 (2018)
11. Vina, J., Sanchis-Gomar, F., Martinez-Bello, V., Gomez-Cabrera, M.: Exercise acts as a drug; the pharmacological benefits of exercise. Br. J. Pharmacol. **167**(1), 1–12 (2012)
12. Yu, Q., Wang, H., Laamarti, F., El Saddik, A.: Deep learning-enabled multitask system for exercise recognition and counting. Multimodal Technol. Interact. **5**(9), 55 (2021)

Advanced Technologies for Training and Learning

Evaluating Incentive Based 3D Virtual Training for Nasopharyngeal Swab Proficiency

Vasavi Gannina[1], Mohammad Burhan Khan[2], J. Cecil[1(✉)], Frédéric Merienne[2], and Binti Mohd Zuki Fatin Shamimi[2]

[1] Center for Cyber-Physical Systems, Department of Computer Science, Oklahoma State University, Stillwater, OK, USA
{vgannin,j.cecil}@okstate.edu
[2] Arts et Metiers Institute of Technology LISPEN, HESAM Université, 71100 Chalon-Sur-Saone, France
mkhan12@okstate.edu, {frederic.merienne, fatin_shamimi.mohd_zuki}@ensam.eu

Abstract. The global emergence of the COVID-19 pandemic has placed an unprecedented strain on healthcare systems worldwide, demanding the need for accurate and widespread testing methods, particularly the utilization of nasopharyngeal swabs for detecting SARS-CoV-2. Proficiency in this critical procedure among healthcare professionals is paramount to ensure both test accuracy and safety. Nevertheless, conventional training methods face numerous constraints, including high costs, limited availability of trainers, and the inherent risk of infection transmission.

In response to these challenges, this study endeavors to explore a novel approach by integrating incentive-based learning techniques with incentive within immersive 3D virtual training environments tailored for nasopharyngeal swabbing. The primary aim of this investigation is to assess the impact of this innovative approach in comparison to conventional 3D virtual training methods on several crucial dimensions, including knowledge acquisition, cognitive load, skill development, and user engagement. To achieve this, the study capitalizes on cutting-edge technologies like virtual reality (VR) to provide a dynamic and realistic training experience.

In essence, this research seeks to provide valuable insights into the effective amalgamation of incentive-based learning strategies with incentive principles within the realm of virtual reality-based healthcare training. The specific focus of this study lies in enhancing proficiency in the nasopharyngeal swabbing technique, a skill of paramount importance during the ongoing COVID-19 pandemic. By pushing the boundaries of educational technology and leveraging the power of motivation, this research aspires to contribute significantly to healthcare education in these challenging times.

Keywords: COVID-19 · Nasopharyngeal swabbing · Healthcare training · Virtual reality (VR) · Healthcare Education · SARS-CoV-2 detection · Pandemic response · Emerging technologies · Proficiency training

© The Author(s), under exclusive license to Springer Nature Switzerland AG 2024
V. G. Duffy (Ed.): HCII 2024, LNCS 14711, pp. 313–325, 2024.
https://doi.org/10.1007/978-3-031-61066-0_19

1 Introduction

The global COVID-19 pandemic has posed an unprecedented challenge to healthcare systems across the world. Amidst this crisis, one indispensable tool in the fight against the virus is the accurate and widespread testing of individuals, with nasopharyngeal swabbing being a cornerstone of diagnostic procedures. Nasopharyngeal swabbing entails the collection of a sample from the upper respiratory tract to detect the presence of the SARS-CoV-2 virus. Proficiency in conducting nasopharyngeal swabs is not only vital for ensuring the precision of test results but also for safeguarding the well-being of both patients and healthcare practitioners.

While the nasopharyngeal swabbing procedure may appear straightforward, it demands precision and skill to minimize patient discomfort and optimize sample quality. Errors during swabbing can lead to false negatives or inadequate samples, potentially undermining the efficacy of testing and contact tracing efforts. Moreover, healthcare professionals are at risk of viral exposure if the procedure is not executed correctly, emphasizing the critical importance of training and proficiency.

Conventional healthcare training methods typically involve didactic lectures and hands-on practice with standardized patients or mannequins. Despite their effectiveness to some extent, these methods are accompanied by inherent limitations such as material costs, trainer availability, and the potential risk of infection during training, particularly when dealing with highly contagious pathogens like SARS-CoV-2 [13].

In response to these challenges, emerging technologies have opened up new avenues for education and training, prominently among them being virtual reality (VR) and incentive-based learning. VR offers immersive, interactive, and safe training environments that can faithfully replicate real-world scenarios, enabling healthcare professionals to hone their skills without endangering patients or themselves. Incentive-based learning, on the other hand, integrates motivational elements into non-game contexts, rendering training engaging and enjoyable while motivating learners to attain specific objectives [22].

This research paper embarks on an exploration of the fusion of incentive-based learning with incentive into 3D virtual training environments tailored for nasopharyngeal swabbing technique instruction among healthcare professionals. The principal aim of this study is to gauge the influence of incentive-based learning with incentive on knowledge acquisition, cognitive load, skill development, and user engagement, juxtaposed against conventional 3D virtual training setups. Consequently, the study endeavors to illuminate the potential of this approach as an efficacious instrument for healthcare education, especially in the prevailing milieu of the COVID-19 pandemic.

The ensuing sections of this paper will delve into pertinent literature regarding incentive-based learning, the role of virtual reality in healthcare training, and the nuances of nasopharyngeal swabbing techniques. Subsequently, the methodology employed in the study will be outlined, followed by the presentation of results and their analysis. Ultimately, the paper will conclude by summarizing the primary findings and suggesting future research directions in this critical sphere of healthcare training.

In summation, this research endeavors to furnish invaluable insights into the judicious amalgamation of incentive-based learning and virtual reality in healthcare training, with a particular emphasis on proficiency in nasopharyngeal swabbing techniques during the COVID-19 pandemic [13, 22].

2 Background

The 3D VR based models and environments can be viewed as virtual prototyps or digital twins [31], which are designed for a range of applications including process design in manufacturing, training medical residents in surgery and other domains such as the Moon Mission, among others [29, 30, 32–35].

The integration of incentive-based learning with incentive and virtual reality (VR) in healthcare training has gained increasing attention due to its potential to address challenges in traditional training methods. Incentive-based learning, the incorporation of motivational elements into non-game contexts, has been applied successfully in various educational domains [20]. In healthcare, it has been used to enhance engagement, motivation, and learning outcomes [23]. Additionally, VR offers immersive and interactive environments for skill acquisition and simulation-based training [4].

Existing research on incentive-based learning in healthcare training demonstrates its effectiveness in improving user engagement and knowledge retention [6]. For instance, incentive-based simulations have been employed in surgical training to enhance surgeons' skills and confidence [12]. Similarly, incentive-based learning has been utilized in rehabilitation settings to encourage patient adherence to therapy and improve recovery outcomes [11]. In the context of COVID-19, healthcare training has faced unique challenges due to the highly contagious nature of the virus. Incentive-based learning has emerged as a promising tool for remote and safe training, reducing the risk of infection during hands-on practice [8].

VR-based training has also shown promise in healthcare education. Studies have reported its effectiveness in medical and surgical training, enabling learners to practice procedures in a risk-free environment [5]. VR simulations have been utilized to train healthcare professionals in scenarios ranging from patient interactions to complex surgical procedures. These simulations offer a level of realism and interactivity that traditional training methods often lack. In the specific context of nasopharyngeal swabbing, VR can provide a platform for practicing the procedure without the need for physical models, minimizing costs and infection risks [15].

While incentive-based learning and VR have demonstrated individual strengths in healthcare training, limited research has explored their combined impact, especially in the context of nasopharyngeal swabbing technique training. This study aims to bridge this gap by assessing the synergistic effects of incentive-based learning with incentive and VR in enhancing knowledge acquisition, reducing cognitive load, improving skill development, and increasing user engagement among healthcare professionals during the COVID-19 pandemic.

3 Designing and Building Simulation-Based Training Environments

A participatory design methodology was employed in the development of a virtual training simulator for the nasopharyngeal swabbing technique. This approach incorporated the expertise and viewpoints of both experienced nurses and nursing students. The purpose of this collaborative effort was to guarantee an accurate and expert guided representation in the virtual learning environment that complies with the principles of the eEML model.

For the development of simulation, Unity 3D simulation engine version 2020.3.42f1 using C# programming language was used. HoloLens 2 headset was used for these research activities. A physical 3D head model representing a person's head, which can be tilted, was utilized for skill evaluation of the swabbing procedure. For the physical swabbing test on the 3D head model, test kits containing the Swab and test tubes for specimen collection were provided.

4 Training Environments

Participants were either trained in the 3D virtual environment or the 3D virtual environment with incentives.

3D Virtual Environment Participants. Participants trained in a 3D simulation, as shown in Fig. 1 for COVID-19 nasal swabbing, were shown a series of 6 steps (Table 1) on how to nasal Swab. They could replay the training simulation as many times as they wished.

Table 1. Nasopharyngeal swab training procedure steps

Step Number	Step
1	Grab a swab from the table near the head model
2	Gently tilt the head of the model back approximately 70°
3	Grab a sterile test tube from the tray near the head model
4	Line the Swab with the model's nasal cavity and begin slowly inserting the Swab into the model's nasal cavity, only insert the Swab approximately 4 in or until resistance is felt
5	Break the Swab and leave the top half inside the tube and place the cap onto the tube, dispose of the other half
6	Place the test tube with the Swab in the sterile tray

3D Training Environment with Incentives. Participants went through the same simulation as the subjects from the 3D training environment. However, they additionally participated in the 3D virtual environment with incentives. Score and rank are awarded to players for each accurate action executed during the course of the simulation, as can been seen in Fig. 2.

Each step from Table 1 in the swabbing procedure was represented as a task as can from Figs. 3, 4 and 5.

They receive text and audio feedback following each attempt at a task, as detailed in Table 2. These points and rank function as a form of incentive, stimulating participants to pay greater effort to the training and try to achieve accuracy.

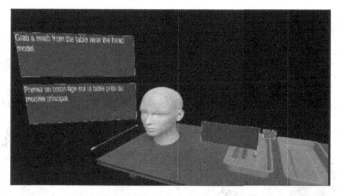

Fig. 1. 3D virtual environment

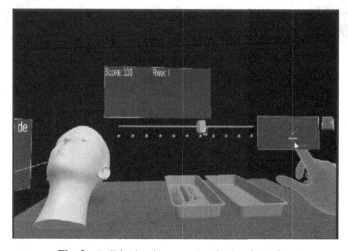

Fig. 2. 3D virtual environment with Score and rank can be seen on the Instruction Panel.

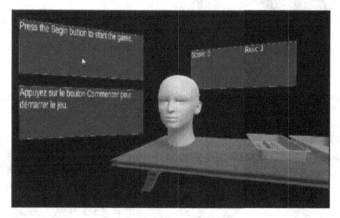

Fig. 3. A slider has been used as for head rotation

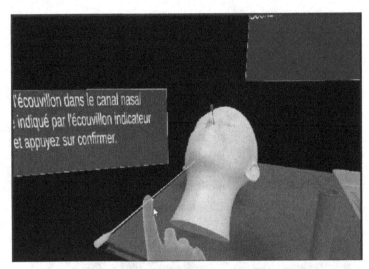

Fig. 4. The red Swab indicates the position where the real Swab has to be placed (Color figure online)

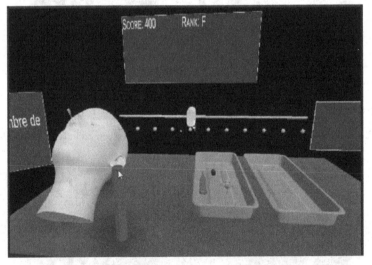

Fig. 5. Slider component for the number of times a swab has to be rotated inside the nasal cavity

Table 2. Voice and text feedback for each attempt in a task

	Correct attempt	Incorrect attempt
Audio Feedback	Success audio	Warning audio
Text Feedback	Promote to next level rank	No change in rank

5 Participants

Twenty participants were involved in this experiment. First ten participants were trained under 3D virtual environment whereas the next ten participants were trained under 3D virtual environment with incentives. Participants for this experiment included nurse trainees from Institut de Formation en Soins Infirmiers, as can be seen in Fig. 6.

Fig. 6. Nurse trainee interacting with simulation

6 Procedure

Upon entering the experimental room, participants were promptly instructed to take a seat. Prior to commencing the experiment, they were required to complete a pre-questionnaire. A comprehensive briefing was provided to the participants, outlining how instructions would be delivered during the course of the experiment. Then, they were asked to wear the HoloLens 2 headset to begin the simulation in a standing position. Based on the training environment, participants received instructions in the simulation to complete the procedure. Upon completing the experiment, participants were requested to complete the post-questionnaire. Following this, assessments were conducted to evaluate their knowledge acquisition, skill acquisition, and memory retention. Impact of cognitive load on the participants was also measured.

7 Assessments

Pre and post-tests [28] were conducted to assess participants' knowledge acquisition and the effectiveness of their learning in the nasal swab procedure. These questionnaires also aimed to evaluate the perceived benefits of the technology, the perceived complexity of the training, and the participant's willingness to use the technology on a regular basis.

The cognitive load was assessed using the NASA Task Load Index (TLX) [1]. To evaluate skill acquisition, participants performed the nasal swab procedure on a 3D head model after completing their training as can have been in Figs. 7 and 8. Additionally, participants were presented with a 3D head model positioned incorrectly and were asked to determine its correctness. If they identified it as incorrect, they were instructed to adjust the tilt position accordingly. The purpose of this Assessment was to evaluate the competence in conducting the swabbing process accurately and safely [2].

Fig. 7. Participants were assessed on their approach to inserting the Swab into the nasal cavity using a physical 3D model (shown in this image).

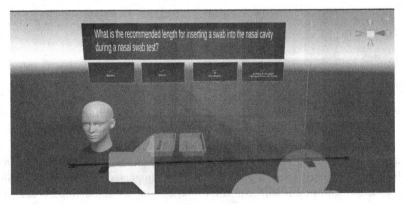

Fig. 8. 3D Assessment

Furthermore, an assessment was conducted to evaluate participants' retention of memory, where they were tasked with identifying objects they recalled from the simulation.

8 Analysis of Pre and Post Questionnaire

Table 3 compares participant responses in two VR environments, one with incentives and one without. The statements include beliefs about technology benefits and ease of use, as well as a preference for system usage. In both environments, participants strongly agreed about the technology's benefits and their desire for frequent use. However, the VR environment with incentives saw a stronger shift from neutral to strong agreement regarding the technology's ease of use compared to the environment without incentives.

Table 3. Participant responses (with and without incentives)

Criteria	Median for 3D Virtual Environment	Median VR Environment with Incentives	Range
I believe that this technology would be beneficial for me	Pre-test: Agree Post-test: Strongly Agree	Pre-test: Strongly Agree Post-test: Strongly Agree	Strongly Agree to Agree
I believe that using this technology would be uncomplicated	Pre-test: Neutral Post-test: Strongly Agree	Pre-test: Agree Post-test: Strongly Agree	Strongly Agree to Neutral
I think I would like to use this system more frequently	Pre-test: Strongly Agree Post-test: Strongly Agree	Pre-test: Strongly Agree Post-test: Strongly Agree	Strongly Agree to Agree

9 Impact on Skill and Knowledge Acquisition

The next set of assessment activities focused on the impact of incentive based learning on knowledge acquisition and skills acquisition after training with the physical head model and the VR based training of the swab testing procedures.

Null Hypothesis. Participants trained in the 3D virtual environment with incentive-based learning would have superior skill and knowledge acquisition compared to those trained without incentive based learning.

The number of participants were 20. Using the results of paired t-tests, the null hypothesis was rejected. The significant differences in pre-and post-test scores for both environments, as evidenced by the t-statistics and p-values (Environment 1: t-statistic of

−5.59, the p-value of 0.00023; Environment 2: t-statistic of −5.25, p-value of 0.00053), show that test scores improved statistically significantly within each environment. Furthermore, the environment with incentives demonstrated a greater increase in average test scores (46.66%) than the environment without incentives (30.30%). This significant difference in improvement supports the rejection of the null hypothesis, indicating that incentive-based learning in a 3D virtual environment resulted in better skill and knowledge acquisition than training without incentives.

The 3D assessment data show that participants in the 3D Virtual Environment with incentives were more successful (90%) in correctly identifying the length of the Swab than those in the standard 3D Virtual Environment (70%). This suggests that including incentives in the 3D learning experience may help participants acquire knowledge better.

However, it is important to note that skill acquisition remained similar in both environments, as none of the participants were able to accurately replicate the head angle required for the Nasopharyngeal swabbing technique on the physical head.

Cognitive Load. An incentive-based version of the training, when compared to a traditional 3D virtual environment, showed a slight increase in mental engagement but a significant decrease in physical demand and frustration levels. In comparison to the traditional setup, there was a noticeable decrease in physical demand (34.5 vs. 52.5) and participants reported less frustration (16.5 vs. 21). However, they felt that their performance was lower (29.5 vs. 50). These results imply that, despite perceptions of lower performance, adding incentives to training can make it less physically taxing and more rewarding.

Null Hypothesis. The addition of cognitive load through incentive-based learning in the simulation would hinder participant's ability to acquire skills and knowledge.

The null hypothesis cannot be rejected at the 0.05 alpha level, as the t-value of 1.56 is less than the critical t-value of ±2.101 for 18 degrees of freedom. This finding indicates that incentive-based learning does not significantly hinder participants' skill and knowledge acquisition. As a result, it can be concluded that including incentives in 3D VR simulations may not hinder from the learning process.

Memory Retention Test. The memory retention test, conducted after training in two different environments, was designed to assess (memory or) recall of objects used in nasopharyngeal swabbing, specifically the Swab, test tube, thermometer, and syringe. The majority of the participants in both environments remembered the Swab and test tube well but had limited recall of the thermometer and syringe. Our initial conclusions were that additional modifications were necessary to the simulation based training experiences to improve such recall tasks.

10   Discussions and Conclusion

This paper's primary conclusion is that incentive-based training significantly improves skill and knowledge acquisition involving participants during the swab training activities. Despite initial concerns about increased cognitive load, the assessment results indicated that incorporating incentives does not hinder the learning process. On the contrary, it appears to reduce physical demand and frustration, thereby improving the training experience. Although both environments effectively taught key aspects of nasopharyngeal swabbing, there is room for improvement in training design to improve recall. Overall, using incentives in a 3D virtual learning environment is a promising way to improve educational outcomes.

In summary, incentive-based learning in a 3D virtual training environment shows promise for healthcare professionals' training in safe procedures. It offers a solution to address their training needs while ensuring safety, particularly in the pandemic era. Future research can further optimize and tailor this approach, improving skill and knowledge acquisition for real-world scenarios.

Acknowledgement. The research activities discussed in this paper were funded through grants from the National Science Foundation (NSF) (grant numbers 2028077, 2106901 and 2050960).

References

1. Katona, J.: A review of human-computer interaction and virtual reality research fields in cognitive InfoCommunications. Appl. Sci. **11**(6), 2646 (2021). https://doi.org/10.3390/app 11062646
2. Sinha, G., Shahi, R., Shankar, M.: Human-computer interaction: a study on user experience design. In: Proceedings of the International Conference on Human Computer Interaction, pp. 123–135 (2023)
3. Meola, A., Cutolo, F., Carbone, M., Cagnazzo, F., Ferrari, M., Ferrari, V.: Augmented reality in neurosurgery: a systematic review. Neurosurg. Rev. **40**, 537–548 (2017)
4. Carmigniani, J., Furht, B., Anisetti, M., Ceravolo, P., Damiani, E., Ivkovic, M.: Augmented reality technologies, systems and applications. Multimedia Tools Appl. **51**(2), 341–377 (2011). https://doi.org/10.1007/s11042-010-0660-6
5. Lu, L., et al.: Applications of mixed reality technology in orthopedics surgery: a pilot study. Front. Bioeng. Biotechnol. **10**, 740507 (2022). https://doi.org/10.3389/fbioe.2022.740507
6. Schiffeler, N., Varney, V., Isenhardt, I.: Escape (the traditional class-) room: gamification and mixed reality in higher education. In: European Conference on Games Based Learning, pp. 614–XXII. Academic Conferences International Limited (2019)
7. Cecil, J., Sweet-Darter, M., Cecil-Xavier, A., Gupta, A.: Role of affordance, visual density and other HCC criteria in designing virtual learning environments to support STEM learning for autistic students. In: Proceedings of the IEEE Frontiers in Education Conference (FIE) (2021). https://doi.org/10.1109/FIE49875.2021.963713
8. Cecil, J., Kauffman, S., Gupta, A., McKinney, V., Pirela-Cruz, M.M.: Design of a human centered computing (HCC) based virtual reality simulator to train first responders involved in the Covid-19 pandemic. In: 2021 IEEE International Systems Conference (SysCon), pp. 1–7. IEEE (2021)
9. Moosavi, M.S., Williams, J., Guillet, C., Merienne, F., Cecil, J., Pickett, M.: Disassociation of visual-proprioception feedback to enhance endotracheal intubation. In: 2022 International Conference on Future Trends in Smart Communities (ICFTSC), pp. 233–236. IEEE (2022)
10. Zhao, K., Guo, X.: Analysis of the application of virtual reality technology in football training. J. Sens. (2022)
11. Gmez-Portes, C., Carneros-Prado, D., Albusac, J., Castro-Schez, J.J., Glez-Morcillo, C., Vallejo, D.: PhyRe up! A system based on mixed reality and gamification to provide home rehabilitation for stroke patients. IEEE Access **9**, 139122–139137 (2021)

12. Barrett, N., Swain, I., Gatzidis, C., Mecheraoui, C.: The use and effect of video game design theory in the creation of game-based systems for upper limb stroke rehabilitation. J. Rehabil. Assist. Technol. Eng. **3**, 2055668316643644 (2016)

13. Koskinen, A., Tolvi, M., Jauhiainen, M., Kekäläinen, E., Laulajainen-Hongisto, A., Lamminmäki, S.: Complications of COVID-19 nasopharyngeal swab test. JAMA Otolaryngol. Head Neck Surg. **147**(7), 672–674 (2021)

14. Cecil, J., Kauffman, S., Cecil-Xavier, A., Gupta, A., McKinney, V., Sweet-Darter, M.: Exploring human-computer interaction (HCI) criteria in the design and assessment of next generation VR based education and training environments. In: 2021 IEEE Conference on Virtual Reality and 3D User Interfaces Abstracts and Workshops (VRW), pp. 524–525. IEEE (2021)

15. By Arcadian. http://www.cortexity.com:8080/nicksblog/images/pharynx.jpg. Public Domain. https://commons.wikimedia.org/w/index.php?curid=789690

16. Clinical Head and Neck and Functional Neuroscience Course Notes, 2008–2009, Uniformed Services University of the Health Sciences School of Medicine, Bethesda, Maryland

17. Kim, D.H., Kim, D., Moon, J.W., Chae, S.W., Rhyu, I.J.: Complications of nasopharyngeal swabs and safe procedures for COVID-19 testing based on anatomical knowledge. J. Korean Med. Sci. **37**(11), e88 (2022). https://doi.org/10.3346/jkms.2022.37.e88. PMID:35315599; PMCID: PMC8938608

18. Pondaven-Letourmy, S., Alvin, F., Boumghit, Y., Simon, F.: How to perform a nasopharyngeal swab in adults and children in the COVID-19 era. Eur. Ann. Otorhinolaryngol. Head Neck Dis. **137**(4), 325–327 (2020). https://doi.org/10.1016/j.anorl.2020.06.001. Epub 2020 Jun 5. PMID: 32646750; PMCID: PMC7274641

19. Purohit, S., Rao, P.K., Rawtani, D.: Sampling and analytical techniques for COVID-19. In: Rawtani, D., Hussain, C.M., Khatri, N. (eds.) COVID-19 in the Environment, pp. 75–94. Elsevier (2022). ISBN 9780323902724. https://doi.org/10.1016/B978-0-323-90272-4.00008-7

20. Kiryakova, G., Angelova, N., Yordanova, L.: Gamification in education. In: Proceedings of 9th International Balkan Education and Science Conference, vol. 1, pp. 679–684 (2014)

21. Aparicio, A.F., Vela, F.L.G., Sánchez, J.L.G., Montes, J.L.I.: Analysis and application of gamification. In: Proceedings of the 13th International Conference on interacción persona-ordenador, pp. 1–2 (2012)

22. McKeown, S., Krause, C., Shergill, M., Siu, A., Sweet, D.: Gamification as a strategy to engage and motivate clinicians to improve care. In: Healthcare Management Forum, vol. 29, no. 2, pp. 67–73. Sage CA: Los Angeles, CA: SAGE Publications (2016)

23. Pesare, E., Roselli, T., Corriero, N., Rossano, V.: Game-based learning and gamification to promote engagement and motivation in medical learning contexts. Smart Learn. Environ. **3**, 1–21 (2016)

24. Molero, D., Schez-Sobrino, S., Vallejo, D., Glez-Morcillo, C., Albusac, J.: A novel approach to learning music and piano based on mixed reality and gamification. Multimedia Tools Appl. **80**, 165–186 (2021)

25. Ulmer, J., Braun, S., Cheng, C.T., Dowey, S., Wollert, J.: Gamification of virtual reality assembly training: Effects of a combined point and level system on motivation and training results. Int. J. Hum. Comput. Stud. **165**, 102854 (2022)

26. Villagrasa, S., Fonseca, D., Durán, J.: Teaching case: applying gamification techniques and virtual reality for learning building engineering 3D arts. In: Proceedings of the Second International Conference on Technological Ecosystems for Enhancing Multiculturality, pp. 171–177 (2014)

27. NASA. NASA TLX (2021). https://humansystems.arc.nasa.gov/groups/TLX/

28. Lewis, J.R.: Comparison of four TAM item formats: effect of response option labels and order. J. Usability Stud. **14**(4) (2019)

29. Gupta, A., Cecil, J., Pirela-Cruz, M., Ramanathan, P.: A virtual reality enhanced cyber-human framework for orthopedic surgical training. IEEE Syst. J. **13**(3), 3501–3512 (2019)
30. Cecil, J., Krishnamurthy, R., Gupta, A.: Exploring immersive simulation-based design frameworks in support of the moon mission. In: Proceedings of the 13th Annual IEEE International Systems Conference, Orlando, Florida, 8–11 April 2019 (2019)
31. Cecil, J., Kanchanapiboon, A.: Virtual engineering approaches in product and process design. Int. J. Adv. Manuf. Technol. **31**(9–10), 846–850 (2007)
32. Cecil, J., Jones, J.: An advanced virtual environment for micro assembly. Int. J. Adv. Manuf. Technol. **72**(1), 47–56 (2014)
33. Cecil, J., Albuhamood, S., Cecil-Xavier, A., Ramanathan, P.: An advanced cyber physical framework for micro devices assembly, special issue on "advanced cps for industry 4.0 - enabling technologies, real-world implementations, and impact assessments. IEEE Trans. Syst. Man Cybern. Syst. **49**(1), 92–106 (2017)
34. Cecil, J., Gupta, A., Pirela-Cruz, M., Ramanathan, P.: A network based virtual reality simulation training approach for orthopedic surgery. ACM Trans. Multimedia Comput. Commun. Appl. (TOMM) **14**(3), 1–21 (2018)
35. Gupta, A., Cecil, J., Pirela-Cruz, M.: A multi-level HXRI-based approach for XR-based surgical training. In: Proceedings of the IEEE Systems Man Cybernetics (SMC) Conference, Hawaii, USA, 1–4 October 2023 (2023)

The Co-design of Simulation-Based Training for Collaboration Between Healthcare Services

Jo E. Hannay[1]([✉])[ID], Sinan S. Tanilkan[2][ID], Trenton W. Schulz[2][ID], and Natalia I. Hansen[1]

[1] Simula Metropolitan Center for Digital Engineering, Department of IT Management, OsloMet, Pb. 4 Street Olavs plass, 0130 Oslo, Norway
johanny@simula.no
[2] Norwegian Computing Center, Pb. 114 Blindern, 0314 Oslo, Norway
{sinan,trenton.schulz}@nr.no

Abstract. As part of developing simulation-based training for better collaboration between healthcare services, we developed instruments for measuring key teamwork constructs *role understanding (responsibility)*, *trust*, *communication* and *collaboration* as experienced during simulation-based training in virtual reality. We co-designed these instruments together with healthcare workers and healthcare students in three workshops and a survey. We followed a method for generating unidimensional *Thurstone scales* with equal-appearing intervals. We then used the instruments in training sessions with healthcare students. We gathered feedback on the simulation and conducted initial analyses on the instrument data. Results are encouraging for the simulation design, but with clear points for improvement. The preliminary analyses from the instruments indicate that they seem to measure the intended constructs as perceived by the training audience. Correlational analyses indicate relationships between these constructs, particularly highlighting the challenge of balancing responsibility with trust and collaboration. Findings advocate the potential in our approach to mirror realistically, and improve, collaborative practices among healthcare professionals.

Keywords: Scenario Design · Measurement Instruments · Healthcare Collaboration · Virtual Reality · Simulation-Based Training · Survey

1 Motivation

National health reforms geared towards efficiency tend to attempt to increase patient throughput by offloading post treatment onto local health services, often without implementing measures for the transfer, reception and treatment at local institutions. Norway and its neighboring Nordic countries have been at the forefront globally in organizing healthcare for its citizens. Nevertheless, recent research has uncovered that personnel with municipal healthcare services might not have the required skills regarding emergencies and general observation

© The Author(s), under exclusive license to Springer Nature Switzerland AG 2024
V. G. Duffy (Ed.): HCII 2024, LNCS 14711, pp. 326–345, 2024.
https://doi.org/10.1007/978-3-031-61066-0_20

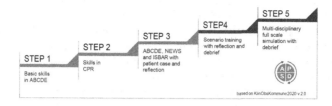

Fig. 1. Steps of the KlinObsKommune framework

abilities [1]. Furthermore, specialist staff at hospitals do not have sufficient knowledge about the skills of municipal healthcare personnel. Collaboration and communication issues due to different fields of expertise, work cultures, non-interoperable processes [2–4] and suboptimal, non-interoperable IT services [5–7] regularly lead to frustration for all involved. In the past years, studies focusing on capability improvement have greatly highlighted the urgent need for enhanced training in emergency response and observation skills among municipal health-care personnel [8]. This is crucial as healthcare personnel face increasingly complex cases due to earlier hospital discharges, emphasizing the necessity for systematic professional development to ensure high-quality patient care.

Healthcare workers in several Norwegian municipalities have in the recent years initiated work to improve on this situation, and developed, among other things, the Clinical Observation in Municipalities Competence Model (KlinObsKommune) [9], which addresses the education of municipal and specialist healthcare personnel in a five-step model (Fig. 1). In Steps 1 and 2, personnel train their skills in systematic patient observation using the *Airway, Breathing, Circulation, Disability, Exposure* (ABCDE) approach [10] and cardiopulmonary resuscitation (CPR). In Step 3, the integration of ABCDE with the *National Early Warning Score* (NEWS) for further clinical observation and decision-making is trained, together with the communication format *Identify, Situation, Background, Assessment and Recommendation* (ISBAR) [11]. Step 4 concerns training the ensuing collaboration within the municipal healthcare system to handle clinical patient deterioration, and Step 5 concerns training the ensuing collaboration between municipal and specialist healthcare systems. Focusing on Steps 4 and 5 is crucial as they address the vital need for enhanced collaboration between municipal and specialist healthcare systems.

Reality does *not*, at present, comply with the KlinObsKommune model. It takes time for Steps 1–3 to be fully in place, and one has to train collaboration skills even when basic skills are lacking [12]. We are therefore developing simulation-based training for collaboration, with the backdrop that basic skills are not in place.

2   Simulation-Based Training

We are developing a series of vignettes for training collaboration between health-care workers in and between healthcare units. A vignette is a small, reusable, temporarily ordered set of events that are ideally self-contained so that they can be reused in multiple scenarios [13]. The idea is that the vignettes can be combined to form a larger parts of patient processing through and across multiple healthcare units and services; for example from the patient's home, via various municipal services to the hospital and back.

Here, we focus on a vignette that starts at the patient's home and which concerns the first stage of collaboration to determine how and where the patient should be treated next. Figure 2 shows the flow of the vignette under development, where a home care worker must detect clinical deterioration in a patient. The worker might not be proficient in ABCDE, NEWS or ISBAR, and in reality, this has led to unfortunate outcomes for patients, when home care workers spend valuable time consulting peers or their administrative nurse in charge (which may be unavailable) or, in a worst-case scenario, may simply leave the premises counting on the next shift to deal with the problem. This vignette was developed earlier in a workshop with health administrators and practitioners to match situations that a home care worker may encounter [14]. In the vignette, the worker should consult the next stage in patient management, which is the emergency room. If the worker cannot perform ABCDE, NEWS or ISBAR satisfactorily, the emergency room nurse is to recognize this and collaborate with the home care worker in performing these procedures over the telephone and to reach a safe decision for the patient, rather than asking the home care worker to call back after all the observations are conducted.

The training sessions are based on deliberate practice principles [15] and integrate the PEARLS debriefing tool [16] to enhance learning [17]. The session consist of the following steps:

1. Introduction and learning objectives
2. Training in the vignette
3. PEARLS debrief with discussions on learning objectives and points of improvement
4. Retraining in the vignette
5. PEARLS debrief with discussions on learning objectives, changes from the first training session and points of improvement in real-life practice

The small circular (orange) symbols in Fig. 2 indicate points of observation during a play and prompts for ensuring the play is completed. For example, at the uppermost phone symbol, there is an observations point as to whether the home care worker makes a phone call, a prompt for making the call if it is evident that the home care worker is not intending to make the call, and a note that the failure to do so is to be discussed in the debrief. All of these activities are denoted *Game Master activities*, reflecting that plays are facilitated by a game master. However, some of theses activities may be covered automatically when computerized simulation systems are involved, and may also be registered by self-reflection in non-facilitated versions of the play; for example, when participants are given the opportunity to train at their own leisure for efficiency reasons.

There are a number of observation points in the diagram, but the current stage of the co-design effort focuses on those highlighted in frames: *role*

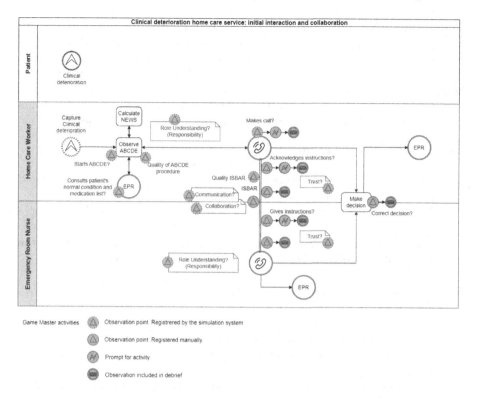

Fig. 2. Work flow in vignette for a clinical deterioration collaboration case

understanding (responsibility), *trust*, *communication* and *collaboration*. These four concepts arose as central points for improvement in the above-mentioned workshop [14].

3 Training Objectives and Key Results

We formulate the training objectives and desired observable outcomes in terms of *Objectives and Key Results* (OKR) [18]. OKRs are used in a variety of ways; including at the organizational, team and individual levels. For the current study, the individual and team levels are appropriate. While we have decided to fix the objectives for the current vignette based on the workshop with healthcare administrators and practitioners [14], we wish to co-design the key results that operationalize the concepts together with the specific health care workers that constitute the vignette's main training audience. The reason for this is twofold: First, this adheres to design principles we state below for increasing the relevance of measurement instruments. Secondly, when searching extensively for suitable measurement instruments in the literature, we found measurement items that concern responsibility and trust as more persistent traits at the institutional and personal levels, but nothing that pertains to these concepts in *a given situation*. For communication and collaboration, there are bodies of work on how to analyze discourse [19,20] and interaction [21–23], but these rely on content and thematic analyses of transcripts of verbal interaction, whereas we are interested in measuring communication and communication as experienced in the situation. In the OKRs below for the vignette in Fig. 2, some suggestions for key results are given, but these are to be determined in the co-design workshops.

Home Care Worker (Individual):
  Objectives:
    – To increase my role understanding, in terms of my responsibility and my importance in this situation
    – To increase my trust in the person with whom I am collaborating
  Key Results:
    – I take better responsibility for making sure to understand the patient's clinical status with the means at my disposal
    – ...

Emergency Room Nurse (Individual):
  Objectives:
    – To increase my role understanding, in terms of my responsibility and my importance in this situation
    – To increase my trust in the person with whom I am collaborating
  Key Results:
    – I take better responsibility for making sure to get the necessary information about the patient's clinical status from the caller.
    – I try harder to instill trust in my collaboration with the home care worker

    – ...

Both (Team):
  Objectives:
    – To improve communication per telephone
    – To improve collaboration per telephone
  Key Results:
    – We are better at constructive communication toward deciding the next step for taking care of the patient
    – We are better at having a shared constructive development toward uncovering the patient's clinical status

    – ...

An objective and its key results speak in terms of changes on underlying constructs; here, *role understanding*, *trust*, *collaboration* and *communication*. A construct consists of a concept together with measurable indicators. This constitutes a reflective measurement model, in which the indicators operationalize the concept [24].

4   The Virtual Reality Application

We opted to create a Virtual Reality (VR) training program for health personnel, allowing healthcare personnel to practice complex scenarios and communication strategies in a controlled environment. Its immersive nature allows for a realistic simulation of healthcare scenarios—enabling practitioners from various disciplines to engage in collaborative tasks in a controlled, risk-free environment. This hands-on approach has the possibility to facilitate a deeper understanding of each other's roles, challenges, and communication styles, which is critical in a multidisciplinary healthcare setting.

The vignette is the first of several that will be developed for collaboration training and implemented in a VR development platform (Unity) for simulation-based training. Apart from the immersive aspects, VR has been chosen for simulating various clinical deteriorations in patients and for enabling distributed training at locations where human markers (enacting ill patients) or physical simulation dolls may not be available.

After registering their name and joining a group (for pairwise training), participants will find themselves in the lobby for the introduction and debrief (Fig. 3). Upon entry, they will see avatars of the other participants in the simulation, read the training objectives, choose their role (home care worker or emergency room nurse), and commence training. can talk to each other in the lobby.

Once the training starts, participants are either a home care worker in a patient's home (Fig. 4) or a nurse taking calls for the municipality's emergency room (Fig. 5). In the patient's home, there is a screen showing basic patient information, the patient's habitual state and page for registering patient

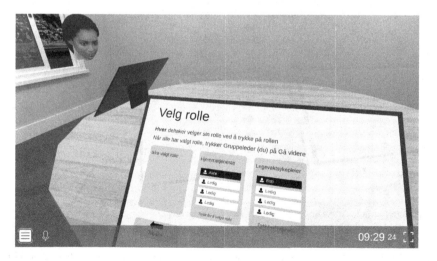

Fig. 3. In the lobby, prior to training, participants choose roles and initiate training. The lobby is also where the debrief takes place.

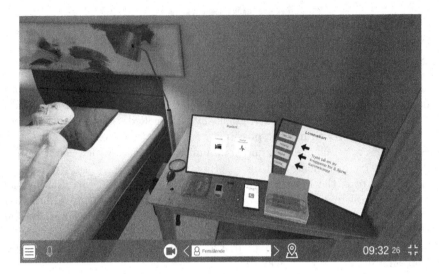

Fig. 4. In the patient home, the home care worker can use tools to check on the status of the patient and call the emergency room to discuss the next steps. Communication with the emergency room should be done using ABCDE and ISBAR.eps

measurements. There are also tools for checking the patient's vital signs and a telephone for calling the emergency room. Further, there is a screen that provides the ISBAR, ABCDE and NEWS procedures. These screens emulate what home care workers usually have on their hand-held devices and on procedural

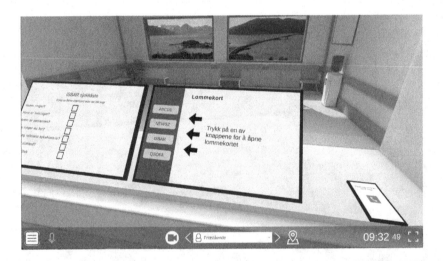

Fig. 5. In the emergency room, the emergency room nurse takes calls from the home care worker, communicates using ABCDE and ISBAR, and comes to a solution for the next step with the home care worker.

quick reference cards. The care worker is to examine the patient and determine what should be done next (possibly with the help of the emergency room nurse).

In the emergency room, the nurse has screens that provide checklists for ABCDE, ISBAR, and NEWS, as well as a medical index used in their daily work for triage and diagnosis. In addition, there is a telephone where the nurse can receive calls from the home care worker. At this point in the simulation, they can only discuss with each other after picking up the phone. Although it is possible in the scenario for the emergency room nurse to call the home care worker, the instructions are to wait for the call and insist on getting information via ISBAR and ABCDE, helping the home care worker to do so, if necessary.

5   Studies

For the co-design of the measurement instruments for the four constructs *role understanding (responsibility)*, *trust*, *collaboration* and *communication*, we conducted three workshops with participants from four municipalities, where home care workers and emergency room nurses played the vignette to experience the situation in the vignette; whereupon they were interviewed on what actions (on the part of either role) they would say were characteristic of each of the four constructs. Several hundreds of statements were elicited in the three workshops. These statements were then used to form a survey in which respondents were to rate the degree to which each statement witnesses the relevant construct. The survey was distributed to healthcare workers, as well as to the training audience for the planned training session at the end. We then used the instrument in an actual training session in an educational setting at a high school that has a program for training health-care workers at the vocational level. Figure 6 summarizes these activities. We will describe each of them in the following sections.

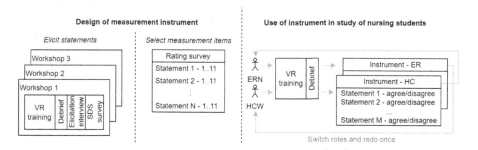

Fig. 6. Overview of the research process: Elicitation of statements (three workshops), selection of measurement items (survey), and the use of the instrument (workshop). Participating actors are emergency room nurses (ER) and home care workers (HC).

5.1 Design Approach for the Measurement Instruments

We declared the following design principles for the co-design of the measurement instruments for the four constructs:

Direct relevance: Those whose skills will be measured will be involved in designing the measurement items

Situational focus: The measurements concern the situation in the vignette

Structured elicitation: The measurement items are to be elicited in a structured manner

The co-design workshops described below observed these principles.

5.2 Co-design Workshops

We conducted three co-design workshops on three separate days with home care workers and emergency room nurses in four municipalities in a region of Norway. Workshops 1 and 2 involved healthcare professionals from one municipality each, while Workshop 3 involved healthcare professionals from the two remaining municipalities. A total of nine pairs of home care workers and emergency room nurses participated in the workshops by playing the simulation pair by pair. In each play, the home care worker used a VR headset and two hand controllers to join the simulation, while the emergency room nurse and the game master joined the simulation on their respective PC desktop clients. The emergency room nurses also had pen and paper for taking notes.

Each play started with a brief introduction from the researchers as to the overall purpose of the workshop. Then the home care worker and the emergency room nurse went to separate rooms. The home care worker was led through basic training in the VR environment for gaining familiarity with the headset and controls and for handling the medical equipment for measuring blood pressure, O^2 saturation and temperature and for examining a virtual patient by sight and touch. The emergency room nurse was familiarized with the virtual emergency room environment and also entered the equipment training area via the desktop client to become familiar with how the virtual equipment functions for the home care worker.

After this, both participants entered the lobby, chose names and the appropriate roles, and were presented with ethics and confidentiality information, as well as the learning objectives (Sect. 3). The simulation started with the health care worker entering the apartment of a patient and the emergency room nurse taken to the telephone dispatch at an emergency room. To help when there was ambiguity in the simulation and to maintain the flow in the simulation, one of the researchers facilitated the simulation as a game master [25]. The game master also gave voice to the patient to respond to home care workers who spoke with the patient. The simulation was then played through once with a PEARLS debrief facilitated by the game master. For these elicitation workshops, retraining was dropped. The game master then invited the participants back to reality and the VR equipment was parked.

We then commenced a structured method for developing unidimensional *Thurstone scales* with equal-appearing intervals [26] for each construct. Based on the experience they had just been through, we elicited potential measurement items by posing directed question for each of the basic constructs and asking participants what it is to act, in the particular situation of the vignette, according to a healthcare professional that does, and does not, exhibit role understanding (responsibility), trust, good communication and good collaboration. The elicitation session took the form of a structured interview on the questions in Fig. 7.

We found that is was better to ask these questions in an interview form, rather than as a survey, as this allowed us to focus the participants and to prompt the participants to consider additional conditions in the situation. For example, if an emergency room nurse would say "the home care worker would have vital readings ready before calling", we could ask, "what if the home care worker doesn't know how to take these readings?"

Providing an interview form was also beneficial for employing the Thurstones scaling method, allowing for a more dynamic interaction, and enabling us as researchers to probe deeper into the initial responses to the questions,

---

1. In the situation you were in, what does a home care worker do who takes responsibility for the patient?
2. In the situation you were in, what does an emergency room nurse do who takes responsibility for the patient?
3. In the situation you were in, what does a home care worker do who does not take responsibility for the patient?
4. In the situation you were in, what does an emergency room nurse do who does not take responsibility for the patient?
5. In the situation you were in, what does a home care worker do who trusts the person they are talking to on the phone?
6. In the situation you were in, what does an emergency room nurse do who trusts the person they are talking to on the phone?
7. In the situation you were in, what does a home care worker do who does not trust the person they are speaking to on the phone?
8. In the situation you were in, what does an emergency room nurse do who does not trust the person they are speaking to on the phone?
9. In the situation you were in, what do a home care worker and an emergency room nurse do who communicate well over the phone?
10. In the situation you were in, what do a home care worker and an emergency room nurse do who communicate poorly over the phone?
11. In the situation you were in, what do a home care worker and an emergency room nurse do who collaborate well over the phone?
12. In the situation you were in, what do a home care worker and an emergency room nurse do who collaborate poorly over the phone?

Fig. 7. Questions used for eliciting statements on the four constructs

ensuring that statements generated for scaling could capture a more comprehensive range of perspectives and situations. Furthermore, this would enhance the scaling process by ensuring that the statements are grounded in real-world experiences, which can facilitate a more accurate analysis (in terms of medians and interquartile ranges; see below) of the responses from the participants.

5.3   The Simulation Design Scale

Although not the main purpose of the elicitation studies, we asked all the participants to answer the Simulation Design Scale (SDS) [27] to get feedback on the simulation design and implementation. As can be seen from the boxplots in Fig. 8, the median responses vary between agree (4) and strongly agree (5). It is worth noting that the statement that is perhaps the most important for the design of the simulation—D13: *The simulation allowed me the opportunity to prioritize nursing assessments and care*—had more variation in responses than most other statements. Still, the median response is 4 (agree).

In conjunction to administering the SDS, we also asked for concrete points for improvement. The most important points concerned confusion on the part of the home care worker when entering the patient's room, due to the open screens next to the patient. These screens display information and entry forms that the home care worker might access on their handheld device at need, but when presented

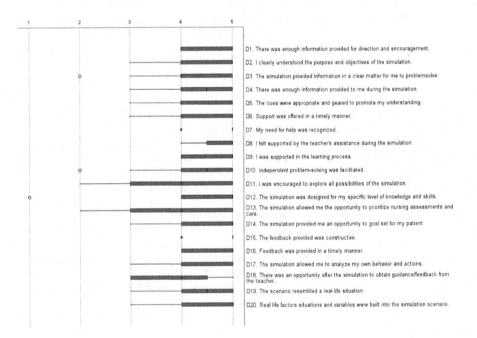

Fig. 8. Results from the SDS survey, with ratings from 1 (strongly disagree) to 5 (strongly agree). The statements D1–D20 and the rating scale can be found in [27].

upon entry, this presented too strong a cue to some participants, who focused their attention on these screens (perhaps thinking there were instructions on what to do in the simulation), rather than attending to the patient. This is part of a general issue of giving the ownership of when to use information, and also when to use medical equipment, to the player. A solution to this is to position all equipment, together with the handheld device, in an emergency rucksack (which they have in real life), which they have to open actively to get access to equipment, after which the handheld device has to be screen unlocked to access any desired information and entry forms.

5.4   Selecting the Measurement Items

After the three elicitation workshops were completed (during Nov. 2023–Jan. 2024), the full set of 298 statements (sorted under their respective constructs) were presented in an online rating form distributed by email to home service workers and emergency room nurses in the four municipalities. The respondents were required to rate each statement according to how much the statement demonstrates the relevant construct (*role understanding* (*responsibility*), *trust*, *collaboration* and *communication*), on an 11-point scale from 1 (very little) to 11 (very much). To encourage responses, each complete response was awarded with a gift voucher of NOK 500. A total of 32 responses were recorded. We also distributed the rating form to the training audience for the planned training session at the vocational high school (gift voucher of NOK 300). Eight students responded, but two responses were invalid, leaving six responses for analysis.

Given the ratings for each statement, we computed the median and the interquartile range (IQR); i.e., the difference between the third and first quartile, selecting the statements with the smallest IQR; i.e., the smallest variance. There were sometimes ties, and some statements selected this way also happened to make less sense, so following [26], we used discretion in choosing statements when necessary. We also had to use statements with tied medians (e.g., 4.5) in place for integral medians (e.g., 5) in some cases.

For the planned training session at the vocational high school, we chose to use the ratings from the training audience for the training session, rather than the ratings from the professional health-care workers. We did this for two reasons. First, for pedagogical reasons, we wanted to show the students that they had themselves contributed to developing the instruments they would be subjected to (thereby also adhering strongly to the first design principle above). Secondly, the student's ratings were more evenly distributed across the 1–11 scale, making it much easier to use the method for developing the Thurstone instruments, than if we had use the ratings of the professionals who rated overwhelmingly at the extremities of the scale. Which rating is the "correct" one is open for discussion. It is possible to administer the instruments based on the professional health-care workers ratings when desired.

For this instance, the resulting instruments to be given to the home care workers are shown in Table 1 and in Table 2 for emergency room nurses. When administered, subjects are to indicate if they agree or disagree with each statement. To

Table 1. The instruments given to home care workers for each of the four constructs: Statements and their weights (the medians from the ratings). Subjects are to indicate if they agree or disagree with each statement.

Home Care Worker	Weight
Responsibility	
I assessed the situation, even though I am a student or unskilled.	5
I did not get along with the person at the emergency clinic and said as little as possible.	4
I made good observations, watched how the patient was breathing and performed ABC, even though I might not have been able to measure.	7
I chose not to call anyone.	2
I had vital measurements ready when I called.	8
I called for expert help due to lack of skills.	9
I took measurements where it was relevant.	6
I renounced responsibility and walked away from the situation.	1
I went in to the patient, saw that the patient was sick, and said I would come back later.	3
I ensured good communication and interaction with the emergency room nurse.	10
Trust	
I felt safe.	9
I contradicted the emergency nurse when I disagreed.	5
I shared what I did not know.	7
I became unsure of my own assessments.	6
I did not call and left the patient in a potentially critical condition.	3
I gave poor information and cooperated poorly with the emergency room nurse.	3
I did not dare to consult with the emergency room nurse.	4
I informed about the patient's condition.	8
Communication	
We ensured that the other person understood what was said.	10
We had hectic and stressed communication.	8
We moved on to other questions before we had clarity on the first one.	5
We let external things influence, such as stress about moving on to other tasks.	4
We talked over each other's heads.	3
We used the same healthcare terms.	9
We spoke over each other.	2
We responded poorly to each other's questions.	1
We were on the same wavelength and immediately said so when we did not understand things.	7
Collaboration	
We had a good dialogue, step by step.	8
The emergency room nurse asked the home care worker: Can you ask the patient about ...	9
We did not come to measures that we considered implementing.	5
We did not follow up on the observations we had made, afterward.	4
We did not catch what the other person in the conversation said.	3
We were both calm, not stressed, talked a little back and forth, considered further observations.	7
We did not listen to each other, were not professional, and had no respect for each other.	2
The emergency room nurse listened to the home care worker and had faith in the measurements they took.	6

Table 2. The instruments given to emergency room nurses for each of the four constructs: Statements and their weight (the medians from the ratings). Subjects are to indicate if they agree or disagree with each statement.

Emergency Room Nurse	Weight
Responibility	
I asked questions, took control of the situation, and built trust.	7
I worked with the home care worker to understand the patient's condition and situation.	6
I did not take the caller seriously, trivialized, and did not understand the responsibility I had for the person calling.	6
I did not follow up and left the responsibility to the home care worker.	4
I did not provide advice or guidance on how to handle the situation further.	4
I listened to the home care worker.	9
I behaved condescendingly towards the home care worker.	3
I said the conditiion would probably pass.	2
I gave feedback/confirmed information that was given.	8
Trust	
I trusted observations given by the home care worker.	10
I felt embarrassed, appeared dismissive, and thought what the home care worker said was not serious.	6
I overrode the home care worker, underestimated the condition, and did not trust what was said.	5
I did not take the home care worker seriously, even though they know the patient better.	4
I came across as competent and conscious in the conversation.	8
I was not cooperative.	3
I took the home care worker seriously, even with their lack of competence.	7
I responded with little engagement.	2
Communication	
We ensured that the other person understood what was said.	10
We had hectic and stressed communication.	8
We moved on to other questions before we had clarity on the first one.	5
We let external things affect us, like stress about moving on to other tasks.	4
We talked over each other's heads.	3
We used the same healthcare terms.	9
We spoke over each other.	2
We were on the same wavelength and immediately said so when we did not understand things.	7
We responded poorly to each other's questions.	1
Collaboration	
We were both calm, not stressed, talked back and forth, considering further observations.	7
The emergency room nurse listened to the home care worker and had faith in the measurements they took.	6
We did not come up with measures that we considered implementing.	5
We did not follow up on the observations we had made, afterwards.	4
The emergency room nurse asked the home care worker: Can you ask the patient about ...	9
We did not catch what the other person in the conversation said.	3
We did not listen to each other, were not professional, and did not have respect for each other.	2
We had a good dialogue, step by step.	8

get a subject's score on a construct, the weights of each agreed statement for the construct are summed and averaged over the total number of statements for that construct. These instruments form the key results for the objectives in Sect. 3.

5.5   Training Session

The training session followed the script in Sect. 2, where the instrument for each role was deployed immediately after each debrief. The retraining was done with switched roles. The students were not trained specifically for any of the two roles, but managed to enact their respective roles in the vignette satisfyingly.

The participants were twelve healthcare students at the vocational high-school level. Three pairs of students underwent training in parallel, and the students performed the PEARLS debrief unfacilitated. This was both deliberate, to examine the viability of unsupervised debriefs, and by necessity, since we did not have enough game masters for these parallel sessions.

After each debrief, the participants were welcomed back to the real world, and asked to complete the instrument for their role in the form of a survey where they would state if they agreed or disagreed to the statements in Tables 1 and 2. Each student played both roles in turn, and thus filled out both instruments.

5.6   Results from the Training Session

The data from the training session consists of the respondents' responses to the instruments for the four constructs (role understanding (responsibility), trust, communication and collaboration), as well timings in the simulation and the decisions for the patient made by the pairs. Table 3 shows participants by pairs

Table 3. Participant scores per pair (A–F) across *responsibility* (R), *trust* (T), *communication* (Com) and *collaboration* (Col), and the pair's decision for the patient. EMS is short for emergency medical services (ambulance).

| Pair | Round | Home care worker | | | | Emergency room nurse | | | | Decision for patient | | |
		R	T	Com	Col	R	T	Com	Col	Call EMS	Observe	Call doctor
A	1	3.8	3.6	3.2	4.3	3.3	3.1	3.9	3.3	x		
A	2	4.5	2.1	2.9	4.1	3.8	2.1	3.4	3.1	x		
B	1	3.3	4.0	2.9	3.8	4.0	3.1	2.9	3.8		x	
B	2	3.7	3.6	2.9	4.3	2.4	2.3	1.9	4.4		x	
C	1	4.5	1.6	4.6	2.3	3.3	3.1	2.4	3.8			x
C	2	3.7	3.6	4.2	3.3	3.3	3.9	5.0	3.8	x		
D	1	2.8	4.0	3.4	4.6	3.6	3.1	2.9	3.1		x	
D	2	4.5	2.1	2.9	2.6	3.6	3.1	3.3	3.8		x	
E	1	4.6	2.1	4.2	5.4	3.8	2.1	4.1	2.6			x
E	2	2.1	5.1	1.8	2.5	3.6	5.3	4.9	3.5		x	
F	1	4.5	3.0	2.3	3.8	3.3	3.1	3.6	3.8	x		
F	2	4.1	3.0	1.0	2.6	3.3	3.1	2.3	3.8	x		

Group Statistics

	Decision	N	Mean	Std. Deviation	Std. Error Mean
Resposibility	Call EMS	10	3.3511	.72125	.22808
	Observe	10	3.7711	.46467	.14694
Trust	Call EMS	10	3.5765	1.05615	.33398
	Observe	10	3.0765	.58408	.18470
Communication	Call EMS	10	2.9779	.85970	.27186
	Observe	10	3.1882	1.12469	.35566
Collaboration	Call EMS	10	3.6260	.70956	.22438
	Observe	10	3.5635	.49347	.15605

Group Statistics

	Call EMS	N	Mean	Std. Deviation	Std. Error Mean
Resposibility	yes	10	3.7711	.46467	.14694
	no	14	3.5516	.74323	.19864
Trust	yes	10	3.0765	.58408	.18470
	no	14	3.1982	1.11726	.29860
Communication	yes	10	3.1882	1.12469	.35566
	no	14	3.2225	.93763	.25059
Collaboration	yes	10	3.5635	.49347	.15605
	no	14	3.5904	.89875	.24020

Fig. 9. Comparison of means between individuals for the decision to call the emergency response service (EMS) and the decision to continue observing (top); and for the decision to call the emergency response service (EMS) and all other decisions (bottom).

and their scores across the four constructs, along with the pairs' decisions for the patient. The patient in this case is suffering from sepsis and should receive attention without much delay, so the most appropriate response of those suggested is to call emergency medical services (EMS), while the least appropriate response would be to continue observing over time. To see if our data revealed any relationships between the decision and the four constructs, we compared the score means of each construct between those individuals who were involved in the decision to call for EMS and those who decided to continue observing; see Fig. 9 (uppermost table). There are only minor and statistically insignificant differences in score means on all four constructs. We also compared score means between the decision to call the emergency response service (EMS) and all other decisions; see Fig. 9 (lowermost table), also with small insignificant differences. Thus, there does not seem to be any relation between how the students in our sample experienced the four constructs and the quality of the decision.

Next, we checked to see if there were any relations between the four constructs. Figure 10 shows correlations between the four constructs for home care workers (uppermost table) and for emergency room nurses (lowermost table). For the home care worker players, there is a significant strong negative correlation ($r = -.925$, $p < .001$) between *responsibilty* and *trust*, that might suggest an inverse dynamic. Within the VR training context, as the perception of taking responsibility increases, the level of trust may decrease, which, ostensibly, could pose potential challenges for collaborative practice. This should be investigated further, and if robust, should be thoughtfully addressed in training vignettes.

Correlations Home Care Workers

		Resposibility	Trust	Communication
Trust	Pearson Correlation	-.925**		
	Sig. (2-tailed)	.000		
	N	12		
Communication	Pearson Correlation	.270	-.388	
	Sig. (2-tailed)	.395	.212	
	N	12	12	
Collaboration	Pearson Correlation	.084	.008	.306
	Sig. (2-tailed)	.794	.981	.333
	N	12	12	12

**. Correlation is significant at the 0.01 level (2-tailed).

Correlations Emergency Room Nurses

		Resposibility	Trust	Communication
Trust	Pearson Correlation	.101		
	Sig. (2-tailed)	.755		
	N	12		
Communication	Pearson Correlation	.378	.546	
	Sig. (2-tailed)	.226	.066	
	N	12	12	
Collaboration	Pearson Correlation	-.656*	.161	-.435
	Sig. (2-tailed)	.021	.618	.157
	N	12	12	12

*. Correlation is significant at the 0.05 level (2-tailed).

Fig. 10. Correlations for home care workers (top) and for emergency room nurses (bottom)

For emergency room nurse players, there was a significant medium-to-strong negative correlation ($r = -.656$, $p = .021$) between *responsibility* and *collaboration*. Here, perhaps, emergency room worker players who take responsibility take charge of the situation and get into a mode of telling the home care worker what to do, rather than trying to figure out what to do together. Indeed, the vignette is designed for *in-situ* instruction of possibly unskilled home care workers by more experienced emergency room nurses, and the instructions to the emergency room nurse players are to help the caller to follow ABCDE and ISBAR.

6 Discussion

The study's findings indicate that there may be nuanced dynamics between *role understanding (responsibility)*, *trust*, *communication*, and *collaboration* in the situation played out in the vignette.

Notably, the negative correlations between *responsibility* and both *trust* and *collaboration* may indicate a phenomenon of taking responsibility in the sense of taking over when trust is low, with low collaboration as a result. This degree to which this is advantageous, is probably situation dependent. The possible dynamics in the challenges that highly responsible individuals may face in collaborative efforts would need further investigation.

7 Limitations

The most prominent threats to validity are the threats to construct and external validity. On the one hand, the entire study concerns the building of constructs in an empirical manner. On the other hand, the manner in which we did this has limitations. First, the number of responses was low, thereby limiting the validity of the instruments we developed. Further, we based the instrument on student input (although we did have input from healthcare professionals), which may not bring valid insights gained from experience into play. On the other hand, involving the training audience in developing the instrument would arguably increase its meaningfulness to the respondents, thereby heightening an aspect of construct validity. Our goal in these studies was to develop methodology, and we think that the methodology is sound, and that better validated instruments can be built using the same methodology with a larger set of respondents. Further, the question of validity also depends on whether the context is participatory for educational purpose or for professional training.

Using students for the training session poses a threat to external validity, in that the results from the training session may not transfer to other relevant settings; e.g., with professional healthcare workers. For example, the negative correlations observed in the data must be replicated in other training sessions if one wishes to use our reflections on the correlations in those settings, and there may then be other underlying causes for those observations than for ours. Also, the perceptions of the four constructs may be different between student and professionals, but this also depends on how general the constructs are across people, which is a construct validity question.

A further threat to validity is the possible selection bias introduced by rewarding responses with gift vouchers. However, we prioritized getting possibly biased responses over few, or no, responses. We are also uncertain as to what the bias would be in this case.

8 Conclusion

It is challenging to develop serious games with high relevance for professionals, and it is not straightforward to find and apply relevant validated instruments to measure the impact of simulation-based training on situational variables. In health care collaboration, difficulties with collaborations are often tacit and not expressed in ways that help on improving on the situation. We posit that using the design principles set forth and used in this article to develop the key results for vignettes formed around given objectives, will prove to be a favorable way to make simulation-based training more relevant.

Acknowledgements. The authors are grateful to the healthcare administrators of the four municipalities and Akerhus University Hospital for facilitating workshops and surveys and to healthcare professionals for their effort and responses during the various workshops. The authors are also grateful to training coordinator and critical care nurse Eva Linnerud for providing insights into the central aspects in our discussion and for the hard work of establishing administrative contacts at the municipalities. We wish to thank Akerhus University Hospital for lending us their VR headsets on short notice when ours failed. This research is funded by the Norwegian Research Council, project no. 321059 *Close the Gap – Simulation-based training for better collaboration within and between healthcare services.*

References

1. Valdersnes, A.K., Venjum, M.L.: Konsept Kompetanse-sentralen: Trygg i egen kommune Designdrevet innovasjonsprosjekt DIP. Tech. Rep, Kjeller Innovasjon, Kjeller, Norway (2016)
2. Gautun, H., Syse, A.:Earlier hospital discharge: A challenge for Norwegian municipalities. Nordic J. Social Res. **8** (2017)
3. Girdham, M.S.: District nurse views on improving the transfer of care from hospital to home. Primary Health Care **26**, 23–27 (2016)
4. Davis, M.M., Devoe, M., Kansagara, D., Nicolaidis, C., Englander, H.: Did I do as best as the system would let me? healthcare professional views on hospital to home care transitions. J. General Internal Med. **27**, 1649–1656 (2012)
5. Melby, L., Brattheim, B.J., Hellesø, R.: Patients in transition-Improving hospital-home care collaboration through electronic messaging: providers' perspectives. J. Clin. Nurs. **24**(23–24), 3389–99 (2015)
6. Brattheim, B.J., Hellesø, R., Melby, L.: Planning for post-hospital care—Local challenges to general benefits of e-messages: hospital staff's perspectives. In: Proceedings of 3rd European Workshop on Practical Aspects of Health Informatics (PAHI), 2015
7. Lyngstad, M., Melby, L., Grimsmo, A., Hellesø, R.: Toward increased patient safety? electronic communication of medication information between nurses in home health care and general practitioners. Home Health Care Manag. Pract. **25**, 203–211 (2013)
8. Sletner, A., Halvorsrud, L.: Systematic observation training (alert) in the municipal health service and the impact on job satisfaction. Sykepleien Forskning **15** (2020)
9. Centre for Development of Institutional and Home Care Services, Klinisk observasjonskompetanse i kommunehelsetjenesten (2021). https://www.utviklingssenter.noklinisk-observasjonskompetanse
10. Krarup, N.H.V., Grove, E.L., Rohde, C.V., Løfgren, B.: Initial assessment and treatment with the airway, breathing, circulation, disability, exposure (ABCDE) approach. Inter. J. General Med. **5**, 117–121 (2012)
11. Stewart, K.: SBAR, communication, and patient safety: an integrated literature review, Honor's Thesis, University of Tennessee Chattanooga, Chattanooga, Tennesee USA (Dec 2016)
12. Toppe, K., Navarsete, L.S.: Representantforslag om å be regjeringen evaluere samhandlingsreformen og fremme sak til Stortinget om nødvendige tiltak for at samhandlingsreformens intensjoner kan nås," Stortinget, Oslo, Norway, Representantforslag Dokument 8:19 S (2018–2019), Oct. 2018
13. Simulation Interoperability Standards Organization, SISO-GUIDE-006-2018 – Guideline on Scenario Development for Simulation Environments (2018)
14. Hannay, J.E., Fuglerud, K.S., Leister, W., Schulz, T.: Scenario design for healthcare collaboration training under suboptimal conditions. In: Duffy, V.G. (ed.) Digital Human Modeling and Applications in Health, Safety, Ergonomics and

Risk Management. Health, Operations Management, and Design, pp. 197–214 (2022). Springer International Publishing, Cham. https://doi.org/10.1007/978-3-031-06018-2_14

15. Ericsson, K.A.: An introduction to Cambridge Handbook of Expertise and Expert Performance: Its development, organization, and content. In: Ericsson, K.A., Charness, N., Feltovich, P.J., Hoffman, R.R. (eds.) The Cambridge Handbook of Expertise and Expert Performance, ch. 1, pp. 3–20. Cambridge Univ. Press (2006)

16. Bajaj, K., Meguerdichian, M., Thoma, B., Huang, S., Eppich, W., Cheng, A.: The PEARLS healthcare debriefing tool. Acad. Med. **93**(2), 336 (2018)

17. Høegh-Larsen, A.M., Ravik, M., Reierson, I.Å., Husebø, S.I.E., Gonzalez, M.T.: PEARLS debriefing compared to standard debriefing effects on nursing students. Professional Compet. Clin. Judgm. Quasi-Experim. Study Clinical Simulation Nursing **74**, 38–48 (2023)

18. Greenwood, R.G.: Management by objectives: as developed by Peter Drucker, assisted by Harold Smiddy. Acad. Manag. Rev. **6**(2) (1981)

19. Chan, C.K.K.: Peer collaboration and discourse patterns in learning from incompatible information. Instr. Sci. **29**, 443–479 (2001)

20. Hogan, K., Nastasi, B.K., Pressley, M.: Discourse patterns and collaborative scientific reasoning in peer and teacher-guided discussions. Cogn. Instr. **17**(4), 379–432 (2000)

21. Krystyniak, R.A., Heikkinen, H.W.: Analysis of verbal interactions during an extended, open-inquiry general chemistry laboratory investigation. J. Res. Sci. Teach. **44**(8), 1160–1186 (2007)

22. Bakeman, R., Gottman, J.M.: Observing Interaction: An Introduction to Sequential Analysis, 2nd edn. Cambridge Univ, Press (1997)

23. Okada, T., Simon, H.A.: Collaborative discovery in a scientific domain. Cogn. Sci. **21**(2), 109–146 (1997)

24. Diamantopoulos, A., Siguaw, J.A.: Formative versus reflective indicators in organizational measure development: a comparison and empirical illustration. British J. Manag. **17**, 263–282 (2006)

25. Tychsen, A., Hitchens, M., Brolund, T., Kavakli, M.: The Game Master. In: Proceedings of 2nd Australasian Conference on Interactive Entertainment, IE 2005. Creativity & Cognition Studios Press, Sydney, AUS, pp. 215–222 (2005)

26. Trochim, W.M.K.: The Research Methods Knowledge Base, 2nd ed. Atomic Dog Publishing (2001)

27. Reierson, I.Å., Sandvik, L., Solli, H., Haukedal, T.A., Husebø, S.E.: Psychometric testing of the norwegian version of the simulation design scale, the educational practices questionnaire and the student satisfaction and self-confidence in learning scale in nursing education. Inter. J. Nursing Stud. Adv. **2** (2020)

Use of Artificial Intelligence for Training:
A Systematic Review

Nina Jiang and Vincent G. Duffy[✉]

Purdue University, West Lafayette, IN 47906, USA
{jiang841,duffy}@purdue.edu

Abstract. With the rapid advancement of artificial intelligence, it has been widely applied in various domains to assist training, including education, medical, automation, and industrial fields. The purpose of this study is to deep dive into the use of artificial intelligence for training by conducting a systematic literature review. Bibliometric data were collected from multiple databases, including Web of Science, Scopus, and Google Scholar through Publish or Perish. The metadata analysis was performed by using VOSviewer, CiteSpace, etc. The results of the analysis indicated the importance of the research topic and the interdisciplinary nature of artificial intelligence-assisted training by clustering the prevalent keywords, such as human factor, deep learning, explainable artificial intelligence, generative artificial intelligence, education, and medical. The research underscores the potential of artificial intelligence in transforming traditional training paradigms. Also emphasizes the limitations of state-of-the-art applications and proposes the need for further exploration in various domains, including the comprehensive evaluation of the system, and personalized artificial intelligence training systems in specific domains.

Keywords: Artificial Intelligence · Human Factors · Training · Bibliometric analysis · VOSviewer · CiteSpace

1 Introduction and Background

Training is an important aspect of the life of a modern society and to maintain competitive advantages (Salvendy 2012). With the innovations of instructional approaches and technological advances in multidiscipline, the training has experienced rapid growth. By incorporating the rapidly advanced Artificial Intelligence (AI) algorithms, AI is gradually applied to various domains for training assistants and evaluation, including Human Factors (HF), medical, education, automation, and industrial.

AI-assisted training is an emerging area that adopts machine learning algorithms as backbones to enhance the learning process through customized training, progress tracking, and providing real-time feedback; thereby creating an effective learning environment. It can apply to various fields to provide different levels of assistance, such as elementary mathematics, college engineering courses, staff training, and medical procedure guidance. Mathletics, which is an AI-powered learning application that provides

© The Author(s), under exclusive license to Springer Nature Switzerland AG 2024
V. G. Duffy (Ed.): HCII 2024, LNCS 14711, pp. 346–363, 2024.
https://doi.org/10.1007/978-3-031-61066-0_21

tailored lessons to students to adapt their levels and progress (Darragh 2021). In K-12 education, AI-assisted training systems can improve children's drawing ability by improving students' painting performance and their performance in color recognition, imagination, expressiveness, originality, and richness (Chen, Lin, and Chien 2022). The large language model in medical training has been demonstrated to effectively achieve decent scores in the United States Medical Licensing Exam (USMLE) and the MedQA exam (Huang et al. 2023; Nagi et al. 2023). Therefore, AI-assisted training led to a paradigm shift in the training process in various areas.

The advantages of applying AI in training have various aspects. Not only does it provide personalized and flexible learning experiences for different user groups, but it also contributes towards accessibility and sustainability as it reduces dependency on location, and physical textbook requirements. The data-driven nature of machine learning models empowers AI to analyze the vast amount of data, which could offer insights into the learning and training effectiveness and deficiencies for the user (W. Li et al. n.d.; Mosqueira-Rey et al. 2023). Furthermore, the Explainable AI (XAI) in the training offers understandable explanations and transparency to build trust, facilitate learning, and ensure accountability (Parchomovsky 2000).

2 Purpose of Study

The purpose of this study is to conduct a systematic literature review of the articles in the field of AI-assisted training in multiple areas to investigate the feasibility and prevalence of adopting AI in the training process. This study aims to offer a comprehensive overview of the achievements in this direction and identify the research gaps in current research. The bibliometric data are collected from various databases: World of Science, Scopus, Google Scholar, and National Science Foundation (NSF) Awards. Then, by using visualization tools to provide a thorough analysis of the collected metadata (Kanade and Duffy 2024).

3 Research Methodology

3.1 Data Collection

In order to gather bibliometric data, multiple databases were utilized. Including Google Scholar, Scopus, Web of Science, and NSF Awards (Table 1).

Table 1 presents the search results on different databases by using various search terms. It can be proved that the search results can be limited by adding more terms. To be noted that Harzing has 1000 articles because the limit per search of Publish or Perish is up to 1000 (Parchomovsky 2000; Kanade and Duffy 2020). The bibliometric data were exported from Web of Science (WOS), Scopus, and Harzing into the text format, including the full records (article titles, source, authors, and abstracts) and cited references.

Table 1. Database and search terms.

Database	Search Term	Number of Articles
Web of Science	"AI in training"	12,775
Scopus	"AI AND assisted AND training"	14,808
Google scholar	"AI assisted training"	1,250,000
Harzing	"AI in training"	1000

3.2 Trend Analysis

The Google Ngram offers users the trend plot in various keywords over time. This trend analysis ranges from 1980 to 2019. As illustrated in Fig. 1, it presents how these terms changed over time for human factors, ergonomic, human-centered design, medical training, safety training, and trustworthiness. Those are core elements for the AI in the training. Figure 1 implies the increased awareness of human-centered training in multiple fields with the development of AI technologies in recent years.

However, the term "AI in training" or "AI-assisted training" was unable to find the Ngram. Therefore, further trend analysis on different databases is employed to support that this topic is an emerging area.

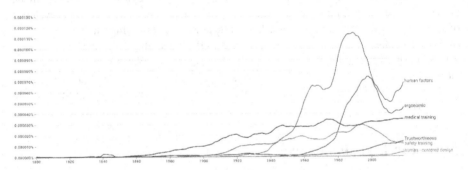

Fig. 1. Google Ngram trend analysis

In order to present the most recent trend analysis, results from Scopus and Web of Science are also provided in Fig. 2 and Fig. 3, which both directly reflect the rapid growth in "AI in training" in recent years by the exponential increase in the volume of related documents.

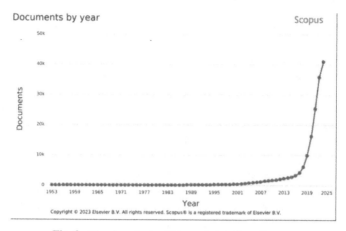

Fig. 2. Trend analysis of the metadata from Scopus

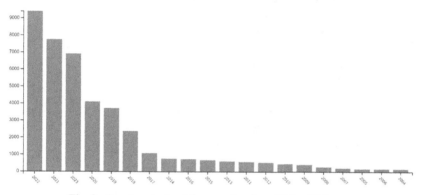

Fig. 3. Trend analysis of the metadata from Web of Science.

4   Results

4.1   Co-citation Analysis

Co-citation in bibliometrics analysis is aimed at analyzing the relationship between two or more published works (scholarly writeups, research papers, or books) when both are cited by some third source (Osareh 1996). It is a way of helping researchers to better understand how the cited work in a particular field relates with and influences each other's. VOSviewer is a powerful co-citation analysis tool (Jan van Eck and Waltman 2022). Initially, the citations must be exported in the required format with all essential information included. Following this, one should select the analysis type and import the dataset, which may be in CSV or another format, into VOSviewer and then configure the necessary parameters (T. Duffy and Duffy 2023; Kanade and Duffy 2022). The confirmation of cited references will be displayed prior to completing the process, as illustrated in Fig. 4. The detailed nodes and their associations of the analysis are depicted in Fig. 5.

Selected	Cited reference	Citations	Total link strength
✓	lee j.d., see k.a., trust in automation: designing for app...	42	63
✓	parasuraman r., riley v., humans and automation: use, ...	31	51
✓	ortony a., clore g.l., collins a., the cognitive structure o...	49	46
✓	tambe p., cappelli p., yakubovich v., artificial intelligen...	31	44
✓	newell a., simon h.a., human problem solving, (1972)	30	42
✓	miller t., explanation in artificial intelligence: insights f...	37	41
✓	adadi a., berrada m., peeking inside the black-box: a s...	50	39
✓	picard r.w., affective computing, (1997)	35	38
✓	glikson e., woolley a.w., human trust in artificial intelli...	17	36
✓	jarrahi m.h., artificial intelligence and the future of wor...	19	35
✓	rickel j., johnson w.l., animated agents for procedural t...	35	35
✓	newell a., unified theories of cognition, (1990)	29	34
✓	devlin j., chang m.-w., lee k., toutanova k., bert: pre-tr...	41	33
✓	anderson j.r., the architecture of cognition, (1983)	21	31
✓	he k., zhang x., ren s., sun j., deep residual learning for ...	40	31
✓	mcneese n.j., demir m., cooke n.j., myers c., teaming ...	21	30
✓	anderson j.r., rules of the mind, (1993)	26	29
✓	hart s.g., nasa-task load index (nasa-tlx)	48	29
✓	20 years later, proceedings of the human factors and e...	19	27
✓	johnson w.l., rickel j.w., lester j.c., animated pedagogic...	20	27

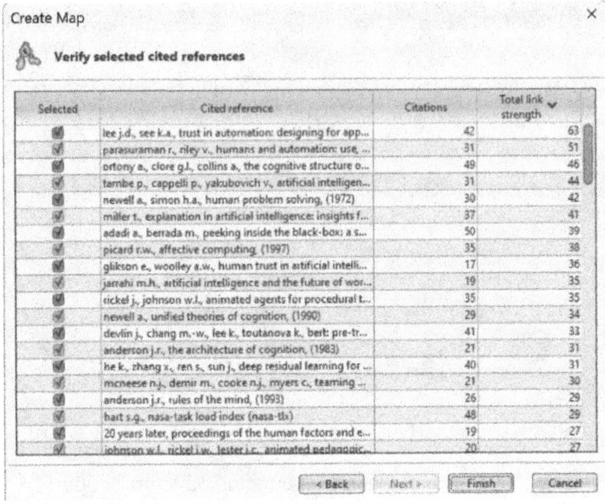

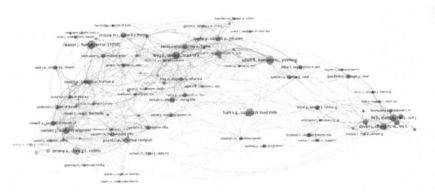

Fig. 4. Verification of selected cited references.

Fig. 5. Co-citation analysis of the metadata on VOSviewer.

The leading countries tree map is present in Fig. 6, including the USA, sequentially featuring the United States, China, England, Germany, South Korea, Canada, Australia, and India, among others. To intuitively illustrate the relationship and collaboration networks, we analyze the geographical location of the co-authors. By examining the geographical distribution of co-authors using CiteSpace and employing Google Earth for visualization, as depicted in Fig. 7 (Yu and Gong 2012). Not only do the results highlight international cooperation but also advise the potential areas for future collaborative research.

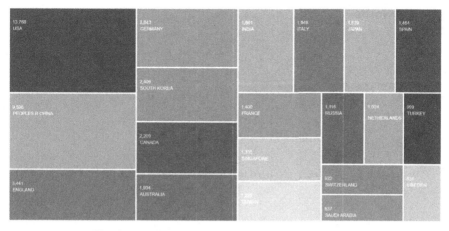

Fig. 6. Tree Map chart of the leading authors' countries.

Fig. 7. Geography network of co-authors.

4.2 Pivot Table

VOSviewer is also used to extract the occurrence of the keywords in this area. As shown in Fig. 8, the top keywords are exported and visualized. Figure 9 presents the density map of the keywords. The label size is proportional to the word's frequencies in the exported metadata from Scopus.

Keywords

■ Occurrences   ░ Total link strength

	Occurrences	Total link strength
Artificial Intelligence	2K	19K
Human Computer Interaction	1K	7K
Human	902	15K
Learning Systems	845	6K
Virtual Reality	799	6K
Machine Learning	721	7K
Personnel Training	658	5K
Decision Making	479	4K
Training	449	6K
E-Learning	447	3K
Deep Learning	409	4K
Algorithms	321	5K
Artificial Neural Network	220	4K
Controlled Study	205	4K

Fig. 8. Keywords analysis in VOSviewer

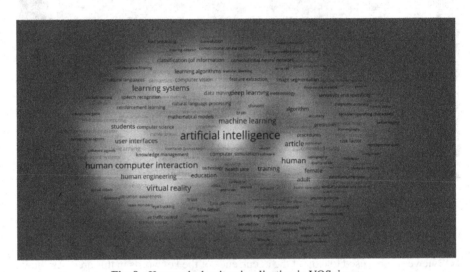

Fig. 9. Keywords density visualization in VOSviewer

4.3 Cluster Analysis

Even though the VOSviewer provides the density visualization of the keywords to present the frequency of keywords in the search topic, it does not inherently reveal the intricate relationships and thematic structures between these keywords.

In order to have a better understanding of the complex bibliometric information, further analysis on CiteSpace is conducted to analyze the metadata (Aydinoglu, Taskin, and Chen n.d.; B. M. Duffy and Duffy 2020).

Cluster analysis in CiteSpace "clusters" of work that share common topics. There are three clustering options: Abstract, Keywords, and Titles. Figure 10 shows the co-citation after cluster analysis by keywords in CiteSpace. The nodes are the subsections under the clustering, which could help us to identify the publications in the topics (Kanade and Duffy 2020).

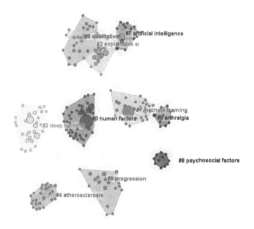

Fig. 10. Cluster results of the keywords analysis in CiteSpace.

The above review on AI in training indicates that this is shaping individualized learning pathways, thus representing a breakthrough advancement regarding the effectiveness of studying and professional development. It becomes increasingly evident that the implications of AI stretch into the more intricate realm of education. Therefore, we deep delve into the application of AI within the educational realm.

As illustrated in Fig. 11, the timeline of the term clustering analysis provides a mapping of the development and interdependence within subject areas throughout time specifically focusing on AI in Educational Research (AIED). The marked lines represent the evolution of several topics and their time dynamic or how they have spread, showing that some themes emerging, others declining, and newer areas of focus like "generative artificial intelligence" developed more recently as technological advances reshaped research interests. This is because it suggests important shifts in priorities such as researchers adapting to developments in technology.

4.4   Leading Papers

Figure 12 presents the Top 20 references with the strongest citations burst in CiteSpace, which was imported from the WOS. It provides detailed information about the cited paper with strength, which is the link strength of the number of co-citations, and the start and end year of the strongest citation.

Table 2 presents the full list of the leading authors that imported from Publish or Perish, which also includes the citation count for each paper. To be noticed, those leading papers are focused on the application of artificial intelligence (AI) in training and

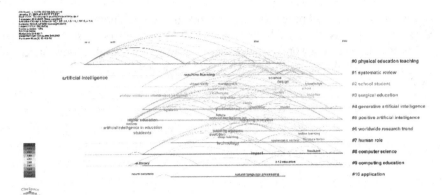

artificial intelligence

#0 physical education teaching
#1 systematic review
#2 school student
#3 surgical education
#4 generative artificial intelligence
#5 positive artificial intelligence
#6 worldwide research trend
#7 human role
#8 computer science
#9 computing education
#10 application

Fig. 11. Timeline of the keywords clustering in CiteSpace.

Top 20 References with the Strongest Citation Bursts

References	Year	Strength	Begin	End	2000 - 2023
Esteva A, 2017, NATURE, V542, P115, DOI 10.1038/nature21056, DOI	2017	11.04	2018	2021	
Gulshan V, 2016, JAMA-J AM MED ASSOC, V316, P2402, DOI 10.1001/jama.2016.17216, DOI	2016	9.06	2018	2021	
LeCun Y, 2015, NATURE, V521, P436, DOI 10.1038/nature14539, DOI	2015	8.11	2018	2020	
Ting DSW, 2017, JAMA-J AM MED ASSOC, V318, P2211, DOI 10.1001/jama.2017.18152, DOI	2017	5.66	2018	2023	
Goodfellow I, 2016, ADAPT COMPUT MACH LE, V0, P1	2016	5.63	2018	2021	
Rusk N, 2016, NAT METHODS, V13, P35, DOI 10.1038/nmeth.3707, DOI	2016	4.5	2018	2021	
Simonyan K, 2015, ARXIV, V0, P0	2015	3.53	2018	2020	
Ronneberger O, 2015, LECT NOTES COMPUT SC, V9351, P234, DOI 10.1007/978-3-319-24574-4, 28, DOI	2015	3.02	2018	2020	
Krizhevsky Alex, 2017, COMMUNICATIONS OF THE ACM, V60, P84, DOI 10.1145/3065386, DOI	2017	5.56	2019	2023	
Bejnordi BE, 2017, JAMA-J AM MED ASSOC, V318, P2199, DOI 10.1001/jama.2017.14585, DOI	2017	4.3	2019	2021	
Poplin R, 2018, NAT BIOMED ENG, V2, P158, DOI 10.1038/s41551-018-0195-0, DOI	2018	4.23	2019	2020	
Silver D, 2016, NATURE, V529, P484, DOI 10.1038/nature16961, DOI	2016	3.7	2019	2020	
De Fauw J, 2018, NAT MED, V24, P1342, DOI 10.1038/s41591-018-0107-6, DOI	2018	3.24	2019	2020	
Lakhani P, 2017, RADIOLOGY, V284, P574, DOI 10.1148/radiol.2017162326, DOI	2017	2.64	2019	2020	
Wang P, 2019, GUT, V68, P1813, DOI 10.1136/gutjnl-2018-317500, DOI	2019	3.84	2020	2021	
Ribeiro MT, 2016, KDD16: PROCE ...... RY AND DATA MINING, V0, PP1135, DOI	2016	3.2	2020	2021	
Litjens G, 2017, MED IMAGE ANAL, V42, P60, DOI 10.1016/j.media.2017.07.005, DOI	2017	5.98	2021	2023	
Jiang F, 2017, STROKE VASC NEUROL, V2, P230, DOI 10.1136/svn-2017-000101, DOI	2017	3.51	2021	2023	
Pesapane Filippo, 2018, EUR RADIOL EXP, V2, P35, DOI 10.1186/s41747-018-0061-6, DOI	2018	3.26	2021	2023	
Tricco AC, 2018, ANN INTERN MED, V169, P467, DOI 10.7326/M18-0850, DOI	2018	3.17	2021	2023	

Fig. 12. Top 20 references with the strongest citations burst in CiteSpace

education across various fields. Most of the studies have been centered on the Health and Medicinal domain which includes surgical training, nursing education, and medical imaging, bringing the efficiency of AI in education and improving the training and diagnostic capabilities in these fields. There are also some researchers interested in the use of AI for educational purposes, as presented by papers that discuss AI models for personalized 12-k, graduate, and medical education.

Figure 13 provides a pie chart view of leading areas in the field of "AI in training". This plot is dominated by Computer Science, with 90,159 documents in the Scopus database. Engineering, Medicine, Mathematics, and Social Sciences also have considerable counts, from around 230 thousand to over 48 thousand. Although Computer Science is the dominant discipline in this field, which takes up 30.3%, it still obvious that there is a wide range of disciplines were covered in the research topic. This indicates the interdisciplinary nature of the research.

Table 2. Leading paper from Publish or Perish.

Cites	Authors	Title	Year
182	N Mirchi, V Bissonnette, R Yilmaz, N Ledwos…	The Virtual Operative Assistant: An explainable artificial intelligence tool for simulation-based training in surgery and medicine	2020
129	B Huval	Method for training and refining an artificial intelligence	2018
128	S Shorey, E Ang, J Yap, ED Ng, ST Lau…	A virtual counseling application using artificial intelligence for communication skills training in nursing education: development study	2019
116	S Maity	Identifying opportunities for artificial intelligence in the evolution of training and development practices	2019
102	M Dubarry, D Beck	Big data training data for artificial intelligence-based Li-ion diagnosis and prognosis	2020
84	EM Brunt, AD Clouston, Z Goodman, C Guy…	Complexity of ballooned hepatocyte feature recognition: Defining a training atlas for artificial intelligence-based imaging in NAFLD	2022
69	HC Lane, MG Core, M Van Lent, S Solomon…	Explainable Artificial Intelligence for Training and Tutoring	2005
52	M Xiao, H Yi	Building an efficient artificial intelligence model for personalized training in colleges and universities	2021

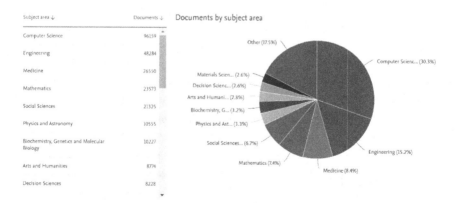

Fig. 13. Scopus Trend Analysis of Number of Documents vs Subject Area

Figure 14 shows a strong representation of Chinses institutions in AI and training. Beyond the academic institutions, corporations like Tencent, Facebook Research, and Google LLC indicate that commercial companies also significantly contribute to the development of AI in training.

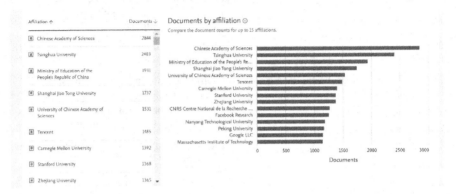

Fig. 14. Documents by authors affiliation.

Figure 15 visualizes the number of documents ranked by each funding sponsor. There are multiple national and international sponsors providing research funding to the researcher, reflecting the importance and recognition of this field. The diversity and distribution of support across these sponsors also imply the interdisciplinary nature of the research.

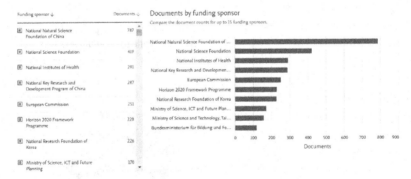

Fig. 15. Documents by funding sponsors.

4.5 Content Analysis

After downloading the papers from Table 2, content analysis is conducted based on the text. The articles were imported to the online Word Cloud tool to generate the word cloud, as shown in Fig. 16. The font size is proportional to the text frequency. This word cloud provides insight into the key concept in the paper.

Fig. 16. Word cloud

5 Discussion

Training is experiencing a big change in how it is designed, delivered, and implemented by the rapid advancements in various disciplines (Salvendy 2012). Based on the above co-citation, keywords, interdisciplinary, and content analysis, we can summarize the current trends and potential research opportunities in AI-assisted training.

In education, AI-assisted training has the potential to change language education and clinical learning. Artificial intelligence and natural language processing (NLP) in learning research (Pack and Maloney 2023) show that artificial intelligence can have a positive effect on language education and clinical medicine (Banerjee et al. 2021). Furthermore, with the rapid development of Large Language Models (LLM) and foundation models, the computational and financial cost of training and finetuning on the designated training tasks will be significantly reduced (Kasneci et al. 2023). However, the majority of LLM are trained on generalized databases, which pose a challenge in delivering domain-specific knowledge for the users (Zhai et al. 2021). Therefore, the customized assisted AI training program is also a promising direction to explore. Such a system could be easily customized for various training tasks to improve the learning experience and outcomes.

The comparison of research publications among three interrelated domains: AIED, Generative AI, and Generative AI in Education is illustrated in Fig. 17. The data is sourced from the Web of Science and encompasses a temporal span from 2014 through 2023.

AI in Education has shown a steady increase in publications over the years, with a significant acceleration starting around 2020. The trend continues to rise sharply through 2023, indicating a growing interest and significant research activity in the application of AI within educational contexts. Generative AI had few publications before 2018, it also shows an increase but remains relatively lower in volume compared to "AI in Education". The trend for "Generative AI" started to become noticeable around 2018 and shows a steady increase in research interest over time, with a sharper rise from 2021 onwards.

Trend analysis of AI in Education, Generative AI, and Generative AI in Education from Web of Science

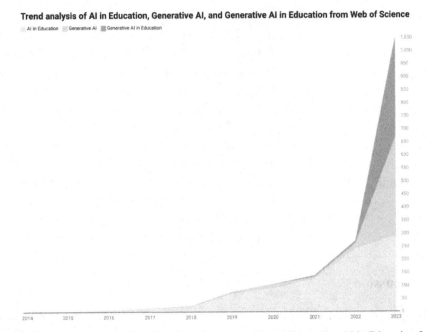

Fig. 17. Trend analysis of AI in Education, Generative AI, and Generative AI in Education from Web of Science.

Generative AI in Education is the latest emerging trend among those three topics in this special intersection of "Generative AI" used in the educational area, whose publications practically appeared around 2020. Following the starting point of zero, from what we can see in Fig. 17, suggests a rapid increase in research publications, particularly from 2021 to 2023. The rapid expansion of generative AI and education implies this field to be a cutting-edge and emerging research topic, aligned with the rise of generative AI and other advanced LLM outside of traditional education. The trends indicate the growing emphasis on AI technologies in education and the appearing acknowledgment of the application of generative models in this field.

Machine learning (ML) and deep learning are also popular topics in this area. Machine learning uses data-driven methods to learn how to predict the results, which could improve the customization of the training process (Mosqueira-Rey et al. 2023). Deep learning, which is a subset of machine learning, has gained prominence by using neural networks to analyze the intricate patterns in large datasets for versatile applications (Lecun, Bengio, and Hinton 2015). For example, in medical education, Fatima rigorously selected 22 studies on AI-assisted medical training (Nagi et al. 2023). This review reveals that AI-assisted training is applied across various domains in the medical education field, including training labs, followed by the surgery domain, orthopedics, ophthalmology, surgery medicine, and behavioral health. Although the research in AI-assisted training has expanded rapidly in recent years, there are still some challenges and underexplored areas.

Although the research in AI-assisted training has expanded rapidly in recent years, there are still some challenges and underexplored areas. The blossoming of deep learning and machine learning has raised concerns about accountability and transparency. This could explain why Explainable AI (XAI) is also a popular topic in this field (Barredo Arrieta et al. 2020; Gunning et al. 2019). Compared to the traditional black box algorithms in deep learning, XAI is able to explain to the user the reason behind the decision. DARPA sponsored an XAI project in 2019 (Gunning and Aha 2019). This program aims to build a foundation for transitioning ML models from the traditional black box approach to an interpretable and transparent mode. ChatGPT-4.0, developed by Open AI, also could provide basic explanations in some areas, like mathematics or physics (Watson and Romic 2024; 2023 et al. 2023).

Interactive AI is one of the potential research opportunities, which already illustrated its effectiveness in the machine learning area by improving the solving methods in the Traveling Salesman Problem (TSP) (Holzinger et al. 2016). Most AI assistant training algorithms only allow unidirectional communication, which means the user will comply with their instructions without questions. However, questions will occur during the training and learning process, and may want to understand why this decision should be taken or not (Salvendy 2012). Thus, an interactive AI-assisted training system, which is related to the active learning approach, could improve the learning experience by including humans in the loop. Bilateral communication in the training process could improve the engagement and adaptability of the user.

Trustiness improvement and evaluation for AI assistance in training is a potential research gap. AI in the training must be trustworthy and communicate that they are trustworthy to encourage users to form appropriate trust in them (Lee and See 2004). Therefore, there is a need for more research on how to customize the training process to enhance trust. Besides, the improvement of transparency and exploitability will enhance the trustworthiness of the system (X. Li et al. 2021). More comprehensive research on the key components of trust in the AI-assisted training process also could be further developed to improve the performance and user experience of AI in the training.

A comprehensive assessment methodology for the LLM application in education is also facing multifaced challenges in AIED, including technical, practical, ethical, and domain-specific evaluation aspects. Although the use of LLMs in education has the potential to revolutionize educational methods (Househ et al. 2023), there are some research gaps in algorithmic bias, cognitive workload evaluation, learning outcome, information overwhelming, overreliance, plagiarism, misinformation, data privacy, and copyright concerns (Abd-Alrazaq et al. 2023). The effective assessment of LLMs in educational assistance, needs to involve assessing their performance in answering domain-specific questions and providing personalized feedback promptly (Shojaee-Mend 2023). Therefore, rigorous domain-specific assessments are crucial to gauge the effectiveness and limitations of LLMs in education. Additionally, LLMs need to be carefully examined to ensure that the generated feedback aligns with educational objectives and ethical considerations when providing personalized feedback (Rose H. et al. 2023). Researchers point out that current GAI and LLMs might be insufficient for the evaluation of complex assignments due to the intricate nature of involved variables and rubrics (Grassini 2023). Thus, to construct a comprehensive assessment methodology of LLMs in education, not only the technical evaluation important, but it is also crucial to evaluate the pedagogical effectiveness, leaner and educator experience, and accessibility, and incorporate the trust and cogitative evaluation into the assess framework to ensure that these systems can enhance learning outcomes and align with the needs and insights of the educational objectives.

6 Conclusion

In conclusion, this study presents a systematic literature review of AI in training by using co-citation analysis, keyword clustering, leading paper analysis, and content analysis on various software. Research indicates that the use of artificial intelligence for training has gained increasing attention across various disciplines, including education, medical, surgery, industrial training, etc. By analyzing the leading paper, the limitations and challenges have also been identified and highlighted. Although it shows superior performance than the traditional training methods in some studies, it also presents limitations, including the significant cost to develop such a system, difficulty in delivering specific domain knowledge, challenges in establishing trustworthiness, lack of comprehensive assessment methodology, and ethical concerns.

7 Future Work

This study includes a systematic analysis of various databases in the field of AI in training and subsection including the AI in education (AIED) and generative AI in education. However, the database for the NSF Awards could be developed to explore current prevalent research subjects and potential research directions. Figure 18 presents a keyword search on the NSF website. The abundance of the search topic indicates the prevalence and multidiscipline nature of AI-assisted training.

Fig. 18. NSF Awards

References

Abd-Alrazaq, A., et al.: Large Language Models in Medical Education: Opportunities, Challenges, and Future Directions (Preprint) (2023). https://doi.org/10.2196/preprints.48291

Aydinoglu, A.U., Taskin, Z., Chen, C.: The CiteSpace Manual (n.d.). https://doi.org/10.1007/s11192-015-1576-8. Accessed 30 Jan 2024

Banerjee, M., et al.: The impact of artificial intelligence on clinical education: perceptions of postgraduate trainee doctors in London (UK) and recommendations for trainers. BMC Med. Educ. **21**(1), 1–10 (2021). https://doi.org/10.1186/S12909-021-02870-X/FIGURES/5

Arrieta, B., et al.: Explainable artificial intelligence (XAI): concepts, taxonomies, opportunities and challenges toward responsible AI. Inf. Fusion **58**(June), 82–115 (2020). https://doi.org/10.1016/J.INFFUS.2019.12.012

Chen, S.Y., Lin, P.H., Chien, W.C.: Children's digital art ability training system based on AI-assisted learning: a case study of drawing color perception. Front. Psychol. **13** (2022). https://doi.org/10.3389/FPSYG.2022.823078

Darragh, L.: The promise of online mathematics instruction programmes: producing the mathematics learner and school mathematics. Res. Math. Educ. **23**(3), 262–277 (2021). https://doi.org/10.1080/14794802.2021.1993977

Duffy, B.M., Duffy, V.G.: Data mining methodology in support of a systematic review of human aspects of cybersecurity. In: Duffy, V.G. (ed.) HCII 2020. LNCS, vol. 12199, pp. 242–253. Springer, Cham (2020). https://doi.org/10.1007/978-3-030-49907-5_17

Duffy, T., Duffy, V.G.: Moderating stress in task design and motivation: a systematic review. Hum.-Autom. Interact. Mob. Comput. 415–430 (2023). https://doi.org/10.1007/978-3-031-10788-7_25/COVER

Grassini, S.: Shaping the future of education: exploring the potential and consequences of AI and ChatGPT in educational settings. Educ. Sci. **13**(7), 692 (2023). https://doi.org/10.3390/educsci13070692

Gunning, D., Aha, D.W.: DARPA's explainable artificial intelligence (XAI) program. AI Mag. **40**(2), 44–58 (2019). https://doi.org/10.1609/AIMAG.V40I2.2850

Gunning, D., et al.: XAI-explainable artificial intelligence. Sci. Robot. **4**(37) (2019). https://doi.org/10.1126/SCIROBOTICS.AAY7120

Holzinger, A., Plass, M., Holzinger, K., Crişan, G.C., Pintea, C.-M., Palade, V.: Towards interactive machine learning (IML): applying ant colony algorithms to solve the traveling salesman problem with the human-in-the-loop approach. In: Buccafurri, F., Holzinger, A., Kieseberg, P., Tjoa, A.M., Weippl, E. (eds.) CD-ARES 2016. LNCS, vol. 9817, pp. 81–95. Springer, Cham (2016). https://doi.org/10.1007/978-3-319-45507-5_6

Househ, M., et al.: Large language models in medical education: opportunities, challenges, and future directions. JMIR Med. Educ. (2023). https://doi.org/10.2196/48291

Huang, Y., et al.: Benchmarking ChatGPT-4 on ACR radiation oncology in-training (TXIT) exam and red journal gray zone cases: potentials and challenges for AI-assisted medical education and decision making in radiation oncology. Front. Oncol. **13**(April) (2023). https://doi.org/10.3389/fonc.2023.1265024

Jan van Eck, N., Waltman, L.: VOSviewer Manual (2022)

Kanade, S.G., Duffy, V.G.: A systematic literature review of game-based learning and safety management. In: Duffy, V.G. (ed.) HCII 2020. LNCS, vol. 12199, pp. 365–377. Springer, Cham (2020). https://doi.org/10.1007/978-3-030-49907-5_26

Kanade, S.G., Duffy, V.G.: Use of virtual reality for safety training: a systematic review. In: Duffy, V.G. (eds.) Digital Human Modeling and Applications in Health, Safety, Ergonomics and Risk Management. LNCS, vol. 13320, pp. 364–375. Springer, Cham (2022). https://doi.org/10.1007/978-3-031-06018-2_25

Kanade, S.G., Duffy, V.G.: Exploring the effectiveness of virtual reality as a learning tool in the context of task interruption: a systematic review. Int. J. Ind. Ergon. **99**, 103548 (2024). https://doi.org/10.1016/j.ergon.2024.103548

Kasneci, E., et al.: ChatGPT for good? On opportunities and challenges of large language models for education. Learn. Individ. Differ. **103** (2023). https://doi.org/10.1016/j.lindif.2023.102274

Lecun, Y., Bengio, Y., Hinton, G.: Deep learning. Nature **521**(7553), 436–444 (2015). https://doi.org/10.1038/nature14539

Lee, J.D., See, K.A.: Trust in automation: designing for appropriate reliance. Hum. Factors **46**(1), 50–80 (2004). https://doi.org/10.1518/HFES.46.1.50_30392

Li, W., Wang, C., Cheng, G., Song, Q.: Transactions on machine learning, and undefined 2023. International Conference on Machine Learning. Par.Nsf.Gov. https://par.nsf.gov/servlets/purl/10418406. Accessed 30 Jan 2024

Li, X., et al.: Interpretable deep learning: interpretation, interpretability, trustworthiness, and beyond. Knowl. Inf. Syst. **64**(12), 3197–3234 (2021). https://doi.org/10.1007/s10115-022-01756-8

Mosqueira-Rey, E., Hernández-Pereira, E., Alonso-Ríos, D., Bobes-Bascarán, J., Fernández-Leal, Á.: Human-in-the-loop machine learning: a state of the art. Artif. Intell. Rev. **56**(4), 3005–3054 (2023). https://doi.org/10.1007/S10462-022-10246-W

Nagi, F., et al.: Applications of artificial intelligence (AI) in medical education: a scoping review. Stud. Health Technol. Inform. **305**(June), 648–651 (2023). https://doi.org/10.3233/SHTI230581

Osareh, F.: Bibliometrics, citation analysis and co-citation analysis: a review of literature I. Libri **46**(3), 149–158 (1996). https://doi.org/10.1515/LIBR.1996.46.3.149

Pack, A., Maloney, J.: Using generative artificial intelligence for language education research: insights from using OpenAI's ChatGPT. TESOL Q. **57**(4), 1571–1582 (2023). https://doi.org/10.1002/TESQ.3253

Parchomovsky, G.: Publish or perish. Mich. Law Rev. **98**(4) (2000). https://repository.law.umich.edu/mlr/vol98/iss4/3

Kirk, H.R., Vidgen, B., Röttger, P., Hale, S.A.: Personalisation Within Bounds: A Risk Taxonomy and Policy Framework for the Alignment of Large Language Models With Personalised Feedback (2023). https://doi.org/10.48550/arxiv.2303.05453

Salvendy, G.: Handbook of Human Factors and Ergonomics: Fourth Edition (2012). https://doi.org/10.1002/9781118131350

Shojaee-Mend, H.: Evaluating the Strengths and Weaknesses of Large Language Models in Answering Neurophysiology Questions (2023). https://doi.org/10.21203/rs.3.rs-3348418/v1

Watson, S., Romic, J.: ChatGPT and the entangled evolution of society, education, and technology: a systems theory perspective. Eur. Educ. Res. J. (2024). https://doi.org/10.1177/14749041231221266

Yu, L., Gong, P.: Google earth as a virtual globe tool for earth science applications at the global scale: progress and perspectives. Int. J. Remote Sens. **33**(12), 3966–3986 (2012). https://doi.org/10.1080/01431161.2011.636081

Zhai, X., et al.: A review of artificial intelligence (AI) in education from 2010 to 2020. Complexity **2021** (2021). https://doi.org/10.1155/2021/8812542

Annotating Virtual Tai Chi Instruction to Improve Learning Outcomes for Older Adults

Natasha Malik(✉) , Andrew Mitchell , Longyun Liao ,
Janelle Gravesande , Bruce Thong, Paula Gardner , Lisa Carlesso ,
Brenda Vrkljan , and Rong Zheng

McMaster University, 1280 Main Street West, Hamilton, ON L8S 4L8, Canada
{malikn25,mitchaj2,liaol13,gravesja,thongb,gardnerp,carlesl,
vrkljan,rzheng}@mcmaster.ca

Abstract. This study aimed to establish design guidelines that can facilitate the development of digital annotations for both real-time and pre-recorded virtual Tai Chi instruction. We designed 13 original annotations for a virtual Tai Chi platform with the help of 11 older adult co-designers. An iterative design methodology was applied in a focus group setting, with participant co-designers grouped into 2 focus groups of 5–6 participants each. Digital annotations were developed and iterated upon over the course of 18 weeks, with the objective of creating annotations that improve the learning experience for older adults in online Tai Chi classes. Subsequently, design guidelines for digital annotation development were deduced from themes that emerged in focus group discussions. We found that digital annotations for virtual Tai Chi should (1) avoid distracting attention away from the instructor, (2) avoid overwhelming users with information, and (3) optimize for clarity and accessibility. Annotations should also (4) account for the variation in experience level amongst practitioners. Experience level and accessibility can both be addressed when users are granted the ability to (5) customize their own annotations whenever possible.

Keywords: Human pose estimation · Older adults · Older adult mobility · Tai Chi · Virtual lessons · Focus groups · Iterative design

1 Introduction

Tai Chi has been described as "meditation in motion" as reflected in the low impact and slow movements of the human body required to perform this form of exercise. As a mind-body exercise, practicing Tai Chi regularly has been shown to result in physical health benefits for older adults, including but not limited to: increased lower extremity strength, improved balance control, enhanced proprioception, postural adaptation, and reduced risk of falls [3,10,11,24]. In addition,

---

N. Malik and A. Mitchell—Both authors contributed equally to this research.

V. G. Duffy (Ed.): HCII 2024, LNCS 14711, pp. 364–383, 2024.
https://doi.org/10.1007/978-3-031-61066-0_22

Fig. 1. The *skeleton and footwork* annotation, an example of a digital annotation shown to participants.

practicing Tai Chi has also been associated with improvements in mood and cognition [24,25] (Fig. 1).

During the COVID-19 pandemic, many group exercise classes including Tai Chi shifted online. As such, instructors used a variety of ways to teach these classes online, such as offering synchronous (live) options or pre-recorded videos [7,12,14]. Participants enjoy the convenience of exercising at home, and they save time and money by participating in virtual programs as opposed to in-person [5,7,12,14]. Furthermore, virtual programming diminishes barriers to participating in group exercise programs, especially amongst individuals with mobility limitations [7].

However, online mind-body exercise programs come with their own set of barriers. These include both living space-related challenges, such as distractions and limited space [1,21,23], and technology-related challenges, such as difficulty navigating systems and poor audio or video quality [1,5,6,20,21,23]. While verbal instructions assist in learning proper form, students primarily rely on observing and imitating an instructor's example to perform a movement themselves [22]. While this task may be nontrivial in-person, online classes pose additional challenges. The lack of depth perception, the size of the video, and reductions in video quality resulting from a participant's device or network connection can all contribute to the added difficulty of this task in an online setting.

Recognizing the importance of pose information, and the challenge of interpreting it correctly from live or pre-recorded videos, we focused primarily on enhancing the visual communication of pose information. Through our discussion with Tai Chi instructors and consultation of Tai Chi instructional books [13], we narrow down to four categories of annotations in this study, namely, body skeleton, footwork, directionality and range of motion, and captioning. By narrowing down the range of annotations, we can take a principled approach that draws on previous experiences, while also incorporating inputs from co-designers. This approach is particularly valuable when navigating intricate design elements such as color, placement, styling, and update frequency, which are largely undecided at the outset.

1.1   Research Goal

The goal of this study was to establish design principles that can facilitate digital annotation development for online Tai Chi classes, as well as develop and test a few key annotation examples. For the purposes of this work, "annotations" are any kind of visual aid overlaid on real-time or pre-recorded video of Tai Chi instruction. The purpose of these annotations is to facilitate learning, which is primarily accomplished by augmenting the information communicated by the instructor's video, but can also be achieved by promoting student engagement and enjoyment. While our interests lie primarily in the inclusion of annotations in a real-time setting, we designed them as much for real-time classes as for pre-recorded videos. Also, while we were interested in the context of Tai Chi classes for older adults, we believe these design principles can be generalised to any video designed to communicate human poses and motions and any audience.

We applied an iterative co-design approach, in a focus group setting, where older adults were recruited to test and provide suggestions and feedback on digital annotation ideas for virtual Tai Chi practice. Our intent was to ensure that the annotations enhance the learning experience of older adult Tai Chi practitioners when engaging online.

1.2   Research Questions and Study Approach

Toward the aforementioned research goal, this study addresses the following two questions:

1. What digital annotations do older adult practitioners find helpful when engaging in online Tai Chi classes?
2. What design guidelines can guide the development of digital annotations that will enhance the learning experience of older adult practitioners engaging in online Tai Chi classes?

The research questions were explored by applying an iterative design methodology with focus groups of older adult participants. Over the course of 18 weeks, six focus group sessions were held lasting one hour each. Ahead of each session, participants were sent videos demonstrating several annotation prototypes. Participants were asked to review and practice Tai Chi with video demonstrations in advance of each meeting, and discuss their thoughts and experiences with each other during the focus group session. Participants were asked to comment on the following aspects of each digital annotation prototype: (1) Was there a particular element that was effective? (2) Did the annotation help to understand particular elements of movement? (such as direction, weight, distribution etc.) and (3) Was there a particular moment that stood as effective for learning and practicing Tai

Chi? Participants were furthermore asked to comment on what was not working, what they would change, and whether they could see themselves using the annotation and why or why not.

In addition to discussing the digital annotation prototypes as presented, participants were also asked to share their ideas on the changes they would make to the annotations, as well as any ideas they had for possible annotation designs beyond those they had already seen. Annotations that were iterated upon were shown at later focus group sessions and participants were asked to discuss the changes made based on their feedback, and some novel annotations were developed from new ideas presented by participants. Table 1 includes a description of all 13 annotations alongside the focus group session(s) at which they were shown and discussed (see Figs. 3, 4, 5, 6, 7, 8, 9 and 10 for visual depictions). We sought participant feedback on both the information presented and on its visual style, such as an annotation's position on the screen, colour, opacity, or perspective.

Table 1. Table of digital annotations and the focus group session(s) where they were shown to participants.

Annotation	Description	Sessions Shown
Skeleton on instructor	Joint skeleton overlaid on instructor	3, 4, 5
Skeleton on mirror	Joint skeleton overlaid on mirrored view of instructor	3
Skeleton on both	Joint skeleton overlaid on both instructor and mirrored view	5
Bubbles on instructor	Joint skeleton composed of bubbles overlaid on instructor	4, 5
Skeleton left view	Left view of joint skeleton displayed in separate box	3
Skeleton back view	Back view of joint skeleton displayed in separate box	3
Footwork diagram	Foot placement displayed in separate box with supporting leg information	4, 6
Moving clock	Clock diagram on the ground which periodically re-centers on instructor	5, 6
Stationary clock	Clock diagram on the ground which does not move from instructor's starting position	5
Form captions	Name of Tai Chi form displayed at bottom of screen	5
Skeleton and footwork	*Skeleton on instructor* and *footwork diagram* annotations simultaneously	6
Skeleton with supporting leg	*Skeleton on instructor* with supporting leg information	6

2 Methodology

Engaging older adults in co-design is a user-centered design practice. User-centered design aims to align the outcomes of a design endeavor with the needs and preferences of the user group for which the design is intended. Including users in the design process is fundamental to the practice of user-centered design. This study applied iterative design and focus group methodology. Throughout the course of this study, we applied the feedback we received from older adult participants in the focus group discussions to subsequent iterations of annotation ideas. Iterative design methodology involves designers and users in a co-design process during which users test ideas or prototypes of the design in question and call attention to any usability problems to mitigate in subsequent iterations [16]. We chose this method with consideration of our research questions. As delineated in Sect. 1.2, we were interested in exploring what digital annotations older adults find helpful when engaging in online Tai Chi classes. Iterative design methodology with focus groups allowed us to explore these questions alongside older adult Tai Chi practitioners, whose feedback and guidance led to subsequent iterations of the digital annotations. This study conducted iterative design on a total of 13 digital annotations over the course of 18 weeks and six focus group sessions, and ideas were iterated upon at least once to allow for the identification of major usability challenges.

In the practice of iterative design methodology, designers routinely present subsequent iterations to users to ensure they have resolved issues as previously identified. Users may then provide further feedback on the changed design, and this process of exchange continues throughout the development process and beyond as applied [16]. In general terms, the first few iterations of a design are most fruitful in revealing "major usability gains", while subsequent iterations have "progressively smaller potential" for improvements [16]. This is because once major problems have been eliminated, the design may become "polished", and leave little room for further improvement [16].

Combining iterative design methodology with focus groups was generative for this study: We found that the focus group setting was conducive for brainstorming with participants and receiving feedback on annotations. Focus group sessions were conducted on Zoom [26], and while this discussion environment allowed for the generation of ideas and for consensus to be reached from participants' feedback, focus groups may incite groupthink—a phenomenon in which conformity places pressure on individuals to sway decision-making in favor of a harmonious conclusion [19]. Furthermore, focus group moderators may influence the discussion and the interpretability of results by taking control of the discussion and asking biased or leading questions [19].

We mitigated these limitations in our study design by asking open-ended questions. Moderators also received internal training on focus group moderation and were instructed to name participants during sessions, so all participants had the opportunity to comment on the discussion and to contribute their perspective. In addition, up to two notetakers were present for the focus group sessions. After each focus group, notes were compiled into a shared document and compared for any discrepancies which were resolved internally. Members of the research team attended each focus group to observe the research activity. Internal discussions across our multi- and interdisciplinary team helped ensure that the interpretability of results was not swayed by siloed thinking.

We collaborated with a Tai Chi instructor, who provided expert knowledge on Tai Chi, recorded baseline videos of virtual Tai Chi instruction for the digital annotation prototypes, and informed the iterations of annotation ideas throughout the course of the study. Before releasing digital annotations to the focus group participants, the concepts were shared internally with the instructor to address any limitations these iterations could potentially create for users in their online Tai Chi training.

2.1 Recruitment

Table 2. Participant demographic information. *Participants 6 and 8 did not participate in the focus group sessions.*

ID	Age	Sex assigned at birth	Time spent training or practicing Tai Chi	Time spent training or practicing online classes featuring sequences of movements
1	67	Male	36 years	Over one year
2	59	Female	Over one year	Over one year
3	62	Female	Over one year	Over one year
4	73	Female	Over one year	2 to 6 months
5	68	Female	6 to 12 months	6 to 12 months
7	70	Female	Over one year	None
9	65	Female	11 years	2 years
10	76	Female	10+ years	None
11	68	Female	20 years	Less than 2 months
12	75	Female	Over one year	6 to 12 months
13	58	Did not disclose	Over one year	2 to 6 months

A total of 11 participants were recruited for the focus groups. Over the course of 18 weeks, six focus group sessions were held. We initially targeted practitioners from the virtual Tai Chi class taught by the instructor involved in our study, and subsequently opened participant recruitment to older adults with previous Tai Chi experience. Contact holders at the McMaster Institute for Research on Aging (MIRA), McMaster's Physical Activity Centre of Excellence (PACE) and the UNIFOR Local 5555 Union division of the McMaster University Retiree Association distributed recruitment materials through email listservs and social media pages. In addition, Table 3 provides our exclusion criteria (Table 2).

Participants were divided into two online focus groups of six and five participants respectively. Participants' ages ranged from 58 to 76 years old, with a mean

Table 3. Exclusion criteria for the focus group study.

Exclusion Criteria
54 years of age or younger
No previous Tai Chi experience
Does not have access to a computer to attend online focus group sessions
Cannot communicate in English

age of 67 years. All participants had spent at least six months practicing Tai Chi, with 10 participants indicating they had over one year of experience. In addition, participants' time spent training in or practicing Tai Chi before this study varied from six months to 36 years. We also asked participants about how much time they had spent training or practicing in online classes featuring sequences of movements. Two participants had no experience participating in online movement classes, one participant had less than two months of experience and four participants had two to 12 months of experience. On the upper end of the scale, four participants had over one year of experience participating in online movement classes. Importantly, focus group composition was based on participant availability, regardless of their Tai Chi experience. We assigned participants to either focus group based on the time they would be available. Focus groups were repeated in their composition until session five, when the groups were combined into a single group. Over the course of the study, four participants withdrew. All focus group sessions were conducted online on the cloud-based video conferencing platform Zoom [26]. Participants viewed the pre-recorded video demonstrations on desktop monitors, laptops, and television screens. Generally, a larger screen size correlated with increased instructor visibility (Table 4).

Table 4. Participant attendance at the focus group sessions. *4 out of 11 participants withdrew from the study before the third focus group session on April 22, 2022.*

Group	ID	February 18	April 1	April 22	May 13	June 3	June 24
1	3	✓	✓	✓	✓	✓	✓
	5	✓	✓	✓	X	X	X
	9	✓	✓	Withdrew			
	11	✓	✓	Withdrew			
	12	✓	✓	✓	✓	✓	✓
	13	✓	X	✓	X	✓	✓
		6/6	5/6	Combined	2/4	Combined	
2	1	✓	✓	✓	✓	✓	✓
	2	✓	✓	X	✓	✓	X
	4	✓	✓	✓	✓	✓	✓
	7	✓	X	Withdrew			
	10	✓	✓	Withdrew			
		5/5	4/5	Combined	3/3	Combined	
Total		11/11	9/11	6/7	5/7	6/7	5/7

2.2 Study Design

Each focus group session was led by one researcher who facilitated the discussion, and up to two researchers who took notes. One to three members of the research team, in addition to the facilitator and notetakers, were also present in the sessions to respond to participant questions and clarify aspects of the digital annotation prototypes. The instructor was not present at any of the focus group sessions. Since the digital annotations were built on videos of his Tai Chi instruction and he was a teacher for some participants in the study, his presence at the sessions would pose a conflict of interest and could have impacted how participants responded to discussion questions. The first focus group session was focused on discussing and learning about participants' current and previous virtual and in-person learning experience of Tai Chi. This discussion provided participants the opportunity to share with the group their experiences practicing Tai Chi, as well as their experiences with digital technology for exercise. The conversation also touched on themes of community and belonging, and the significance of the role of the Tai Chi instructor in shaping learning experiences. Significantly, the first session helped build rapport within the focus groups and with members of the research team. In the second focus group session, video demos of virtual Tai Chi instruction were shared with participants. The videos served as baseline videos on which the digital annotations were later overlaid and helped evaluate the effectiveness of specific annotations compared to virtual instruction without annotations.

From focus group sessions three to six, we conducted iterative design. At each session, we presented prototypes of digital annotations that were developed in response to participants' needs and wants, as shared in the first and second sessions. Annotation ideas were prioritized based on their feasibility. We shared video demonstrations with participants at least 24 h before each session and played clips from each video at the focus group session. Participants were asked to provide feedback on the annotation presented and discuss the usefulness of the idea for practicing Tai Chi virtually. Following each focus group session, we continued developing digital annotation prototypes by incorporating feedback from the participants, as well as from members of the research team. If participants' responses to an annotation were overwhelmingly negative, we did not continue its development. If participants' responses to an annotation were overwhelmingly positive with no comments for improvement, we did not produce any further iterations. If an annotation was positively received by participants with comments for improvements, we continued development with future iterations. Some annotation ideas, such as the *bubbles on instructor* annotation discussed in Sect. 3.1, were presented by participants as potential ideas that they would like to see in development. We decided not to design any audible annotations, as sound could interfere with the Tai Chi instructor's verbal instruction in virtual classes. In addition, we organized sessions to show a mix of annotation iterations based on feedback and new annotations, and we changed our development plans based on participant feedback by prioritizing the iteration of annotations that were regarded as useful to practicing Tai Chi online.

3   Results

The following section presents the annotations we developed and prototyped over the course of this study, which are summarized in Fig. 2.

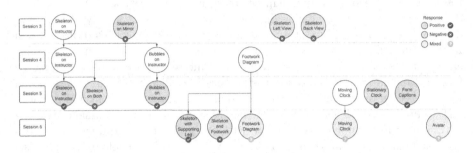

Fig. 2. The annotation ideas evaluated over the course of the focus group study, and the focus group's response to the final iteration of each idea.

3.1   Skeleton Annotations

Fig. 3. Left: The first iteration of the *skeleton on instructor* annotation. Center: The second iteration of the *skeleton on instructor* annotation. Right: The third and final iteration of the *skeleton on instructor* annotation.

Skeleton on Instructor. This annotation uses keyjoints extracted by the HPE process to draw a stick figure skeleton on top of the instructor. This is intended to accentuate the instructor's poses and movements, and make it easier for participants to follow from the video. Use of skeletons such as this is a common way to take advantage of technology to make pose clearer [2,22].

Feedback on the first iteration (Fig. 3, left) was positive, but participants found the many different colours distracting. Participant 3 shared "there's too much colour there for me... If it were maybe one colour or two colours, I can deal with. Here it is too much colour". Participants 1 and 12 agreed. Participants also found the skeleton's head confusing and did not see a need for the head to be annotated since the instructor's head is visible.

In response to this feedback, the lines of the second iteration (Fig. 3, center) were all bright cyan, and the head joints were removed. Participants considered this an improvement, but still found the skeleton to occlude the instructor more than necessary. For the third and final iteration (Fig. 3, right), the entire skeleton was made transparent, and the hand joints were removed. Feedback on the second iteration indicated that while the annotation is helpful, being able to clearly see the instructor is most important. Also, participants found that the hand segments of the joint skeleton only distracted from the real movements underneath, rather than effectively communicating any information about the instructor's hand movements. The final iteration of this annotation received very positive feedback from participants. Participant 2, for example, stated "I really liked it, I found that the lines aren't distracting. I was focused on both Bruce and the annotation. I really liked it". Participant 3 agreed and stated that "of the three overlays, this was my favourite". Participant 12 liked that "You can see his hand movements clearly".

Fig. 4. Left: The first and only iteration of the *skeleton on mirror* annotation. Right: The first and only iteration of the *skeleton on both* annotation.

Skeleton on Mirror. This annotation (Fig. 4, left) uses a keyjoint skeleton just as the previous annotation, but the skeleton is drawn on the mirrored view of the instructor instead of the camera view. The purpose of this annotation is the same as the previous annotation, but using the mirrored perspective rather than the camera perspective.

Feedback on this annotation was negative; in general, participants wanted to watch the near view of the instructor, only looking to the mirrored view for clarification on the position of obstructed parts of the instructor's body. However, the skeleton overlaid on the mirrored view was very distracting to participants, drawing their gaze away from the main view. Additionally, since the mirrored view of the instructor occupied a smaller part of the screen, the annotation was markedly obstructive. Participant 5 stated "I'm trying to utilize the mirror to see what's going on since I can't see the front of him. With having all the different coloured lines all over his body, now I really can't see. It's almost like he's been camouflaged".

Skeleton on Both. This annotation (Fig. 4, right) is a combination of the previous two annotations; the keyjoint skeleton is overlaid on both the near and mirrored views of the instructor.

Feedback on this annotation was negative for the same reasons as the *skeleton on mirror* annotation, as the mirror component was still found to be distracting. The combination of both skeletons obstructed the view of the instructor in both views. Participant 12 expressed that it is "too much visual information at the same time for me... it is confusing for my brain".

Fig. 5. Left: The first iteration of the *bubbles on instructor* annotation. Right: The second and final iteration of the *bubbles on instructor* annotation.

Bubbles on Instructor. This annotation is similar to the *skeleton on instructor* annotation, but the circles and lines representing the keyjoint skeleton were replaced with bubbles. This annotation idea was suggested by the focus group after seeing the first iteration of the *skeleton on instructor* annotation. In session 3, participant 4 asked "Have you thought of dots? I guess they call them bubbles. Might not be as confusing as lines. We may be able to follow the arm a little better because there's more pieces. More fluid". The purpose of this annotation, and information communicated by it, are the same as the *skeleton on instructor* annotation, but with an appearance some may find more visually appealing.

Feedback on the first iteration (Fig. 5, left) was positive, but participants suggested representing the skeleton with a greater number of smaller bubbles in order to make the lines of each limb clearer. We followed the given feedback for the second and final iteration (Fig. 5, right), to which participants responded very positively. Participants 2, 3 and 4 in particular really liked it. The "fluidity" that bubbles convey, was considered suitable to represent the practice of Tai Chi. Participant 4 expressed that "The bubbles come across as more fluid. Tai Chi is a fluid practice... I like this for the fluidity that it gives to the motion".

Skeleton Left and Back View. This annotation uses the same skeleton as the *skeleton on instructor* annotation, but instead of overlaying the skeleton on the instructor, the skeleton was shown in a separate black box at the bottom-left of the video. The skeleton was also shown from a different perspective than the camera's view of the instructor. Two perspectives were evaluated: a view from the left side (Fig. 6, left), and a view from behind (Fig. 6, right). The intention was for the alternate perspective to add information that participants can use to understand the instructor's positioning in 3D space.

Fig. 6. Left: The first and only iteration of the *skeleton left view* annotation. Right: The first and only iteration of the *skeleton back view* annotation.

Feedback on both annotations was negative; participants found it overwhelming to follow the instructor's movements in multiple areas of the screen at the same time. Participant 5 stated "I think this is just too much, I can't look at three places at once". Participant 3 agreed: "I think that's very accurate, because if you look at the annotation here, you are missing what he's doing there". Additionally, the bright colours of the annotation distracted participants from focusing on the instructor: Participant 3 shared "The bright colours on the annotation draw my eyes as opposed to Bruce".

3.2 Footwork

Fig. 7. Left: The first iteration of the *footwork diagram* annotation. Right: The second and final iteration of the *footwork diagram* annotation.

This annotation uses the same keyjoint information as the previous annotations for two different purposes. First, the foot position and orientation as viewed from above the instructor's head was shown in a black box at the bottom-left corner. Second, the average of all keyjoint 3D positions was taken, and this position was compared to each foot's position to roughly estimate which foot was supporting the instructor's weight. This was displayed by the colour of each foot in the box: grey if the foot was off the ground, bright red if the foot was supporting the instructor's weight, and dark red if it was on the ground but not supporting weight. Both feet were considered to be supporting the instructor's weight if the weight was evenly distributed across both feet.

This annotation was designed based on suggestions from the Tai Chi instructor to our team. Knowing how weight should be distributed is important for performing Tai Chi correctly, but it is difficult for instructors to communicate this information as there is no obvious visual sign. Communicating this information through an annotation allows students to better understand the forms performed by the instructor.

The second iteration (Fig. 7, right) included the addition of an extra icon representing a torso for reference, as well as minor implementation improvements over the first (Fig. 7, left) which made the annotation more accurate.

Feedback from the focus group on this annotation was mixed. The negative feedback was similar to that on the *skeleton left view* and *skeleton back view* annotations: watching two different areas of the screen was overwhelming. The positive feedback was that the footwork information was very helpful for effectively understanding the instructor's poses in 3D. Participants agreed that while the annotation would be distracting in the context of learning a form for the first time in a live online Tai Chi class, the annotation might prove helpful in any context where the same form was repeated several times, such as in a pre-recorded training video that can be re-watched or classes featuring a large amount of repetition. In these contexts, the learner can watch a different area of the screen each time a form is repeated depending on the information they feel they are missing.

Feedback from the focus group on this annotation was mixed. The negative feedback was similar to that on the *skeleton left view* and *skeleton back view* annotations: watching two different areas of the screen was overwhelming. The positive feedback was that the footwork information was very helpful for effectively understanding the instructor's poses in 3D. Participant 1 shared "I'm learning a different form now, something like this would be useful... the feet are very important".

Participants agreed that while the annotation would be distracting in the context of learning a form for the first time in a live online Tai Chi class, the annotation might prove helpful in any context where the same form was repeated several times, such as in a pre-recorded training video that can be re-watched or classes featuring a large amount of repetition. In these contexts, the learner can watch a different area of the screen each time a form is repeated depending on the information they feel they are missing.

3.3   Directionality

This annotation shows a clock-like circle on the floor under the instructor to be used as a visual and verbal reference for directionality, orientations, and range of movements. This system is used by the Tai Chi instructor who collaborated with us in his usual classes, represented using paper and tape on the floor (Fig. 8, left). The orientation and angles of the instructor's movements and poses are much more difficult to perceive in video form than they are in-person. In order to address this, the Tai Chi instructor on our team uses this clock system; while a student might not be able to understand the angle between the instructor's feet from the video, if the instructor's feet are aligned with the familiar angles of 12 o'clock and 2 o'clock the student can use these as a point of reference to guide their own pose. The system used by the instructor involves two overlapping

Fig. 8. Left: The instructor's physical clock system. Center: The first iteration of the *moving clock* and *stationary clock* annotations. Right: The second and final iteration of the *moving clock* annotation.

clocks to be used as reference in two different parts of the sequence of forms. However, this system has limitations: the meaning of the clock system is not always readily apparent until it has been explained, the two overlapping systems can be confusing to some students, and, notably, that some forms involve moving away from the center of this clock system. These annotations are intended to serve the same purpose as the physical clock system, but without some of these drawbacks. The annotations were prepared manually using video editing software.

The *stationary clock* annotation correspond with the physical version; the clock was placed under the instructor's feet at the start of the video, and not moved thereafter. The *moving clock* annotation began in the same position, but moved several times throughout the video. The Tai Chi instructor identified the instances in the video when he transitioned from one Tai Chi form to the next, and the clock re-centered on the instructor at these moments. The first iterations of both versions (Fig. 8, center) used a circle with 8 notches around the circumference, corresponding to cardinal directions as a compass does. The second iteration (Fig. 8, right) of the *moving clock* instead has 12 notches, as an actual clock, and re-centers more often than the first iteration.

Feedback on the *stationary clock* annotation was negative, and participants preferred the *moving clock* when asked to compare. Feedback on the *moving clock* was mixed. Participants found that if the clock does not re-center on the instructor, the clock's frame of reference quickly becomes irrelevant to the instructor's movements, defeating its purpose. Some participants found the *moving clock* mildly helpful, while others did not find it helpful; in general participants who had experience in this Tai Chi instructor's classes belonged to the former group, while the rest belonged to the latter. Many of these participants who were unfamiliar with the clock reference system used by this Tai Chi instructor also found the physical version of the clock confusing and unhelpful. This suggests that the clock is not universally helpful, but could be helpful in classes where the instructor regularly uses this reference to teach.

Fig. 9. The first and only iteration of the *form captions* annotation.

3.4 Form Captions

This annotation (Fig. 9) consists of captioning the name of the Tai Chi form at the bottom of the screen while each form is being performed by the instructor. The form names and timings were provided by the instructor. This annotation was also prepared manually using a video editing program; a live version of this annotation would require a human activity recognition model that is able to accurately identify the instructor's Tai Chi form. Human activity recognition technology has been successfully applied to other mind-body exercises [9,15], but not yet to Tai Chi.

Feedback on this annotation was positive. Participants found the simple reminder of the form's name helpful, and the identification of when each form transitions to the next useful, and they found that it did not distract from the instructor. This may be because they do not change frequently, so there is very little movement to draw attention away from the instructor. This may also be due to subtitles and other similar captions being commonplace in entertainment, so people may be already be used to ignoring them when they are not needed. In addition, participants shared that the form captions help to learn the sequence. Participant 1 expressed "You're going to have to memorize it eventually... having the captioning facilitates that".

3.5 Combinations

Fig. 10. Left: The first and only iteration of the *skeleton and footwork* annotation. Right: The first and only iteration of the *skeleton with supporting leg* annotation.

Skeleton and Footwork. This annotation (Fig. 10, left) is a combination of the final iteration of the *skeleton on instructor* annotation and the final iteration of the *footwork diagram* annotation. We wanted to evaluate the possibility of including multiple different annotations at the same time.

As anticipated, feedback on this annotation was negative. Participants found both annotations at once to be an overwhelming amount of distracting information.

Skeleton with Supporting Leg. This annotation (Fig. 10, right) is also a combination of the *skeleton on instructor* and *footwork diagram* annotation ideas. However, rather than showing both annotations on different areas of the screen, the footwork diagram was not shown, and the segments overlaid on the instructor's feet and shins and coloured as the feet were in the *footwork diagram* annotation. The intention was to sacrifice the additional foot position information of the footwork diagram in exchange for a less distracting annotation.

Feedback on this annotation was very positive. Participants appreciated the supporting foot information from the footwork diagram, and they found including this information on the keyjoint skeleton to be less distracting. Participant 3 shared that this annotation is their favourite: "One of the best, it showed weight and balance all on one annotation, it was easier to look at one thing". Participants 12 and 4 agreed that it is helpful and that they "like it very much". Overall, we consider this to be our most successful annotation.

4   Design Guidelines

The results of the focus group study led us to five design principles that can inform annotation design. These principles align with the literature on Universal Design; the seven principles of Universal Design are equitable use, flexibility in use, simple and intuitive use, perceptible information, tolerance for error, low physical effort, and size/space for approach/use [4,8].

4.1   Avoid Distracting from Instructor

The Tai Chi instructor should always be the center of attention. Annotations may augment practitioners' experience, but they must not distract practitioners from the instructor. It is very easy for the bright colours and clear lines of digital annotations to draw practitioners' attention away from the instructor, and this has a negative effect on practitioners' learning experience. If the annotation is overlaid on the instructor, then it must not overly obstruct practitioners' view of the instructor. This was demonstrated with the iterative design of the *skeleton on instructor* annotation. If the annotation is not overlaid on the instructor, then it must contain information that is designed to be glanced at, such as the *form captions* annotation.

4.2   Avoid Information Overload

Even when annotations are not overly distracting individually, they can quickly overwhelm practitioners when combined. If practitioners feel that there are too many different elements drawing their attention, annotations can frustrate practitioners and prevent them from effectively engaging with the class. This risk is only magnified by older adults' sensitivity to visual distractions [18]. Therefore, when designing annotations, there must not be too many different visual components communicating information simultaneously, particularly for components that draw more attention to themselves.

4.3   Ensure Clarity and Accessibility

As discussed above, annotations should communicate information effectively at a quick glance in order to avoid distracting participants. For annotations to communicate information as effectively as possible, they must be clearly distinguishable from the video on which they are overlaid. Annotation colours must be chosen that have very high contrast with the background and be consistent; for example, we found that cyan (#00FFFF) was effective on the backgrounds we used. Similar considerations should be applied to any displayed text. For example, white text outlined in black is clear on most backgrounds (Fig. 9). Text should also be large enough to be easily readable, even on small screens. These considerations are particularly important for older adult practitioners; as contrast sensitivity decreases with age, the need for high-contrast visuals increases to maintain annotation accessibility [17].

4.4   Account for Variation in Experience Level

A pattern arose over the course of the focus group study: when participants disagreed on the value of an annotation, their difference of opinion often mirrored their different levels of experience. Some participants acknowledged explicitly that certain annotations would be helpful for beginners, but less helpful for more experienced Tai Chi practitioners. For example, in session 3, Participant 3 expressed "I think it depends on where you are in terms of learning [this practice] . . . how helpful the annotation would be" Participants 5 and 12 agreed. Beginners benefit from annotations that communicate information which clarifies the instructor's pose, while experienced practitioners understand these forms already and tend to use the instructor's movements more as a visual reminder of the forms.

4.5   Promote Customization and Sense of Control

The desire to customize annotations was often reported by focus group participants, which in practice would address the problem of variation in experience level discussed in the previous design guideline. Beginners may appreciate the information communicated through the *footwork diagram* annotation while experienced Tai Chi practitioners find it distracting: the needs of both users can be met if they are given the ability to turn individual annotations on and off. This extends beyond difference in experience to personal preference; the *bubbles on instructor* annotation (Fig. 5) contains the same information as the *skeleton on instructor* annotation (Fig. 3), as they both display the same joint skeleton, but some participants preferred one while some preferred the other.

5   Conclusion

This study contributes an understanding of the needs and desires of older adult Tai Chi practitioners when engaging with a virtual environment to exercise and learn the mind-body exercise. Tai Chi instructors and digital technology designers can apply the findings of this study when designing and applying digital technologies, such as digital annotations, to enhance the online learning experiences of older adult Tai Chi practitioners. Study participants also highlighted the importance of practicing Tai Chi in a community environment, as social connectedness impacted their motivation to return to in-person classes and contributed to feelings of belonging. While further work on the technology required to generate these annotations in real time is needed before a live system can be deployed, the design principles developed through this study can guide the development of digital teaching techniques that meet the needs of older adult practitioners so they may experience positive learning and health outcomes through online engagement.

Acknowledgment. This work was supported by a Catalyst Grant from McMaster University's Institute for Research on Aging (MIRA) and the NSERC funded Smart Mobility for the Aging Population (sMAP) CREATE Program at McMaster University. We thank the study's participants for their contributions as co-designers. We thank David Chung for his work on annotation mock-ups. We thank contact holders at MIRA, McMaster University's Physical Activity Centre of Excellence, and at Unifor Local 5555 Union Division of McMaster University's Retiree Association for their assistance with participant recruitment. We thank Bruce Thong for his contribution of expert knowledge as a Tai Chi chief instructor and consultant for Michael DeGroote Pain Clinic at McMaster University Medical Centre, and for the Retiree Chapter of Unifor Local 5555 union division of McMaster University's Retirees Association.

Disclosure of Interests. The authors have no competing interests to declare that are relevant to the content of this article.

References

1. Addington, E.L., Sohl, S.J., Tooze, J.A., Danhauer, S.C.: Convenient and live movement (CALM) for women undergoing breast cancer treatment: challenges and recommendations for internet-based yoga research. Complement. Ther. Med. **37**, 77–79 (2018)
2. Anderson, F., Grossman, T., Matejka, J., Fitzmaurice, G.: Youmove: enhancing movement training with an augmented reality mirror. In: Proceedings of the 26th Annual ACM Symposium on User Interface Software and Technology, pp. 311–320 (2013)

3. Bubela, D., Sacharko, L., Chan, J., Brady, M.: Balance and functional outcomes for older community-dwelling adults who practice tai chi and those who do not: a comparative study. J. Geriatr. Phys. Ther. **42**(4), 209–215 (2019)

4. CAST: Universal design for learning guidelines (2018). http://udlguidelines.cast. org

5. Corriveau, H., Tousignant, M., Gosselin, S., Boissy, P.: The use of telerehabilitation to provide an exercise program to improve balance in a post-stroke population: preliminary results. In: Donnelly, M., Paggetti, C., Nugent, C., Mokhtari, M. (eds.) Smart Homes and Health Telematics, pp. 58–65. Springer, Heidelberg (2012). https://doi.org/10.1007/978-3-642-30779-9_8

6. Donesky, D., Selman, L., McDermott, K., Citron, T., Howie-Esquivel, J.: Evaluation of the feasibility of a home-based teleyoga intervention in participants with both chronic obstructive pulmonary disease and heart failure. J. Altern. Complement. Med. **23**(9), 713–721 (2017)

7. Emard, N., et al.: Virtual mind-body programming for patients with cancer during the covid-19 pandemic: qualitative study. JMIR Cancer **7**(2), e27384 (2021)

8. Gassmann, O., Reepmeyer, G.: Universal design: innovations for all ages. In: The Silver Market Phenomenon: Marketing and Innovation in the Aging Society, pp. 101–116 (2011)

9. Gochoo, M., et al.: Novel IoT-based privacy-preserving yoga posture recognition system using low-resolution infrared sensors and deep learning. IEEE Internet Things J. **6**(4), 7192–7200 (2019)

10. Hackney, M.E., Wolf, S.L.: Impact of Tai Chi Chu'an practice on balance and mobility in older adults: an integrative review of 20 years of research. J. Geriatr. Phys. Ther. **37**(3), 127–135 (2014)

11. Hsieh, C.C., et al.: The effectiveness of a virtual reality-based tai chi exercise on cognitive and physical function in older adults with cognitive impairment. Dement. Geriatr. Cogn. Disord. **46**(5–6), 358–370 (2018)

12. Huang, A.J., Chesney, M.A., Schembri, M., Pawlowsky, S., Nicosia, F., Subak, L.L.: Rapid conversion of a group-based yoga trial for diverse older women to home-based telehealth: Lessons learned using zoom to deliver movement-based interventions. J. Integr. Complement. Med. **28**(2), 188–192 (2022)

13. Jwing-Ming, Y., Yang, J.: Tai Chi Chuan Martial Power: Advanced Yang Style. YMAA Publication Center (2015). https://books.google.ca/books? id=VNrroQEACAAJ

14. Kwok, J.Y.Y., Lee, J.J., Choi, E.P.H., Chau, P.H., Auyeung, M.: Stay mindfully active during the coronavirus pandemic: a feasibility study of mhealth-delivered mindfulness yoga program for people with parkinson's disease. BMC Complement. Med. Ther. **22**(1), 1–12 (2022)

15. Luo, Z., et al.: "left arm up!" interactive yoga training in virtual environment. In: 2011 IEEE Virtual Reality Conference, pp. 261–262. IEEE (2011)

16. Nielsen, J.: Iterative user-interface design. Computer **26**(11), 32–41 (1993)

17. Owsley, C., Sekuler, R., Siemsen, D.: Contrast sensitivity throughout adulthood. Vision. Res. **23**(7), 689–699 (1983)

18. Parimoo, S., Choi, A., Iafrate, L., Grady, C., Olsen, R.: Are older adults susceptible to visual distraction when targets and distractors are spatially separated? Aging Neuropsychol. Cogn. **31**, 1–37 (2022)

19. Rosenbaum, S., Cockton, G., Coyne, K., Muller, M., Rauch, T.: Focus groups in HCI: wealth of information or waste of resources? In: CHI 2002 Extended Abstracts on Human Factors in Computing Systems, pp. 702–703 (2002)

20. Sawyer, L.M., et al.: Rapid conversion of tai chi classes from face-to-face to virtual during the covid-19 pandemic: a quality improvement project. In: Nursing Forum, vol. 57, pp. 491–496. Wiley Online Library (2022)
21. Selman, L., McDermott, K., Donesky, D., Citron, T., Howie-Esquivel, J.: Appropriateness and acceptability of a tele-yoga intervention for people with heart failure and chronic obstructive pulmonary disease: qualitative findings from a controlled pilot study. BMC Complement. Altern. Med. 15(1), 1–13 (2015)
22. Semeraro, A., Turmo Vidal, L.: Visualizing instructions for physical training: exploring visual cues to support movement learning from instructional videos. In: Proceedings of the 2022 CHI Conference on Human Factors in Computing Systems, pp. 1–16 (2022)
23. Snyder, S., Silva, R.F., Whisenant, M.S., Milbury, K.: Videoconferenced yoga interventions for cancer patients and their caregivers during the covid-19 pandemic: a report from a clinician's perspective. Integr. Cancer Ther. 20, 15347354211019112 (2021)
24. Sungkarat, S., Boripuntakul, S., Chattipakorn, N., Watcharasaksilp, K., Lord, S.R.: Effects of tai chi on cognition and fall risk in older adults with mild cognitive impairment: a randomized controlled trial. J. Am. Geriatr. Soc. 65(4), 721–727 (2017)
25. Tse, A.C., Wong, T.W., Lee, P.H.: Effect of low-intensity exercise on physical and cognitive health in older adults: a systematic review. Sports Med.-Open 1(1), 1–13 (2015)
26. Zoom Video Communications, Inc.: Zoom. https://zoom.us/

Training Support Method with Loudness Changes in Music

Ruiyun Wang[✉], Jiayun Huang, Yuchen Jin, and Shin Takahashi

University of Tsukuba, 1-1-1 Tennodai, Tsukuba, Ibaraki, Japan
{wang,huang,jin}@iplab.cs.tsukuba.ac.jp, shin@cs.tsukuba.ac.jp

Abstract. Many methods using music to support training have been proposed. Most of these methods achieve the effects of improving poses and supporting training by changing the melody according to the postural state during training. In this study, we propose a training support method using changes in sound loudness, based on the idea that elements of music and sound other than melody (tempo, pinch, and loudness) may also be applicable to training support. Specifically, by changing the loudness of each part of pop music commonly heard in daily life in conjunction with body movements, the accuracy of movements is presented as feedback in real time. In this paper, we describe a prototype that supports training by linking hand or foot movements to changes in the loudness of the singing vocals and an experiment that investigated whether the proposed method positively affects postural accuracy and the training experience using the prototype.

Keywords: Natural User Interface · Training support · Music loudness · Physical training

1 Introduction

Various interaction methods have been proposed to support daily training. Among these, sound-based methods offer advantages such as not requiring the user to look at a screen or attach devices to the body. Sound-based methods assist posture and motivation improvement by adjusting the music's tempo or melody based on the user's movements have been proposed [6,8,9,17]. However, discussion on utilizing other elements of music (e.g., timbre, rhythm, volume) for training support remains limited. Our study explores the possibility of applying another musical element - loudness to training support.

We propose a training support method using changes in music loudness. Our method achieves training support by mapping the movements of different body parts to the loudness of various music components (e.g., vocal, bass, drums, guitar). For instance, when performing squats, the position of the knees could be reflected in the loudness of the guitar, and the correct hip position could be assessed through the loudness of the vocal (Fig. 1). By indicating the position of various body parts using the loudness of individual music components, we aimed to achieve posture improvement. Simultaneously, by providing real-time

V. G. Duffy (Ed.): HCII 2024, LNCS 14711, pp. 384–395, 2024.
https://doi.org/10.1007/978-3-031-61066-0_23

control over the music, we anticipate improving motivation to continue training and fostering a sense of reward after posture improvement.

In this paper, we present a preliminary study aimed at exploring the perceptibility of changes in the loudness of vocal parts within music. Additionally, we introduce and evaluate a novel prototype designed to aid the movement of an individual body part. This prototype operates by adjusting the loudness of singing vocals within a musical composition, thereby facilitating targeted movement support.

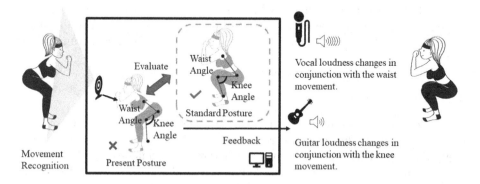

Fig. 1. Squat support using music loudness

2   Related Work

2.1   Sound and Training Support

Music is utilized in numerous training support systems. Khan et al. developed a musical exercise platform for the visually impaired using MIDI sound melodies [6]. Newbold et al. used unstable melodies for moderate stretching [9] and improve squatting poses [8]. Ghai et al. discussed whether the angle of the knee can be monitored by changes in the pitch and loudness of real-time white noise [4]. Keesing et al. proposed an exercise game to support HIIT (High-Intensity Interval Training) by changing the tempo corresponding to movements [5]. HealthSit assisted lower back stretching with spatial music [13].

Apart from music, training support methods often design voice interfaces based on the coach's verbal instructions. EyesFreeYoga provides real-time verbal feedback on differences from its reference poses based on coach's instruction [12]. Commercial exercise games also use virtual coaches to support training. For example, RingFit Adventure [11] and Fitboxing [10], fitness software from Nintendo, use a virtual coach to provide audio instructions and encouragement to the player during training.

2.2   Training Support Without Using Sound

Visual feedback is one of the main methods being used. Clarke et al. proposed a method to synchronize a training guide video with the user's movements [2]. Physio@Home uses multiple cameras to present the user's movements simultaneously with the guide video [15]. SleeveAR provides guidance and performance feedback with images projected onto the arm and floor [14]. For interactions aimed at improving poses, BodyLights employs markers projected by a wearable 3D-printed projection device to aid in aligning and refining the body's movements and orientation during training [16].

In addition to visual feedback, vibration is used frequently as well: GymSoles presents the center of gravity of the body during squats with vibrations that strike the feet [3]. Zhang et al. presented incorrect poses during running by vibration [18].

2.3   The Positioning of Our Research

Although music is often used to provide feedback in existing movement support methods, there has been no proposal to correlate music loudness with body movement. Moreover, questions such as whether music loudness can be used for support, the extent of support music loudness can offer, and how to utilize music loudness for support have not been explored. The loudness that changes in accordance with body movement has the potential to provide posture feedback and improve posture, while changes in loudness without altering the music's structure may have the advantage of minimally impacting the listening experience. In our research, we proposed a movement support method that correlates the loudness of various parts of music with the movement of different body parts. Through a loudness perception experiment, we analyzed the possibility of using musical loudness for support. Additionally, we implemented a support system for movements of a single body part and evaluated the effectiveness of musical loudness support on two types of movements with different levels of difficulty, discussing how loudness can be used in movement support.

3   Loudness Perception Experiment

In this experiment, we investigate how well changes in the loudness of singing vocals in music can be perceived, and assess the feasibility of utilizing vocal loudness variations to support training involving movement of a specific body part. Participants listened to music featuring progressively increasing vocal loudness and provided feedback on their perceptions of the loudness levels.

3.1   Music Used in the Experiment

One of the objectives of the proposed method is to facilitate training support using music that users listen to regularly. Consequently, for the music used in the experiment, we chose two pop music tracks with relatively clear rhythms: a female singer's 'South Of The Water'[1] and a male singer's 'I'm Alright'[2] (original loudness: -23LUFS). From each piece of music, we extracted 15 segments of varying durations to correspond with body movements of different speeds. Specifically, we selected five segments each for durations of 0–5, 5–10, and 10–15 s. We gradually increased the loudness of the vocals in each segment linearly from 0% to 149.8% of the original track (+3.5 dB), thereby creating a total of 30 music stimuli for the two pieces of music. Out of these 30 music stimuli for the experiment, 24 (8 segments each for 0–5 s, 5–10 s, and 10–15 s) were used for the experiment, and 6 (2 segments each for 0–5 s, 5–10 s, and 10–15 s) were used for practice.

3.2 Participants and Procedure

The participants were eight graduate students, ranging in age from 24 to 29, who were not majoring in music (4 males and 4 females).

Before the experiment, time was taken to familiarize the participants with the music used in the experiment. They were given files of the experimental music (total listening time of approximately 7 min for the two songs) and were asked to listen to both tracks at least twice a day for more than four days.

To ascertain the participants' familiarity with the experimental music, we asked them about their frequency of listening to the tracks. Additionally, we played the first ten seconds of the music and requested they identify the corresponding song titles. The perception experiment proceeded only after the participants successfully named the correct songs.

Practice time to get accustomed to the experimental software was provided before the experiment. During the practice time, participants listened to six practice music stimuli. They answered the loudness of the singing voice by manipulating a slide bar within the experimental software using a mouse, continuing this process until they became adept at using the software.

During the experiment, the 24 music stimuli were each presented randomly three times. Participants indicated the perceived loudness multiplier (perceived value) relative to the original loudness by adjusting the slider bar.

3.3 Results

Table 1 shows the average perceived loudness of the experiment participants when the loudness of the singing was adjusted to 149.8% of the original track. We can observe a noticeable difference in the perceived loudness that correlates with the duration of the music stimulus. For music stimuli of 5 s or less, the average value of the perceived maximum loudness was 67.8% of the original track. It indicated that it was difficult to accurately predict loudness when the duration of the music stimulus was relatively short. The participants mentioned they felt difficulty in correctly perceiving loudness due to the rapid change.

---

[1] South Of The Water, ACTIONS!, 2012.
[2] I am Alright, Angels in Amplifiers, 2014.

Table 1. Average perceived value at maximum singing loudness (149.8% of the original track)

Duration of the Music Stimulus (s)	Average Perception of Loudness (%)
0–5 (Average: 3.9)	67.8
5–10 (Average: 8.0)	96.9
10–15 (Average: 12.8)	106.3

As the duration of the music stimulus increased, a trend was observed where the accuracy of loudness perception improved. The average value of the perceived maximum loudness for 5–10 s was 96.9%, and for 10–15 s, the value was 106.3%. Most of the participants recognized the singing voice after the loudness exceeded 30% of the original song and felt a linear change after it exceeded 50%. As an example, the perception results of one participant (P7) for a 14-second music stimulus are shown in Fig. 2. The singing voice was perceived after the loudness exceeded approximately 26.8% (-41LUFS, -27 dB) and a linear change was felt after it exceeded 53.5% (-36LUFS, -26 dB).

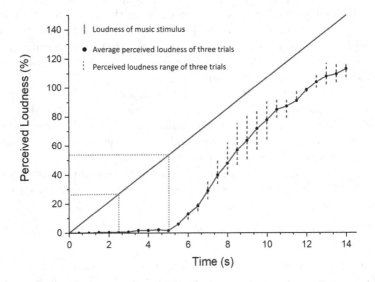

Fig. 2. P7's perception of loudness for a 14-second music stimulus

4   Prototype System

We implemented a prototype system to support two training exercises that involve movements of a single body part: keeping arms horizontal (Training

1 (T1), Fig. 3) and keeping legs vertical (Training 2 (T2), Fig. 4). The standard method for doing both training involves lifting the hands or legs slowly from a natural and relaxed position at a constant speed (for 10 s), maintaining the hands or legs and the torso in a vertical position for 30 s, then slowly lowering the hands or legs at a constant speed (for 10 s) to return to the relaxed position. During the training, muscles in the torso and arms or legs are engaged. Throughout the training, the loudness of vocals changes based on the movements of the hands or legs. When the hands or legs are in the designated positions to be maintained, the loudness adjusts to the loudness corresponding to the original music parts' loudness.

Fig. 3. T1: Keeping arms horizontal

Fig. 4. T2: Keeping legs vertical

We utilized the skeletal recognition of Microsoft Azure Kinect [7], which includes a built-in depth camera, for the recognition of the positions of the arms and legs by angle A1 (Fig. 2) between the right arm and the torso and angle A2 (Fig. 3) between the right leg and the torso. We establish a correlation between the loudness of the vocal and angle A1 or A2. Due to detection issues in Kinect's skeleton recognition, especially during T2 where only one leg is often detected, and assuming T1 is left-right symmetric, only the data from the right side of the body (the side facing Kinect) is used to affect the vocals' loudness in the implementation. The loudness of vocals is linearly correlated with changes in joint angles. Based on the loudness perception experiment's findings that users tend to perceive vocals' loudness as smaller than its actual value, the loudness of vocals in the relaxed position is expressed as 15% of the original loudness, while the designated correct positions (hands or legs and torso at 90°) is expressed as 120% of the original loudness. The music utilized in the implementation is South Of The Water, the same song in the loudness perception experiment. Participants listened to the music during training while wearing AirPods 3 [1].

5   Evaluation Experiment

We conducted an evaluation experiment with the prototype system to assess the effectiveness of support for single-part movement training through vocal loudness changes.

5.1   Participants and Procedure

We recruited eight participants, separate from those involved in the loudness perception experiment, comprising four females and four males, all aged between 20 and 29, majoring in subjects other than music and physical education, with good health. Among the participants, four had regular exercise habits, and three of them specifically practiced bodyweight training.

It is assumed that users are familiar with and accustomed to the music used for assistance. To ensure this familiarity, participants received the experimental music in WAV format three days before the scheduled experiment day and were asked to listen to the music at least three times a day. Additionally, before the experiment, participants were asked to wear the AirPods, listen to the music once, and adjust the system's loudness to an appropriate level they felt, which remained fixed during the experiment.

At the beginning of the experiment, the participants were explained about the overview of the proposed method, the objectives, and the flow of the experiment. Subsequently, the participants were asked to perform two types of training (T1 and T2) using the system. They were informed about the correlation between changes in vocals' loudness and body movements, understanding that harmonious vocals' loudness represents that the correct positions have been achieved. After detailing the methods for changing loudness, we verified that each participant had the physical capability to perform the training. Participants were also informed that they could stop the training if there were physical exhaustion and were encouraged to take sufficient rest during the experiment. Participants were asked to have practices to familiarize themselves with the correlation between vocals' loudness and body movements. During the practice, participants were asked to try raising both hands and both legs at various speeds and angles.

During the experiment, participants were required to perform T1 and T2 three times under two conditions: one with no change in vocal loudness (i.e., listening to the original song as is) and the other with changes in vocal loudness. A rest period of at least five minutes was provided between each training, ensuring that participants had taken sufficient rest. Finally, evaluation of the proposed method was collected through a questionnaire and a brief interview.

5.2   Results and Discussions

Table 2 presents the results of the questionnaire. In the survey, participants were asked to rate four items on a 7-point Likert scale: the ability of changes in vocal loudness during training to reflect body movements (Correspondence) and

Table 2. Answers of the questionnaire in 7-point Likert scale

	Correspondence	Improvement	Motivation	Reward
P1	7	3	4	6
P2	5	5	6	6
P3	7	4	6	5
P4	5	6	4	5
P5	7	6 .	7	6
P6	7	6	7	7
P7	7	7	6	7
P8	6	7	6	7
Average	6.4	5.5	5.8	6.1

improve posture (Improvement), the effectiveness of loudness feedback in motivating to continue training (Motivation), and the potential for obtaining a sense of reward after improving poses (Reward).

Additionally, Fig. 5 illustrates the changes in angle A1 while participants performed the T1, and Fig. 6 shows the changes in angle A2 during the T2. It's worth noting that the data used in the figures exclude outliers caused by instances where Kinect failed to correctly recognize skeletons.

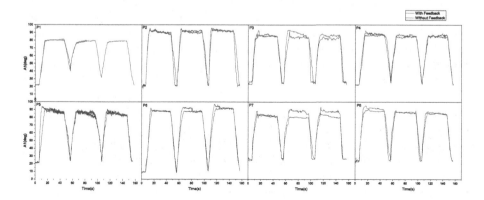

Fig. 5. Changes in angle A1 during training T1

Posture Improvement. The results of the question Correspondence and Improvement were an average of 6.4 points and 5.5 points, respectively. From these results, it can be inferred that many participants were able to grasp their postures to some extent from the feedback of vocals' loudness and found the feedback to be useful for improving postures.

Looking at Fig. 6, the effects of the proposed method can be speculated, especially in the challenging T2 training where grasping and maintaining poses

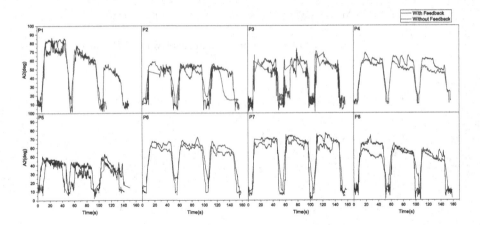

Fig. 6. Changes in angle A2 during training T2

are difficult. Comparing the feedback presence and absence in Fig. 6 (blue and red lines), participants P2, P4, P5, P7, and P8 maintained a position closer to the standard (angle of 90°) when there was feedback on vocals' loudness. Additionally, it was observed that participants adjusted poses more often when feedback was present. Differences in the frequency of these adjustments can be inferred from the data, such as P1 and P4 in Fig. 6.

Positive comments about pose improvement in the T2 training were also obtained from interviews. For example, P4 mentioned, "The support for maintaining difficult poses is good." P7 stated, "When performing T2, I worked hard to maintain the correct poses to hear the correct loudness of singing vocals." and P8 commented, "By the feedback, I realized that the position of lifting my leg was not perfect. However, I couldn't adjust my pose due to lack of strength." These comments align with the results in Fig. 6, indicating the effectiveness of the loudness feedback for T2. Furthermore, P1 commented that the support for challenging training was difficult: "I focused on maintaining poses, so I couldn't pay attention to improving my poses from the changes in vocals' loudness."

On the other hand, the training T1 had lower difficulty, making it easy to grasp and maintain correct poses. Therefore, the pose improvement was not prominently observed in this experiment. Only P7 showed relatively noticeable arm adjustments in Fig. 5. From the interview, it was found that P7 could grasp the position of the hands from the vocals' loudness. "I felt the loudness was small, so I raised my hands." To investigate the support effect for subtle pose adjustments, future experiments may involve training with more noticeable deviations from the standard poses(e.g., plank, where the lower back tends to drop). Additionally, considerations are being made for the use of devices or methods that allow for more accurate collection of movement data.

Motivation and Reward. The average score for the question on Motivation was 5.8, while for Reward, it was 6.1. From these results, it can be inferred that the proposed method had a certain degree of motivational effect on supporting the training.

From Fig. 6, the support effect during T2 is noticeable. For instance, P1 ceased after attempting T2 twice without feedback; however, with feedback, P1 was able to successfully complete it three times. Similarly, P2 discontinued the third attempt of T2 midway without feedback, but with feedback, was able to adjust and hold the pose until the end of the third attempt. The effect of maintaining poses for longer periods appeared alongside the pose improvement, suggesting that the posture improvement effect is realized on the basis of the motivational effect.

In interviews, four participants positively acknowledged the training support effect. For instance, P1 mentioned, "I wanted to hear the feedback of vocals' loudness, so I was able to complete three times of T2," P2 stated, "With feedback, I focused more on my pose improvement, and the thought of giving up on training decreased," P5 commented, "The changes in vocals' loudness increased sense of immersion in training and concentration on movements," and P8 expressed, "Training became enjoyable with the changing vocals."

Furthermore, to enhance the support effect, there were many voices expressing a desire for personalized music recommendations based on individual music preferences and types of training. Advice was also given to expand beyond pop music to include other music genres. Additionally, comments suggested that providing information on training duration and the number of repetitions simultaneously could positively impact motivation.

Comprehensive Impression. Many participants commented that they could adjust their posture naturally in response to changes in loudness, with many describing the method as "a very interesting proposal" during interviews. Specifically, P2, P5, and P7, who regularly engage in weight training, shared particularly positive feedback in their interviews, expressing a desire for a system that could support them in their daily training routines.

P2 commented that "the proposed method works very well for anaerobic exercises, but it is not suitable for aerobic exercises (with intense movements) because I do not want a sudden change in loudness (during training)." P4 holds the same idea and suggests that the tempo of the music should be changed to support aerobic exercises.

Moreover, we got a suggestion that feedback should be presented by combining music and words. In the future, we plan to explore the possibility of using a combination of vocal and music to provide more accurate and effective support.

6   Conclusion and Future Work

In this study, we proposed an interaction method that utilizes the loudness of vocals for training support. The proposed method aims to achieve effective interaction by dynamically changing the loudness of each part of the music in sync with the user's movements during training, with the goal of supporting pose improvement and enhancing training motivation.

The loudness perception experiment confirmed the duration of music and the range of loudness within which linear changes can be perceived. Based on the results, an evaluation experiment using a prototype support system was conducted. The experiment involves two training types, T1 (relatively simple) and T2 (difficult), to assess the support effectiveness of the proposed method for training involving the movement of a single part of the body. The proposed method demonstrated effects in improving poses and supporting training for exercises where grasping and maintaining poses were relatively challenging.

Due to detection issues with Kinect, subtle pose adjustments during the experiment could not be analyzed directly from joint data. Therefore, for future work, we plan to increase the variety of training types, record training situations more precisely with other methods, and conduct evaluation experiments allowing for a more comprehensive analysis of the support effectiveness.

Furthermore, as the support effectiveness for T1 was not prominent in this experiment, it suggests that the current support method may not be able to present subtle differences in angles. We plan to explore adjustments in the correlation between movement and loudness changes to see if more nuanced differences can be presented.

Additionally, based on the participants' comments about the need for the feedback of personalized music recommendations, we aim to apply the proposed method to a broader range of music genres and explore the realization of a music recommendation system based on user preferences and training conditions. For example, recommending fast-paced or slow-paced music based on the difficulty level of the training is an idea for exploration.

References

1. Apple: Airpods3 (2021). https://www.apple.com/jp/airpods-3rd-generation/
2. Clarke, C., Cavdir, D., Chiu, P., Denoue, L., Kimber, D.: Reactive Video: adaptive video playback based on user motion for supporting physical activity. In: Proceedings of the 33rd Annual ACM Symposium on User Interface Software and Technology, pp. 196–208 (2020)
3. Elvitigala, D.S., Matthies, D.J., David, L., Weerasinghe, C., Nanayakkara, S.: Gymsoles: improving squats and dead-lifts by visualizing the user's center of pressure. In: Proceedings of the 2019 CHI Conference on Human Factors in Computing Systems, pp. 1–12 (2019)
4. Ghai, S., Schmitz, G., Hwang, T.H., Effenberg, A.O.: Auditory proprioceptive integration: effects of real-time kinematic auditory feedback on knee proprioception. Front. Neurosci. **12**, 142 (2018)
5. Keesing, A., Ooi, M., Wu, O., Ye, X., Shaw, L., Wünsche, B.C.: HIIT with hits: using music and gameplay to induce HIIT in exergames. In: Proceedings of the Australasian Computer Science Week Multiconference, pp. 1–10 (2019)
6. Khan, R.A., Jeon, M., Yoon, T.: "Musical Exercise" for people with visual impairments: a preliminary study with the blindfolded. In: International Conference on Auditory Display, 2018 (2018)

7. Microsoft: Azure kinect (2021). https://azure.microsoft.com/ja-jp/services/kinect-dk/

8. Newbold, J.W., Bianchi-Berthouze, N., Gold, N.E.: Musical expectancy in squat sonification for people who struggle with physical activity. Georgia Institute of Technology (2017)

9. Newbold, J.W., Bianchi-Berthouze, N., Gold, N.E., Tajadura-Jiménez, A., Williams, A.C.: Musically informed sonification for chronic pain rehabilitation: facilitating progress & avoiding over-doing. In: Proceedings of the 2016 CHI Conference on Human Factors in Computing Systems, pp. 5698–5703 (2016)

10. Nintendo: Fit boxinge (2018). https://fitboxing.net/

11. Nintendo: Ringfit adventure (2020). https://www.nintendo.co.jp/ring/index.html

12. Rector, K., Bennett, C.L., Kientz, J.A.: Eyes-free yoga: an exergame using depth cameras for blind & low vision exercise. In: Proceedings of the 15th International ACM Sigaccess Conference on Computers and Accessibility, pp. 1–8 (2013)

13. Ren, X., Yu, B., Lu, Y., Chen, Y., Pu, P.: Healthsit: designing posture-based interaction to promote exercise during fitness breaks. Int. J. Hum.-Comput. Interact. **35**(10), 870–885 (2019)

14. Sousa, M., Vieira, J., Medeiros, D., Arsenio, A., Jorge, J.: Sleevear: augmented reality for rehabilitation using realtime feedback. In: Proceedings of the 21st International Conference on Intelligent User Interfaces, pp. 175–185 (2016)

15. Tang, R., Yang, X.D., Bateman, S., Jorge, J., Tang, A.: Physio@Home: exploring visual guidance and feedback techniques for physiotherapy exercises. In: Proceedings of the 33rd Annual ACM Conference on Human Factors in Computing Systems, pp. 4123–4132 (2015)

16. Turmo Vidal, L., Zhu, H., Riego-Delgado, A.: Bodylights: open-ended augmented feedback to support training towards a correct exercise execution. In: Proceedings of the 2020 CHI Conference on Human Factors in Computing Systems, pp. 1–14 (2020)

17. Yin, B., Bailey, S., Hu, E., Jayarekera, M., Shaw, A., Wünsche, B.C.: Tour de tune 2-auditory-game-motor synchronisation with music tempo in an immersive virtual reality exergame. In: Proceedings of the 2021 Australasian Computer Science Week Multiconference, pp. 1–10 (2021)

18. Zhang, X., Huang, M.C., Ren, F., Xu, W., Guan, N., Yi, W.: Proper running posture guide: a wearable biomechanics capture system. In: Proceedings of the 8th International Conference on Body Area Networks, pp. 83–89 (2013)

Design Research on VR System Integrating Task-Based Teaching and Learning for Manual Skills Training in Dental Students

Zhihao Cheng, Siu Shing Man[✉], and Hua Ming Peng

School of Design, South China University of Technology, Guangzhou 510006,
People's Republic of China
2073803526@qq.com

Abstract. This study employed Task-Based Teaching and Learning (TBTL) in Virtual Reality Assisted Dental Training (VRADT) to seamlessly integrate Virtual Reality (VR) into the overall dental training process. This new integration focused on addressing the current deficiency in manual skills among dental students during school training and clinical internships. This study involved a comprehensive review of VRADT and TBTL literature, culminating in the proposal of a TBTL—VRADT Integration Model. Utilizing survey methodology (34 valid responses) and user interviews (5 dental students), the study explored dental students' perspectives on the application of VR in tooth extraction procedures. The TBTL—VRADT model was illustrated in the context of VR-assisted dental student training for tooth extraction. Employing the Kano model (34 valid responses), essential features for VR systems in tooth extraction procedures were identified. The study concluded with the design of a high-fidelity VR system prototype based on the TBTL—VRADT and Kano models. The TBTL—VRADT model facilitated the integration of meaningful tasks throughout VR-assisted dental training, effectively harmonizing VR with the overall dental training process. This model played a pivotal role in planning the comprehensive design of VR systems for Virtual Reality Assisted Dental Training (VRADT). The TBTL—VRADT model significantly enhanced practical manual skills training for dental students, improving their proficiency in hands-on procedures.

Keywords: Virtual Reality Assisted Dental Training · Task-Based Teaching and Learning · Manual Skills Training

1 Challenges Faced by Dental Students

1.1 Current Situation

The significance of manual dexterity for dental students in their clinical internships and future medical careers is self-evident. However, the manual dexterity of dental students has not received sufficient cultivation and practice during the educational process. Recently, the author utilized web scraping techniques to extract data from two prominent

© The Author(s), under exclusive license to Springer Nature Switzerland AG 2024
V. G. Duffy (Ed.): HCII 2024, LNCS 14711, pp. 396–411, 2024.
https://doi.org/10.1007/978-3-031-61066-0_24

knowledge-sharing platforms in China, namely "Baidu" and "REDhub", by entering the key search term "manual dexterity of dental students." Then, 749 and 4720 relevant entries were obtained from platforms, respectively.

Subsequently, the author focused on six key terms related to perceived poor manual dexterity, namely "poor manual dexterity," "clumsy hands," "handicap," "handicapped," "dexterity," and "very poor manual dexterity." The entries associated with these keywords were then subjected to statistical analysis. The results indicated that among the entries on "Baidu," 24% of dental students expressed self-perceived poor manual dexterity; on "REDhub," this proportion surged to a substantial 59%. The following Table 1 presents detailed statistical results.

Furthermore, an examination of selected entries reveals that poor manual dexterity significantly impacts the confidence levels of dental students and influences their future career planning. The findings underscore the pressing need to address and enhance the manual dexterity of dental students during their education to mitigate the negative impact on their self-confidence and future professional trajectories.

Table 1. Detailed statistical results about relevant entries.

key terms\Platforms	Baidu	REDhub
Entries about poor manual dexterity, clumsy hands, "handicap", "handicapped", dexterity, very poor manual dexterity	182	2794
Entries about others	567	1926
Sum	749	4720
Percentage of entries about poor manual dexterity, clumsy hands, "handicap", "handicapped", dexterity, very poor manual dexterity	24%	59%

During clinical internships, the suboptimal manual dexterity of dental students can result in many adverse consequences, impacting patient safety, student confidence, and the professional reputation of educational institutions [1]. From a patient perspective, the inadequate manual skills of students, manifested through incorrect selection or usage of surgical instruments and a lack of proficient surgical techniques, may lead to procedural errors, thereby elevating the risk of patient injury and complications, potentially culminating in severe medical incidents. The ineptitude displayed by students in the treatment process can also induce discomfort in patients, subsequently diminishing their satisfaction with the provided treatment.

For the students, deficient manual dexterity poses challenges in the competitive job market, particularly in fields requiring highly developed surgical skills. The repercussions extend beyond the academic setting, as students with suboptimal hands-on abilities may encounter difficulties securing employment opportunities that demand high surgical proficiency. Consequently, addressing and ameliorating the deficiencies in manual dexterity during clinical internships is imperative for the individual student's future career prospects and the overall safety and satisfaction of patients undergoing dental procedures.

1.2 The Reasons for Poor Manual Dexterity Among Dental Students

The deficient manual dexterity observed among dental students may be influenced by various factors, prominently including: limited practical opportunities, inadequate simulation training equipment, insufficient realism in simulation training, disparities in teaching methodologies, clinical environment pressures, lack of feedback and guidance, and a deficit in proactive learning. Experimental teaching in dental education serves as a bridge to clinical practice. However, constrained by limited laboratory conditions and faculty resources, students face restricted access to laboratories. Some experimental projects incur high costs, leading to inadequate supplies of experimental materials. The high prices of certain experimental equipment make it impractical to ensure each student's possession of a complete set. Limited sources for obtaining experimental specimens and specific storage requirements further complicate the situation.

As a result of these challenges, some crucial experimental projects face difficulties in implementation, thereby restricting the enhancement of teaching quality and effectiveness in dental education. Insufficient clinical resources in schools contribute to a shortage of patient exposure opportunities for students during practical operations. Additionally, inadequate investment in advanced simulation training equipment hinders students from engaging in comprehensive simulated exercises in low-risk environments. Existing simulation training devices often fail to effectively replicate real clinical scenarios, causing students to feel ill-prepared for actual environments. Consequently, students may experience nervousness and anxiety, potentially impacting their manual stability and operational accuracy in the presence of real patients.

Compounding these issues, some students exhibit inherently poor manual dexterity and lack enthusiasm for improving these skills. Consequently, they fail to actively participate in additional learning and practice opportunities, leading to a detrimental cycle. Although the causes of deficient manual dexterity among dental students are multifaceted, addressing these challenges requires a commitment to enhancing traditional dental education environments and methodologies at the foundational level.

2   The Application of Virtual Reality in Dentistry

2.1   Virtual Reality-Assisted Dental Training (VRADT)

Overcoming various limitations of traditional teaching models, virtual simulation technology provides a pathway for simulating real learning experiences. Researchers believe that the cross-integration and innovative development of next-generation information technologies, such as Virtual Reality (VR) and digital surgical design with modern dental technologies are effective approaches to enhance the quality and scale of dental education, aiding in improving students' enthusiasm for learning and shortening the training time for dental professionals. Currently, an increasing number of educators are exploring the application of these technologies in dental education [2].

Domestic universities are establishing virtual simulation experimental teaching centers to enhance teaching quality and efficiency more effectively. The introduction of VR technology into dental education has led to the establishment of a virtual simulation teaching resource platform for dentistry, significantly overcoming limitations imposed by various experimental conditions. This contributes to consolidating students' theoretical knowledge and effectively cultivates their practical operational abilities.

Currently, many researchers have applied VR technology in various areas of dental education, achieving significant success. In orthognathic surgery, Chinese researcher Liu Hanghang implemented VR technology in early clinical internship teaching. The students in the VR teaching group demonstrated significantly higher scores in professional assessments compared to the traditional teaching group's average scores. Additionally, the VR teaching group's ratings for the difficulty of learning during the internship were significantly lower than the average difficulty ratings of the traditional teaching group. This approach breaks through the constraints of teaching time and space, addressing challenges related to the complex anatomical structures of the facial region and the limited field of view in orthognathic surgery teaching operations. In oral anatomy and physiology, research by Reymus M and colleagues utilized VR to teach root canal anatomy to dental undergraduates. The results indicated that VR simulation can enhance dental students' understanding of root canal anatomy, and they highly appreciated the integration of VR simulation into endodontic courses. From a teaching perspective, VR in root canal anatomy instruction offers considerable advantages over 2D radiography and CBCT scans [3]. Sukhdeep Murbay's study has significant implications for the field of dental restoration. The research introduced the Moog Simodont Dental Training Simulator (VR) into the preclinical course of the direct restoration module in dental surgery courses, using both manual and digital methods to evaluate the performance of undergraduate dental students. The study demonstrated a significant improvement in student performance using the Moog Simodont Dental Training Simulator (VR) [4]. In a study by Baoping Zhang and colleagues, aiming to explore assessment methods in clinical implant dentistry courses and evaluate the effectiveness of a virtual simulation platform, experimental results concluded that virtual simulation education, especially involving jawbone simulation models, can enhance students' implantology performance and training. This research has important implications for implant dentistry, particularly considering the current increase in demand for clinical oral implant procedures. Furthermore, VR technology has played a crucial role and shown research advancements in various dental fields, including periodontology and dental pulp disease studies [5].

2.2 Benefits and Drawbacks of Virtual Reality-Assisted Dental Training

From the current studies about virtual reality-assisted dental training(VRADT) in various fields of dentistry, it can be observed that VR technology has the potential to visualize abstract medical concepts, assisting students in gaining a deeper understanding and establishing a three-dimensional and hierarchical sense of complex structures. This aids in memory retention, improves learning efficiency, stimulates students' enthusiasm for learning, and cultivates their abilities for practical innovation and independent learning [1].

Researchers primarily employ VR technology to present virtual simulation platforms and three-dimensional models of oral and maxillofacial structures, including dental models, dental arch models, skull models, jaw movements, comprehensive dental treatment units, and simulated patients, among others. These models help students better comprehend the diagnosis and treatment processes of oral diseases, understand and master the anatomical structures of various parts of the human oral cavity, and become familiar with dental instrument usage methods and procedures. Consequently, this provides a simulated learning platform to enhance the manual dexterity of medical students [6].

However, in the current application of VR to dental education research, there are not only some technical issues, such as the realism of the models, but also problems related to subjects experiencing dizziness. While VR technology advances, there are still technical limitations in graphical and perceptual details compared to real-life situations. This may affect students' understanding of actual anatomical structures.

2.3 Shortcomings of Virtual Reality-Assisted Dental Training Research

The application of VR in dental education can be improved by considering dimensions beyond technical limitations, particularly in enhancing the teaching process for VR-assisted dental training. However, there are two current shortcomings in the research on VR-assisted dental training: First, the results in existing studies are inconsistent, depending on how researchers integrate VR into the dental education process. Some studies suggest a lack of statistically significant differences in experimental data between control and experimental groups. The seamless integration of VR into the dental education process is crucial, directly impacting the design of educational content and the success of teaching outcomes. However, there is a lack of focus on whether better methods, such as task-based teaching and learning, are needed to integrate VR more effectively into dental education. Second, researchers have primarily concentrated on the effectiveness of VR technology in specific domains, neglecting an exploration of which functionalities are crucial in the application of VR to dental education systems. There is a gap in research regarding the overall system design and the important aspects of human-computer interaction within VR applied to dental education.

3   Task-Based Teaching and Learning (TBTL)

3.1 The Application Fields of Task-Based Teaching and Learning

The approach centered around tasks is referred to as Task-Based Teaching Method or Task-Based Learning Teaching and Learning (TBTL). TBTL, originating from Kolb's Experiential Learning Theory in 1984, has been widely applied in education. Over the years, TBTL has been extensively used in language learning processes and various educational domains such as vocational training, science education, arts education, physical education, and information technology education. In a study conducted by Munir Hussain Anjum investigating the impact of TBTL on learners' oral skills, it was found that the subjects using the task-based teaching method showed statistically significant differences in average scores for oral skills compared to those using traditional teaching methods. The post-test scores of the former were significantly higher than those of the latter. The research results support the effectiveness of TBTL as a language teaching method [7]. Domestic researcher Chen Yong explored the application of task-based teaching in organic spectrum analysis courses, closely following the forefront of subject development, task-oriented, aiming to explore the enhancement of students' abilities in learning theoretical knowledge in class, autonomous learning, and problem-solving. Zhang Ziyang investigated how the use of task-based teaching methods in physical education practices could effectively enhance the interest of junior high school students in sports. TBTL is widely applied in various educational fields to address issues such as the complex and diverse structure of relevant disciplines, the complexity of knowledge, and the difficulty of memorization. This provides a strong reference for applying TBTL to dental education.

3.2 The Integration of Task-Based Teaching and Learning with Technology

While TBTL has many advantages, it is not considered a perfect teaching method, and it is continually being optimized. The enhancement of TBTL through technology has been a focal point of research. González-Lloret and Ortega proposed a conceptualization of task-based language teaching in computer-assisted environments, where tasks are integrated into technology not only as a medium but also as an opportunity for "learning language through practice" [8]. In an experimental study, Lin integrated technology into task-based language teaching to explore students' self-regulated learning in a gamified learning environment. She found that technology-enhanced task-based language teaching improved students' autonomy, interest, and cognitive learning [9]. Technology integration into TBTL is increasingly studied, and the incorporation of TBTL into new technologies, such as VR, is seen as a significant future direction. Furthermore, combining TBTL with technology tends to diminish the traditional role of teachers in education.

In 2020, Kurhila and Salla conducted a study that combined TBTL with computer program intervention in Finnish language learning. They used the LanCook kitchen program based on task-based language learning principles, linking the real scenario of a kitchen with knowledge related to the Finnish language. Learners adjusted the interactive process based on their needs and decided whether and how to respond to the computer's prompts. The computer's role was similar to that of a teacher, providing instructions (initiating), students were expected to perform the required actions (responding), and the computer accepted or rejected the actions (feedback). The study illustrated how a real-world learning environment, such as a kitchen, and its authentic ecological context demonstrated how learners could regulate language learning based on learning goals and the progress of interactions. Student engagement was a key feature in promoting learning, as students were active agents of their own learning. This research provides important insights and possibilities for applying TBTL to self-directed student learning [10].

3.3 The Framework of Task-Based Teaching and Learning

According to the perspectives of Ellis and Shintani, the purpose of task-based teaching method is to engage learners in meaning-centered activities through the execution of tasks [11]. Lynch and Maclean (2000) argue that TBTL is rational because the tasks chosen in TBTL are replicated in a way that represents real tasks [12]. To implement TBTL, researchers have proposed various models for teaching stages.

The TBTL framework proposed by Wills primarily consists of pre-task, task cycle, and language focus stages. In the pre-task, the theme and task are introduced. The task cycle involves pairs or groups working together. Learners prepare for the next stage by making statements, informing the whole class how they completed the task. They then report on the task to the entire class, and the teacher provides critical assessment of each group's presentation. The language focus stage is further divided into analysis and practice [13].

Ellis's (2003) Task-based Language Learning Framework model differs significantly from Wills's framework. Ellis suggests that only the task-based language learning stage is effective, and other stages before and after the task do not truly impact the task-based language learning process [14]. According to Nunan, task-based learning involves five elements: goals, input, process, roles, and environment [15]. This study will further investigate based on Wills's TBTL framework, as it provides a clearer delineation of the steps involved in the task (see Fig. 1).

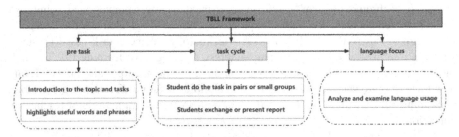

Fig. 1. Wills's TBTL framework.

4 TBTL-VRADT Integration Model

Based on the previous research on VR-assisted dental training(VRADT) and the exploration of the potential application of TBTL in dental education, a fusion model of TBTL and VR-assisted dental training (TBTL-VRADT) is summarized. This model integrates Wills's TBTL framework with some adjustments. Wills's framework emphasizes pre-task, task cycle, and language focus, all applied to the language teaching process. However, a further analysis of these three components reveals their correspondence to three stages of the learning process (see Fig. 2).

The first stage involves setting clear objectives and preliminary learning and understanding of language knowledge, such as grasping the words and grammar needed. This stage is an individual's preliminary learning, mainly preparing for the application of language knowledge in the next stage. The second stage is crucial, focusing on consolidating and applying knowledge. In this stage, meaningful tasks are completed to further apply the language acquired in the first stage, achieving the effect of knowledge consolidation. The third stage involves joint analysis and evaluation of language knowledge by students and teachers. It can be seen that Wills's framework emphasizes not the

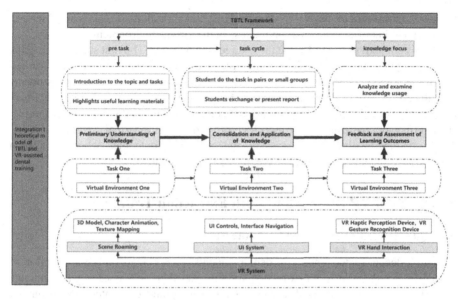

Fig. 2. TBTL-VRADT Integration Model.

type of knowledge being learned but how different stages of the learning process are meaningfully linked.

In previous studies on the application of VR in dental medicine, researchers have paid little attention to how VR is integrated into the systematic teaching process of dental training. Instead, VR technology has been applied to a small part of the training process, with a focus on investigating the effectiveness of VR intervention in training outcomes. This is where the significance of combining TBTL with dental training lies in making the VR-assisted dental training process more systematic and helping to stabilize the training outcomes.

The fusion model comprises two major modules. The first part is the TBTL framework, with its core concept aligned with Wills's teaching framework. However, its application scope is no longer confined to language but extends to a broader range. In this model, "knowledge" represents that the TBTL framework can be applied to multiple domains.

The second module describes how the VR system corresponds to the three parts of the TBTL framework. Leveraging the current advancements in VR technology, VR systems can provide rich three-dimensional scenes and multimodal interactions. Common VR modules used in the field of dental medicine include scene roaming, UI, and VR hand interactions. With the powerful features of VR systems, they can offer dental medicine learners learning scenarios in virtual environments.

Merely completing dental medicine training tasks, real surgical tasks, and various tasks related to using dental instruments in a virtual environment is insufficient. For instance, learners are likely to forget quickly if they do not promptly reinforce or apply what they have learned about using various dental instruments in the virtual environment.

However, in this model, the VR system provides tasks for all three stages, representing the complete knowledge acquisition process in the virtual environment.

In this context, the tasks for the three stages are outlined. The first stage's task helps dental medicine students clarify learning objectives and browse and memorize learned dental medicine knowledge. For example, this task is designed to familiarize students with the correct use of dental instruments. The second stage's task encourages learners to apply the knowledge acquired in the first stage to practical situations. For example, students may be challenged to use tools for tooth extraction in a virtual scenario correctly. The third stage involves tasks assessing student learning outcomes, where the system may require students to complete a specific task for evaluation.

5   Design of VR System for Tooth Extraction Training

5.1   Questionnaire Survey and User Interviews

To gain a deeper understanding of dental students' perspectives on the application of virtual reality (VR) in tooth extraction training and their self-assessment of manual dexterity, this study employed a questionnaire survey and user interviews to gather insights into students' real thoughts.

Among the 34 valid responses collected (Reliability Analysis: The Cronbach's Alpha Coefficient is 0.665), 27.78% of respondents considered their manual dexterity to be average, 22.22% expressed dissatisfaction with their current manual dexterity, and 33.33% were very dissatisfied with their manual dexterity. Therefore, the questionnaire results indicate that the majority of students believe their manual dexterity needs improvement.

Regarding the question "If virtual reality is applied to cultivate manual dexterity in the field of dentistry, would you be willing to use it or recommend it to classmates?" 33.33% of dental students expressed willingness, and 41.76% indicated they were willing to use or recommend it to friends. Hence, dental students are highly anticipating the application of virtual reality in tooth extraction training to enhance manual dexterity (see Fig. 3).

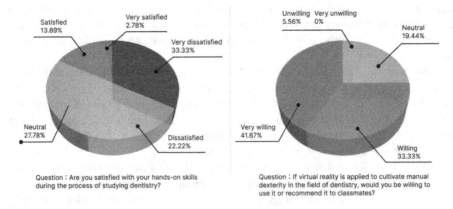

Fig. 3. Survey Statistical Results.

Due to location constraints, 30-min online interviews were conducted with 5 dental students to understand their current level of manual dexterity and their views on applying virtual reality to tooth extraction training. The specific interview outline and main content are detailed in Table 2.

From the interview content, it was found that dental students are not satisfied with their manual dexterity, as they have limited opportunities for hands-on practice in their regular studies, mainly focusing on theoretical knowledge. They believe that virtual reality training can allow them to practice multiple times without real patients, and they express great anticipation for this approach.

5.2 TBTL-VRADT Integration Model for VR-Assisted Tooth Extraction Training

Based on the instantiation research method, this study illustrates the application of the TBTL-VRADT Introduction Model in VR-assisted tooth extraction training. Tooth extraction is a common procedure in dental training, but limited school resources and a scarcity of real samples have led dental students to grasp theoretical knowledge better while lacking practical experience. Consequently, this has resulted in a deficiency in their hands-on skills during the tooth extraction.

For routine tooth extraction, the standard procedure involves preparing the necessary instruments, ensuring correct tooth positioning, disinfecting and anesthetizing the tooth and surrounding area, loosening the tooth by separating the gum, repositioning the tooth socket with cotton balls, and advising the patient on postoperative care. Applying the TBTL-VRADT Introduction Model in VR-assisted tooth extraction training aims to make the training process more systematic, allowing for repeated practice in a virtual environment.

Applied in the VR-Assisted Tooth Extraction Training, the TBTL-VRADT Introduction Model also includes the three stages of the entire learning process (see Fig. 4).

The first stage is the pre-task, where the main objective is for students to clarify their goals: mastering the process of tooth extraction to improve hands-on skills, gaining a preliminary understanding of the tooth extraction process, the required instruments, and understanding oral structure. In this stage, the VR system provides a virtual environment and tasks conducive to understanding this knowledge. For example, it offers realistic 3D oral models, instruments required for tooth extraction, and a simulated instrument display, allowing students to repeatedly use surgical instruments in a virtual environment and dissect oral models to become proficient in tool usage.

The second stage is the task cycle, designed to encourage students to apply the knowledge learned in the first stage to the complete process of simulated tooth extraction. Students can understand the knowledge points and enhance operational memory through this process. The task focus stage is the most meaningful, simulating a real surgical process, allowing learners to operate boldly without fear of mistakes. The system provides students with a clear task in the virtual environment: extracting the lower left first molar of the patient. In the process of completing this task, students naturally consolidate the just-learned knowledge.

Table 2. Interview outline and main content.

Topic	Questions	Answers
Personal Information	Please briefly introduce yourself, including your name, age, current academic stage, and major	The average age is 23 years old, majoring in Dentistry
Manual Dexterity	How do you perceive your manual dexterity when performing dental procedures?	I am relatively strong in theoretical aspects, but when it comes to practical operations, especially for some complex surgeries, I feel that my hands-on ability is relatively insufficient
Views on VR in Tooth Extraction Training	Are you familiar with the application of virtual reality in tooth extraction training? What are your thoughts on using virtual reality for tooth extraction training?	I believe virtual reality training can allow us to simulate operations multiple times in a safer, more controlled environment
Advantages of VR Training	In your opinion, what are the advantages of using virtual reality for tooth extraction training? Do you believe this technology can help improve students' manual dexterity? Why or why not?	I think virtual reality training can increase interest in learning, provide a safer environment for practicing, allow for multiple repetitions without risks, and offer real-time feedback
Practical Application and Effects	If you have experienced virtual reality tooth extraction training or other simulations, could you share your feelings and experiences? In actual tooth extraction procedures or other training, do you feel that previous virtual reality training has contributed to your confidence and skills?	They have not experienced virtual reality training for tooth extraction, but they are very eager to try tooth extraction training through VR technology
Challenges of VR Training	What challenges do you anticipate when using virtual reality for training?	I am concerned about the differences between virtual and real environments; I feel that virtual reality may have some technical issues

The third stage is knowledge focus, where the system assesses and provides feedback on students' learning achievements, allowing students to understand the learning effectiveness and plan further studies. In this stage, the system offers a virtual environment for assessment, such as participating in a game that involves selecting the corresponding

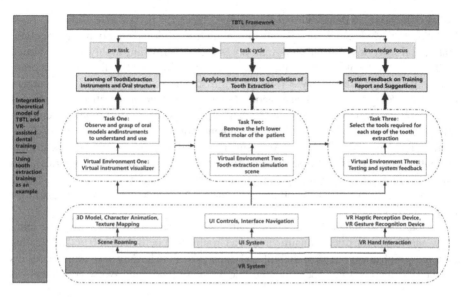

Fig. 4. TBTL-VRADT Introduction Model in VR-assisted tooth extraction training.

tools for each step of tooth extraction. After the task, the system scores and informs students about areas that need improvement.

Applying the TBTL-VRADT Introduction Model to VR-assisted tooth extraction training can clarify the role of each teaching module in the instructional process. Additionally, meaningful tasks are used to integrate these modules. This, in turn, helps the VR system establish relationships between different scenarios, ensuring that the connection between scenes is based on meaningful tasks.

5.3 KANO Model

Applying the TBTL-VRADT Introduction Model to VR-assisted tooth extraction training establishes meaningful connections between different scenes within the VR system through tasks. Additionally, it is essential to identify the actual functionalities required by dental students because various system features will be utilized during the tooth extraction training process, and the design of these features will impact the overall training experience. Therefore, the authors conducted a KANO questionnaire survey to understand the required functionalities of dental students for the application of virtual reality in tooth extraction training.

To explore the functionalities dental students require in a VR system for tooth extraction training using the TBTL-VRADT Introduction Model, the author identified ten features through a combination of questionnaire surveys, user interviews, and desktop research. These functionalities, analyzed using the KANO model, include Sensory Simulation (replicating the tactile sensations, resistance, and vibrations during surgery for a lifelike experience), Emergency Situation Simulation (replicating potential urgent scenarios such as bleeding or nerve damage), Surgical Process Recording (capturing and documenting students' virtual surgery processes for review and analysis), Team Collaboration Mode Selection (establishing a multi-user virtual environment for collaborative oral surgeries), Virtual Oral Anatomy Modeling (providing highly realistic virtual tooth models for anatomical simulation), Communication Skills Cultivation (incorporating features for pre-surgery consultations, in-surgery reassurance, and post-surgery reminders), Surgical Instrument Practice (allowing students to practice with various virtual oral surgical instruments like forceps, retractors, etc.), Multimodal Interaction (integrating visual, auditory, and tactile elements for a comprehensive sensory experience), Real-time Feedback and Assessment (providing immediate feedback to help students correct errors and assess their skill levels in tooth extraction surgeries), and Real-time Simulation of Surgery Time (simulating time pressure during virtual surgeries to enhance students' work efficiency). The KANO model was applied to prioritize these functionalities.

A total of 34 valid KANO questionnaires were collected for this study. The reliability analysis of the questionnaire yielded a Cronbach's coefficient of 0.960, indicating extremely high questionnaire reliability. The analysis of the KANO questionnaire results for the ten functionalities, including the calculation of Better and Worse coefficients, is presented in Table 3.

Table 3. KANO questionnaire results for the ten functionalities.

Function	KANO Attribute	Better Coefficient	Worse Coefficient
Sensory Simulation	Attractive Quality	58.62%	−20.69%
Emergency Situation Simulation	Indifferent Quality	55.56%	−29.63%
Surgical Process Recording	Indifferent Quality	51.85%	−37.04%
Team Collaboration Mode Selection	Indifferent Quality	51.85%	−29.63%
Virtual Oral Anatomy Modeling	Indifferent Quality	51.72%	−20.69%
Communication Skills Cultivation	Indifferent Quality	48.15%	−22.22%
Surgical Instrument Practice	Indifferent Quality	48.15%	−40.74%
Multimodal Interaction	Indifferent Quality	46.43%	−21.43%
Real-time Feedback and Assessment	Indifferent Quality	46.43%	−28.57%
Real-time Simulation of Surgery Time	Indifferent Quality	44.44%	−25.93%

The results indicate that only Sensory Simulation is considered an attractive feature among the ten functionalities, while the remaining nine functionalities fall under the indifferent category. Refer to Figure Five for a detailed breakdown. Despite this, it was discovered through discussions with dental students who completed the questionnaire that they still desire to incorporate these functionalities into the VR system, aiming for a comprehensive VR learning system with all the features.

6 High-Fidelity Prototype Diagrams for the VR System Assisting Tooth Extraction

The perception simulation in the VR system is crucial for tooth extraction training, as it allows students to have a more realistic tactile sensation when gripping surgical instruments and provides strong feedback on the collision between instruments and the oral model to adjust the force accordingly. The other nine indifferent functions are also important, and their specific application depends on the particular scenario.The high-fidelity prototype design of the VR system for assisting tooth extraction training is shown in Fig. 5.

In the first stage, when students perform tasks such as grasping various instruments and observing and dissecting oral models, gaining a preliminary understanding of the tooth extraction process, the use of instruments, and the oral structure, the VR system needs to have functions such as virtual oral model dissection, instrument grasping, and multimodal interaction combining audio and video.

In the second stage, as students lead the simulated complete process of tooth extraction, the system can provide functions such as team collaboration mode selection, communication dialogue, emergency situation simulation, surgery time simulation, surgery process recording, and real-time feedback and assessment. Particularly, the real-time feedback and assessment function can alert students when they make mistakes during a step, prompting them to pay closer attention to identified issues and reinforce their practice.

In the third stage, when students participate in the game "selecting the corresponding tools for each step of tooth extraction," the system can provide real-time feedback and assessment and real-time simulation functionality.

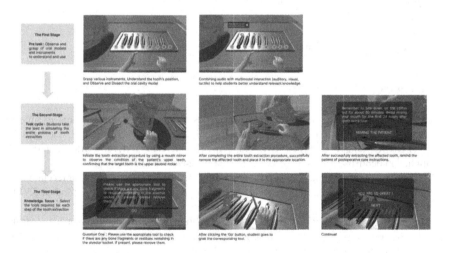

Fig. 5. High-fidelity prototype design of the VR system for assisting tooth extraction training.

7 Conclusion

Task-based teaching methods have been widely applied across diverse educational domains, demonstrating efficacy and suitability. In the context of oral instruction training, this study integrates task-based teaching methods within the pedagogical framework, stringing together the training processes of pivotal projects in oral medicine. The present research introduces the TBTL-VRADT integration model, strategically amalgamating task-based teaching methods, virtual reality (VR) systems, and oral medicine instruction. This model seamlessly incorporates meaningful tasks throughout the entire VR-assisted oral medical training process, thereby integrating VR with the comprehensive workflow of oral medical training.

Subsequently, leveraging the TBTL-VRADT integration model as a foundation, the overall design of the VR system for Virtual Reality Assisted Dental Training (VRADT) is meticulously planned, encompassing the connections and interactions between each scene within the VR system. Finally, grounded in the case study methodology, the model is applied to the VR system design for tooth extraction training. This application gives students a holistic understanding of the tooth extraction procedure and hands-on experience in a virtual environment. The system facilitates functional support during the student's participation in the tooth extraction process, aiding in the nuanced comprehension and refinement of practical skills. In the future, the TBTL-VRADT integration model holds promise for broader application in hands-on training for dental students, thereby elevating their manual dexterity and aligning with the rigorous standards of scientific publications in the field.

Acknowledgments. This research received no specific grant from funding agencies in the public, commercial, or not-for-profit sectors. I am very grateful to my supervisors Hua Ming Peng and Siu Shing Man, for their careful teaching.

Disclosure of Interests. All authors disclosed no relevant relationships.

References

1. Pulijala, Y., Ma, M., Pears, M., et al.: Effectiveness of immersive virtual reality in surgical training—a randomized control trial. J. Oral Maxillofac. Surg. **76**(5), 1065–1072 (2018)
2. Huang, T.K., Yang, C.H., Hsieh, Y.H., et al.: Augmented reality (AR) and virtual reality (VR) applied in dentistry. Kaohsiung J. Med. Sci. **34**(4), 243–248 (2018)
3. Reymus, M., Liebermann, A., Diegritz, C.: Virtual reality: an effective tool for teaching root canal anatomy to undergraduate dental students–a preliminary study. Int. Endod. J. **53**(11), 1581–1587 (2020)
4. Murbay, S., Chang, J.W.W., Yeung, S., et al.: Evaluation of the introduction of a dental virtual simulator on the performance of undergraduate dental students in the pre-clinical operative dentistry course. Eur. J. Dent. Educ. **24**(1), 5–16 (2020)
5. Zhang, B., Li, S., Gao, S., et al.: Virtual versus jaw simulation in Oral implant education: a randomized controlled trial. BMC Med. Educ. **20**(1), 1–10 (2020)
6. Haleem, A., Javaid, M., Khan, I.H.: Virtual reality (VR) applications in dentistry: an innovative technology to embrace. Indian J. Dent. Res. **31**(4), 666–667 (2020)

7. Anjum, M.H., Kayani, M.M., Jumani, N.B.: The effect of task-based language learning (TBLL) on developing speaking skills of secondary school learners in Pakistan. Int. J. Engl. Linguist. **9**(2), 283–291 (2019)
8. González-Lloret, M.: Technology for task-based language teaching. In: The Handbook of Technology and Second Language Teaching and Learning, pp. 234–247 (2017)
9. Lin, C.: The impact of technology-assisted task-based language teaching on self-regulated learning. In: 2021 International Conference on Advanced Learning Technologies (ICALT), pp. 285–287. IEEE (2021)
10. Kurhila, S., Kotilainen, L.: Student-initiated language learning sequences in a real-world digital environment. Linguist. Educ. **56**, 100807 (2020)
11. Ellis, R., Shintani, N.: Exploring Language Pedagogy Through Second Language Acquisition Research. Routledge, London (2013)
12. Lynch, T., Maclean, J.: Exploring the benefits of task repetition and recycling for classroom language learning. Lang. Teach. Res. **4**(3), 221–250 (2000)
13. Willis, J.: A Framework for Task-Based Learning. Intrinsic Books Ltd. (2021)
14. Ellis, R.: Task-Based Language Learning and Teaching. Oxford University Press, Oxford (2003)
15. Nunan, D.: Task-Based Language Teaching. Cambridge University Press, Cambridge (2004)

Author Index

Printed in the United States
by Baker & Taylor Publisher Services